Unlikely Environmentalists

Unlikely Environmentalists

CONGRESS AND

CLEAN WATER,

1945–1972

Paul Charles Milazzo

 University Press of Kansas

Published by the University Press of Kansas (Lawrence, Kansas 66045), which was organized by the Kansas Board of Regents and is operated and funded by Emporia State University, Fort Hays State University, Kansas State University, Pittsburg State University, the University of Kansas, and Wichita State University

Library of Congress Cataloging-in-Publication Data

Milazzo, Paul Charles.
    Unlikely environmentalists : Congress and clean water, 1945–1972 /
Paul Charles Milazzo.
        p.   cm.
    Includes bibliographical references and index.
    ISBN 0-7006-1475-3 (cloth : alk. paper)
        1. Environmental protection—Government policy—United States—History—
20th century.   2. Water—Pollution—Law and legislation—United States—History—
20th century.   3. Environmental law—United States.   4. United States. Federal Water
Pollution Control Act.   5. United States. Congress.   I. Title.
    GE180.M55 2006
    363.739′45097309045—dc22   2006019964

British Library Cataloguing-in-Publication Data is available.

Printed in the United States of America
10 9 8 7 6 5 4 3 2 1

CONTENTS

This book began as an effort to reinsert Congress into the post-1945 political history of the United States. The body of historiography I encountered during graduate school focused almost exclusively on the presidency in matters of national policymaking. Adherents of the "organizational synthesis," in particular, looked to the interest groups, experts, and bureaucrats who orbited the executive branch to explain why the federal government expanded the way it did during the twentieth century. Scholars like Steven Skowronek, Brian Balogh, and Theda Skocpol, who emphasized the contingent nature of "modernization," usually depicted the legislative branch as an inveterate opponent, rather than a willing architect, of big government. If such "top-down" history marginalized Congress, however, the view was not much better from the bottom up. Historians who studied social movements or cultural experiences viewed legislative machinations as remote from and largely irrelevant to the authentic struggles of local people and communities.

To "bring Congress back in" to narratives of American political development, I searched for a policy area that fused "top-down" and "bottom-up" storylines and featured legislators as the first responders on the federal level. The environment was a perfect choice. The rise of the environmental regulatory state ranks as one of the most far-reaching transformations in American government since World War II. Grassroots activism and shifting cultural ideals helped bring about this change, particularly in the sixties and seventies, but I soon realized that Congress did more than just respond reflexively to the prevailing zeitgeist. Water pollution control policy provided a particularly useful case study in this regard, since, beginning in the fifties, legislators' concern about national water quality both outpaced public concern and predated the environmental movement. As such, a congressional focus prompts us to reconsider the periodization of post-World War II environmental politics.

Likewise, paying heed to the institutional structure of the legislative branch can tell us something new about the substance of environmental policy and how it came to be. It is less important to know that the 1965 Water Quality Act became law during the Johnson administration or that the 1972 Clean Water Act did so during the Nixon years than it is to understand that both laws were the products of Congress's "committee era." This, too, suggests a new periodization—but that is not all. Historians like Julian Zelizer have underscored how standing committees and their powerful chairmen shaped important federal policies, like taxation, that fueled the growth of the modern American state. Beyond the power of the purse, Congress's internal structure and dynamic also determined why legislators played a more assertive role than did the executive branch in placing emerging policy priorities like pollution control on the national agenda.

As I came to discover, the institutional exigencies of the legislative branch often prescribed the ideas, interests, and values that informed environmental policy and law. As a consequence, the persons or organizations articulating them did not always conform to conventional wisdom about what constitutes an "environmentalist." The title of this book, and the chapters to follow, indicate that the roots of environmental policy extended in multiple directions and drew inspiration from more varied sources than either political or environmental historians realized. Likewise, they suggest that practitioners in both fields will find richer stories to tell when Congress is given its due.

Much like J. R. R. Tolkien, I found that this tale grew in the telling. Along my way there and back again, I incurred many debts, which I gladly acknowledge here.

Christopher Beam and Elaine Ardia at the Edmund S. Muskie Archives and Special Collections Library helped me locate critical source materials and photographs. Richard Hunt and his staff at the National Archives' Center for Legislative Archives uncovered many treasures, including ten untouched cartons jammed with the Senate Public Works Committee's water pollution files. Their dedication to congressional research made my work easier and much more enjoyable. So, too, did Don Ritchie and Richard Baker in the Senate Historical Office, who patiently fielded my many queries. And House photo historian Fred Beuttler slogged through a daunting, unprocessed collection to find the visuals I requested.

Army Corps of Engineers historian Marty Reuss helped me track down manuscript collections and interviewees, answered questions, and even hired me as a research contractor. Char Miller and Adam Rome cheerfully encouraged my labors by editing essays or commenting on conference papers where I worked out some of the book's main themes. Martin Melosi and Jeffrey Stine gave the initial manuscript a careful reading and offered many trenchant comments. Jeffrey also lent advice, secondary works from his personal library, and kind words of support that made the project less onerous.

It is impossible to study the post-1945 Congress properly without talking to the dedicated staff members who kept it running. All the staffers I interviewed were forthcoming, generous with their time, and enthusiastic about telling their stories. I thank Jerry Sonosky, Leon Billings, Thomas Jorling, Don Nicoll, Theodore Schad (who, sadly, passed away in October 2005), Ron Linton, Lester Edelman, William Hildenbrand, and Barry Meyer for allowing a stranger into their homes and offices to answer questions about a bygone era. Barry Meyer was kind enough to lend me the official Senate history of the 1972 Clean Water Act, an invaluable bound volume that I delighted in using because it happened to be Senator Jennings Randolph's personal copy.

A fellowship with the University of Virginia's Miller Center of Public Affairs supported my research. I want to thank Sid Milkis, Brian Balogh, and their staff (particularly Chi Lam) for their dedication in creating a community of young scholars who care about political and policy history. The connections I made there enlightened both mind and spirit. The late Hugh Davis Graham, my Miller Center mentor, proved every bit the gentleman he was reputed to be and made sure to introduce me to Fred Woodward, my editor at the University Press of Kansas. It was wonderful to work (alas, all too briefly) with a historian I admired so much. Among the constellation of academic stars affiliated with the Miller Center and the *Journal of Policy History*, Julian Zelizer, one of the nation's foremost congressional scholars, offered more guidance and assistance than I deserved. I also thank my Miller Center/University of Virginia compatriots Sarah Phillips, Peter Kastor, Andy Morris, David D'Andrea, Joe Thorndike, and Meg Jacobs for their friendship and support.

Before coming to the University of Virginia for graduate work, my history professors at Amherst College—Gordy Levin, David Blight, Kevin Sweeney, and Robert Gross—inspired me to follow in their footsteps. Once at Virginia, Joseph Kett, Charles McCurdy, Mel Leffler, Michael Holt, and Olivier Zunz helped me go the distance. I owe a great debt in particular to Ed Russell, whose intellect, insight, and friendship proved invaluable. Once I crossed the mountains with degree in hand, my colleagues at Ohio University offered advice and encouragement: Lon Hamby, Kevin Mattson, Robert Ingram, Norm Goda, Michael Grow, Steve Miner, and especially Patrick Griffin, who taught me the difference between writing a dissertation and writing a book.

This book is a testament to the patience and dedication of Brian Balogh, my graduate advisor and friend. His brilliance as a historian is matched only by his kindness and good humor, which provided a light in dark places when all other lights seemed to go out. I thank him for all he has done and forgive him for overstating the quality of Italian food to be found in Charlottesville.

I can never repay my parents for all they have given me, or all the burdens they have borne on my behalf. I love them very much and hope I have made them proud. Finally, I thank Laura for putting up with me, for bearing our beautiful son, Samuel Joseph, and for making this last line possible: "And he lived happily ever after to the end of his days."

Introduction

By the middle of the twentieth century, pollution had become a predicament that spared few rivers, lakes, or streams in the United States—and no wonder. The continent's water resources bore a considerable burden for a burgeoning nation. These waters nourished its population's agriculture, buoyed its industry, transported its goods, and supported its cities, even as their beauty continued to stir the souls of its intrepid vacationers and outdoor enthusiasts. As the country emerged victorious from World War II, Americans pursued postwar prosperity with well-deserved optimism but soon discovered that the by-products of that prosperity befouled the very waterways that sustained it. Between 1900 and 1950, the population of the United States doubled from 76 million to 151 million, and its industrial capacity expanded by 700 percent. World War II in particular sparked a dramatic burst in production and urbanization that accelerated these upward trends. As populace and productivity increased, so too did the volume, intensity, and complexity of pollution from municipal and industrial sources.

Pollution did not have to be "unnatural" to cause problems. Domestic sewage contains mostly organic materials, which provide a hearty meal for aquatic microscopic organisms. Their feasting decomposes fecal wastes into phosphorus and nitrogen, but receiving waters pay the tab in the form of dissolved oxygen to complete the necessary chemical reactions. In 1920, the total "oxygen demand" exerted by such waste loads nationwide was equivalent to that of the raw sewage produced by 40 million people. By the mid-fifties, despite the construction of 6,500 municipal treatment plants nationwide, the "population equivalent" of municipal pollution alone had ballooned to 75 million people; organic wastes from manufacturing effluent approached twice that volume. As a consequence, oxygen deficiencies plagued waterways with heavy urban-industrial concentrations, particularly in the Northeast and the Midwest. Lakes Erie and Michigan, along with the Upper Mississippi, Calumet, Delaware, Hudson, Merrimack, and Ohio Rivers (and their tributaries) suffered frequent fish kills, putrid odors, and zones practically devoid of life—except for eels, suckers, and an overabundance of algae that thrived in waters with excessive amounts of nitrogen and phosphorus.[1]

Although public health officials made great advances in the first half of the century in neutralizing waterborne diseases, much of what flowed into America's waters confounded conventional knowledge or treatment technology. This included inorganic industrial wastes like metal filings, pickling liquors, phenols, and acids. During and after World War II, an expanding chemical industry produced dozens of new synthetic compounds each year, discharging complex by-products whose effects on streams were largely unknown. Perhaps the fastest-growing sector was petrochemicals. Oil and petroleum derivatives not only spilled into the densely industrialized Ohio River, but also the Houston ship channel, Galveston Bay, and other waterways in the Southwest where the majority of the nation's oil refining took place.[2]

Not all the culprits were industrial by-products, however. From burgeoning towns and suburbs, manufactured consumer items like synthetic detergents, lawn fertilizers, and insecticides flowed through sewers, washed into local streams during rainfall, or penetrated into groundwater, where they resisted decomposition. Nor were all pollutants complex or exotic. Rivers already prone to siltation, like the Mississippi, Delaware, and Potomac, carried even denser loads when activities that promoted run-off (commercial agriculture, logging, real estate development, and damming) accelerated. Rain seeping through abandoned and exposed coal mines leached sulfuric acid into Appalachian streams. Heat emitted from steam electrical power plants during the cooling process elevated water temperatures to levels that reduced oxygen or endangered aquatic wildlife. And high salt concentrations threatened the potability of water drawn from western rivers heavily tapped for crop irrigation, from rivers vulnerable to the Atlantic Ocean's incursion in times of drought, and from subterranean tables in areas as diverse as Michigan, Florida, Oklahoma, and California.[3]

For most of the country's history, polluted waters remained, in the words of President Dwight Eisenhower, a "uniquely local blight." What was unique, in fact, was the federal system outlined by the Constitution, which delimited the authority of the national government and vested individual states with the power to police both public health and private markets. When it came to pollution, few Americans, Eisenhower included, had a problem with this arrangement. Of course, pleas for a more forceful federal response arose from some corners, particularly those associated with sport fishing or conservation. But these voices were few. Politically influential business leaders preferred environmental regulations that were minimal and overseen by local officials who were accountable. Local officials, meanwhile, guarded their spheres of influence and resisted federal encroachment. And citizens retained a vigilant distrust of a distant, centralized state. As late as 1950, the most prominent federal water pollution statute on the books was a weak, temporary law that extended no authority to enforce standards or punish recalcitrant violators.

Within little more than two decades, however, all that changed. Nothing heralded the new era quite like the 1972 Federal Water Pollution Control Act Amendments, more commonly known as the Clean Water Act. This groundbreaking law coupled stringent standards and tough federal enforcement with unprecedented programmatic objectives, including a goal to *eliminate* discharges into the nation's waters by 1985. Its passage confirmed that water pollution had graduated from a uniquely local blight to occupy an unequivocal place on the national agenda.

How and why did this transition occur when it did? The primary explanation offered by historians and other observers is the rise of environmentalism, and with good reason. Just as happened in the struggle for civil rights, heightened citizen awareness and participation helped transform the environmental policy landscape—and American society. By the late sixties and early seventies, grassroots activists, public interest advocates, and ordinary voters had united to voice their apprehension about the fragile state of the natural world. They converted anxiety into political capital and prodded government officials to reexamine the costs associated with unchecked growth. This mass movement channeled the New Left's faith in direct action as well as its sense of urgency and moral imperative. But it also amplified a diffuse chorus of local concerns, which in turn reflected a deeply rooted shift in public values. In the years after World War II, a growing population of middle-class, urban, and educated Americans became more enthusiastic "consumers" of natural amenities, attuned to the benefits of open space, fresh air, and clean streams for human health and well-being. From this perspective, then, environmentalists combined the forces of cultural change and grassroots politics to challenge entrenched interests and compel the federal government to take a more active, aggressive role in regulating pollution.[4]

Such a singular focus on mass movement environmentalism, however, has obscured the full panorama of people, organizations, ideas, and events that gave rise to the environmental regulatory state. It is the purpose of this book to reveal what the traditional storyline has neglected by weaving the history of the federal water pollution control program into a broader narrative of political and institutional development after World War II. This more inclusive approach acknowledges the impact of familiar activists and agendas. But it also reveals influential advocates for pollution control where no one previously had bothered to look for them. Indeed, the spotlight falls on a less-celebrated, though no less significant cast of characters whose activities, properly accounted for, reconfigure the boundaries of environmental politics. These were the "unlikely environmentalists."

The classification is a loose one, and purposely so. Unlikely environmentalists include those persons or bureaucracies whose efforts on behalf of water quality would register as unexpected, counterintuitive, and even ironic when measured against popular and scholarly assumptions about the origins of environmental law. The label is also applied to more renowned environmental politicians and professionals whose careers and motivations, once reexamined, defy conventional depictions. It does not, however, imply merely cynical or ulterior motives. Richard Nixon's surprising contributions to federal pollution control policies, for example, though well chronicled in these chapters, remained products of political expediency that failed to hold his interest. If opportunism were all that defined unlikely environmentalists, there would be little to recommend them. But there is more to them than that.

Unlikely environmentalists remind us that the federal government's interest in redressing polluted streams after 1945 also grew out of a set of priorities distinct from those voiced by the grass roots. These alternative influences have been eclipsed by the long shadow cast by the environmental movement, but recovering them is crucial. By interpreting environmental policy simply as the product of upheaval, or as the outgrowth of a single set of values, we risk overlooking the continuity and diversity of other discourses—technical, institutional, and political—that played a part in its evolution.

Advocates of economic development, missile system designers, and dam-building bureaucrats may not have represented the typical audience at an Earth Day rally. On first inspection, their interests appear indifferent or even inimical to the cause of clean water. Yet they did not serve exclusively as a force of opposition in environmental politics. In the course of pursuing their own agendas within well-established organizational channels, these ubiquitous actors in the nation's political life took an active interest in water pollution and proceeded to shape how policymakers devised solutions to the problem. They did so not only prior to the onset of a tangible environmental movement, but afterward as well.

The institution at the center of this process was the U.S. Congress. In recent years, students of post-1945 political history have come to recognize the extent to which the legislative branch, not just the executive, took the initiative in "state-building," or the expansion of the federal government's administrative capacity. True, Congress conceded the advantage to the "imperial presidency" in terms of in-house expertise, staff support, media relations, control of classified information, and a centralized administrative structure equipped for rapid responses to national crises. But ever since the nineteenth century, the legislature has modernized in its own way. It grew as the nation's population did and responded to an ever-increasing workload with a system of standing committees that accommodated both the need for policy specialization and the demands of new legislative careerists. After World War I, in both the House and the Senate, formal and informal rules coalesced to promote the autonomy of committee chairs and detach them from the strict discipline of party leadership. By the end of World War II, a constellation of independent chairmen exerted near total control over the pace and substance of legislative output. Although some reveled in obstruction, others established their committees as hubs for policy networks that served as fertile ground for new government initiatives.[5]

The story of water pollution control is a story of congressional state building. The legislative branch acted more assertively than the executive branch to make a federal case of water quality in the postwar era. Moreover, Congress's responsiveness to the issue was a function of its own internal evolution over the course of the twentieth century. Its decentralized institutional structure and behavioral norms encouraged legislators to pursue novel policy initiatives, often outpacing public demand for them. At the same time, however, these initiatives often grew out of—and were filtered through—existing committee jurisdictions and the ingrained networks of interest groups, experts, and federal bureaucracies attached to them. Congress, then, served as the arena where unlikely environmentalists operated and thrived. It was there that older agendas, reflecting long-standing national values and priorities, continued to receive their fullest airing. They provided a ready template for legislators seeking to define a new role for the federal government in environmental regulation, a template that persisted and adapted to the challenges issued by the movement culture of the sixties and seventies.[6]

To tell this story, the book is organized into three parts. Part One focuses on the most prominent set of values and priorities influencing the early politics of water pollution control, which I refer to collectively as the "developmental discourse." For much of the twentieth century, when Americans worried about water, they usually worried about running short of it. Improving and impounding local watercourses ranked among the highest priorities for business and civic leaders nationwide, even in eastern communities blessed with more humid climes.

Such collective enthusiasm for water resources development found institutional expression in Congress. Committees specializing in public works and reclamation projects mediated between solicitous interest groups and the federal construction agencies eager to oblige them. These insulated policy units, or "iron triangles," as political scientists call them, directed a generous dispersal of government funds to build dams, reservoirs, and diversions along virtually every free-flowing stream that could bear them (and some that could not). Following World War II, as the demand for water surged amid an unprecedented urban-industrial take-off, Congress responded with annual public works budgets that soared into the billions.

Federal water pollution control policy during the post-1945 era evolved as an adjunct of this extensive congressional pursuit of water development. In the fifties and sixties, conventional concerns about water quantity often shaped legislative approaches to water quality. Contemporary policymakers interpreted pollution as part and parcel of a national water resource problem, since it impeded the reuse of limited supplies and exacerbated deficiencies that seemed to pose an ominous threat to regional economic growth. As a matter of jurisdiction, the same public works committees that dispensed local pork barrel projects to engineer an end to scarcity also presided over the fledgling expansion of what would become the federal government's largest environmental regulatory program. This institutional pedigree left its mark on the substance of water quality legislation.[7]

The unlikely environmentalists introduced in Part One are precisely those legislators who discovered water pollution in the process of doling out pork and promoting development. Some used this "distributive politics" to muster new constituencies in support of federal environmental regulation at a time when business opposition was strong and public environmental consciousness was not. John Blatnik (D-Minn.), chairman of the House Subcommittee on Rivers and Harbors, shepherded the first permanent water pollution control legislation through Congress in 1956 by recasting it in the more familiar New Deal mold of government-promoted natural resource development, employment, and economic growth. Others, like the Senate's reigning king of pork, Robert Kerr (D-Okla.), had little use for an expanded regulatory state but did wish to justify Congress's multibillion-dollar public works bills in the face of executive branch condemnation. He used the prestige of a select committee in 1959–1960 to underscore the linkage between water quality and quantity, depicting federally funded dams in Oklahoma and waste treatment plants in Ohio as part of the same national blueprint for prosperity. Kerr embraced pollution control to deflect criticism of special interest politics and localism in the public works budget; Blatnik exploited special interest politics and localism to promote pollution control. What they both shared, however, was the power of the congressional committee chair to marshal institutional resources, from staff support to purse strings, to shape policy.

Even the nation's foremost environmental lawmaker took his career cues from Congress's post–World War II committee system, not the will of the people or an inherent love of nature. Edmund Muskie (D-Maine) earned a reputation as the Senate's "Mr. Clean" in the sixties and seventies, with a résumé that boasted some of the nation's most important pollution control statutes. Yet Muskie was not just an unlikely environmentalist, he was also an unwilling one, at least initially. A New Deal–style Democrat and former governor, Muskie came to the Senate in 1958 seeking prestige for himself and economic development for his poor, rural state. His committee assignments, for reasons beyond his control, portended neither. Placed on the Senate Public Works Committee but denied the chairmanship of the coveted Rivers and Harbors Subcommittee, in 1963 he found himself saddled with a temporary subcommittee on air and water pollution control, an assignment he bemoaned as marginal and irrelevant to his broader ambitions.

But the chairmanship he didn't ask for—and didn't want at first—allowed Edmund Muskie to pursue an alternative path to power. Muskie soon learned to broker another indispensable congressional resource besides pork: knowledge. The junior senator realized that his modest subcommittee offered him more than just a primer on smog and sewage. It also provided an institutional base to publicize an emerging social problem, develop legislation to address it, and cultivate constituencies to lobby for continuous policy implementation. In short, it allowed him to become a legislative entrepreneur. Muskie leveraged his authoritative knowledge to build consensus—in committee, in Congress, and among a myriad of interests in both the public and private sectors—to create a more viable federal water quality program at a time when relatively few Americans demanded one.

As a consensus builder, Muskie continued to rely on a set of traditional assumptions that pervaded the postwar policymaking system. He, too, viewed water pollution control as a way to conserve a scarce natural resource essential for regional development. Unlike his predecessors, however, he moved beyond distributive politics to devise a developmental mode of environmental regulation. To augment national water supplies, his 1965 Water Quality Act sought to establish regionally specific ambient stream standards and impose some of the costs of cleanup on industrial dischargers. The legislation's potential to promote local water resource planning may have motivated the senator and his colleagues more than the prospect of punitive action against recalcitrant polluters. But Muskie's emphasis on resource management catered to both developmental and environmental concerns. It did not overlook aesthetic or health-oriented justifications for water quality regulation so much as it subsumed them within a broader utilitarian framework. This policy outlook comported with the political climate of the early sixties, when the Johnson administration's newfound interest in "natural beauty" and ecology coexisted with its stated intention to develop and manage the water supply of every river basin in the country. It also comported with the atmospheric climate, as the most severe northeastern drought of the twentieth century dramatically underscored the link between water quality and quantity in dense urban concentrations.

Without recourse to a broad base of grassroots support or a powerful national environmental lobby, Muskie looked to two other pillars of postwar policymaking—experts and federalism—to overcome entrenched opposition to his initiative. The legislation featured multiple safeguards to preserve local control and deferred to the sanitary engineers who dominated state regulatory boards. As such, the limits of political acceptability dictated the structure of Muskie's pollution control program. Nevertheless, he also sincerely endorsed its cooperative, technician-centered approach as the best regulatory option for promoting long-term enhancement of water quality.

Unfortunately for Muskie, prevailing assumptions about development, expertise, and localism were in transition even as he was locking them into law in 1965. By the latter half of the sixties, their perceived legitimacy had waned. Once a mass environmental movement emerged as a tangible political and cultural force, Muskie's careful consensus building, deference to federalism, and developmental outlook not only became less necessary—these became political liabilities. Faced with a whole host of challenges from aggressive interest groups, new sets of experts, the media, other congressional committee chairs, and even a Republican White House, the senator was soon forced to reconsider his regulatory philosophy.

While accounting for this undeniable upheaval in environmental politics during the late sixties and early seventies, Part Two of the book taps the vein of underlying continuity that also played a crucial role in shaping the substance of policy. The focus shifts from development to a second postwar ethos, less familiar but no less prominent or pervasive. I have dubbed it the "systems discourse." It refers to a broad affinity in the political culture for a distinct archetype: the autonomous, self-regulating unit, be it mechanical, natural, social, or administrative. A diverse cross section of Americans assumed that an apposite understanding of such systems would enable them to appreciate—and manage—complexity. The penchant for "systems thinking" penetrated a wide range of public policies during the sixties. In the case of water pollution control, it not only gave voice to new kinds of experts, but it also captured the public imagination in ways that stimulated grassroots demands for change.

Ecology—or more specifically, ecosystems ecology—emerged as a systems-oriented science whose mainstream cultural appeal helped fuel the rise of the modern environmental movement. Popular interpreters appropriated the discipline's holistic principles to emphasize nature's complex, interdependent relationship with human society. From this perspective, ecology offered ordinary Americans an intellectual framework for interpreting the environmental consequences of unchecked development, reexamining technological hubris, and appreciating the "balance" of nature. For disaffected young activists taking a sober second look at the market or the military-industrial complex, an ecological worldview also registered as an authentic alternative.

Ecology's resonance in legislative policy circles during the mid-to-late sixties, however, often had more to do with its compatibility with traditional institutions and ways of thinking. Indeed, postwar ecosystems ecology emerged from the very military-industrial ethos that the counterculture condemned. Practitioners of the so-called New Ecology imported to the study of nature the same interdisciplinary, mechanical, and management-oriented perspective that grew out of World War II operations research and Cold War aerospace engineering. For this reason, professional ecologists found that they shared a common vernacular with members of Congress. Systems analysis, at once holistic and technocratic, enjoyed a pervasive appeal among legislators and bureaucrats seeking to use the administrative capacity of the federal government to address a host of new issues and problems. As systems analysis merged with social science and migrated into the civilian realm, policymakers believed they had discovered a planning tool to bring just about any large, complex, interdependent system under efficient control—including the natural environment that ecologists described.

The first serious tests to Edmund Muskie's authority and his committee's jurisdiction grew out of this broader systems framework. First, rival legislators, ambitious staffers, and a few influential academics applied the insights of ecology to environmental administration. Their efforts culminated with the landmark National Environmental Policy Act of 1970 (NEPA), legislation its sponsors believed would bring rational management to both the environment and federal environmental bureaucracies. Implicit in this vision of a comprehensive policy for the "total environment" was a challenge to Muskie's piecemeal, and decidedly unecological, approach to pollution control. Likewise, the success of Earth Day in April 1970 confirmed that a mass movement had coalesced around ecological values. A diverse cross section of the American public now perceived threats to nature with a greater sense of urgency and expected the federal government to enforce tough new standards of environmental protection. A new professional class of public interest lobbyists also lent clout to this diffuse constituency, which had traditionally lacked an organizational presence in Washington. As these advocates condemned the Muskie subcommittee's air and water legislation for kowtowing to corporate polluters and acquiescing to "captured" local officials, their demands for stronger federal regulation found a receptive audience elsewhere in Congress, not to mention an opportunistic Nixon White House. Edmund Muskie, once a legislative entrepreneur, suddenly found himself behind the curve.

The cumulative impact of these transformations in the political landscape helped usher in a revolution in the American regulatory state. In the fifties and sixties, environmental statutes had granted state administrators considerable discretion, refraining from pushing the technological envelope or demanding hard deadlines for air and water quality improvement. Edmund Muskie's groundbreaking Clean Air Act of 1970 and Clean Water Act of 1972, however, abandoned such restraints in an effort to reassert his committee's policy leadership—a task made easier thanks to its superior knowledge, experience, and staff support. These long, dense, complex statutes marked a sea change in environmental law. They concentrated regulatory power at the federal level, promulgated strict national standards and timetables, and placed the burden of proof on polluters during the enforcement process.

It is tempting to attribute such regulatory innovations, and Muskie's change of heart, solely to public clamor or political one-upsmanship with the White House. Yet the Clean Water Act cannot be explained solely in terms of partisan competition, the environmental movement, or the pressures exerted by the movement's most prominent interests and actors. As Part Three of this book argues, the groundbreaking 1972 statute represented both the culmination of a policy process that began in the fifties and a synthesis of the various discourses policymakers engaged in during that time. Although environmentalism exerted an undeniable influence on the final text, developmental agendas with deep institutional roots continued to inform the deliberations of senators and staff. Moreover, when ecological concepts and values finally penetrated the Senate Public Works Committee, they did so as part of a broader conversation about administrative management that was steeped in the language of systems and prompted by a rather diverse cast of characters, from the Army Corps of Engineers to California's aerospace industry. In short, the story of one of the postwar era's most complex and influential pieces of environmental legislation remains incomplete without considering the enduring contributions of unlikely environmentalists.

The Senate Public Works Committee's internal operations take center stage in fleshing out this broader history. Since 1963, Edmund Muskie had always cultivated an active, independent staff as well as an atmosphere of open debate among members of both parties. This management style left a tangible imprint on the substance of all his environmental legislation, but on none more than the Clean Water Act.

Muskie was not alone in needing help as legislative workloads grew in magnitude and complexity. The population of support personnel exploded in Congress only after the reforms of the seventies, but their total numbers grew steadily between 1947 and 1971, from 290 to 780 in the Senate and 193 to 779 in the House. Staff size and autonomy varied from committee to committee, but in both chambers legislative entrepreneurs formed productive partnerships with ambitious staffers culled from various professional backgrounds. Staff members often took the initiative in drafting statutory language or otherwise filtering the sources of information that informed it. In the early seventies, Public Works Committee staffers conceived some of the Clean Water Act's more radical features and helped channel the ecological knowledge that inspired them. Even so, the final product grew out of an extended conversation among the senators themselves behind closed doors. During their colloquy, they vetted the feasibility of the legislation's objectives, the precision of the language used to express them, and the most effective means to implement them in light of past failures. Party affiliation certainly colored individual opinions, but the senators' cooperative efforts and collective identity as legislative policy specialists tended to trump partisan differences. The result was a water pollution bill whose content surprised both sides of the political divide.[8]

The Senate's version of the Clean Water Act was a decisive break with the past, and it aroused considerable opposition. The Nixon administration rallied business interests, state officials, and sanitary engineers to protest what they considered the legislation's unreasonable costs, impractical goals, and inflexible, centralized administrative structure. The House Public Works Committee provided a sympathetic forum for these detractors. Its members did not belong to a specialized subcommittee on pollution control and did not share their Senate counterparts' pessimism about the existing state-federal program. They proceeded to fight a contentious battle to defend the autonomy of local communities and mitigate the impact of the strict, technology-based controls associated with Muskie's bill. These, they argued, would compel federal administrators to consider too narrow a range of variables when making regulatory decisions.

Ironically, many environmentalists were making a similar argument about administrative discretion in an effort to reconcile Muskie's legislation with the National Environmental Policy Act. The senator may have ultimately embraced ecology, but he never wavered from his belief that specialized experts deserved exclusive jurisdiction over matters of pollution control. NEPA's defenders and congressional patrons did not share Muskie's sanguinity about specialization, however. Rather, they looked to NEPA's main instrument, the "environmental impact statement," to broaden the base of expertise employed to protect the "total environment." Much to his chagrin, in 1972 Muskie found himself defending the Clean Water Act's provisions from both its foes as well as its putative friends.

This is a book about water pollution control that seeks to muddy the waters. By extending the time line, expanding the list of players, diversifying the set of relevant ideas and influences, and multiplying the venues where policy was made, it complicates conventional accounts of environmental politics in the United States. Yet such complexity is appropriate if, in the words of one prominent scholar, "the environmental management state deserves to join the national security state and the welfare state as a central concern of political historians." The rise of modern environmentalism undoubtedly represented a critical turning point in American political culture, but its transformative aura has prompted us to detach the government response that followed from its broader postwar political and institutional context. Unlikely environmentalists will help us recover that context and connect the natural world to the larger story of post–World War II American political development.[9]

PART I

Development

Setting the Agenda

John Blatnik and the Developmental Politics of Water Pollution Control

The October 1960 edition of the journal *Wastes Engineering* featured a retrospective article written by Gordon McCallum, a top administrator in the Public Health Service's water quality program. Addressing a readership of fellow sanitarians, the author proclaimed the 1950s as the profession's "Decade of Reawakening." Complacency that had derived from the successful conquest of waterborne diseases earlier in the century, he wrote, had receded in the face of significant postwar challenges. Sanitary engineers were now mobilizing to cope with a phenomenon few had foreseen during the Depression: growth. A mushrooming urban population and industrial economy generated unprecedented volumes of sewage, petrochemicals, pesticide run-off, and other wastes, all of which flowed ineluctably into the nation's waterways. This pollution problem grew more serious with each passing day.[1]

But rather than characterize pollution control as a defensive response to economic growth and its consequences, McCallum emphasized how essential it had become for sustaining that growth. The administrator asserted that the nation's "abatement needs transcend a narrow interpretation of their relation to health" in the postwar era. Instead, he described the policy objective as one of making "a constant water supply meet an increasing demand by having the right quantity of the right quality where it is needed." For local communities, controlling pollution had literally become a matter of economic survival. Exhorting the League of Virginia Municipalities in 1958, McCallum pointedly asked his audience whether they knew of a more economical means of obtaining water than from the stream passing through your town. . . . Suppose the water has been withdrawn and returned polluted town after town until it reaches you in a condition that is unsuitable for domestic or industrial use. Will you be happy about going to a costly alternative source for water supply—if one is available? . . . Will you be happy in failing to attract new industries or even having water to support normal community growth? This is not just a question of esthetics, recreation or even health—it is one of basic economics. It will affect your pocketbook and the pocketbooks of everyone in your community.[2]

The spectacle of a public health administrator who justified water pollution control in the name of economic development does not fit with our assumptions about the origins of modern environmental policy. Twenty-first-century observers are predisposed to view environmental protection and development as mutually exclusive. But Gordon McCallum saw pollution control, resource conservation, and regional growth as mutually reinforcing. Restoring water quality represented another way to augment national water supplies at a time when Americans demanded record volumes for an ever-widening array of uses.

The post–World War II Congress championed such developmental priorities. The imperative to pursue state-sponsored economic growth not only reflected public preference—it had become ingrained in the very structure of the committee system. Although legislators remained attuned to novel ideas and new interests, an agenda like water quality regulation met resistance because it threatened the power and profits of others. In 1955, prior to the emergence of environmental lobbyists or even a tangible environmental movement, only an imaginative, motivated legislator could get it through. But he could do so only by exploiting the venerable rhetoric that celebrated development and the institutional channels that delivered government resources, better known as "pork."

That legislator's name was John Blatnik. His career as an environmentalist was not only unlikely, but also, for the most part, unfamiliar. A New Deal partisan from the Iron Range of Minnesota, Blatnik had about as much interest in championing water pollution control as most of his colleagues, which is to say, not much. But in 1955, he found himself saddled with an unenviable task: trying to sell an indifferent Congress on a modest amendment to a lame-duck water pollution control law. Luckily, he also found himself in charge of a public works subcommittee (Rivers and Harbors) with a long tradition of distributing government resources in the name of regional development. Had any other congressional entity claimed jurisdiction over water pollution, the history of the policy might have been different. But in the middle of the twentieth century, when legislators heard "water," they thought of channels, locks, dams, and jobs. Blatnik tapped into this developmental mind-set to redefine the issue and pass the first permanent Federal Water Pollution Control Act in 1956. By doing so, he helped insert pollution control into a broader national agenda.

John Blatnik cannot claim credit for the more expansive and ambitious water pollution legislation of the sixties and seventies, but the developmental approach he adopted proved surprisingly durable. Over the next decade, overcoming apathy and outright opposition remained the primary challenge for the legislative "entrepreneurs" who sought to establish an effective federal water quality program. Both the rhetoric of economic growth and the popularity of distributive politics continued to provide invaluable political leverage.

Modest Beginnings and Meager Prospects

By modern standards, the 1956 Federal Water Pollution Control Act was a modest bill, but its even more humble predecessor reflected the obstacles and indifference John Blatnik would face. Congress did not get around to passing the first-ever Water Pollution Control Act until 1948, and soon after it did legislators concluded that the national abatement program it created was too feeble to take seriously. Even so, no one seemed particularly motivated to do much about it. Water pollution had become a more noticeable problem during the thirties and forties, but it did not register as enough of a crisis among national policymakers to warrant upsetting the traditional balance of federalism. The 1948 act made sure that the states retained their undisputed dominion over matters of implementation and enforcement, and it limited the surgeon general, the federal government's leading health official, to providing technical services and modest financial assistance to municipalities and local agencies.[3]

The statute's rather convoluted regulatory procedures illustrate how faithfulness to federalism undercut programmatic effectiveness. Congress restricted the scope of federal enforcement authority to "interstate waters and tributaries thereof," excluding any watercourse that did not flow across or form part of state boundaries. The surgeon general could concern himself only with pollution problems that endangered "the health or welfare of persons in a state other than that in which the discharge originated." In such cases, the statute authorized him to notify the polluter and appropriate state agency of the problem and specify a time limit for its abatement. Absent any response, a second notice was forthcoming.[4]

Next, the surgeon general had the option of convening a public hearing board to recommend "reasonable and equitable measures" to secure abatement. If the polluter chose to ignore the board's recommendation, the administrator of the Federal Security Agency (the parent agency of the Public Health Service at the time) could request the attorney general to bring suit against the polluter in federal court—provided that the state where the discharge originated gave its consent. The incentive to do so was minimal, since state officials owed more allegiance to local industries than to any aggrieved parties in distant jurisdictions downstream. Even if the suit made it to court, the statute instructed the judges to give "due consideration to the practicability and to the physical and economic feasibility of securing abatement of any pollution proved." In sum, anyone seeking to enjoin a particular polluter on interstate waters faced a rather ponderous bureaucratic procedure, a state veto, and a considerable burden of proof before the judiciary. Carried through to the end, the entire process could take four years.[5]

Although Congress granted the temporary law a three-year extension in 1953, doubts about its feasibility had already begun to surface. The appropriations committees stopped funding grants-in-aid to state pollution control programs in 1952 and never even bothered to set money aside for the act's modest loan program for waste treatment plant construction, arguing that the amounts authorized were too small to have any tangible effect. In 1955, the House Committee on Appropriations denied a requested increase of $145,000 for enforcement activities since, to that point, not a single abatement order had ever been issued under the statute. A committee report put the matter bluntly, calling the Water Pollution Control Act, "in the final analysis, almost unenforceable."[6]

And yet, when the Department of Health, Education, and Welfare (HEW) introduced a series of amendments designed to strengthen the act that same year, Congress seemed content to consider only the most incremental improvements. HEW's legislative package included a number of new features. First, the bill excised the most blatant impediments to federal enforcement: state veto power over abatement suits and the required second notice to polluters. It also granted hearings boards subpoena power to compel testimony in pollution control cases and deleted the obligation for courts to review the "physical and economic feasibility" of any abatement methods prescribed by the boards. Finally, in order to measure the detrimental impact of waste discharges with more technical and legal precision, and to assist industries and municipalities in estimating treatment requirements, HEW proposed that the states adopt a voluntary system of interstate water quality standards.[7]

HEW administrators demonstrated little inclination to defend their innovative proposals, however, when faced with resistance from state officials, industrial interests, and skeptical members of the Senate Public Works Committee. Witnesses characterized water quality standards as cumbersome, obtrusive, and unnecessary, while Oklahoma's Robert Kerr, chairman of the Rivers and Harbors Subcommittee and founder of the Kerr-McGee Oil Company, expressed similar reservations. HEW's assistant secretary could not backpeddle fast enough. He described the standards as "a preventative mechanism rather than an enforcement device," which granted the surgeon general no discretion to act independently without state cooperation; indeed, the procedure was entirely optional. The committee deleted the standards provision anyway, along with the subpoena power for hearing boards. But it did accept HEW's recommendations with respect to the state veto and the judicial "economic practicability" test. It also expedited the process of notice and public hearings—the estimated time from initial discovery to court action, optimistic administration officials predicted, would be reduced from four years to two. Content with this modest agenda, the committee delivered the revised bill, S. 890, to the House of Representatives, where, quite unexpectedly, the politics of water pollution got personal.[8]

Life's a Blitch: John Blatnik Discovers Water Pollution

Members of the House Committee on Public Works did not betray much enthusiasm for pollution control when the Rivers and Harbors Subcommittee took up the Senate bill. Indeed, John Blatnik, the subcommittee chairman, exemplified that indifference. In June 1955, the Minnesota Democrat dreamed of paved asphalt, not glistening streams. With the pending interstate highway act monopolizing his attention, Blatnik gave little thought to a peripheral measure that he expected would pass with minimal debate or effort on his part. His lack of engagement came through during the hearings, where he demonstrated little knowledge of the Senate bill's content, nor of the alternative bills under consideration, including one introduced under his own name. The man colleagues would later call "the father of water pollution control" hardly seemed worthy of the sobriquet.[9]

Blatnik began to focus on clean water only when unexpected opposition to the Senate bill distracted him from his pursuit of pavement. On the last day of the current session of Congress, he learned from House Speaker Sam Rayburn that a member of his own subcommittee had objected to the bill's consent privilege, a rule suspending floor debate that was normally reserved for uncontroversial measures. The member in question was Iris Faircloth Blitch, a first-term representative from Georgia who expressed strong reservations about the legislation's modest enforcement provisions. The chairman later speculated that Blitch had acted on behalf of the paper and chemical manufacturing interests in her state; but whatever the reason, her one-woman blockade suddenly subjected the bill to a potential floor fight, a fight Rayburn wanted to avoid as recess approached. At the Speaker's request, Blatnik reluctantly agreed to withdraw it until the next session, but the delay rankled him. The Public Works Committee's highway bill had suffered a defeat that summer, and as Blatnik prepared for a major battle in 1956, he was in no mood for such detours.[10]

As Blatnik's aide, Jerry Sonosky, recalled, the chairman's annoyance over this unforeseen snag, and what he perceived as the corporate arrogance behind it, sparked a more personal interest in what would become his signature policy issue. No environmental crisis or upsurge in citizen lobbying accounted for this change of heart. Instead, Blatnik acted out of pique. "If they didn't like S. 890," he told Sonosky upon departing for Minnesota in August 1955, "give them one they really won't like." Despite the tough talk, however, the 1956 Water Pollution Control Act that Blatnik sponsored proved, at best, only marginally more effective than its predecessor in matters of enforcement.[11]

Nevertheless, Blatnik's involvement did inspire a shift in strategy and emphasis that set the tone for the water pollution control policy process in the postwar era. As chairman of the House Subcommittee on Rivers and Harbors, the Minnesota Democrat understood the intrinsic appeal of federal water resource projects among members of Congress. By packaging pollution control as an extension of such government-sponsored economic development and exploiting his subcommittee's institutional advantages, he marshaled the necessary support for the first permanent federal water quality program.

Blatnik's success hinged on two factors. First, he broadened the issue's appeal by casting it in the context of economic growth. Second, he exploited his command of distributive politics—the time-honored tradition of giving away government resources to maximize constituent happiness—to overcome entrenched opposition. Both tactics reflected his New Deal pedigree.

Defining the Issue: Pollution Control and Development

For Congress to take water pollution control seriously, John Blatnik and his staff needed to frame the problem in a way that appealed to his colleagues' sense of urgency. In other words, they had to define the issue as one that policymakers ought to choose as a priority over other competing demands and allocate scarce government resources to redress. Political scientists refer to this process as agenda setting, and it became even more important in the post–World War II era as a burgeoning list of social issues tempted members of the executive and legislative branches to increase the state's administrative capacity.[12]

The strategy that Blatnik chose becomes clearer when viewed in the broader context of his personal history and political upbringing. John Anton Blatnik was born in Chisholm, Minnesota, on 17 August 1911, the son of Slovenian immigrants. The small town where his family had settled was located in St. Louis County, along the Mesabi Iron Range in the northeastern section of the state. It supported a rural economy: area farms cultivated alfalfa and raised dairy cows, while local forests sustained a timber crop. But iron mining constituted the primary economic activity in Chisholm, and when the Depression hit in the early thirties it devastated the region, with the unemployment rate topping 50 percent.[13]

Although the bleak economic outlook strained family resources and dashed Blatnik's dreams of going to medical school, he still managed to attend college. After a two-year stint teaching in a one-room country school, he received his degree from the State Teachers College in 1935. From 1935 to 1937, Blatnik served as an educational advisor for the Superior National Forest Civilian Conservation Corps (CCC); over the next four years he taught high school chemistry and became the assistant superintendent of schools for Saint Louis County. His experience as an administrator led to a successful bid for a state senate seat in 1940. When the war interrupted his term, he enlisted in the army and spent the next three and a half years in the Army Air Corps Intelligence and the Office of Strategic Services, serving behind enemy lines in Italy and Yugoslavia. Upon his return in 1946, he ran for Congress, successfully unseating the Republican incumbent in northeastern St. Louis County, Minnesota's sixtieth district.[14]

The crucible of rural depression in Chisholm forged Blatnik's later conviction that the government had an important role to play in supporting economic expansion and the development of natural resources. His experience in the CCC, coupled with firsthand observations of how an unstable mining sector victimized working families, convinced him of the importance of state and federal conservation programs. To sustain the region's economy in the future, Blatnik believed, the government would need to make preemptive efforts to prevent the depletion of the Mesabi Range's rich ore loads. Wartime demand for iron soon made this a pressing issue.

Some of Blatnik's earliest initiatives as a state politician dealt directly with natural resources development. In 1940, he attended a presentation given by Edward Wilson Davis, an electrical engineer working for the University of Minnesota's Mines Experiment Station. Davis and his colleagues had labored for decades to perfect a viable commercial process for extracting the fine iron particles embedded in taconite, a hard rock found in abundance in northeastern Minnesota. If the state encouraged the development of the taconite industry, Davis argued, it could slow the exhaustion of iron ore, buttress the tax base, and prevent a steady erosion of jobs. Blatnik responded enthusiastically to Davis's ideas and agreed to sponsor a proposal for a special tax incentive program. The ensuing 1941 Minnesota taconite tax law removed taconite from the state's ad valorem tax rolls in an effort to promote industrial diversity.[15]

Blatnik pursued a similar agenda in Congress. As a national legislator, he was most concerned with the underlying issue of employment. Having run on the Democratic-Farmer-Labor Party ticket, a Depression-era party unique to

*Representative John Blatnik
(D-Minn.). Courtesy of the
Minnesota Historical Society.*

Minnesota and indicative of the state's progressive political tradition, he supported a wide variety of programs dedicated to regional economic development, vocational training, and other measures that promised to avert future
depressions and create jobs. The congressman enjoyed particularly strong
support from organized labor and retained a healthy suspicion of corporate
business leaders, but still managed to cooperate with them in pursuit of his
developmental agenda.[16]

His committee assignment also contributed to his policy outlook. As chairman of the Rivers and Harbors Subcommittee, Blatnik's authority in Congress stemmed from his capacity to accommodate solicitous interest groups
and dispense water projects to local communities. He also remembered how
Depression-era government expenditures under the New Deal's Works Progress Administration (WPA) and Public Works Administration (PWA) had
provided employment opportunities and an economic infrastructure for his
ailing home state. For Blatnik, then, promoting economic stimulus via federally funded public works suited both the institutional imperatives of the

legislative branch and the political imperatives of a more aggressive brand of postwar, progrowth Keynesianism. In this regard, the failure of the 1955 highway bill devastated Blatnik precisely because he viewed it as a major job producer, as well as a "multi-billion dollar tax revenue feature."[17]

When the congressman set out to resurrect the defunct water pollution bill in the summer of 1955, he drew upon this developmental framework to redefine the issue. He also drew upon another institutional resource that proved increasingly important in the postwar Congress: energetic staff support. Blatnik had hired Jerry Sonosky, a law student and fellow resident of Chisholm, to supplement his small staff in 1954. Sonosky's combination of intelligence, ambition, loyalty, and Democratic idealism allowed him to play an unusually large policymaking role for someone of his age and experience. In addition to handling the normal responsibilities of a congressional aide— letter writing, constituent services, and reelection campaigns—Sonosky assisted Blatnik with Public Works Committee staff duties. The water pollution bill represented his most important assignment to date. The young attorney interpreted the legislation as an opportunity to rein in recalcitrant corporate polluters and establish a precedent for federal regulatory intervention in what had long been considered a state matter. As the Blitch affair had demonstrated, however, the strong opposition of both industry and many local officials meant that precedent would have to be modest. Water quality standards or subpoenas were not feasible, but passing a bill that eliminated the state veto on abatement suits would give a foot in the door, at least, for stronger enforcement mechanisms in the future.[18]

Yet even so subtle a refinement risked rejection, both he and Blatnik realized, if the terms of the debate went unchanged and they failed to exploit the federal government's ability to distribute benefits and promote regional growth. With help from the Library of Congress's Legislative Reference Service, Sonosky figured out how to package pollution control to appeal to the broadest audience. Once Blatnik returned to Minnesota, Sonosky contacted Wallace R. Vawter, a senior specialist in engineering and public works at the Legislative Reference Service, to request a comprehensive background study in preparation for future hearings and draft revisions. His subsequent report, entitled "Water Supply and Use," made an indelible impression on the young attorney.

The report defined water pollution as a potential threat to the nation's water supplies and economic growth, a predicament most likely to resonate with postwar policymakers. Rather than addressing pollution in traditional terms, as a public health issue, Vawter chose to frame it more expansively as part and parcel of a national water resources problem. Although total water supply in the United States remained constant, the study asserted, unprecedented postwar growth in population and industry led to an ever-increasing demand for water to support a variety of functions, ranging from domestic and industrial use, to irrigation, power production, and recreation. National usage in 1955 amounted to approximately 262 billion gallons per day, as compared to only 40 billion gallons per day at the turn of the century. The projected figure for 1975 was 453 billion gallons per day. Although Vawter admitted that an ample overall supply of water existed to serve the nation's needs for the foreseeable future, the pollution problem exacerbated regional irregularities in distribution, as well as seasonal shortages, and ultimately posed a long-term threat to a "continuing expanding economy."[19]

A national pollution abatement program, Vawter asserted, offered one of the most cost-effective means to conserve the nation's most valuable natural resource. "Although much attention has been given to conservation of water through construction of dams for storage," he concluded, "relatively little government support has been given to pollution control," which had to be regarded as "an essential—and less costly—supplement to dams and aqueducts in the total conservation picture." Pollution, he surmised, wasted water. Pollution control, on the other hand, conserved stream quality, allowing repeated reuse.[20]

From the Vawter report's perspective, then, the question of quality proved inseparable from that of quantity. Sonosky realized that this approach to water pollution control bore incalculable advantages for the chairman of the Rivers and Harbors Subcommittee. Congressional enthusiasm for water development projects in the twentieth century was well established. Federal expenditures for such purposes totaled $12.3 billion between 1931 and 1954; much of this amount actually pertained to postwar appropriations, as the rate of spending in the fifties approached four times that of the New Deal thirties. Sonosky suspected that redefining pollution control as an adjunct to this widely accepted water development program and its supply-oriented focus held much more political promise than other justifications.[21]

The economic development angle also resonated with a general public more attuned to shortage than sewage. Explosive postwar growth in urban

areas taxed the water-delivery infrastructures of most municipalities, as local utility companies struggled to come up with the funding and manpower
to deliver fresh water to their customers. Severe droughts also afflicted the
East and the Midwest throughout the fifties, squeezing urban water systems
and making shortages and use-restrictions a common rite of summertime.
In 1953, 1,100 systems nationwide were forced to restrict water use to some or
all of their 24 million customers, while in 1955 sixty-six areas of the country
experienced deficiencies affecting a total of 18 million people.[22]

The media helped reinforce the link between national growth and water supply during the 1950s. Articles appeared regularly in popular periodicals, questioning whether such periodic shortages presaged more chronic
national water supply problems in the future. Their conclusions varied, but
all underscored the underlying connection between water and prosperity.
An oft-cited 1954 article in *Fortune* ranked the availability of water among
the most critical factors, alongside labor and transportation, in determining industrial plant location nationwide. Moreover, a spate of government
reports throughout the decade—including the President's Materials Policy
Commission (Paley Commission, 1952), the Commission on Organization of
the Executive Branch of the Government (Hoover Commission, 1955), and
the Presidential Advisory Committee on Water Resources Policy (1956)—revisited the question of national water resources policy in the context of economic development.[23]

When John Blatnik convened hearings on his revised water quality bill in
March 1956, he framed the legislation in a developmental context. Blatnik
conceived of pollution control in much the same way he had the taconite refining process in the forties: as a legitimate avenue for government-initiated
resource conservation. The influence of the Vawter report was evident in his
appeal. Water use for all purposes was on the rise, he noted, estimating that
by 1975 the country would require an increase in the current water supply of
145 percent, or the equivalent of eleven Colorado rivers, to meet its needs.
"Pollution is a waste of water," he echoed, "just as effective in reducing a
water resource for use as is a period of drought." Like Vawter, Blatnik characterized pollution control as "a valuable and economical supplement" to
traditional conservation measures like storage impounds, permitting
"repeated re-use of the same water as it flows from city to city and industry
to industry."[24]

The chairman rarely strayed from this rhetorical strategy. When, during the floor debate, he veered extemporaneously into what Sonosky called a "health tirade," his staff quickly decided to have the remarks expunged from the *Congressional Record*. They judged the health angle their weakest argument, since waterborne communicable diseases and epidemics had become far less prevalent in the postwar era. Instead, Sonosky inserted the text of Blatnik's original remarks, which emphasized the nation's dwindling water resources.[25]

Issue Definition and Distributive Politics

Incorporating water quality concerns into a prominent postwar developmental discourse may have been necessary for legislative success, but it was not sufficient. John Blatnik's initiative still had powerful enemies; he needed to recruit more than just casual friends.

A policy like pollution control generally provides benefits to diffuse national constituencies while concentrating the costs of regulation among discrete interests, namely the polluters who have to pay for the cleanup. As a consequence, those threatened interests are more motivated to organize and oppose the policy than the putative beneficiaries are to support it. Blatnik realized that well-financed business lobbyists—from the National Association of Manufacturers to representatives of the powerful steel, chemical, or paper industries—held considerable sway over their representatives in Congress. They often dominated state legislatures and the state bureaucracies that regulated water pollution. State pollution control administrators, meanwhile, resented federal encroachment into their regulatory domain and actively campaigned against new enforcement initiatives.[26]

On the other hand, Blatnik could not hope to draw support from a national environmental movement, for none existed in 1955. Pollution did not yet arouse a grassroots response detectable in Washington, nor did conservation interest groups wield much influence in the capitol on issues unrelated to land preservation. Organizations like the Izaak Walton League and the National Wildlife Federation dutifully backed federal legislation, but the magnitude of their political clout paled in comparison to big business and state pollution control experts. When spokespersons for the Manufacturing Chemists Association asserted that there had been "no showing of need for increasing the federal government's enforcement power in the field of water pollution abatement," the remarks aroused little public resistance or rebuttal. Given these circumstances, Blatnik had no choice but to try to attract more influential benefactors who did not yet realize what pollution control could do for them.[27]

The second crucial dimension of agenda setting, then, involved broadening the scope of political conflict. Policymakers like John Blatnik tried to redefine issues by encouraging alternative interests with different priorities to participate in policy debates traditionally dominated by just a few prominent voices. This was crucial, since most federal policies in the twentieth century took form within a variety of government "subsystems," each composed of a specific congressional committee or subcommittee, a set of discrete interest groups, and an executive agency. These insular subsystems, or "iron triangles," dealt with arcane matters of little interest to the average citizen and tended to exclude anyone uninvolved with the specific issue at hand, be it farm price supports or railroad shipping rates.[28]

As chairman of the Rivers and Harbors Subcommittee, Blatnik knew all about the nature of iron triangles, since he served as a central participant in one of the oldest and most prominent among them. He also recognized that if his subcommittee were ever to launch a viable federal water pollution control program, he would need to counteract the influence of state administrators and manufacturing interests by appealing to other, well-established constituencies who heretofore had had little stake in water quality legislation. By mobilizing new, previously apathetic participants, Blatnik hoped to overcome entrenched opposition to his initiative.[29]

Blatnik knew jobs and pork best, so he used them to promote pollution control. Generally speaking, when the government dispensed resources, it made more friends and fewer enemies than when it redistributed them through zero-sum decisions that determined winners and losers. So to expand the scope of participation, the Minnesotan decided to deemphasize the controversial politics of regulation in favor of the less-divisive tradition of distributive politics. During the winter of 1955–1956, Sonosky had focused predominantly on the enforcement language of the House bill, working in concert with sympathetic officials from HEW's general counsel's office. Upon reviewing their work, Blatnik shifted gears and began raising questions about sewage treatment facility construction needs. The chairman had in mind a federal matching grant program to help finance local plant construction (in contrast to the limited loans authorized by the 1948 act). The idea was firmly grounded in New Deal precedent, since the WPA had earmarked millions of dollars for treatment plants in the thirties as part of a broader public works agenda. During World War II, the exigencies of mobilization brought a temporary halt to the construction and dried up federal funding, which did not resume after 1945.[30]

Data provided by the Public Health Service underscored the connection between dollars and clean water. In 1955, the United States had a population of 165 million people, 95 million of whom lived in cities or communities that had a sewer system. By the agency's reckoning, existing treatment facilities served 55 million of the population that lived in communities with sewer systems adequately, 16 million inadequately, and 24 million not at all. But regardless of the degree of treatment applied to municipal wastes, annual net loads discharged into the nation's watercourses had a polluting impact equivalent to the raw sewage of 55 million people. To make a dent in the problem, the agency estimated that spending for treatment plant construction nationwide had to increase by at least 23 percent over the next 30 years (the rate during the fifties averaged $230 million per year, or $2.42 per capita). Specifically, over $5 billion would be needed to fund nearly 6,700 new treatment plants. Local communities bore the burden of financing these facilities, either through increased taxation or through bond issues.[31]

Blatnik anticipated that cities and counties would rally to pollution control legislation offering federal construction grant assistance as part of the package. Citing his own experience with the Minnesota Municipal Association, the congressman noted how smaller towns and municipalities, with their limited tax bases, already struggled to build needed public housing, roads, and libraries, which had more visceral appeal among taxpayers than sewerage systems and waste treatment plants. Without the sort of federal aid the New Deal used to provide, he claimed, these communities could never afford the sanitary infrastructure they needed. As expected, organizations like the American Municipal Association and the U.S. Conference of Mayors responded enthusiastically to the proposed grant program; an American Municipal Association representative actually assisted Sonosky in drafting the specific provisions. These interest groups represented thousands of local city and county officials nationwide, Democrats and Republicans alike. They were staffed with skilled lobbyists who had established channels of access to many members of Congress over the years. In short, the municipalities seemed like an ideal choice for a potent new constituency to support a national pollution control program.[32]

But they were not Blatnik's only choice. He also turned to his most reliable and influential political base—organized labor. From the beginning, the Minnesota congressman viewed a federal waste treatment construction grant program as a state-sponsored vehicle for creating jobs. Similar priorities had motivated New Deal public works projects, but even more recent federal legislation, like the 1946 Hill-Burton Hospital Survey and Construction Act, continued to provide employment opportunities in the course of financing critical public amenities. Unions quickly grasped the significance of clean water from the perspective of bricks, mortar, and wages. Moreover, Blatnik pitched the bill's enforcement provisions to labor leaders as a means to promote regional industrial equity. Southern states already were luring northern manufacturing concerns with "right to work" laws that discouraged union activity. Establishing a uniform federal regulatory regime for controlling water pollution, Blatnik suggested, would prevent Sunbelt politicians from leveraging more northern jobs with weak local water quality standards.[33]

Protecting Blatnik's flank on the water pollution bill, labor forces realized, also promised residual benefits in areas of greater immediate concern, as the fate of clean water and interstate roads once again became intertwined. Congress expected to reconsider the abortive federal highway bill in 1956, a proposed government spending program that both Blatnik and the unions interpreted as an employment bonanza. In 1955, New Mexico senator Dennis Chavez had sponsored a successful amendment to the legislation, exempting contractors from the provisions of the 1931 Davis-Bacon Act, which required payment of "prevailing wage rates" to workers on federal construction projects. The AFL-CIO and the major construction unions urged the extension of Davis-Bacon to the interstate highway program to preserve the sanctity of local collective bargaining agreements. The Associated General Contractors of America, the American Road Builders Association, and the Chamber of Commerce all opposed the measure. Blatnik's assistance in the prevailing wage fight made quid pro quo support of pollution control worth the unions' effort and thus helped secure one of the largest, best-organized, and most influential constituencies as a new participant in the policy process.[34]

By January 1956, then, John Blatnik and his staff had refashioned the subcommittee's environmental legislation into an instrument of economic development, designed to conserve a natural resource essential for growth, stimulate job creation, and protect regional labor markets. They mobilized new constituencies to lobby for water pollution control by exploiting the capacity of the Public Works Committee to distribute government benefits to localities. And they fashioned a new formidable alliance of conservation groups, unions, and county/municipal organizations that offered enough political clout to challenge the monopoly of influence formerly exerted by industries and state officials. Only one question remained: exactly what kind of regulatory law could distributive politics deliver?

Distributing Pollution Control

The construction grant program turned out to be the most popular new feature of the 1956 Water Pollution Control Act, but its appeal proved insufficient to carry stronger abatement measures along in its wake. Blatnik still had to negotiate with the bill's opponents and give ground on its already modest enforcement provisions. In effect, the congressman's legislation offered federal public works money in lieu of federal police power. This pollution control strategy realistically stood the best chance of success in the political context of the mid-fifties. But the compromises it entailed rendered cleaner water a more elusive goal.

The structure of the grant program itself militated against a more systematic prioritization of urban waste treatment needs. The 1956 act authorized $50 million annually for ten years; no one grant could exceed 30 percent of a project's total cost, or $250,000, whichever was smaller. Sonosky adapted an allocation formula similar to that found in the Hill-Burton Hospital Act of 1946, which factored both the population and the per capita income of states into the equation. But since Blatnik worried that large cities would consume the bulk of state allowances, he also decided to add a provision setting aside half of the total authorizations for small cities and towns. This built-in bias toward less-wealthy, less-populated areas helped disperse program benefits as broadly as possible, a wise strategy for building congressional support. But it also steered federal money away from the metropolitan areas that suffered the most serious sewage disposal and water quality problems.[35]

Of course, Sonosky was left to define "small," a legal category determined more in reference to politics than demographics. He set an initial population ceiling of 100,000, only to be informed—emphatically—by another of Blatnik's administrative assistants that such a figure would exclude Duluth from consideration. The Minnesota native, who had recently begun referring to himself and his colleagues at HEW as "the Sewer Gang," dutifully increased the limit to 125,000.[36]

Blatnik himself acceded to more extensive changes to make the bill's enforcement sections acceptable to critical state officials. Despite the glacial pace for formal public hearings or court proceedings, local administrators lamented the surgeon general's independent power to initiate abatement actions without consultation. They insisted that federal enforcement should not commence until state or interstate agencies had been allowed to confirm that a problem existed and to decide what, if anything, needed to be done about it.

Blatnik and his staff bowed to these demands by adding an informal "conference phase" where a consensus on the problem might be reached and abatement activities suggested. A more formal public hearing followed six months later if the secretary of HEW determined that reasonable progress had not been made in the interim. The emphasis throughout the entire process remained on cooperation and negotiation—deferring to local experts whenever possible to take corrective measures and avoiding direct confrontation until all other avenues had been explored. Although these concessions proved sufficient to mollify state bureaucrats, the House-Senate Conference Committee still found it necessary to reinsert the "economic feasibility" test back into the judicial phase to appease other detractors. They needn't have worried; with all the new procedural delays, the chances of ever taking a polluter to court had actually grown more remote. In fact, only one court action was ever filed under the act in the decade following its passage.[37]

Yet despite these allowances, Blatnik still needed to invoke the institutional advantages of his subcommittee chairmanship to save the legislation from an uncertain fate. In the spring of 1956, the members of the House Rules Committee leaned toward rejecting the measure. To ensure its safe passage to the chamber floor, Blatnik needed to convince one person to switch his vote. He did so by offering a hold-out from Mississippi the channel-dredging project he had long desired in Pascagoula. Such subtle maneuvers led Jerry Sonosky to admire how Blatnik "made pollution controllers out of every member of Congress who had a channel to dig, a harbor to deepen, a bridge to build, [or] a post office to name."[38]

Distributive politics also trumped partisan politics. During the subsequent floor debate on 13 June, Republicans mounted a vocal attack on the grant program, charging that it would set an expensive new precedent for federal involvement in state and local matters. Unsuccessful motions to recommit the bill and delete the grant program split the members along party lines. The final vote in its favor, however, was considerably more lopsided, 338 to 31. Regardless of party, few representatives proved willing to turn their backs on federal subsidies that stood to benefit nearly every congressional district.[39]

Executive Resistance

By mobilizing new constituencies with a vested interest in the 1956 act's construction grant program, John Blatnik hoped to keep water pollution control on the federal government's agenda for the foreseeable future. The chairman could expect unions, counties, and municipalities to lobby his subcommittee for the program's expansion over time, just as organizations like the National Rivers and Harbors Congress had worked in tandem with the Army Corps of Engineers to secure funding for local water development throughout the twentieth century.

The Public Health Service seemed like the executive agency poised to occupy the third leg of Blatnik's new "iron triangle." It certainly had an easier case to make for sewage treatment plants than the Corps did with many of its pork barrel projects. When the Public Health Service factored the Census Bureau's revised population estimates into its own projections of urban sewage in 1958, for example, officials concluded that both the number of treatment plants and the sophistication of the technology they employed would need to increase in order to keep pace. That meant considerably more money would be required to overcome construction backlogs and facility obsolescence than they had estimated just three years ago. What better justification for federal assistance?[40]

But the Public Health Service was no Army Corps of Engineers. Rather than seize the bureaucratic opportunity Blatnik's new program offered them, agency officials demurred. In fact, HEW, which oversaw the Public Health Service, testified before the House Public Works Committee as one of the most outspoken critics of federal grants-in-aid. One chronicler of early water pollution legislation dubbed HEW's aversion to this "bountiful spending program" as "one of the great anomalies in the annals of bureaucracy." HEW's position reflected its careful deference to state sovereignty and concomitant hesitance to encroach in areas where local administrators traditionally exercised discretion.[41]

It also reflected the Eisenhower administration's frugality. The White House demonstrated little enthusiasm for spending federal dollars on waste treatment plant construction. Accordingly, the president moved to counter Blatnik's subsequent 1958 proposal to increase authorizations and dollar-ceiling limits on individual grants and recommended sharp cutbacks in the program for fiscal year 1959. Administrative opposition culminated with the February 1960 veto of a new set of amendments designed to raise annual grant authorizations from $50 million to $90 million. The veto message referred to water pollution as a "uniquely local blight" and asserted that "primary responsibility for solving the problem lies not with the federal government but rather must be assumed and exercised, as it has been, by the state and local governments." Notwithstanding his efforts to make water pollution control more palatable by distributing government benefits and diverting attention from controversial regulatory issues, John Blatnik still had to confront questions about the proper limits of federalism.[42]

This skirmish over funding constituted only a single battle along a much broader front. In the late fifties, a Democratic-controlled Congress and a Republican executive branch waged war to determine the proper level of federal expenditures required for future water resource development, particularly in the arid West. As it happened, this wave of congressional concern for dams and reservoirs buoyed the fortunes of pollution control in subtle and unanticipated ways.

The story of how these parallel policies intersected at decade's end confirms that John Blatnik's developmental approach to pollution control was neither anomalous nor idiosyncratic. When Congress commissioned a select committee in 1959 to establish, in technical detail, the case for a comprehensive water resources program, its final report identified pollution control as an integral component of that program. This was not at all what the committee had intended. Nor could any of its members take credit for Blatnik's hard-won water pollution legislation in 1956 or later in 1961. But as the next chapter details, the conclusions of the Senate Select Committee on National Water Resources evolved logically from the same sorts of assumptions about water supply and economic growth that Blatnik had articulated. As such, the Select Committee's well-publicized efforts on behalf of its developmental agenda contributed to a political atmosphere conducive to Blatnik's own initiatives. In 1960, congressional policymakers fought President Eisenhower for more dams and more sewage treatment plants. They simply saw them as different means to the same end.

The Solution to Pollution Is Dilution
The 1960 Senate Select Committee on National Water Resources

There is no greater monument to federally sponsored resource conservation and economic development than a dam. In the twentieth-
century American West, where perpetual water scarcity stood as an
obstacle to regional growth, the federal government's money, administrative capacity, and technical expertise combined to raise soaring
walls of concrete and steel, harnessing the flow of wild rivers behind
them. In the thirties, forties, and fifties, the Bureau of Reclamation
and the Army Corps of Engineers scrambled to regulate entire river
systems at the behest of local interests and their congressional representatives. The structures they built provided irrigation to make
the desert bloom and agribusiness boom, while generating the electricity that nurtured postwar urban-industrial growth. The precedent
established during the New Deal and World War II set the tone for the
golden age of federal water development over the next two decades.[1]

There is no greater monument to the environmental consequences of technology and progress than a dam. The postwar politicians, administrators, and engineers who subscribed to the developmental ethos disregarded aesthetics and ecosystems as they
pursued their ambitious construction agenda. In the fifties, a new
generation of conservationists protested the taming of great rivers and the inundation of scenic canyons, defending the intangible
benefits of nature when measured against additional kilowatts or
acre-feet. But while the construction agencies cared little for solving
environmental problems and their challengers cared little for dams,
neither viewed dams as solutions to environmental problems.[2]

In 1960, a coalition of experts working for the Senate Select Committee on National Water Resources made the connection in an unlikely way. After an exhaustive investigation, they concluded that maintaining water quality sufficient to promote regional economic growth had displaced navigation, irrigation, or even hydropower as the most pressing justification for government development of water resources. This was somewhat surprising, since the members of the Select Committee for whom these experts worked did not care all that much about water pollution. Representing predominantly western states, the senators simply desired an authoritative, technically based rationale for extending the federal largesse that had benefited their region since the thirties. What they wanted, in short, was a prescription for building more dams. And that is what they got, since the experts also concluded that more dams meant more reservoir storage, and thus more fresh water to dilute the wastes threatening regional economic development.

In the process, congressional actors derived a novel national environmental policy prescription from the most traditional of political agendas—regional public works projects. They did so by processing complex technical information against a legislative backdrop of partisanship, localism, and pork, then devising an analytical model that paid lip service to all three, yet still pointed to something new. Once again, distributive politics and the promise of economic development vaulted water pollution control into the national spotlight.

The Select Committee staff and the preceding chapter's protagonist, Representative John Blatnik, traveled different routes to the same destination. In 1955–1956, Blatnik sought to legitimize federal water pollution control by framing it in the context of government water resources development. Committee staffers justified continued government water resources development by emphasizing the need for water pollution control. Either way, policymakers saw quality and quantity as two sides of the same coin. Pollution control represented a way to make water supply meet water demand, clearing the way for economic growth and prosperity.

Blatnik and the committee held something else in common: neither would let a penurious president interfere with its agenda. Dwight Eisenhower considered both water pollution and the politics of water development uniquely local blights. His battle to curb Congress's insatiable appetite for pork created a backlash that helped launch the Select Committee in 1959. The Select

Committee's findings about water quality, meanwhile, made Blatnik's fight for an expanded federal waste treatment construction grant program appear more urgent than ever.

The president never meant to conjoin the two issues. But the developmental priorities that pervaded postwar national politics and structured the legislative policy process discouraged such tidy partitions. They also produced some unanticipated institutional alliances. In the late fifties, when Eisenhower criticized federal funding for waste treatment plants, the Public Health Service (PHS) dutifully backed his defense of localism and deference to federalism. Little did he realize that the very same agency's technical expertise would inform the methodology the Select Committee later employed to calculate national water demand and justify massive federal funding of dams and treatment plants. Congress's receptivity to a multitude of experts, ideas, and bureaucratic agendas ensured that strange bedfellows of this sort continued to shape the substance of postwar water pollution policy over the next decade, even after the environmental movement rose to prominence. In the meantime, a frugal Republican executive discovered just how legislators could produce new environmental initiatives from older developmental imperatives—and make a politically appealing, albeit expensive, case for both.

Spending Money Like Water

Despite Eisenhower's dedication to federalism and fiscal moderation, he faced an uphill battle in keeping the size and cost of the government in check during the fifties. National security expenditures, coupled with domestic priorities like social security, health, and education, accounted for a growing portion of the overall federal budget. "Under these circumstances," Budget Director Maurice Stans noted in 1959, "federal investment in water resources development must compete with other federal programs serving national needs if the federal budget is to be maintained on a sound basis."[3]

The president's efforts to rein in spending and impose more executive branch control over public works did not dampen congressional enthusiasm for water development. It led to a series of clashes between the two branches during Eisenhower's second term, a conflict that must be viewed in the context of an unprecedented postwar push to harness the nation's water resources. World War II and the Korean War had forced the diversion of national resources almost exclusively toward military ends. The end of tensions signaled a rush to make up for lost opportunities. By the time the Public Works Committees reported their $1.6 billion River and Harbors bill in 1956, Congress had already approved a backlog of approximately $8 billion in uncompleted projects.[4]

Eisenhower did not oppose federal water development in principle, but Congress's freewheeling public works authorization process ran counter to his vision of a "corporate commonwealth." In this idealized American polity, professional managers mediated between the government and a myriad of interest groups, promoting social harmony and consensus while steering a course between the unfettered free market and statism. Water development politics, being at once local, interest group–driven, and congressionally centered, eschewed such disinterested expertise and fiscal moderation. The Public Works and Interior Committees chafed at executive branch efforts to subject water development planning to more uniform procedures—like Bureau of the Budget Circular A-47, a Truman-era directive that dictated specific cost-benefit standards for all proposed federal water projects. The Republican administration made every effort to strengthen these criteria, but it also took more direct aim at the purse strings.[5]

Between 1956 and 1959, the Eisenhower administration vetted annual Rivers and Harbors legislation in an effort to weed out unjustifiable authorizations. The president's pocket veto of the 1956 bill, for example, cited thirty-two projects, set to cost over $530 million, that had skirted conventional standards of review. Eisenhower also requested "no new starts" on water projects in his 1958 and 1959 annual budget messages, to provide what he described as a much-needed "breathing spell." Legislators responded by packing the public works bills in each of those years with over sixty new unbudgeted items costing hundreds of millions. The president vetoed both bills, insisting that "overspending in respect to water resources" was "harmful to the United States and to the proper development of these resources themselves." But Congress managed to override the veto in 1959, approving almost $1.2 billion in water development projects and affirming an earlier House report that declared "an overwhelming bipartisan rejection" of the "no new starts" policy. Partisanship, however, was never far from the surface of this battle.[6]

Westerners Nationalize Water Resources Policy

With the 1960 presidential elections looming, Democrats in the Senate sensed an opportunity to seize the water issue, redefine it on Congress's terms, and convert the Republican administration's fiscal caution into a political liability. To do so, they had to counter Eisenhower's negative portrait of parochial, special interest politics and emphasize the nationwide relevance of federally sponsored water development. Given the affinity of western states for subsidized water, senators from beyond the hundredth meridian, like Clinton Anderson (D-N.Mex.) and James Murray (D-Mont.), took the lead in casting their region's prosperity as the sine qua non of a national agenda. From their bases on the Interior Committee and its Subcommittee on Irrigation and Reclamation, these influential westerners hatched Senate Resolution 48, which created the Select Committee on National Water Resources in the winter of 1959.[7]

The Select Committee became the vehicle for western Democrats to present their case to the public. S. Res. 48 charged the committee with writing a report by January 1961 after "making exhaustive studies of the extent to which water resources activities in the United States are related to the national interest" and determining the demands for water and water development for the years 1980 and 2000. Report writing on this subject was not exactly new. Executive branch committees had composed no fewer than eight major studies of water resource policies since the close of World War II. All of them suggested that more comprehensive stream regulation was essential in the future. President Truman's 1952 Materials Policy (Paley) Commission in particular had cast the supply of good-quality water as a limiting factor for industrial manufacturing and projected increased municipal, agricultural, and recreational water demands that threatened to tax existing supplies. But the reports had also recommended more centralized executive branch planning and oversight, so Congress had duly ignored them.[8]

This time, things would be different. Mike Mansfield (D-Mont.), who introduced S. Res. 48 in January, argued that the Select Committee would distinguish itself from its executive branch predecessors by drafting its report as a definitive guide for a "comprehensive legislative program," delineating "the amount, the character, and the timing of water-resource development necessary to meet national requirements in the years ahead." In other words, a report by Congress for Congress would lay out a course of action without trying to reinvent the legislative policymaking process.[9]

Legislators preferred to focus on the broader implications of the executive branch studies—namely, that failure to plan for future water needs could threaten the United States' economic growth, standard of living, and security. In testimony before Clinton Anderson's Subcommittee on Irrigation and Reclamation, a parade of western witnesses endorsed S. Res. 48 in precisely this context. Although not hesitating to point out the benefits to their own region that an aggressive water development strategy portended, they made a point to cast such development through a national lens. From this perspective, the water scarcity that perpetually gripped the West was less a regional idiosyncrasy than a harbinger of future national conditions, given popular predictions of increasing population and per capita water use. "This is not a western problem, it is a national problem," Mansfield surmised, "and the time may not be too far distant when water will be more valuable than oil."[10]

The rhetorical strategy of nationalization proved effective, but the western slant of the Select Committee did not go unnoticed. In one of the more penetrating retrospective analyses, written in 1962, Wayne State University political scientist Roy Hamilton accused the committee of acting as an overt regional advocate. Its unmistakable pedigree represented his most damning evidence: all but four of its seventeen senators had hailed from arid or semi-arid states. Given this composition, Hamilton maintained, the Select Committee's conclusions were bound to be a "self-fulfilling prophesy," since "no western Senator . . . would dream of establishing a select committee to report on the problems of water supply and then proceed to have the members appointed to the committee who were unable to think of water supply as a problem."[11]

Hamilton suggested that the Select Committee's policy analysis could never have transcended its preexisting political agenda. The experts and information it employed reflected member bias. The Select Committee's recommendations seemed all the more self-evident given that much of the data it solicited appeared to come from federal agencies with vested interests in developing water in the West. Was it any wonder, Hamilton mused, that the final committee report indicated that $50 billion in water development would be required by 1980, including the full regulation of five western river basins?

Hamilton had no doubt that the Select Committee's final report would have a definitive impact on water resources policy in the future but concluded that the nation's eastern states would inevitably be shortchanged in the process.[12]

Roy Hamilton did not exaggerate the Select Committee's western bent, nor did he underestimate the final report's impact on water resources policy in the 1960s (its recommendations inspired both the Water Resources Research Act of 1964 and the Water Resources Planning Act of 1965). In dismissing the predictability of the messenger, however, Hamilton overlooked the less predictable content of the message. The Select Committee sought to promote a national developmental agenda that delivered significant benefits to the West. Yet it ended up doing so by introducing a new issue that few westerners, or anyone else, cared about—pollution control—and casting it as the central component of the nation's water resource management program. By assuming that the committee's policy output was overdetermined, the political scientist underestimated Congress's capacity to acquire and process an impressive range of information, even in the most partisan climates.[13]

Anatomy of a Select Committee

Although the tone of the Select Committee's mission was set from the top down, politics alone did not dictate how staffers pursued solutions to discrete technical problems. They tapped a wide variety of professional networks, seeking assistance from academic experts, private consultants, and government bureaucrats. This flexible response was typical of committees prior to the seventies, when the number of permanent support personnel remained small. Nevertheless, it granted certain players a measure of access and influence that belied their less prominent position in the field of water resources development, allowing them to reorient the staff's technical deliberations.[14]

On the surface, the choice of Senator Robert Kerr (D-Okla.) as chair seemed to confirm Roy Hamilton's charge that the committee was little more than a front for regional pork. Although Kerr had earned millions as an Oklahoma oilman, his humble rural upbringing instilled a deep-seated reverence for the power of water to transform dust into prosperity. As his state's governor in the forties, and then its senator from 1949 until his death in 1963, Kerr made comprehensive development of natural resources, or "land, wood, and water," his number one priority, particularly in the Arkansas White and Red River basins.[15]

Kerr's chairmanship of the Subcommittee on Rivers and Harbors and Flood Control solidified his influence in the Senate even before his later involvement with the space program. Assuming command of the subcommittee in 1955 enabled Kerr, in the words of one biographer, "[to expand] a narrow concern for Oklahoma's water development into a broad policy position that touched the interests of almost every other Senator and large numbers of congressmen."[16]

The hierarchy of priorities evinced in Kerr's legislative dealings turned Eisenhower's "corporate commonwealth" on its head. "I represent myself first, the state of Oklahoma second, and the people of the United States third, and don't you forget it!" he once admonished a colleague. For Kerr, what was good for Oklahoma was good for the nation, and pork was good for both of them. He was instrumental in packing new starts into the public works bills of the late fifties and bristled at the intrusive presence of the executive branch in the appropriations process. During a 1957 debate on the rivers and harbors bill, he warned his colleagues against becoming the captives of the Budget Bureau. He even deflected the criticism of frugal cold warriors by raising the troubling specter of "a pagan Communist nation" making "more efficient use of soil and water resources than the most advanced and enlightened nation in the world."[17]

Despite Kerr's visceral allegiance to the gospel of water development, the senator's preferences had little direct impact on the methodology of the technical investigations that informed the substance of the committee's recommendations. This remained the realm of the professional support staff. Though he could easily have filled these positions with like-minded cronies, Kerr realized he needed the weight of independent expertise on his side to convince nonwestern colleagues. He also had enough confidence in his own authority to entrust the research to more impartial water resource professionals. Two in particular, Edward Ackerman and Theodore Schad, determined the structure of the committee's influential study and marshaled the array of experts who executed it.

Edward Ackerman's contribution predated Kerr's tenure as chair. A distinguished professor of geography at the University of Chicago, Ackerman had served as an administrator in the Tennessee Valley Authority and the

Civil Works Branch of the Bureau of the Budget, as well as as a staff member of the Hoover and Paley Commissions. He also headed the Water Resources Program of Resources for the Future (RFF), an independent policy research organization. Ackerman consulted with Clinton Anderson informally in the weeks leading up to the Select Committee's formation and in April began preliminary planning for a two-phased study commensurate with its ambitious mandate. The first phase would consist of a series of twenty-eight technical studies designed to answer the essential questions Congress had asked: how much water development was needed, when and where it was needed, and at what cost? Though the details were complicated, at bottom these studies needed to provide quantitative assessments of current water supplies, current uses, projections of future demand, and the means to meet that demand. The second phase would consist of a staff analysis of legislative options, which would include a comprehensive study of technical, economic, and other factors expected to influence national water development over the next two decades.[18]

It fell to Theodore Schad, the committee's staff director, to implement Ackerman's blueprint. Schad was a Johns Hopkins–educated civil engineer employed as a water resources specialist by the Library of Congress's Legislative Reference Service. He had developed his expertise during stints with the Army Corps of Engineers and Bureau of Reclamation in the 1940s. As an analyst for the Bureau of the Budget in the late fifties, Schad assisted in drafting Eisenhower's veto messages for the Rivers and Harbors Acts and helped to defend Budget Circular A-47 when it came under attack from none other than Senator Kerr. As a consequence, both Kerr and his staff aides were familiar with his work, deeming him knowledgeable, organized, and competent. Ackerman likely recommended Schad, since they knew each other from their earlier days at the Bureau of the Budget. Thus the two men most responsible for the composition of the Select Committee's report had both faithfully served the executive agency leading the charge to rein in Congress's water development programs.[19]

Schad's choice of expert assistance reflected his own professional background, the nature of Ackerman's study, and the institutional options available to him in Congress. Given the vast amount of background information required for phase one, not to mention the looming January 1961 report deadline, the staff director relied as much as possible on executive branch agencies to prepare the technical reports. He also turned to a number of informal advisors from federal water agencies in particular, along with a small cadre of outside consultants. These included Ackerman, Ackerman's colleague from the University of Chicago geography department, Gilbert White, and renowned sanitary engineer Abel Wolman, with whom Schad had studied at Johns Hopkins. His university mentor now served with White and Ackerman as the staff director's "brain trust," analyzing information submitted by federal agencies, reviewing drafts of the committee's report, and contributing separate formal studies pertaining to multipurpose water development and water reuse.[20]

Schad scrambled to formulate an organizational framework sufficient to support the most ambitious synthesis of water-related information yet undertaken. Ackerman's outline specified what information was needed but said less about how it might be presented to Congress and the public in a meaningful way. The staff director drew his inspiration from an unheralded source: a 1957 thesis written for the Industrial College of the Armed Forces by Douglas Woodward, a U.S. Geological Survey geologist. It caught the attention of only a small circle of water resource insiders, but Schad happened to be one of them. Woodward's study was the first he had seen that attempted with any real sophistication to relate physical supplies of water to projections of present and future demands. Although it focused on industrial needs, the study also estimated the dependable yield of water by region in relation to projected usage. Woodward indicated that total daily demand by 1980 would reach 597 billion gallons, a significantly higher estimate than Truman's Materials Policy Commission had made (350 billion gallons per day) just five years earlier.[21]

Schad concluded that this research model, once endowed with more methodological sophistication, could accommodate a broad range of data and provide the answers the Senate was looking for. Although the staff director judged Woodward's regional analysis too perfunctory, he realized that such area-specific knowledge about water supply and demand was important—and generally unavailable. The 1952 Materials Policy Commission had incorporated regional demographic data from the Census Bureau into its water demand projections but made no attempt to divide the United States into river basins or study each region as a discrete unit. The Select Committee's study would be the first to relate natural variations in water supply to estimates of population growth, levels of economic activity, uses of water, and the maintenance of water quality for reasonably homogeneous regions.[22]

The decision to go with a comprehensive water supply-demand study granted RFF an even greater say in the committee's technical labors. RFF's water specialists had cited Woodward in their own work and concluded independently that the thesis would benefit from further regional refinement. The organization retained University of New Mexico economics professor Nathaniel Wollman (no relation to Abel) to do the necessary research. Ackerman then brokered an agreement that enabled Wollman to produce the desired study for the Select Committee, in exchange for the latter's unique access to federal data. This symbiotic arrangement made Schad's job easier and pleased knowledgeable observers in the water resources field, who believed RFF would encourage innovation and free the committee staff from excessive reliance on federal water development agencies.[23]

These observers were correct. Although Roy Hamilton assumed that construction-oriented agencies had supplied the most critical information and ideas, the magnitude of their influence was not as definitive as he believed. Their technical input did not dictate how the RFF study would measure aggregate water demands or what it would recommend to meet them. The agency that had the greatest say in how these parameters were defined was the PHS, and the policy it advocated was pollution control.[24]

The Public Health Service and the Pollution Control Paradigm

The PHS's contribution proved somewhat ironic, given the agency's struggle to secure a niche in the water resources field after 1945. On the one hand, its cooperative, client-based relationship with the states led the agency to resist more direct regulatory responsibilities, deferring instead to local administrators on how best to handle the growing pollution problem. Yet as the traditional threat of waterborne disease receded—owing to advances in sanitary engineering fostered by the PHS itself—and national attention shifted from health to economic growth, PHS officials complained of increasing bureaucratic marginalization within the federal government's water supply and river basin development programs. As Assistant Surgeon General Mark Hollis saw it, a medical as opposed to a construction orientation seemed like a liability once priorities had shifted from "maintaining bacterial quality to the logistics of quantity to meet . . . ever-increasing demands."[25]

The PHS sought to leverage its water quality expertise by serving as a technical consultant in federal multipurpose water development ventures. A 1958 internal report emphasized that the PHS was "uniquely qualified to determine the water supply requirements of municipal and industrial users, and to make water quality studies of existing and proposed raw water supplies." The agency performed these services for the Corps of Engineers and the Bureau of Reclamation under Title III of the 1958 Rivers and Harbors Act. Better known as the Water Supply Act of 1958, the law required proposed reservoir projects to provide for municipal and industrial storage needs, as well as traditional priorities like irrigation, flood control, or power generation. Elsewhere, the PHS's ambitious 1957 Arkansas–Red River Water Quality Conservation Study emphasized that pollution abatement could maximize the water resources developed in multipurpose projects. Local and federal officials valued these services, since water quality data, though increasingly critical to the planning process, was hard to come by. Likewise, the Select Committee staff relied upon the PHS for data pertaining to trends in both urban water usage and the magnitude of stream pollution from municipal and industrial sources.[26]

The PHS owed its special influence with the committee staff to the unique access of its liaison officer, Melvin Scheidt. Trained as a civil engineer at Johns Hopkins, Scheidt was a relative newcomer to the organization, working previously at the Bureau of the Budget as the public works coordinator. As fellow alumni of Johns Hopkins and the Bureau of the Budget, Scheidt and Theodore Schad knew each other well. Scheidt developed a close working relationship with Schad and the staff of RFF, which allowed him to vet Nathaniel Wollman's methodology and assure that it accounted for "water quality management"—controlling water quality as a means of maximizing usable quantity.[27]

Although the precise extent of Scheidt's influence is difficult to measure, water quality did figure more prominently in RFF's supply-demand model than in any previous study. Unlike his predecessors, Wollman distinguished activities involving actual physical water losses (irrigation, soil conservation, municipal supplies, certain types of manufacturing) from "flow uses" (recreation, navigation, hydroelectric power, municipal and industrial sanitation) that returned the water to its course, albeit in an altered condition, making it available for other functions downstream. Permanent ("net") losses represented a small percentage of gross water "consumption," since the majority of "used" water remained in the channel. So, as the PHS emphasized, "the problem of quantity, in the last analysis, frequently breaks down to a problem of quality, since deterioration in the quality of water resulting from previous uses can ultimately render it unfit for most further use, even though it is still available in sufficient quantity for such purposes." The United States was not running out of water, according to the PHS. It was "running out of clean water."[28]

Schad and Wollman's supply-demand model also departed from past studies in its deliberate effort to measure and account for waste assimilation as a discrete "flow" use. In so doing, it reflected the conventional wisdom that waste assimilation represented a legitimate function of lakes and streams. Since no treatment technology yet existed to remove all polluting substances from industrial and municipal sewage, communities still had to rely on receiving waters to dilute the remaining effluent.[29]

The central issue the Select Committee staff began to ponder, then, was the relationship between regional water requirements and the quality required to support them, assuming that the same water had to be reused many times over. Wollman and Schad decided to designate an arbitrary level of 4 parts per million of dissolved oxygen as the average water quality for any given region. They realized that 4 parts per million represented a more stringent standard than most states employed, particularly for streams flowing past urban-industrial complexes. But on average, that much dissolved oxygen could sustain aquatic life and recreation and would also enable repeated reuse for other functions as the water flowed downstream. Although they did not immediately grasp the consequences of their decision, Schad and Wollman's choice of a working standard of quality set the tone for their entire model.[30]

The technical complications associated with their assumptions quickly mounted. The staff had accepted the assignment of quantifying waste loads as a function of anticipated water usage, estimating the biological oxygen demand (BOD) of those loads and then determining the requisite levels of treatment and dilution required to maintain the stated quality standard. All of these variables, Scheidt emphasized, were functions of the specific characteristics of individual streams, defying easy generalization. Prompted by these misgivings, Schad contacted the PHS directly to request some method for approximating pollution loads for an entire river basin. Agency officials informed him that conventional analysis for a single basin would take up to five years to complete. Without a reasonable methodological compromise, Schad realized, they could never complete the study on schedule.[31]

At Scheidt's urging, the committee staff decided to farm out the problem to an external expert in the hope of securing a workable statistical model. He suggested George Reid, a professor of civil engineering and sanitary science at the University of Oklahoma and the director of the university's Bureau of Water Resources Research. He knew Reid as a PHS consultant to the Corps of Engineers in the Southwest, where he conducted municipal water supply studies for proposed reservoir projects in accordance with the 1958 Water Supply Act.[32]

Reid's water supply research influenced the work he would undertake for the committee and, ultimately, the conclusions of the Select Committee Report itself. His communication with Schad commenced in August 1959, while he worked on municipal estimates for projects in Kansas and Oklahoma. Reid was shocked to discover just how prominently water for supplemental waste dilution—planned releases from dams and reservoirs to enhance the volume of well-oxygenated receiving waters—figured in developing criteria for future supplies. For many reservoir projects, the need for such flow regulation turned out to be greater than the municipal and industrial water requirements of the developing areas in question. Although supplemental dilution was no substitute for sewage treatment, he concluded, cities and towns could not rely on treatment alone. Even the best current technology did not remove excess nitrogen and phosphorus, organic nutrients that induced excessive algae growth and depleted a stream's remaining oxygen. Reid went so far as to suggest that the future growth of an area should be limited by the availability of stream flow, and by extension, dams and reservoir storage, for sanitary dilution.[33]

Schad harbored doubts that dilution capacity would ever represent an absolute limiting factor on economic growth, but Reid offered the expertise he needed on short notice. With data supplied from RFF, the PHS, and the U.S. Geological Survey, the Oklahoma professor set about developing a series of methodological shortcuts to determine a number of relevant variables for the committee's study: a stream's capacity to assimilate waste, the magnitude of future pollution loads, the costs of various levels of proposed treatment, and the amount of supplemental dilution water required in light of such treatment to maintain average regional water quality at the 4 parts per million standard.[34]

The staff director's initial reservations resurfaced when he reviewed a draft of Reid's work in March 1960. He later confided to one of Abel Wolman's colleagues in the Johns Hopkins Sanitary Engineering Department that the Oklahoman's methods yielded results "which are quite high for dilution, higher, in fact than any of us think would ever be achieved," since building dams and reservoirs for flow augmentation was not the cheapest option available. Schad understood, of course, that the push for simplification colored Reid's work. A number of reviewers subsequently balked at the mathematical shortcuts Reid employed, particularly his attempts to calculate rates of waste decomposition and stream reoxygenation, which varied widely across individual stretches of water.[35]

Although Schad comprehended the shortcomings of Reid's study, he never seriously considered shelving his conclusions. Noting that Reid's work "appears to be the key to the entire projection of future needs," Schad assumed his methods would have to be more "carefully developed and applied" in the future. For the present, his figures were incorporated into the RFF supply-demand study, which in turn served as the foundation of the staff's "phase one" draft report, distributed for consultant review at the end of March. Wollman's analysis for the Ohio River Basin was completed first and set the tone for the rest of the study. Relying heavily on Reid's techniques, he determined that flow requirements for waste dilution, even assuming a dissolved oxygen standard less than 4 parts per million, exceeded all other consumptive losses or flow requirements by a wide margin. By the year 2000, 19 billion gallons per day would be required for dilution alone, a flow met in the Ohio Basin only 70 percent of the time. Additional storage of 5 to 8 million acre-feet would be needed by century's end to guarantee the necessary flow. Applying this method nationally, the RFF staff concluded that five or six basins would be unable to meet projected needs for waste dilution in 1980; even more would fall short by 2000.[36]

The preeminence of pollution over all other water resource issues took the committee staff by surprise. It so dominated demand estimates that dilution requirements became, by default, the "ruling flow" of the RFF study. They assumed that a region could meet all requirements for water provided its supply was equal to or greater than the sum of consumptive losses plus the water required for dilution of waste. Rough tabulations of total national storage requirements based on the Ohio Basin projections reached 250 million acre-feet by 1980 and 482 million acre-feet in 2000. Schad later informed the chair of the Johns Hopkins University Sanitary Engineering Department that those figures "threw a terrific scare into my consultants, particularly Dr. [Abel] Wolman," who feared that publicizing such unexamined storage estimates "might set off a mad spree of reservoir building without knowing just what we are doing." The consultants' reservations inspired the RFF staff to downplay those numbers and derive different combinations of sewage treatment and storage in order to determine the cheapest option for specific regions.[37]

What ultimately distinguished the RFF study of water resources were the twin pillars of supplemental dilution and waste treatment. As Nathaniel Wollman described it, "The demand for water in its most general meaning is a demand for sustained flow after accounting for losses, to take care of the biochemical demand still remaining in the effluent discharged from treatment plants. . . . By relating surface flow to level of waste treatment, both of these become intrinsic elements of a 'water resource program.'" In effect, the national water resources program prescribed by the Senate Select Committee became "a program of reservoirs and waste treatment plants." The final report earmarked $42 billion out of a total of $54 billion in recommended expenditures for waste treatment, with 60 percent of the dam-regulated flow funded by the remaining $12 billion designated to maintain water quality after treatment. Roy Hamilton's accusations notwithstanding, the report allotted the bulk of this money to be spent east of the 96th meridian; 72 percent of treatment costs, for example, pertained to the East. But the question remained: how would the committee's western boosters react to the staff's conclusions?[38]

Congress and the Politics of Expertise

Members of Congress have a litmus test for information reminiscent of the physician's Hippocratic oath: first, do no harm. Most legislators seek information not for its own sake, but as a means to exercise power over the policy process. They are often more concerned that information will harm them or undermine their positions than whether it actually serves to help them. For this reason, legislators generally do not allow the experts they employ much discretion. Rather, legislators turn to experts in order to frame problems and solutions more effectively. The chairman of the Select Committee on National Water Resources proved no exception.[39]

Up until this point, Senator Kerr had remained aloof, deferring to the professional judgment of his personnel. With phase one's technical studies and projections nearing their final form in the spring of 1960, his staff director looked ahead to the more introspective second phase of the committee report. Schad expected it to deal with the sorts of issues that had resonated in the water resources field for years, and which former budget analysts felt particularly inclined by training and experience to address, including methods of cost-benefit analysis and interagency relationships. But his boss had other plans. Kerr had departed Capitol Hill for Oklahoma in order to digest the staff's work, and he was pleased with what he read. So pleased, in fact, that upon his return to Washington, he informed his staff director that phase one would become, in and of itself, the basis for the Select Committee's final report. The speculative analysis of phase two was to be dropped entirely.[40]

In opting to eliminate phase two, Kerr exhibited an astute sense of what was required both to maximize the impact of the Select Committee's work and to deflect potential critiques of institutional arrangements he favored. A dozen executive branch reports had revisited matters of cost-benefit analysis and interagency relationships since the thirties; none had managed to overcome the political inertia inherent in attempting to reorganize the water resources bureaucracy. Avoiding a repetition of these arcane bureaucratic battles stood to make the Select Committee's report more palatable to both its congressional audience and the public. Of course, the chairman also had no intention of allowing the staff to tamper with a decentralized bureaucratic structure that delivered his handpicked water projects and buttressed his base of power in the Senate.[41]

Nor did Kerr's approval of the preliminary phase one report represent an act of selfless deference to expertise. Although the staff produced the information in a nonpartisan fashion, its subsequent interpretation would take place in a decidedly politicized sphere. When the chairman reviewed the report, he judged first that it did no harm. The report's emphasis did not detract from an aggressive policy of water resources development at all—it sim-

A meeting of the consultants to the Senate Select Committee on National Water Resources. Standing: Senator Robert Kerr (D-Okla.), Don McBride. Left to right around table: Len Mosby, Irving Fox, Ed Ackerman, Abel Wolman, Ted Schad, Herb Gee, W. G. Hoyt, Gilbert White. Courtesy of the Carl Albert Center Congressional Archives, University of Oklahoma.

ply incorporated pollution control as an operative variable into that policy. In fact, by bringing the matter of water quality to the forefront, the report succeeded brilliantly in framing water resources in a national context. The staff report may not have beaten the drum for specific western proposals and may have emphasized a problem beyond the traditional purview of either the Bureau of Reclamation or the Corps of Engineers, but it underscored, with professional and scientific authority, that comprehensive development of water resources stood as an imperative for the entire country. In the process, it took nothing away from Oklahoma. To that end, the report meshed seamlessly with Kerr's sense of regional and national priorities.

Other members of the Select Committee reacted with less enthusiasm.

Democrats like Frank Moss (D-Utah), Claire Engel (D-Calif.), Gale McGee (D-Wyo.), and their staffs were relative newcomers to the Senate with ambitious plans for the federal development of the West's water resources. The report's substantial focus on pollution, and its conspicuous lack of recommendations for specific projects in western states, troubled them. A number of senators were also disturbed that the draft committee report used a 2.5 percent growth rate, rather than the 5 percent rate endorsed in July's Democratic national platform, to calculate future water supply and demand.[42]

Kerr's approach to his duties as chairman served to mute these ripples of dissension. The Oklahoma senator refrained from using subcommittees, despite the variety of topics the Select Committee addressed, to prevent individual members from exerting undue influence in pet areas of interest. Kerr also acted to shield the staff's work from revision. When his colleagues moved to raise objections during meetings of the full committee, Kerr responded by beginning to read the more than fifty-page draft, word-for-word, inviting them to engage in a painstaking session of microediting. Opposition quickly evaporated. The Select Committee published its final report with a codicil of minority opinions, but the impact of this dissent proved negligible.[43]

By the time Senator Kerr presented the Report of the Select Committee on National Water Resources to the Senate on 30 January 1961, it said all he wanted it to say. RFF's completed study indicated that water demands would increase to 559 billion gallons per day, or 51 percent of total stream flow, by 1980, and 888 billion gallons per day, or 81 percent of stream flow, by 2000. Because water would be widely reused, the margin between aggregate supply and demand was not as close as it appeared, but the maintenance of quality to permit reuse would become the paramount concern. The report recommended "a positive program for developing and using natural [water] supply," including the full development of the resources of five western regions by 1980. Although advocating no specific projects, the committee did make a number of broad recommendations, calling for up-to-date federal and state plans for river basin development; more state activity in water resources management; federally coordinated research; and periodic assessment of water supply-demand relationships.[44]

The enthusiastic public and political response to the Select Committee's report confirmed Kerr's instincts. Declaring it "by far one of the most popular in recent years," the Government Printing Office distributed 5,000 copies in the first month of publication alone and estimated total distribution would reach 20,000, or ten times that of the average Senate committee report. The report's popularity led the effusive editors of the *Journal of the American Water Works Association* to proclaim that "water, like sex, has fundamental appeal."[45]

In the more abstemious realm of politics, the executive branch lent prompt affirmation to the Select Committee's work. The outlook and recommendations of the final report assumed a central place in President Kennedy's Message on Natural Resources Policy, delivered to Congress on 23 February 1961. Kennedy wasted no time distancing himself from his predecessor's stance, bluntly rejecting a "no new starts policy" that "denied the resource requirements and potential on which our economic growth hinges." He instructed the director of the Bureau of the Budget to implement, wherever possible, "the very excellent and timely report of the bipartisan Senate Select Committee on National Water Resources." He also pledged an intensified program of water pollution control, urging passage of the legislative amendments vetoed by Eisenhower the year before. "To meet all needs—domestic, agricultural, industrial, recreational," the president noted, "we shall have to use and re-use the same water, maintaining quality as well as quantity."[46]

The report of the Senate Select Committee on National Water Resources represented the culmination of a process, characteristic of the post–World War II Congress, in which diffuse technical information was acquired, analyzed, and converted into knowledge useful for promoting policy. Congress may have lacked the institutional capacity of the executive branch, but the Select Committee employed its own informal web of experts, culled from universities, private think tanks, and the Legislative Reference Service to produce "a more serious and scholarly document," in the words of Nathaniel Wollman, than its critics presumed. Robert Kerr, an actor thoroughly enmeshed in the politicized environment Hamilton postulated, sanctioned the "scholarly document" because he judged it beneficial to his broader political purposes. Regional politics did not preclude the production of complex policy analysis within Congress so much as it framed how that analysis would be used.[47]

The RFF study reflected the prevailing mind-set of water resource professionals circa 1960, meaning that it exhibited certain underlying assumptions that politicians like Kerr shared. The staff recognized that much of their supply-demand model relied on shortcuts and conjecture. They knew, for example, that their definition of pollution excluded inorganic chemicals, toxic substances, radioactive waste, and pesticides, and that their methodology for determining dilution requirements employed many mathematical and biological generalizations. They even suspected, correctly, as it turned out, that cost and other complicating factors made dams an impractical antidote for water pollution in urban areas. But the staff continued to interpret future national requirements for water as a function of economic growth—and economic growth as an independent variable. By contrast, when Theodore Schad led a new National Water Commission in the next major comprehensive analysis of U.S. water resources in the early seventies, his staff projected future water demand as a function of specific value choices and social policy decisions, growth being but one among many.[48]

To be sure, an unexamined commitment to development did not preclude the Select Committee staff from diagnosing the nation's water pollution problem. Although proponents of pollution control had made a similar case throughout the 1950s, the committee's comprehensive, quantitative presentation underscored the point in an authoritative way: quality had become the controlling variable in the federal government's water resources policy, where for the first half of the century it had been only a marginal concern. But the Select Committee never contemplated or recommended stricter enforcement activities directed at industrial polluters. Robert Kerr objected to the modest provisions in John Blatnik's 1961 legislation to strengthen the federal government's police powers. He relented only begrudgingly, and not without securing a section of the bill that authorized the Corps of Engineers and Bureau of Reclamation to consult with the PHS, determine the volume of water required for supplemental dilution of a stream's waste effluent, and build that additional capacity into pending reservoir projects. Such solutions remained faithful to the recommendations of the Select Committee's experts—and its original mission.[49]

The Passing of the Old Guard

The data and conceptual framework generated by the Senate Select Committee on National Water Resources reinforced the idea that water pollution control should serve as a method to supplement finite regional water supplies and promote economic growth. This policy perspective remained influential in Congress well into the sixties but failed to bolster the political fortunes of two prominent players who had espoused it to great advantage. Ironically, the 1961 Federal Water Pollution Control Act Amendments signaled the waning relevance of both the PHS and John Blatnik, just as their stars appeared ascendant.

Despite its critical contribution to the Select Committee report, the PHS failed to convince Congress that it possessed the capacity or the commitment to manage water quality in the long run. The tenor of the debate emerging from both the House and the Senate favored upgrading the water pollution control program's status within HEW, which meant elevating it out of the "sub-basement" in the PHS and establishing a more independent administration within HEW.[50]

Representative John Dingell (D-Mich.) acted on behalf of prominent conservation organizations in his efforts to compel such a bureaucratic reorganization—the most tangible policy contribution conservationists made in the early sixties. Dingell, chairman of the Subcommittee on Fisheries and Wildlife Conservation, viewed enforcement as a critical component of federal pollution control and often complained that the surgeon general and other top PHS officials failed to carry out the program with sufficient vigor to protect fish and wildlife resources. "Because of the orientation of the Surgeon General's Office over a long period of years," he told the House Public Works Committee, "efforts have been made . . . to convert the water pollution activities into a kind of polite research." Likewise, conservation spokesmen criticized the PHS's narrow "medical" approach to pollution control at a time when policymakers desired to treat water quality in the broader context of national water resources management. Such characterizations undoubtedly proved frustrating for an agency that had long sought to demonstrate its relevance in just such a context. Although the PHS continued to conduct important research, Congress, the executive branch, and the public looked to other bureaucratic options for managing river basins and regulating water quality.[51]

The momentum generated by the 1960 presidential election and the Select Committee's final report helped John Blatnik build upon the legislative foundation he had established in 1956. But Blatnik's legislation had succeeded in generating its own inertia over the last five years. Although organized labor served as an important catalyst early on, the nation's cities and counties soon emerged as the most vocal and influential advocates for the federal grant program. Between 1957 and 1961, the government awarded more than $213 million nationwide for over 2,500 construction projects costing a total of $1.25 billion, with every federal dollar generating $4.50 in local matching funds. The program's success energized municipalities and worked to undermine the Eisenhower administration's opposition. The 1961 Water Pollution Control Act Amendments increased authorizations for treatment plant construction by between $30 and $50 million annually.[52]

Despite these accomplishments, the influence and leadership of John Blatnik gradually dissipated as institutional changes within Congress shifted the locus of environmental initiative from the House to the Senate. Although Blatnik remained active in the politics of pollution control, he did not guide the subsequent transformations in federal policy or administrative capacity as enforcement and prevention became more pressing issues. What did persist, however, was the predominance of developmental values and priorities that continued to inform Congress's newest environmental entrepreneur—an unassuming senator from Maine named Edmund Muskie.

The Education of an Entrepreneur
Edmund S. Muskie and the Subcommittee on Air and Water Pollution

A cold rain fell outside the state courthouse in Augusta, Maine, two weeks before Christmas in 1959. Inside, Robert Kerr presided over the latest field hearings conducted by the Senate Select Committee on National Water Resources. The heterogeneity of the nation's water problems compelled the Select Committee to convene hearings in twenty-four localities during its tenure. Most of the early ones had taken place out west, but Senator Kerr's road show now swung east, making stops in the Great Lakes states and in New England.

The Select Committee chose its hearing sites in response to petitioning senators, and the one that took place in Augusta was no exception. Given the turbulent history of New England's political conflicts over water and power, it was hardly surprising that Edmund S. Muskie had solicited Kerr to visit Maine. Although barely a year into his first term in the Senate, Muskie had recently served as his state's governor (1955–1958) and understood the significance of hydroelectric power in a region plagued by high energy costs. But state administrators also struggled to reconcile the competing demands of water users engaged in industry, fishing and gaming, recreation, and agriculture. As they planned for future growth in population and production, Maine's officials braced for a run on the state's water resources and expected the viability of the economy to depend increasingly on multipurpose dams and similar public works.[1]

Muskie also recognized that stream pollution represented an increasing threat to water supplies. In his brief opening statement before the Select Committee, he noted that the disposal of untreated sewage and industrial waste had seriously deteriorated the quality of receiving waters, while conflicting with "other desirable uses." He insisted, however, that the state had created a Water Improvement Commission and the necessary program of stream classification to "permit the greatest utilization of this valuable resource." Muskie went on to assert that long-term practical solutions to water pollution problems rested less with enforcement than with technological innovation and "applied research."[2]

Despite these facile assurances, the hearings evinced a less optimistic picture of Maine's water pollution problem and the state's handling of it than Muskie let on. According to a local League of Women Voters representative, agency directors responded so evasively to questions concerning "such clearly neglected areas as pollution control" that "the Committee was obliged to probe" for basic information. She described the senators as "obviously astonished" at the cumbersome pollution abatement program in Maine nominally overseen by the Water Improvement Commission (WIC) and at the "speciousness of industry arguments which threaten industrial removal if abatement is enforced." Questioned closely by Kerr, WIC's commissioner admitted that the legislature, not the commission, assigned classifications to individual streams, defining their desired condition in reference to anticipated uses. Given the political clout of paper manufacturing companies and other industrial interests, the legislature had never adopted any classifications designed to improve water quality. Not only did the system exempt existing polluters, it did not yet apply to Maine's major rivers, the Androscoggin and the Kennebec. As Kerr saw it, the WIC conferred little more than a "license to pollute."[3]

The commissioner's report on municipal sewage treatment proved even more sobering. He admitted that most of the state's twenty-one treatment plants were obsolete and inefficient and served only a small percentage of Maine's inhabitants. According to the PHS, Maine treated only 11 percent of its municipal sewage and had increased the percentage of waste treated between 1945 and 1957 by only 2 percent, the worst performance in the entire nation.[4]

Edmund Muskie would gain renown in the sixties and seventies as the Senate's "Mr. Clean," the leading authority on pollution control and sponsor of some of the most important environmental legislation of the postwar era. But on this day in 1959, the junior senator could only look on as Robert Kerr, the conservative oilman from Oklahoma, assumed the role of environmental crusader, cross-examining reluctant witnesses and exposing the futility of Maine's cleanup efforts, often to the delight of onlookers. History remembers neither man in this way, and for good reason. Kerr had no stomach for the federal regulatory power that Muskie would later endorse to redress the nation's pollution problem.[5]

The anomalous goings-on in Augusta remind us that Muskie's career as an environmental policymaker began in Congress, not in Maine. Beginning in 1963, the senator would use his position as the chair of the Public Works Committee's Subcommittee on Air and Water Pollution to manufacture congressional and public support for stronger pollution control laws. Like John Blatnik before him, Muskie acted as a legislative entrepreneur. He dedicated himself to a policy that had yet to generate significant grassroots support but stood to benefit millions of Americans—not to mention Muskie's own position of power within the legislative branch.

Unlike Blatnik, however, Muskie did not wield influence or overcome opposition by distributing pork. Rather, his institutional currency in the Senate was knowledge. He leveraged the authority of his autodidactic expertise to persuade colleagues and ordinary citizens to expand government regulation of water quality. He did so, however, while continuing to draw upon the developmental discourse that had made pollution control relevant to men like Kerr and Blatnik in the first place and that continued to resonate with the public in the mid-sixties. As with his predecessors, natural resource development took on a special significance early in Muskie's political life. So Maine is the place to begin the story of the senator's environmental career after all—but not for the reasons Muskie himself claimed.

Muskie in Maine

Biographers first discovered Edmund Muskie in the early seventies, as his prospects for the presidency gained momentum. Since his reputation as the foremost legislative expert on pollution issues defined his political identity, the senator made sure to locate the origins of his environmentalism in the pastoral ethos of his New England home. As he recalled in his own autobiography, "My journey toward a place in the environmental sun began in my own backyard.... there you were, viscerally, an outdoorsman and a conservationist.

If you were born in Maine, you got interested in doing something about it when that beauty was threatened."[6]

Like most down east natives, Muskie encountered an intimate juxtaposition of bucolic nature and industrial blight in Maine that informed his sense of place. Born to Polish immigrant parents in 1914, Muskie grew up in Rumford, an isolated town of 10,000 situated at the confluence of the Swift and Androscoggin Rivers in the western part of the state. Rumford's rustic landscape was dominated by the Oxford Paper Company's pulpwood processing plants, which poured raw mill wastes into the adjacent streams and belched thick chemical clouds into the air. Muskie's ambition and intelligence allowed him to escape the confines of the mill town via Bates College and Cornell Law School. After a stint in the navy during World War II, he returned to set up private practice in the town of Waterville, where he also began his career in local Democratic politics. He spent three terms in the state legislature, then served as the district director of the Office of Price Stabilization in 1951 and as Maine's Democratic National Committee Chairman in 1952 before running successfully for governor in 1954—the first Democrat to do so in a popular election in Maine in the twentieth century.[7]

Memories of home played a part in Muskie's gubernatorial campaign, but it was Rumford's economy, not its environment, that shaped the substance of his platform. Economic development remained his administration's number one priority. Maine was a poor state, ranked in the lowest quarter nationally for per capita income. The region was dotted with small towns and rural communities like Rumford, the majority of which depended upon a single factory or mill. The most prominent industries—pulp and paper processing, textile and shoe manufacturing, fish and shellfish production—relied on a cheap workforce to ensure profits and vigorously opposed any policies, such as state-sponsored industrial diversification or a minimum wage, that might undermine the unskilled, low-wage labor market they enjoyed. The Republican Party's perennial dominance of state politics had managed to keep such threats at bay for decades. As contemporary political scientists marveled at the business community's monopolistic control of local and state government, the postwar economic boom enjoyed by the rest of the nation seemed to pass Maine by.[8]

The forces aligned with and against Muskie would have been identical even if he had chosen pollution control as the defining issue of his administration instead of development. By emphasizing the link between economic and political stagnation, the candidate tapped a well of populist discontent shared by unionists, farmers, small businessmen, and professionals. The same intransigent polluters who stymied the Water Improvement Commission and ignored local pleas to abate environmental nuisances represented the very concentration of industrial power that the Democrats condemned. A popular antipathy for arrogant corporate polluters did exist in Maine in the fifties and sixties, as evinced by the applause that Senator Kerr's cross-examinations provoked during the Select Committee's hearings. But an inchoate collection of concerned citizen groups could not yet match the political clout of big business or offer a compelling alternative to untrammeled growth, and would not do so until the later sixties.[9]

Reminiscent of John Blatnik, Governor Muskie viewed government stewardship and development of natural resources as a means to ensure economic security. During the campaign he pledged to create a centralized Department of Conservation, with jurisdiction over the state's forests, inland fish and game, sea and shore fisheries, minerals, and waterways. He described water pollution in 1955 as a problem that had "serious economic implications for existing industries," especially recreation and tourism, and argued that a modest control program would attract new businesses to Maine by providing "an abundant supply of clean water." Since Muskie expected water shortages to grow more acute in other parts of the country, he insisted that the state could not allow pollution to erode its competitive advantage. The governor grew particularly frustrated when a manufacturer he had tried to lure to Bedford chose to locate out of state because of the degraded condition of the Saco River.[10]

Although Muskie looked to a "partnership with free enterprise" to promote "progressive development and sound conservation" of natural resources, industrial interests continued to resist any kind of environmental regulatory program. The union president at International Paper warned Muskie in 1954 that pollution control was a political "hot potato" and that he feared the company would abandon its plant in Franklin County "if forced too much on anti-pollution." The governor got the message. "Patience, ingenuity, and cooperation on the part of all those interested will be required . . . if we are to avoid undue burdens for existing industries and our municipalities," the governor emphasized in his public statements. To his credit, Muskie convinced the legislature to strengthen the state's anemic water improvement law and stream classification process in 1957 and vigorously pursued federal grant money for waste treatment plants. But by the time Robert Kerr visited Augusta in 1959, observers were already referring to Maine's water quality efforts as "more amusing than effective."[11]

By that time, Muskie had moved on to Washington and the Senate. Over the next few years he continued to champion economic growth by supporting initiatives for area redevelopment, public works, manpower retraining, and similar programs benefiting Maine. Although pollution had not been a priority, in 1963 his priorities would change.

Power, Policy, and Institutional Imperatives: The Postwar Congress

Neither the sublime memory of Maine's pristine wilderness nor the hue and cry of his constituency drove Edmund Muskie to transform himself into the preeminent congressional authority on pollution. Rather, his career path reflected a series of responses to the internal structure and norms of the legislative branch. The junior senator recognized that developing expertise in the arcane fields of pollution and urban policy offered the most direct avenue to maximize his power and influence within the Senate. Muskie's environmental turn must be viewed in this organizational context.

Unlike most institutions in the twentieth century, Congress became more modern as it became less hierarchical. In the years leading up to World War II, a combination of institutional and partisan reforms diminished traditional sources of authority like the Speaker of the House and the Democratic Caucus, solidified the seniority system, and dispersed power to the standing committees. Over the next two decades, the committee system achieved its most enduring stability. Part of this stability derived from a lack of turnover in House and Senate membership—more than 80 percent tended to be reelected from one term to another. Once seniority replaced leadership discretion as the mechanism for distributing institutional resources, electoral longevity enabled members to secure committee chairs and build independent bases of power. Largely free from external interference or sanction, chairs exercised nearly total control of their committees' agendas and staffs and enjoyed considerable legislative autonomy.[12]

Congressional committees and their chairs became even more prominent players in the postwar policymaking process. Oklahoma's Robert Kerr had a greater impact on the geography of the nation's infrastructure, both with regard to water projects and space installations, than perhaps any other individual in government. Southern conservatives like Kerr, who encountered little electoral competition in their respective districts, benefited most from the seniority system and held a disproportionate number of committee chairs. They frequently blocked policies endorsed by liberals in areas such as education, housing, and civil rights.[13]

Apart from the politics of distribution and obstruction, congressional committees served as decentralized, specialized units that brokered another resource indispensable for policy development: knowledge. Chairs mastered complex information from a wide range of sources and garnered reputations as specialists in their particular fields. Legislators generally deferred to committee expertise, especially as the substance of policy grew more complex. Specialization also constituted one of the more valued norms of conduct, or "folkways," of the Senate, where members were encouraged to develop expertise on issues related to their committee assignments. Senior members expected freshmen to forgo immediate political rewards and serve an "apprenticeship," accruing knowledge and seniority that would eventually translate into power and prestige. The institutionalization of expertise in the committee system contributed to the Senate's endemic conservatism in the postwar period.[14]

The 1958 election that brought Edmund Muskie to Washington had a profound impact on the partisan balance and institutional configuration of the Senate. Capitalizing on recession and political scandal, the Democrats gained fifteen seats, increasing their number from forty-nine to sixty-four. The influx of new members altered the demographic and ideological profile of the upper chamber. Nearly all the freshman hailed from electorally competitive northern states, and most—including Muskie, Michigan's Philip Hart, and Minnesota's Eugene McCarthy—were liberals. But the election did not simply shift the Senate's center of gravity to the left; it created an ideological gap between senior members—mostly conservative Southern Democrats who occupied positions of influence—and their newly arrived colleagues. Between the 86th and the 91st Congresses, conservatives held over half of all committee chairs. Northern Democrats soon found that the Senate's committee system, together with its conservative folkways, stood as serious obstacles to policy change and career advancement.[15] Though unable to alter the distribution of committee chairs, the Class of 1958 did force certain changes in the Senate's traditional mode of operations. Most notably, the leadership acquiesced and suspended the apprenticeship norm, allowing liberals to engage almost immediately in active policymaking. Freshman likewise benefited from advantageous assignments on "prestige committees" like Finance, Appropriations, or Armed Services. With such a unique opportunity to develop expertise and influence in important policy areas, Edmund Muskie had no intention of embarking on a career in pollution control in 1959. His top committee choices included Foreign Relations, Judiciary, and Commerce, all of which offered more appetizing fare than soot or sewage.[16]

Muskie's decision to pursue an unglamorous specialty in environmental policy reflected a pragmatic adjustment to the institutional exigencies he encountered in the Senate during his first term. The most compelling of these proved to be the rancor of Lyndon Johnson, the Democratic majority leader. An inauspicious run-in early on with the influential Texan altered the course of Muskie's career. Alongside Robert Kerr and Georgia's Richard Russell, Johnson stood as one of the most powerful figures in the Senate and ranks as the most successful majority leader of the twentieth century. His effectiveness stemmed less from policy expertise than from his mastery of parliamentary procedure and his renowned ability to secure consensus by cajoling fellow Democrats. Johnson's control over individual committee assignments proved to be an invaluable means of persuasion. The so-called Johnson Rule relaxed the Democratic Steering Committee's strict adherence to seniority and allowed every new Democratic senator a seat on one of the more sought-after committees. As with most favors Johnson bestowed, however, such advantageous placement incurred a corresponding political debt.[17]

Muskie soon learned the perils of resisting the "Johnson treatment." During their introductory meeting, the majority leader worked the freshman with his trademark charm in an effort to win backing on a proposed change in the Senate's cloture rule, a parliamentary procedure designed to limit southern filibustering of civil rights legislation. Johnson empathized with Muskie's transition from the spotlight of the governor's mansion to the relative anonymity of the Senate, where members faced an overwhelming number of complicated issues. "There'll be times, Ed," Johnson intimated, "when you won't know how you're going to vote until they start calling the M's." Muskie, not quite convinced that Johnson's tactic on cloture would work, took the advice to heart. When pressed to commit his vote, Muskie earnestly, if somewhat dryly, replied, "Well, Lyndon, we haven't gotten to the M's yet." Johnson evidently mistook Muskie's phlegmatic demeanor for sass, referring to him later on as "chickenshit," the all-purpose moniker for persons and things LBJ found displeasing. Muskie's subsequent assignments reflected the Texan's displeasure. The Democratic Steering Committee passed him over for his top three choices and placed him instead on the less appealing Banking and Currency, Government Operations, and Public Works Committees.[18]

Johnson used the Public Works Committee as a repository for incoming members with a penchant for independence and an inclination toward liberal activism. He relied on Robert Kerr's overwhelming presence on the committee to keep a tight rein over his charges. Johnson first employed this strategy, at Kerr's urging, with Patrick McNamara, the former union leader and newly elected senator from Michigan in 1954. He also trusted Kerr to contain other newcomers between 1958 and 1962: Jennings Randolph (West Virginia), Steven Young (Ohio), Frank Moss (Utah), Lee Metcalf (Montana), and Muskie, among others. By the early sixties, at Robert Kerr's behest, the Senate Public Works Committee had become a liberal enclave. But Kerr's containment plan failed to consider one salient variable: his own mortality. Felled by a sudden heart attack in December 1962, the Oklahoma senator surrendered control to those he had sought to restrain when Patrick McNamara assumed command in 1963.[19]

The most pressing question the new chairman faced at the start of the 88th Congress, and the one that affected Edmund Muskie's career most directly, involved the assignment of subcommittee chairs. The proliferation of subcommittees stands out as another of Congress's notable postwar institutional adaptations. Although the Legislative Reorganization Act of 1946 streamlined the committee structure, it could not diminish the magnitude or complexity of Congress's workload, and subcommittees multiplied to pick up the slack. Subcommittees also helped to alleviate the regional disparity in the Senate's distribution of power. They provided a critical outlet for junior liberals to publicize problems, develop policy expertise, and gain prestige. Between 1957 and 1968, the number of subcommittees in the Senate grew from 86 to 103, while the percentage of southern subcommittee chairs declined from 45 percent to 31 percent.[20]

Senators enjoyed longer terms and more freedom from parochial affairs than their colleagues in the House and had the luxury of pursuing novel policy matters. Subcommittees served them as vehicles for exploring issues that affected broad national constituencies, such as consumer health and safety or the environment, but attracted relatively little attention.

Still, Edmund Muskie wanted no part of the Subcommittee on Air and Water Pollution. The push to create it in 1963 had come from an outsider: Abraham Ribicoff. The former secretary of HEW and Connecticut's senator-elect acted on the advice of his new legislative assistant, Jerry Sonosky, who had moved over to HEW after leaving John Blatnik's office in 1961. Although the energetic aide lobbied successfully on his boss's behalf, Ribicoff was assigned to the Government Operations Committee instead. While he and Sonosky went on to national prominence investigating pesticides in 1963, McNamara decided to put Muskie in charge of the new, low-wattage subcommittee. The junior senator had dreamed of taking over Robert Kerr's coveted Rivers and Harbors chairmanship, dispensing pork rather than managing the miscellaneous pollution-related bills introduced in the Senate in 1963. When the committee's staff director, Ron Linton, reluctantly began to explain the assignment to Muskie, he didn't get much farther than the word "air" before the dejected senator interrupted him: "Air? What the hell do I care about air coming from Maine?"[21]

Despite this inauspicious beginning, Edmund Muskie made the most of his opportunities and within eighteen months had transformed himself into the leading Senate expert on both air and water pollution. The senator's superior intellect and work ethic served him well in an institution where colleagues valued specialization and unassuming dedication to legislative duties. According to Linton, Muskie "spent lots of time mastering arcane issues you would normally leave up to staff and staff would leave to technical consultants." Muskie also excelled at distilling relevant technical details and communicating salient policy issues to a general audience. His effectiveness as a leader stemmed from the credibility he garnered as an articulate expert, whether dealing with the specifics of pollution control on the Public Works Committee, state-federal relations on the Government Operations Committee, or metropolitan planning and housing on the Banking and Currency

Committee. Muskie used his professional authority to build broad public and congressional consensus; his reasoned discourse could be persuasive even among those who disagreed with him. Observers hailed the senator's efforts on behalf of the Johnson administration's Model Cities program, for example, as the key to that bill's eventual passage in 1966.[22]

Muskie also benefited from two institutional characteristics unique to the Public Works Committee: independent staff support and nonpartisanship. Because the medium of Muskie's influence was knowledge, the role of staff proved critical to his success. Muskie relied to a great extent on his administrative assistant, Don Nicoll. A journalist and Maine Democratic Party operative during the fifties, Nicoll served as Muskie's most trusted aide between 1962 and 1971, as well as the primary staff architect of the pollution control programs developed during the sixties. Although Muskie's stoic personality tended to keep his associates at arm's length, the two worked effectively together, and Nicoll enjoyed a significant degree of freedom. So too did Ron Linton, the committee's staff director, to whom McNamara entrusted an "unheard of" degree of discretion on legislative issues and day-to-day decisions. Linton coordinated staff work for the Pollution Subcommittee, collecting and organizing information that presented a range of options he hoped would provide members with a sound basis for discussion and deliberation.[23]

The committee's lack of formal partisan divisions or acrimony fostered an atmosphere conducive to reasoned exchange. Its personnel structure maintained no formal distinction between majority and minority staffers. With McNamara's blessing, Linton decided to treat the committee staff as a single unit, sharing all the same documentation and meeting together regularly to hash out legislative substance and text.

The process of consensus building within the Public Works Committee represented the first critical step in environmental policymaking during the sixties, a task ideally suited to Ed Muskie's personality and management style. By all accounts, Muskie acted as an honest broker who strove to build a sense of trust among his colleagues. He encouraged thorough debate and dialogue on pollution control strategies, courted the participation of minority members, and was amenable to compromise. His alliance with Delaware's Caleb Boggs, another former governor and the ranking Republican on the subcommittee, helped expedite the passage of major air and water quality measures. Unanimous committee support for subcommittee legislation, combined with

Senator Edmund Muskie (D-Maine) conducts a hearing of his Subcommittee on Air and Water Pollution in 1966. Senator Caleb Boggs (R-Del.) sits to his right. Courtesy of the Edmund S. Muskie Archives and Special Collections Library.

Muskie's skillful floor management, reinforced his aura of authority and typically produced overwhelmingly favorable Senate majorities. The 1963 Clean Air Act passed by a voice vote; the roll call tally for the 1965 Water Quality Act was 68 to 8. The 1966 Clean Water Restoration Act and the 1967 Air Quality Act both passed without a single dissenter.[24]

Muskie's personal qualities and institutional advantages help explain why the locus of environmental policymaking swung from the House to the Senate in the sixties. As the thrust of pollution control policy shifted toward prevention and federal enforcement activities, John Blatnik found it increasingly difficult to build consensus in the House Public Works Committee. It featured a membership three times as large as the Senate's, with a number of southern conservatives and representatives from industrially oriented districts who strongly resisted federal regulation. Blatnik proved unable to overcome their opposition solely through his mastery of distributive politics. Though a skillful political broker, the Minnesota Democrat possessed neither a mind capable of mastering technical policy details nor staff support with the kind of enthusiasm for pollution control that Sonosky had displayed in the fifties.[25]

The efforts of Edmund Muskie and his colleagues to reconstruct the federal water pollution control system culminated in October 1965 with congressional approval of the Water Quality Act, the most important legislation of its kind during the sixties. The act provided a new rationale, a new administrative structure, and a new regulatory mechanism for protecting the nation's lakes and rivers. For subcommittee members, those two and a half years involved a reciprocal process of learning and educating. They had to master the details of a new policy, assess the practical and political feasibility of proposed solutions, and refine legislation in response to interest group feedback.

Muskie also exploited the institutional prestige of the Senate to raise national awareness of the scope and severity of the water pollution problem. Though some of the methods he used to convince an apathetic public to support federal water pollution laws were novel, his argument often hinged on familiar ideas.

Building Support

In retrospect, it seems odd that Ed Muskie would need to work so hard to build a national constituency for water pollution control legislation between 1963 and 1965. Evidence of a pollution problem in the early sixties and growing public dissatisfaction with it is not that difficult to detect. As in Maine, local activists throughout the country brought increasing pressure to bear on area pollution control officials to redress fish kills, the loss of recreational opportunities, leaking suburban septic tanks, and other aesthetic and health concerns. In the Midwest and Great Lakes regions, such activity helped precipitate federal enforcement conferences. These proceedings, in turn, amassed a wealth of technical data that revealed the extent of the problem in unprecedented detail. Such findings attracted media coverage and buttressed the cause of local conservation groups. Hundreds of thousands signed petitions

in Ohio urging the cleanup of Lake Erie, following an enforcement conference in August 1965.[26]

Though important, such place-based activities did not, in themselves,
generate the sustained publicity or momentum necessary to dictate policy
choices on the national level. They did not yet add up to a mass movement
with the cultural resonance to capture the public's imagination or the political clout to overcome entrenched opposition to stronger pollution control
laws in Washington. As late as 1965, only 17 percent of Americans responding to a Gallup poll listed the reduction of air and water pollution as goals
worthy of government attention. Muskie began work two years prior to this,
at a time when national conservation groups still lacked a cohesive strategy
on pollution issues. Ron Linton had to solicit representatives from such organizations to appear before the subcommittee and prep them to "say what we
wanted them to say."[27]

Muskie made publicity and public education an important part of his
subcommittee's agenda between 1963 and 1966. He followed Robert Kerr's
lead in June 1965, scheduling a series of field hearings and using the prestige of a Senate forum to focus attention on local water pollution problems
in eight different cities. Those hearings happened to coincide with the House-
Senate conference committee negotiations on the Water Quality Act. Muskie
also built issue awareness by maintaining a rigorous speaking schedule with
frequent media appearances.[28]

The subcommittee also turned to a more unorthodox use of media to
raise public awareness in 1963: the first-ever Senate-produced documentary
film. This effort grew out of Ron Linton's background in journalism, as he
thought of ways to reach the wider American audience that did not read
government reports. Despite Pat McNamara's initial incredulity, he signed
off on the project, which ended up costing about $200,000. Linton secured
a camera crew from PHS's Communicable Disease Center and an air force
plane to shuttle them around to numerous shooting locations around the
country. Henry Fonda even agreed to serve as the narrator, although he otherwise refused to appear on screen, much to Linton's disappointment. The
senators appeared in wooden cameos, however, in an effort to explain how
their legislative activities would help "meet our water needs." The final product, entitled *Troubled Waters*, targeted an audience of schools, civic groups,
and similar community-based institutions.[29]

The film's depiction of the pollution problem suggested how committee members themselves interpreted it, as well as what message they believed would resonate with the public. *Troubled Waters* attempted to bring the issue home to Americans by juxtaposing graphic images of pollution with scenes of ordinary citizens using water for a variety of purposes. Fonda spoke of "the great purifier of the Earth," as visions of baptisms, bathing children, and scrubbing surgeons filled the screen. "Water can purify itself too," the narrator added, "if given enough time and space between the jobs men ask it to do." The water pollution problem came about precisely because the nation, with its growing population and industrial base, was running out of both time and space between use and reuse. "If America's waters are troubled," Fonda surmised, "it is because they are overworked." A succession of characters expressed the consequences in a personal way, from a housewife standing at her kitchen tap ("Why can't we get any decent drinking water in this town anymore?"), to an old fisherman ("They shouldn't be allowed to dump all that crud in our trout stream"), to a button-down businessman ("how can you expect me to stay in business here, if I can't even use this water in my plant?").[30]

The script defined pollution broadly to include industrial and municipal sewage, thermal discharges, pesticides, detergent suds, agricultural runoff, acid mine drainage, radioactive materials, and oil. The shots were edited to show water users in uncomfortable proximity to these wastes—children splashed near an industrial outflow pipe and a water skier glided beneath a plane's pesticide trail. The director took full advantage of the capabilities of color film, showing the effluent in all its vivid hues: from the reds of a meatpacking plant in Kansas City and the blacks of a Maine textile factory, to steel mill browns, white detergent suds, and green algae.

Such a dramatic visual medium provided an ideal way to depict the aesthetic assaults and health-oriented risks of water pollution, but the producers wanted to emphasize the specter of shrinking supplies as well. At the finale, Fonda evoked the image of Babylon, the great ancient civilization transformed into a barren desert: "To live, man must use and pollute the water. But if he abuses it and fails to do his best to restore its natural purity, then water will no longer be able to serve him. And factories will close, farms will dry up, people will disappear, and the lesson of Babylon will not have been learned. The population and industry of America are growing every day; the water supply remains the same."

Though melodramatic, the Babylon analogy reflected the mind-set of Public Works Committee members and their perceptions of the film's audience. *Troubled Waters* justified water pollution control as a way to meet practical human needs in an expanding urban-industrial society. As the committee members saw it, water shortage still had a more immediate personal significance than water pollution for the majority of Americans. Binding the two together, as John Blatnik and the Select Committee had tried to do, still made sense in 1963.

As luck would have it, prevailing weather patterns in the Northeast soon reinforced this connection more effectively than any movie or hearing could. Between 1963 and 1967, the northeastern United States experienced its most severe drought of the twentieth century. This multiyear dry spell had tangible political and policy consequences. The national dialogue on water pollution control legislation took place as the endemic conditions of the parched West imposed themselves upon one of the nation's most humid regions. The weather did not alter the substantive questions that needed to be faced: the proper jurisdiction for the federal government, the amount of money to be spent, how clean the water should be, and who precisely was to make such decisions. But the drought brought the specter of scarcity home to urban easterners. Not only did it exacerbate pollution problems—it rendered national water development concerns more credible and dramatically reinforced the relationship policymakers had long emphasized between the quality and quantity of water.[31]

The plight of New York City proved emblematic of the Northeast's water crisis. The city relied on distant reservoir systems in the Catskills and the Delaware River watersheds to serve the bulk of its water supply needs. It shunned more proximate, polluted options like the Hudson or East Rivers, which continued to absorb the city's waste effluent, more than a third of which, or half a billion gallons annually, remained untreated. But the decision not to renovate or reuse nearby streams appeared shortsighted as the drought continued unabated in the summer of 1965. Mayor Robert Wagner had already enacted a series of compulsory conservation measures in April that brought the reality of shortage home to the city's profligate water users, restricting activities like washing cars and watering lawns. Despite curbs on consumption, reservoir capacity dwindled steadily and officials warned of a potential "water famine" by the fall. In July, New Jersey, Delaware, and Penn-

Figure 4. The severe
northeast drought of the
mid-sixties underscored
the link between water
quantity and quality in
urban areas. Copyright
1965 by Bill Mauldin.
Reprinted courtesy of the
William Mauldin Estate.

sylvania pressured New York to contribute 275 million gallons per day from
its shrinking out-of-state reservoirs to recharge the Delaware's estuaries and
protect the potable supplies of the Philadelphia-Camden area from saltwater
intrusion. Two days later, Mayor Wagner allowed the city to supplement its
supplies with treated water from the Hudson.[32]

By that time, the media had seized upon the predicament of the largest city
in the country as both an allegory of poor planning and an indication that
the nation's water resource priorities were in transition. Commentators underscored the relationship between the quality of major urban streams and
the quantity of water available for urban use. The *New Republic* cited the
drought as conclusive evidence that "the Northeast must begin to use its water
several times over. . . . pollution can no longer be tolerated." Speaking specifically of the Hudson, *Newsweek* asserted that "the desecration of one of

the nation's scenic resources is bad enough," but "the destruction of the river as a water resource is criminal." New York's tribulations seemed to indicate that eastern cities were not prepared to meet the growth in water demand predicted by the Select Committee on National Water Resources.[33]

The northeastern drought shaped the public's perception of both national water quality issues and government efforts to address them. Although public health problems and the loss of recreational opportunities were becoming increasingly common occurrences in metropolitan areas, water shortage altered local economies and lifestyles in a way that provoked a sense of emergency. Historians have credited the Johnson administration for promoting a "New Conservation" in the mid-sixties that began to cast natural beauty and urban quality of life issues as central to the Great Society. In August 1965, however, as the president dispatched "water crisis teams" to northeastern cities and Interior Secretary Stewart Udall described New York as tottering "on the edge of disaster," urban quality of life depended most immediately on adequate water supplies.[34]

Policymakers and media observers alike characterized pollution control as the most efficient means to salvage and supplement the Northeast's dwindling water resources. In a retrospective analysis characterizing 1965 as an "epochal" year in the country's water history, the New York Times singled out the recent "radical shift in national opinion, especially in the East, from a long unbudgeable apathy about water to urgent concern about problems of supply and pollution." Such sentiment had a tangible influence during Congress's deliberations on the pending water quality legislation. Increasing citizen awareness of the nation's deteriorating water quality undoubtedly contributed to the eventual passage of the Water Quality Act, as Muskie hoped it would. But so did the weather. "When all is said and done," one congressional aide remarked in October 1965, "our best friend on the water pollution bill was the Northeastern drought. If anything gives a guy courage to thumb his nose at a lobbyist, it's 400 housewives screaming about watering their lawns."[35]

Developing a Water Quality Policy

Skillful public relations efforts and a well-timed drought helped overcome political inertia, but, even so, enacting the 1965 Water Quality Act required

Muskie to apply all the knowledge and authority he had accrued as a legislative specialist in the Senate. The law's objectives—to reduce the volume of pollution and improve stream quality over time—represented a new policy direction and demanded an enhanced degree of government regulatory activity that business interests, and many state officials, did not willingly countenance. When Muskie's mastery of detail failed to overcome opposition in the House of Representatives, he needed the White House's help with arm-twisting. Regardless, in both its strengths and its weaknesses, the statute bore all the markings of its sponsor's legislative style: a pragmatic approach to problem solving, qualified deference to technical experts, enduring faith in federalism, and careful attention to consensus.

Muskie's handiwork managed to raise public expectations about pollution control while remaining grounded in some of the more traditional elements of water politics, including economic development, pork, and local control. When subcommittee members and staff began to ponder the water pollution problem in 1963, they drew their initial inspiration from the Senate Select Committee on National Water Resources. The staff's preliminary report cited Select Committee data and assumed that the nation's total dependable reserve of fresh water would be inadequate to sustain its developing economy in the coming years, making additional waste treatment and reuse essential. Nathaniel Wollman, the economist who had conducted supply-demand studies for the Select Committee's final report, testified as the subcommittee's lead-off witness in June 1963. Nor did Muskie ever entirely abandon the Select Committee's rhetoric on water shortages, pollution, and growth.[36]

The subcommittee diverged from the Select Committee's policy recommendations on supplemental storage for waste dilution, however, favoring treatment as the primary remedy for pollution control. This preference conflicted with that of industrial interests, who preferred federally funded dams to the capital costs associated with internal plant process changes. Members and staff took their cue from leading experts, including Nathaniel Wollman himself, who had recently revised his data, methodology, and assumptions. He concluded that it would be "foolhardy" to "commit the nation to a large construction program that technological advances in process engineering and waste treatment might make obsolete."[37]

Interest group politics inevitably informed the subcommittee's policy choices as well. Private polluters did not have recourse to public funding to offset treatment costs, but municipalities did, and their influence remained substantial. John Blatnik's construction grant program had drawn Hugh Mields, the lead lobbyist for the U.S. Conference of Mayors, into the fray during the late fifties. Mields became a vocal advocate for more treatment plant funding on behalf of the nation's 300 largest metropolitan areas but also believed that municipalities would expedite their building efforts if federal law called on them to upgrade existing water quality. Mields worked so frequently with the subcommittee staff during legislative drafting that he became Ron Linton's closest friend and eventual business partner.[38]

The subcommittee's evolving attitude toward waste treatment and water quality improvement reflected both a reliance on and reaction against the sanitary engineering profession. Muskie understood that any viable federal water pollution control system would depend on the sanitarians' technical knowledge and deferred to their authority on state-level water quality boards. Over the course of the twentieth century, sanitary engineers had adopted a regulatory strategy that fused administrative expertise with the principles of voluntarism, compromise, and localism. Shunning confrontation or legalistic coercion, they applied their technical skills to balance the needs of various interest groups in matters of water quality and use, a consensus-building effort one historian aptly labeled "cooperative pragmatism." They rejected uniform water quality regulations, choosing instead to determine local treatment requirements in reference to a number of variables, including a stream's capacity to assimilate waste and an individual community's water usage priorities.[39]

Although members and staff made liberal use of the profession's expertise, some of its established orthodoxies gave them pause. On the one hand, the subcommittee harbored no illusions about the role streams served as sinks for pollution. "To say that we must cease discharging wastes is unrealistic," the 1963 staff report noted, adding that "disposal of treated wastes . . . through the medium of water is a necessary and legitimate use of this resource." But no stream, they believed, should be reduced to the status of a "mere carrier of waste." Staff members questioned the practice of allowing dischargers to pollute streams up to their calculated absorptive limit, or "assimilative capacity." Muskie and Don Nicoll drew upon their experience with the S. D. Warren Paper Company and other manufacturers who repeatedly tried, and failed, to predict the assimilative capacity of Maine's waterways in lieu of treating mill effluent. When waste overloads converted large stretches of rivers into hydrogen sulfide–spewing, anaerobic sewers, chemists and engineers readily admitted the uncertainties inherent in their methods.[40]

At a minimum, the subcommittee sought to remedy the nation's most grossly polluted waterways, like the Ohio River or New York's Raritan Bay. Although many engineers in government and some in industry had come to accept the need to reduce excessive pollution loads, they still determined treatment re- quirements in reference to a stream's carrying capacity and desired function and refused to install technology they did not deem economically feasible. Sewage plants around Raritan Bay and in the Ohio River Basin removed only larger floating solids and in some instances provided chlorination. In 1963, federal officials feared that efforts on the Ohio River would "not be enough to insure safe water for a multiplicity of uses," especially since industrial treatment works lagged far behind municipal ones. The PHS estimated that the current annual volume of organic industrial waste (excluding inorganic toxics) was more than double the total municipal load nationwide.[41]

In an era of burgeoning waste loads and water demand, the subcommittee concluded, ensuring adequate water supplies for all legitimate uses required more than passive abatement strategies resigned to containing damage after the fact. "It is only through the enhancement of the quality of water," Muskie declared on the Senate floor in October 1963, "that we can assure maximum utilization of this resource" for "multiple purposes, including industrial, ag- ricultural, recreational, public water supply, and fish and wildlife." Muskie's experience in the governor's mansion taught him that industry pressure usu- ally prevented public officials from building a mandate for improvement into local stream designations. So the legislation he introduced teamed the federal government with the states to set enforceable standards for *ambient* water quality (the condition of the stream itself). It sought to hold industries and municipalities accountable for reducing their waste loads over time so that local watercourses could support all the beneficial uses Muskie cited.[42]

Standards were expected to serve as the baseline for remedial actions as well as to provide an essential blueprint for water use planning. Muskie de- sired uniform, predictable regulations that told dischargers what would be ex- pected of them and that enabled local officials to prepare long-term abate- ment strategies. Using ambient standards as an engineering base for treat- ment works, industries and municipalities could "develop realistic plans for new plants or expanded facilities, without uncertainties about waste disposal requirements on interstate waters." At that time, this sort of proactive planning was not feasible. By 1963, thirty-six states had passed legislation to establish water quality standards, but only twenty-two actually followed through, with varying degrees of comprehensiveness and stringency. The senator likewise touted his new regime as a means to sidestep the enforcement conference process, replacing a "subjective method of drawing up ad hoc standards under the present law" with "procedures for deciding on standards under which the communities and the affected industries participate."[43]

From the beginning, however, the subcommittee's strategy faced practical and political obstacles. Ambient standards needed to be coupled with another set of standards that dictated the content ("type, volume, or strength of matter") of effluent exiting outflow pipes. But persistent industrial opposition prevented Muskie from writing effluent limits into his legislation. Absent an explicit legislative mandate, the subcommittee took it on faith that the states would promulgate their own industrial effluent standards in the process of implementing ambient standards.[44]

Despite such limitations, Ed Muskie and Don Nicoll articulated a rational justification for a federal ambient standards system that they applied to both water and air pollution control throughout the sixties. When Muskie weighed policy alternatives, he focused on the ultimate objective: what was the program trying to achieve, and how would one know if it succeeded? The senator wanted his legislation to articulate clearly stated goals that the public would understand and accept. The goal in this instance was enhancing the overall quality of individual streams. Effluent limitations, while necessary, offered only a means to that end. Effective regulation over the long run required planning and enforcement mechanisms that remained flexible enough to adjust to local exigencies, especially in watersheds with multiple dischargers. Muskie concluded that regulated interests would accept modifications of an established abatement plan only if the bottom line—the desired condition of the stream itself—remained clear and fixed. Federal officials, Nicoll speculated, could expend all their political capital negotiating specific discharge standards, but if those standards later proved ineffective, the government would be forced to go through the "horrendous exercise of convincing people that you hadn't gotten it quite right but you knew what you were doing this time around." Nicoll and Muskie believed that progress would occur over time as technical knowledge accrued and dischargers were held accountable for improving water quality.[45]

Muskie went out of his way to vest the standard-setting process with enough flexibility to accommodate unique local conditions, be they political, economic, or environmental. Although the HEW secretary was authorized to establish standards on interstate waters, he could not do so unilaterally, without giving area officials ample time to do the job themselves. Muskie also made a point not to confuse regulatory consistency with homogeneity. He disavowed *national* water quality standards, or those that applied uniformly to all waterways. Natural and economic variables varied so widely, he believed, that water quality designations had to reflect "the differences in water uses, the intensity of water uses, and the availability of water river by river and portion of river by portion of river." Decisions concerning the development of water resources remained a local responsibility. The federal government provided incentives for communities to maintain the highest quality water possible, but could not impose a single standard for all.[46]

It was Muskie's willingness to protect the prerogative of the states in matters of environmental regulation that enabled him to secure legislative consensus within the Public Works Committee. His critical alliance with Caleb Boggs grew out of a mutual respect for federalism. Muskie credited Boggs and his staff with authoring the "lion's share" of the language pertaining to state and local participation in the standards-setting process. The chairman's efforts to preserve the integrity of federal-state relations, however, militated against his stated interest in fostering water quality enhancement. The subcommittee intended to push dischargers to install more advanced treatment works than they otherwise would and believed that breakthroughs in technology would follow on the heels of ambitious ambient requirements and more federal grants for research and treatment plant construction. But the deference to local interests built into the legislation provided multiple opportunities to weaken standards. Nor did the subcommittee's bill do much to speed or strengthen the current program's tortuous enforcement procedures.[47]

Critics still feared that Muskie's legislation would upset the balance of federalism. In October 1963, Senator John Sherman Cooper (R-Ky.), the most conservative member of the Public Works Committee, registered a rare public dissent with his colleagues. He characterized the pending bill, S. 649, as a radical departure from past practice, because the HEW secretary's power to "fix standards" and "look into the future of a stream as well as to its present use" gave this person "a kind of zoning authority over all river basins in the United States." Industrial interests lobbied both houses of Congress, attempting to reduce the secretary's authority and ensure that any standards would be susceptible to further administrative and judicial revision.[48]

Support within the executive branch and the House of Representatives proved crucial to overcoming this opposition, but it was not immediately forthcoming. The House took no action on S. 649 after the Senate approved it in October 1963, and the White House swamped Congress with major legislative initiatives on civil rights, poverty, health care, and tax reform in 1964. Executive staff considered water pollution only a second tier issue. Muskie's bill appealed mainly as a way to placate John Dingell (D-Mich.) and strip program administration from the PHS, "the maximum distance the Administration should go," according to LBJ's budget director.[49]

The Johnson administration rediscovered water pollution as it embraced the "New Conservation." In his "Message to Congress on Natural Beauty," in February 1965, the president spoke of uplifting "the dignity of man's spirit" by turning the federal government's attention to improving "the total relationship between man and the world around him." In addition to wilderness areas, outdoor recreation, and scenic rivers, the administration began to focus on problems like noise, overcrowding, and pollution that affected urban environments. Johnson's February address endorsed Muskie's efforts by calling for legislation that would provide "a national program to prevent water pollution at its source rather than attempting to cure pollution after it occurs." It also demanded a "swift and effective enforcement procedure" that S. 4, the Muskie bill recently reintroduced and passed by the Senate, still did not offer. Upon consulting with congressional staff members, conservation groups, and urban organizations, administration officials agreed to forgo amendments that might delay enactment.[50]

Even without additional enforcement measures, Muskie and the Johnson administration struggled to overcome the strong resistance to S. 4 in the House. In March, a majority coalition in the Public Works Committee decided to dump water quality standards entirely and reported what HEW officials described as a "very weak and ineffectual bill." Although John Blatnik indicated that he favored standards, he preferred to pass a bill that created a new Federal Water Pollution Control Administration independent of the PHS, rather than risk an extended debate on a program that he suspected HEW lacked the personnel or technical knowledge to implement. The chairman faced intense pressure to abandon federal water quality standards from the petroleum industry and farm interests.[51]

With the assistance of the White House, Muskie labored to strengthen Blatnik's resolve during contentious conference committee negotiations in the summer of 1965. The Senate contingent rebuffed a compromise proposal submitted by the House in late July because it bore the stamp of the Manufacturing Chemists Association. The association tried to tie the standard-setting procedure to the cumbersome enforcement system, while blurring the distinction between "water quality criteria" (descriptive guidelines) and "standards of water quality" (formal prescriptive limits on pollution). Don Nicoll, who had drafted the Senate's more precise language, resisted these efforts. The administration also worked to counter petroleum lobbyists, who sought to weaken standards by subjecting them to judicial review before state and federal officials had even finalized them.[52]

The final version of the 1965 Water Quality Act represented a complex fusion of state and federal authority that coupled a mandate for enhancement with a byzantine administrative procedure designed to achieve it. The statute created a new Federal Water Pollution Control Administration (FWPCA) in HEW to oversee the program. The states had until 30 June 1967 to establish water quality standards for interstate streams, which were to consist of two distinct elements: water quality criteria and a plan for the implementation and enforcement of those criteria. If a state did not act to set standards, or the secretary of HEW judged them inconsistent with the act, the secretary could publish his own proposed standards following a public hearing. If the state did not voluntarily adopt the secretary's standards after six months, he was empowered to promulgate them unilaterally. But the legislation also provided for a review process before a special hearing board, convened upon the request of the governor of an affected state, which had the authority to modify the secretary's standards. The act retained its predecessors' enforcement procedures but also authorized the secretary to seek abatement through court action if the standards were violated, after giving violators 180 days' notice. Judges were expected to consider the "practicability and the physical and economic feasibility" of the standards when reviewing enforcement orders.[53]

With the Water Quality Act, Muskie made the most of what was politically possible in 1965, but the legislation also reflected his vision of how environmental regulation should operate in a federalist framework. Having established his reputation as the foremost pollution control expert in Congress, Muskie used his authority to block subsequent changes to the program that he regarded as detrimental—even if they stood to strengthen it. When the White House proposed a "Clean Rivers Demonstration Program" in February 1966 that tied federal funding and stricter enforcement measures to the Interior Department's centralized river basin planning program, Muskie resisted it in the name of state and municipal autonomy. Though the senator acceded to the transfer of the FWPCA to Interior in May 1966, his 1966 Clean Water Restoration Act gutted the administration's original proposal and authorized $3.55 billion over the next six years for waste treatment grants. The Public Works Committee thus continued to reinforce the connection between pollution control and pork.[54]

Muskie's strategy made sense while developmental assumptions about pollution control remained credible pillars of national policy, and the senator himself ranked as Congress's undisputed specialist. By 1966, however, alternative ways of thinking about environmental protection had already found expression at the grassroots levels and in policy circles beyond the Public Works Committee. As the decade progressed, the language of economic growth and the logic of decentralized regulatory authority ceased to resonate with citizens who had come to view rivers and lakes as intrinsically valuable, delicately balanced systems under stress, rather than as resources or commodities per se. To protect these natural amenities, they demanded a more vigorous, coordinated government response than Muskie's legislation allowed.

Muskie spent his early career in the Senate trying to build a national environmental constituency, but he was unprepared for the political and cultural changes that heralded its arrival. This emerging social movement and the ecological discourse that accompanied it brought repeated challenges to his legislative authority and policy preconceptions. Ecology offered a holistic alternative to the prevailing developmental mind-set, holding out the promise that complex natural systems could be both comprehended and rationally managed. This mode of "systems thinking" boasted a broad spectrum of practitioners who sought to shape environmental policy in ways Muskie did not foresee.

PART II
Systems

4

Thinking in Systems
The Rise of Professional Ecology

The word "ecology," *Time* observed in February 1970, "is often used in ways that suggest an attitude rather than a discipline." The magazine's assessment appeared two months prior to the first Earth Day, just as national environmental consciousness was waxing, but historians since then have concurred with the sentiment. At the turn of the decade, they concluded, ecology "referred not just to a scientific discipline, but to the interconnectedness of life, the balance of nature, the beneficent aspect of the planet that humans threatened, and the environmental movement [itself], which was sometimes called 'the ecology movement.'"[1]

Just five years earlier, the most prominent environmental legislator of his day, Senator Edmund Muskie, had made the case for his 1965 Water Quality Act without reference to any of these things. Of course, Muskie cared about the impact of pollution on natural beauty and human health. But as late as the mid-sixties, he also felt comfortable justifying pollution control as a policy that would provide the quantities of clean water necessary for future growth and economic development.

By 1965, however, an "ecological attitude" had already prompted some Americans to reassess the developmental values and priorities that members of Congress and most of the nation took for granted. By the late sixties and early seventies, ecology, as disseminated in popularized form through various mass media outlets, provided a new intellectual framework and vocabulary for ordinary citizens to interpret environmental harm, assess the intrinsic worth of "pristine" nature, and contemplate public policy options. In short, ecology seemed to offer a challenge to and an alternative for the developmental discourse long predominant in the nation's political culture.

The most influential prophets of popular ecology—Aldo Leopold, Rachel Carson, and Barry Commoner—conveyed a common ethical imperative to a wide audience with finely crafted prose. Although each addressed different issues, they all managed to rethink postwar conceptions of progress, development, and environmental management, while giving voice to many Americans' underlying ambivalence about the era's celebrated scientific and economic advancements. In particular, they cautioned that science and technology tempted humans to view their societies as separate and independent from the natural world. This sense of estrangement obscured mankind's reliance on the normal functioning of natural cycles and systems and bred a certain disregard for nature's inherent value and fragility.

Likewise, the authors used ecological ideas to critique the common assumption, nourished as well by technological hubris, that nature existed as something that could be mastered and controlled. Carson's best-selling exposé on synthetic pesticides, *Silent Spring* (1962), argued that the widespread efforts to eradicate pests with chemicals, though well meaning, contravened the "complex, precise, and highly integrated system of relationships between living things" and placed humans and nonhumans alike at risk. Commoner's books, *Science and Survival* (1963) and *The Closing Circle* (1970), echoed the same concerns when discussing radioactive fallout or the synthetic byproducts of the modern industrial economy. Leopold's *A Sand County Almanac* (1948) presented an ethical rationale for valuing biotic communities based on their inherent "integrity, stability, and beauty" rather than on traditional economic calculations.[2]

Yet for all their cachet, none of these writers had actually trained as professional ecologists. Carson was an editor for the Fish and Wildlife Service and a well-known nature writer; Leopold was a forester and repentant game manager; Commoner alone held a Ph.D., but he had trained as a plant physiologist. Nevertheless, all three talked the talk of academic ecologists to make a moral case about the proper relationship between society and nature. Carson spoke of food chains and the biomagnification of toxins. Leopold waxed eloquent about evolution's capacity to create stable, diverse, and adaptable biotic communities with interconnected cycles of energy and nutrients. Commoner converted fundamental ecological ideas into engaging aphorisms like "everything is connected to everything else" and "everything has to go some-where." Taken together, this holistic perspective, with its appreciation for nat-ural cycles and systems, seemed to offer an alternative to what many in the late sixties and early seventies perceived as the self-destructive technological myopia of the "military-industrial complex."[3]

Ironically, much of ecology's systems-oriented vocabulary owed its origins to World War II, the Cold War, and the very scientific establishment that Car-son, her cohorts, and a new generation of environmentalists critiqued. His-torians have noted the extent to which post-1945 ecosystems ecology relied on mathematics, thermodynamics, and certain other quantitative sciences that gained currency during wartime. The discipline also benefited from the funding provided by the Atomic Energy Commission (AEC), an agency virtually synonymous with the military-industrial complex. In this context, Donald Worster has argued, ecologists adopted a concomitant "managerial ethos," or the confidence that natural communities could be managed effi-ciently, rather than exploited, when understood from a research perspective that was at once holistic, mechanical, and economic. While the purveyors of popular ecology borrowed certain technical concepts and an affinity for in-terdependence from these professionals, the latter continued to retain an un-derlying faith in modern science, statistical analysis, and productive systems management not endorsed in *Sand County* or *Silent Spring*.[4]

When members of Congress began looking in new environmental pol-icy directions, they often found the science of ecology appealing, precisely because of its affinity with traditional Cold War technical discourses. This is not to say that ecology did not provide a novel way of viewing and ap-preciating natural communities, or a foundation to rethink developmental priorities. Legislative hearings on wetlands in the mid-sixties, for example, celebrated their diversity, complexity, and productivity as justifications to halt the drainage and development of what had once been considered use-less "swamps." Many legislators were likewise familiar with and influenced by Carson's and Leopold's published works. Nevertheless, those interested in applying ecological expertise to pollution control and other broad problems of environmental administration most appreciated the discipline's familiar optimism about systems analysis and management. Ecologists seemed to ap-proach natural systems in much the same way engineers and other scientists approached mechanical, military, or administrative ones.[5]

Policymakers began to take an interest in ecosystem ecology because it offered a way to bring large, complex, interdependent entities under efficient control. And ecology suggested an attitude as much as a discipline for legislators, too. Unlike the ecological popularizers, however, theirs was an attitude that reflected the technocratic, political, and policy culture of the post–World War II era.

Congress did not absorb ecological knowledge by osmosis. Starting in the mid-sixties, certain committee chairs took the lead in sponsoring large-scale ecological research and exploring its potential implications for federal environmental policy. Others, like Edmund Muskie, did not. This is rather ironic, given that professional ecologists ended up informing the substance, objectives, and underlying principles of Muskie's 1972 Clean Water Act more directly than any comparable environmental legislation. To begin to explain how and why they did so, it is instructive to focus on three individuals whose careers embodied the professional and political development of ecology during the sixties.

The Public Works Committee's most important conduits for ecological knowledge were not Carson, Commoner, or Leopold, but rather Thomas Jorling, Gene Likens, and George Woodwell. The story of how Jorling, an attorney/ecologist, became the committee's minority counsel and the other two, both distinguished researchers, became its scientific advisors unfolds in the next chapter; their specific influence on legislative policy is recounted in subsequent chapters. Their prior professional experiences reflected the ways in which ecology as a systems-oriented science rose to prominence and captured the attention of Congress during the sixties. Jorling made it his mission to rouse the discipline from its political slumber and seek out access to receptive committees in an effort to enhance its status on Capitol Hill. Likens's and Woodwell's research suggested how pollution and other environmental disruptions could be analyzed empirically at the level of the ecosystem, providing a technocratic way to address the problem that legislators like Muskie eventually found compelling and politically valuable.

Neither Muskie nor his committee, however, contributed much to ecology's initial emergence in the realm of environmental policy. In the mid-sixties, they remained focused on prosaic issues related to air and water quality standard-setting and federal sewage treatment grants. But as this chapter and the next suggest, legislative entrepreneurs with environmental interests

and committees of their own soon turned to ecology and ecologically oriented ideas to carve out their own policy niches. When Thomas Jorling came
to the nation's capital, he found his profession's prospects better served in
these other arenas.

Mr. Jorling and the Ecologists Go to Washington

Jorling's career trajectory parallels the ecological profession's own path to
policy relevance in the sixties. After graduating from Notre Dame in 1962 with
a degree in biology, his interest in plant ecology led him to Washington State
University for graduate studies. But the insulated life of a research scientist
did not satisfy Jorling's yearning to tackle pressing public policy issues. After
a few months of course work, he became convinced that "the real import of
science could not be served on the basis of its research and teaching aspects
alone, and that the broader questions of science and society required a different background." To that end, he enrolled in Boston College Law School,
where he received his degree in 1966. Far from abjuring his scientific roots,
the young attorney described his turn to the legal profession as the product
of "a singular desire to make, for myself at least, ecology relevant."[6]

The lawyer-ecologist soon headed to Washington to try his hand at a relevant career in the public sector. An idealistic letter to Stewart Udall landed
him a job in the Solicitor's Office of the Department of Interior, but his two
years there failed to provide an adequate outlet for his training or interests.
His fortunes improved in 1968 when he accepted an invitation to join the office of the general counsel at the Smithsonian Institution. Beginning in 1964,
Secretary S. Dillon Ripley had overseen the expansion of the Smithsonian's
resources and programs in ecology, reorienting its research agenda away from
taxonomic biology in favor of ecosystem dynamics and biological interde-
pendence. Jorling described his new post as "an extraordinary opportunity,
one which I feel is more suitable for my abilities than any other." The work of
the general counsel's office often reflected the Smithsonian Institution's new
mission and involved Jorling in the ongoing development of ecological and
environmental research legislation. During that same period, he completed
his master's degree in plant ecology and worked with the Smithsonian's new
Office of Ecology to familiarize himself "with the whole range of issues that
come under the general heading of environmental quality."[7]

Jorling was eager to use his position to serve as a liaison between the realms of science and law, prodding local attorneys and ecologists alike to become more active in environmental public affairs. His membership in the Ecological Society of America (ESA), the discipline's primary professional organization, proved invaluable for networking. Jorling's activities in the ESA during the late sixties coincided with a period of growth and transition for the ESA as well as for the science it represented.

The organizational evolution of the ESA reflected the new demands placed on practitioners of ecology as they were drawn into a public arena increasingly solicitous of their professional knowledge. Compared to their counterparts in Britain, American ecologists had been slow to organize, founding their own professional association only in 1915. Throughout the interwar years, membership remained largely static. In 1936, even the ESA's president admitted that ecology hardly offered the most attractive field of specialization among biologists. Nevertheless, research methodologies progressed in the intervening years, particularly in the wake of World War II, and the number of ecologists in the United States actually tripled between 1945 and 1960.[8]

Despite a postwar spike in the profession's ranks, the ESA continued to limit itself to the sponsorship of research and education, making no real effort to inject its collective voice into matters of public policy. Its hesitance reflected its members' skittishness about addressing the social implications of their work. Even as federal funding of ecological research increased under the auspices of the AEC in the 1950s, academic ecologists rarely participated in policy debates regarding the effects of atomic radiation, despite evidence of public concern. Ecologists also proved to be ineffective self-promoters. Although the ESA inaugurated an Ecological Study Committee in 1958, this modest effort to reach a broader public audience and enhance the "function and status of ecology in science and society" had minimal impact. The committee largely failed to tap the growing mass interest in nature and outdoor recreation or to popularize an ecological vocabulary that would later become so pervasive.[9]

The catalyst that thrust the profession into the public spotlight emerged from outside the circle of academic ecology with the publication of *Silent Spring* in 1962. ESA members were quick to identify the sea change that Carson's book portended. "*Silent Spring* created a tide of opinion which will never again allow professional ecologists to remain comfortably aloof from public responsibility," an ESA report contended. Failure to provide the authoritative voice sought by policymakers and citizens, ecologists feared, would leave a vacuum for self-proclaimed experts to fill. S. Dillon Ripley recalled that the post-Carson landscape prompted the ESA to "abandon its former position of 'no comment' on matters of public interest" and establish a more active Committee on Public Affairs in 1962. As the introverted ESA tentatively prepared to engage policy issues, it also had to accommodate the swelling ranks of the profession. The number of American ecologists doubled during the sixties, while the ESA added an estimated 500 to 600 new members annually.[10]

It was in this context that Thomas Jorling set about to marry ecology and public policy, primarily by exhorting prominent members of the ESA to intensify their political activities. During his tenure with the Smithsonian he frequently corresponded with the organization's presidents, offering advice, assistance, and networking opportunities. Not long after meeting incoming ESA president John Cantlon at a 1968 conference in Madison, Wisconsin, Jorling wrote him to encourage ESA active participation in Washington. The ESA's scientists, he insisted, had to be capable of communicating with lawyers, administrators, and legislators without resorting to the "scare tactics and polemics" that were best "left to the conservationist." Since the ESA still had no permanent organizational presence in the capital, Jorling offered to broker meetings between Cantlon and a number of insiders who were sympathetic to ESA interests and cared about environmental quality, including Russell Train, the president of the Conservation Foundation, and environmental experts at the Library of Congress's Legislative Reference Service.[11]

As the Smithsonian's legislative counsel, it is unsurprising that Jorling identified Congress as the most important point of access for those ecologists seeking greater government resources and policymaking influence. He sensed a growing congressional interest in ecological research and "a unique opportunity to shape meaningful legislation" that the profession could exploit to secure funding for desired programs. In February 1968, Jorling urged ESA representatives and Smithsonian staff members to brainstorm strategies for maximizing the organization's input into the legislative process. He also counseled his fellow ecologists to "take the initiative" in advocating their views to lawmakers. "It is not enough to have the truth on your side," he emphasized; "we must . . . do the legwork to convince people of the importance of ecology."[12]

Jorling read the mood in Washington accurately. Over the last few years, certain policymakers, including members of Congress, had begun to view ecology as a discipline relevant to the federal government's environmentally oriented programs. In 1964, Interior Department secretary Stewart Udall exhorted ecologists to share their expertise with public and private decision makers. President Johnson's Science Advisory Committee (PSAC) later called for a study of ecosystems in its influential 1965 report, *Restoring the Quality of Our Environment*, as a baseline to evaluate pollution problems. A year later, Senator Gaylord Nelson (D-Wisc.) held hearings on (unsuccessful) legislation authorizing the Interior Department to conduct and sponsor basic ecological research, particularly as it pertained to land use or resource policies.[13]

For Jorling, however, the most important patron of ecology in 1968 was Representative Emilio Daddario (D-Conn.), who chaired the Subcommittee on Science, Research, and Development in the House Committee on Science and Astronautics. Daddario's interest in the discipline grew out of his (and his staff's) independent investigations of pollution control and its technological dimensions. He believed that other congressional analyses of the issue had overlooked the role that federal research and development policy might play in guiding federal pollution control programs. Daddario held hearings on the adequacy of abatement technology during the summer of 1966, where a number of witnesses, including one who had helped draft the 1965 PSAC Report, advocated ecology as an applicable knowledge base. After the subcommittee's report recommended stepped-up support for ecological research, Daddario used his subcommittee as a forum to consider several such research programs and to conduct colloquia on "environmental quality," broadly defined. The Smithsonian's expanded ecological programs made S. Dillon Ripley a frequent witness and exposed Jorling to Daddario's activities firsthand. The congressman's receptivity to the profession, not to mention his subcommittee's oversight of the National Science Foundation's budget, provided an opportunity that Jorling believed ecologists could not ignore.[14]

Emilio Daddario helped usher American ecology belatedly into the post–World War II world of large-scale, government-supported scientific research. This is not to suggest, however, that ecologists had no access to state funding prior to the late sixties. Between 1950 and 1965, the AEC's quest to comprehend the physiological and environmental effects of ionizing radiation led it to inaugurate programs in ecology at Oak Ridge, Brookhaven, Hanford, Savannah River, and other national laboratories. By the 1960s, the AEC supported most ongoing ecosystems studies in the United States. That said, such federal munificence never approached the levels that had transformed physics, engineering, or medicine into paradigms of post–World War II "big science." Nor did broader authority or prestige follow automatically from the AEC's institutional support.[15]

Thomas Jorling's desire to bolster ecology's influence in Washington reflected not only the profession's reticence but also its lesser status relative to the other biological and physical sciences. The number of Ph.D.s in ecology continued to pale in comparison to these disciplines. Since most American universities still considered ecology a subbranch of botany or zoology, few independent programs existed. And unlike projects in nuclear physics or weapons engineering, where teams of experts worked with multimillion-dollar budgets, AEC-sponsored ecosystems studies were modest in scope. Moreover, since this applied research tended to track rather closely with the agency's specialized needs, it seldom imbued members of the ecological profession with an overt sense of mission pertaining to environmental protection.[16]

The exclusion of ecologists from influential positions in the federal scientific establishment posed similar obstacles to policy formulation. Vietnam-era competition for funding, the open hostility of other fields like microbiology, and general apathy toward ecological research underscored the critical need for well-placed advocates, but results were often disappointing. During the Johnson administration, the ESA tried and failed to place an ecologist on the President's Science Advisory Committee. The governing board of the National Academy of Science (NAS) featured no ecologists at all until decade's end, a fact reflected in numerous policy decisions. In January 1967, the NAS established an Environmental Studies Board with a sweeping mission to coordinate its environmental programs. Although the board included five individuals with corporate affiliations and backgrounds in industrial research, no one with expertise in environmental biology made the cut. "The National Academy doesn't know enough about ecology to know how ignorant it is," vented ESA president LaMont Cole, who criticized NAS's habit of entrusting ecologically oriented studies to scientists trained in other fields.[17]

A similar sort of snub brought what would become the ecological profession's greatest windfall—the International Biological Program (IBP)—to the attention of Emilio Daddario. In 1959, European biologists conceived the IBP as an analog of the successful International Geophysical Year (1957–1958), hoping to stimulate significant research programs on the "biological basis for productivity and human welfare." As program planning evolved in the United States and abroad throughout the sixties, ecosystems ecology came to define the IBP's mission and methodology, in part because the other biological sciences viewed the endeavor ambivalently. Yet, in 1965, the NAS established the U.S. National Planning Committee for the IBP, with Roger Revelle, an oceanographer, as its chairman.

The appointment of a nonecologist was at odds with ESA's own recommendations on the IBP—and a sore spot among many in the organization. But Roger Revelle was a member of the House Panel on Science and Technology and had close contacts with George Miller, chairman of the Committee on Science and Astronautics. Revelle informed Daddario about the workings of the program, and his subcommittee later took up its cause. Thanks in part to Daddario's persistent advocacy, the funds Congress appropriated in 1970 made the U.S. contribution to the IBP the world's largest and made possible an unprecedented series of lavishly funded, large-scale studies of representative biomes in the United States.[18]

Emilio Daddario and his subcommittee ultimately put their faith in ecology because the practitioners of that science spoke a language that appealed to them, the language of systems. As more legislators turned their attention to environmental problems in the late sixties, they gravitated to solutions in keeping with the technical methods and administrative ethos prevalent in other policy areas. Most ecologists in the years after 1945 treated their basic unit of study, the ecosystem, as a self-contained, self-regulating entity that could be quantitatively described and rationally managed. This way of thinking about discrete systems first emerged in a military context during World War II. It grew to define how the public and private sectors developed complicated weapons programs and attempted to coordinate sprawling defense-related bureaucracies during the Cold War. By the time "systems analysis" had begun to spread to the civilian realm in the 1960s, many members of Congress had internalized this mode of problem solving, especially those, like Daddario, who specialized in issues of science and technology.

The IBP's decision to adopt ecosystems ecology as its methodology dovetailed nicely with the congressional affinity for systems solutions to complex social problems. The allure of the "self-governing machine," a metaphor invoked during the Daddario subcommittee's IBP hearings in 1967 and 1968, reflected the technological optimism that both policymakers and scientists shared in the post–World War II era. This common ground facilitated the political support for ecology that Thomas Jorling sought. By 1970, of course, a popular ecological discourse had risen to challenge older developmental assumptions about nature. In the sixties, however, what resonated with legislators was not simply a popular discourse, but a professional discipline grounded in systems thinking—and a by-product of the military-industrial complex.[19]

The Rise of Systems Thinking

Ecology's technocratic appeal to postwar policymakers has roots back to World War II. No circumstance proved capable of mobilizing the scientific establishment to serve the state quite like total war. It gave rise to an impressive range of technological innovations, from nylon to nuclear fission, as well as an array of symbiotic institutional relationships that later flourished in the context of the Cold War. The war also fostered a management philosophy alternatively labeled "systems engineering" or "systems analysis," which advocated the application of scientific methods to administer complex systems in the most objective, rational manner possible.

The ability to describe how a discrete system functioned with mathematical precision, so as to optimize its operation, became the hallmark of systems analysis as developed in the postwar era. Its precursor, operations research (OR), arose in the early years of the war, when British and American scientists helped develop and assess military strategies for new weapons technologies. OR analyzed "deployed systems," or operations currently in use, like bombing runs or missile trajectories. By contrast, systems analysis purported to evaluate a range of management alternatives for future programs. To that end, think tanks such as the RAND Corporation—a hybrid institution created jointly by the air force and Douglas Aircraft in 1946—advanced a holistic planning approach that valued interdisciplinarity, the objectivity of scientific and engineering methods, and rigorous quantification. RAND's mathematicians, economists, and game theorists focused primarily on strategic defense policy and, increasingly after 1952, on the issues surrounding nuclear deterrence.[20]

Cold War systems managers applied similar methodologies to coordinate large-scale military and civil projects—like guided missile systems or the space program—that involved a multitude of private contractors and government agencies working in tandem. The success of such programs and the prestige of RAND encouraged Secretary of Defense Robert McNamara to adopt systems techniques to rationalize his agency's unwieldy budget in the 1960s. The former Ford Motor Company president appreciated how the new methods enabled planners to articulate overarching missions supported by objective analysis—the perfect antidote for the military's fragmentation and inefficiency. In August 1965, Lyndon Johnson issued an executive order requiring all government agencies to institute a variation of McNamara's mission-oriented Planning Programming and Budgeting System (PPBS).[21]

The prospect of managing complex social systems encouraged the migration of systems analysis into the civilian realm in the fifties and sixties and led experts in government and industry to integrate social science into systems planning. As expectations for multipurpose river basin development grew more ambitious, for example, water resource planners looked for ways to assess competing social objectives and provide policymakers with informed design alternatives. The Harvard Water Program, a multidisciplinary research and training facility, pioneered a technique known as "multi-objective analysis" in the late fifties that used sophisticated mathematical models and computer simulations to evaluate river basins as interdependent social units. Over the next decade, the federal government formally adopted the multiobjective approach as the preferred method for water resource planning. Likewise, in the field of pollution control, the Daddario subcommittee advocated systems analysis and PPBS to "place pollution abatement on a comparable basis with other national technology programs."[22]

During the same period, practitioners of postwar ecology readily adopted a similar systems discourse. Oxford University botanist Arthur Tansley first coined the term "ecosystem" in 1935 while reassessing the process of ecological succession, or the maturation of plant communities from simpler to more complex and stable forms (for example, from meadows to forests). The prevailing model, espoused by the prominent American plant ecologist Frederic Clements, depicted such communities as single, holistic organisms, or "super-organisms," rather than as systems of integrated components. Tansley worried that this organismic metaphor fostered methodological complacency among ecologists by encouraging simple description in lieu of functional analysis. His basic definition of an ecosystem incorporated both biotic and abiotic variables, whose interactions could be measured and, in theory, predicted.[23]

Tansley's ecosystem concept provided his postwar successors with an experimental framework to model the workings of nature using the principles of thermodynamics, chemistry, microbiology, and other quantitative sciences. Perhaps the most influential implementation of Tansley's ideas came with the work of Raymond Lindeman. His seminal 1942 paper, "The Trophic Dynamic Aspect of Ecology," ushered in modern ecosystems research, or what would come to be known as "the new ecology," by the 1950s and 1960s. Developed under the tutelage of preeminent Yale ecologist G. Evelyn Hutchinson, Lindeman's research formally undermined the distinction, typical of prewar ecology, between living communities and the nonliving environment.[24]

Following Hutchinson's lead, Lindeman stressed the centrality of "biogeochemistry" to ecosystem function, or the flux (back and forth movement) of materials between living and nonliving components of the biosphere. His advisor's pioneering work in limnology prompted him to explore how both energy and matter shuttled between organic and inorganic forms. First, Lindeman reconsidered the concept of the "food chain" articulated in Charles Elton's classic 1927 work *Animal Ecology*. He shifted the focus from food, per se, to the transfer of energy across "trophic levels" of diverse species organized according to feeding habits (decomposers, photosynthetic organisms, herbivores, and carnivores). This "trophic-dynamic" approach healed the prewar breach between botanists and zoologists and made microbiology central to ecological research. More important, it married ecology to the laws of thermodynamics, providing ecologists with the tools to measure energy storage and transfer efficiencies among trophic levels, ecosystem inputs and outputs, and the rate of biological productivity. Likewise, Lindeman emphasized how nutrients and other matter moved through perpetual sequences of synthesis and degradation. Photosynthetic organisms transformed inorganic compounds into complex organic molecules, while consumers and decomposers broke organic materials back down into inorganic form. Gauging these ecosystem nutrient cycles became a staple of the profession.[25]

As the post–World War II generation of ecologists refined the ecosystem concept, the metaphorical appeal of the self-regulating machine—no less

holistic than Tansley's "super-organism"—led them to assimilate basic principles of wartime operations research and systems analysis. If the machinery of nature did in fact operate according to the laws of thermodynamics
and energy econometrics, it seemed appropriate to play up the connections
with mechanical systems. The new field of cybernetics provided an intriguing bridge. Norbert Wiener, one of the pioneers of both systems analysis and
cybernetics, described the latter as "the science of control and communication, in the animal and the machine." For Wiener, "control" involved the
conveyance of messages that changed the behavior of the recipient. His experience with artillery devices during the war informed his interpretation.
These weapons employed sensors and circuits that transmitted targeting information through feedback loops, providing for automatic correction and
recalibration.[26]

Raymond Lindeman's mentor, G. Evelyn Hutchinson, took the lead in
applying cybernetics to ecological research. Hutchinson's theoretical work
treated biogeochemical cycles and population dynamics as analogous systems: self-correcting, mutually responsive to negative feedback, and tending
toward equilibrium. His influential 1946 paper, "Circular Causal Systems in
Ecology," delivered at the Macy Conference on Cybernetics, presented natural systems as self-balancing. Feedback mechanisms allowed discrete environments to remain constant or to return to normal upon disturbance. Any
deviation in one direction caused a reaction in the opposite direction until
equilibrium was attained, a process that Hutchinson insisted could be expressed mathematically.[27]

The self-regulating unit that Hutchinson postulated became the foundation of ecosystem ecology during the fifties and sixties, although it was
another of his graduate students, Howard Odum, who rendered the concept most accessible. Odum built his reputation during the fifties with the
path-breaking research he conducted for the Office of Naval Research and
the AEC. In these studies, Odum treated complex ecosystems—a salt marsh
in Silver Springs, Florida, and an irradiated coral reef at Eniwetok Atoll in the
Bikini Islands—as black boxes, perfecting techniques to quantify their biogeochemical cycles and metabolic energy budgets. He subsequently imported
Hutchinson's emphasis on biogeochemical cycles into his brother Eugene's
seminal *Fundamentals of Ecology* (1953), by far the most influential ecological textbook of the postwar era. Its lucid prose and conceptual clarity helped

define the ecosystem as "any entity or natural unit that includes living and nonliving parts interacting to produce a stable system in which the exchange of materials between living and nonliving parts follows circular paths."[28]

The Odums' writings and research over the next decade continued to articulate ecosystem function using the lexicon of cybernetics. During this same period, the ecosystem gradually assumed paradigmatic status among many plant and animal ecologists. A majority of those who conducted research for the AEC were weaned on *Fundamentals of Ecology*, as terms like "homeostasis," "steady state," and "feedback loop" became common vocabulary in ecological monographs. By 1964, Eugene Odum officially hailed the arrival of "the new ecology," distinguishing it as an essential division of biology rather than a mere extension of biochemistry or physiology. Since the ecosystem was the discipline's "basic unit of structure and function," he further described the new ecology as "a systems ecology." Natural systems, Odum insisted, needed to be analyzed holistically, lest the complexity and diversity of their internal feedback mechanisms be overlooked. He predicted that the increasing use of computers, mathematical models, and information theory would assist ecologists in their efforts to understand such complex processes. The ascendance of the IBP in the early seventies seemed to signal the culmination of this vision.[29]

Despite Odum's optimism and the IBP's prominence, however, the holistic conception of nature as a self-regulating machine did not remain a consistent article of faith among all ecologists. By the seventies, in fact, some within the profession were suggesting that the qualities of randomness, instability, and disequilibrium best characterized the way ecosystems functioned. But even before then, population ecologists and others within the discipline had resisted Odum's emphasis on homeostatic balance. The IBP, whose expansive scope and complexity actually militated against theoretical syntheses or conceptual breakthroughs, failed to unite them. And regardless of subdiscipline, many ecologists who preferred independent, small-scale research questioned the need for a "Manhattan Project" like the IBP in the first place.[30]

This growing fragmentation within the profession hardly prevented members of Congress from drawing upon ecosystems ecology's mechanical and management-oriented conception of nature as an inspiration and a resource. The discipline's most direct contribution to the substance of environmental legislation in the seventies, however, owed little to the IBP, or even to its benefactor, the Daddario subcommittee. The two academic ecologists who helped transform federal water pollution control policy, Cornell University's Gene Likens and Brookhaven's George Woodwell, pursued their research independently of the IBP. Moreover, they found their most receptive audience in a Senate committee that had displayed little interest in ecology throughout much of the sixties.

Pollution in a Systems Context

Much like the Odums, Gene Likens and George Woodwell sought balance. For them, ecology involved the study of natural systems in dynamic equilibrium and the factors disrupting that equilibrium. Quantitative analysis of biogeochemical cycling, they believed, offered a glimpse at how ecosystems responded to human-induced disturbances over time. The implications of their work for the federal government's environmentally oriented activities drew them into policy debates ranging from forestry practices to the uses of DDT. But it was the Public Works Committee that ultimately retained the two as ecological advisors in 1970. In 1971, their input helped convince Edmund Muskie to reframe the objectives of his subcommittee's pending water pollution control legislation in explicitly ecological terms and to revise its long-standing regulatory strategy.

It is all too easy to attribute the updated philosophy of the 1972 Clean Water Act to the broad cultural currency that popular ecological ideas enjoyed at the time. In fact, a more subtle combination of political, practical, and technical considerations prompted the newfound receptivity that Muskie and his colleagues exhibited toward ecology in the early seventies. The subsequent appeal of Woodwell's and Likens's research, in particular, reflected the saliency of all these factors. To a great extent, however, the Clean Water Act's grounding in postwar ecosystems ecology stemmed from the committee's positive response to the language the two ecologists spoke. That language, in turn, grew out of a body of work that was thoroughly representative of the quantitative, systems-oriented science ecology had become by the sixties.

As congressional experts, Likens and Woodwell spoke to the issue of water pollution, but as researchers they actually spent much of their time in the woods. After receiving his doctorate in zoology and limnology from the University of Wisconsin in 1962, Gene Likens moved on to Dartmouth and the

nearby Hubbard Brook Experimental Forest, a major center for hydrological research in New England. Nestled within a bowl-shaped valley in north-
central New Hampshire, this 3,000-square-hectare range of hardwoods and
conifers subsumed several contiguous watersheds that were drained by Hubbard Brook's meandering tributaries. Likens teamed with a Dartmouth colleague, plant ecologist Herbert Bormann, to investigate the cycling of minerals and nutrients through the aquatic pathways of this forested ecosystem.
In 1963, they coauthored a National Science Foundation proposal for a study
that would become one of the most successful and influential of its kind.[31]

Like the IBP biome project, research at Hubbard Brook shared a grounding in the new ecology and employed interdisciplinary teams of experts with
diverse training in the physical sciences. But Bormann and Likens's less hierarchical management style allowed their smaller groups of researchers more
autonomy, which led to greater innovation and cost-effectiveness. By the late
seventies, scientists affiliated with Hubbard Brook had published over two
hundred articles and books.[32]

Hubbard Brook implemented the first comprehensive series of controlled
experiments designed to measure the process of biogeochemical cycling
within and among entire ecosystems. The scientists paid particular attention to nutrients with sedimentary cycles, such as phosphorus, calcium, and
magnesium, all of which were more susceptible to disruption by human activity and amenable to analysis through geochemistry, hydrology, and me-
teorology. Research focused on measuring nutrient flux within and across
ecosystem boundaries, determining total chemical budgets for individual
ecosystems, and relating them to broader biospheric cycles. They hoped
that the resulting baselines would illuminate how human activities—clear-
cutting, pollution, and pesticide and fertilizer use, for example—disrupted
normal patterns.[33]

Hubbard Brook's methodology turned on the intimate relationship between the hydrological cycle and the nutrient cycle. Precipitation transported
nutrients in, water leached them from soil and rocks, and stream flows bore
them away. The topography of individual watersheds (the surrounding forest land drained by a tributary) defined the limits of the ecosystems under
study. Bormann and Likens chose six sheds in the northeastern corner of
the experimental forest. They measured meteorological inputs through a
network of precipitation gauging stations and geological outputs through

concrete weirs constructed at the foot of each watershed. Data taken at the weirs allowed them to ascertain both the volume of water and the quantities of chemical substances exiting the sheds and to tally nutrient budgets for magnesium, phosphorous, calcium, sodium, potassium, and several other elements. Doing so enabled the ecologists "to predict with fair accuracy both the output and the concentration of chemicals in the stream water draining from our mature, forested ecosystem." Such information, they concluded, "would seem to have considerable value for regional planners concerned with water quality."[34]

Having demonstrated how the chemistry of stream water depended on processes of control inherent in the forest ecosystem, Bormann and Likens decided to study a system subjected to stress. In conjunction with the Forest Service, they set about in the winter of 1965–1966 to cut down every beech, maple, and birch tree growing in Watershed Number Two, leveling almost 16 hectares of forest and shrubs. They hoped to determine the impact of clear-cutting on stream flow, as well as the effects of such forest manipulation on "nutrient relations and on eutrophication of stream water." Likens noted that the experiment resembled some of the "semi-serious" proposals raised during the northeastern drought of the mid-sixties to "cut those trees in New England that were wasting water by evapo-transpiration, to produce more liquid water for the thirsty megalopolis between Boston and New York City."[35]

Their research indicated that clear-cutting significantly polluted the stream that drained the denuded Hubbard Brook forest. Not only did deforestation increase the total volume of run-off, the net export of dissolved minerals was up to fifteen times greater than in undisturbed ecosystems. The stream water became more acidic, the nitrate concentration grew to exceed the maximum concentrations allowable for public drinking supplies, and increased nutrient levels in the water fostered dense algal blooms. In 1971, environmental opponents of the Forest Service's clear-cutting practices provoked an angry backlash from professional foresters by citing these findings during public debates—much to the chagrin of the two ecologists, who preferred to view themselves as neutral experts rather than advocates.[36]

George Woodwell proved more willing to involve himself in matters of public policy. Woodwell, who received his Ph.D. in botany from Duke in 1958, treated ecosystems as self-regulating units in the theoretical tradition of Lin-

deman, Hutchinson, and the Odums. He also retained a Darwinian framework reminiscent of his predecessors, viewing ecosystem stability, or "integrity," as a product of natural selection. Integrated through millions of years
of evolutionary competition and adaptation, plants and animals coexisted
within optimally balanced "natural communities" that displayed complex yet
predictable patterns of structure, function, and development.[37]

Woodwell's research explored how ecosystems responded to short-term
disturbances, like pollution or radiation, that prompted deviations from
"evolutionary background levels" and diminished biological complexity and
diversity. In the Irradiated Forest Experiment at Brookhaven National Labs,
for example, he exposed two types of natural communities—a field of weeds
and a deciduous forest—to gamma emissions considerably beyond the evolutionary experience of target plant life. The choice of environments was not
arbitrary. It corresponded to the typical sequence of ecological succession in
the Northeast, where simple weed patches yielded over time to increasingly
advanced plant life, and finally to an oak-pine "climax community"—the
most stable, diverse, and complex ecosystem found in the region. Experimental results suggested that early successional stages were much more resistant
to stress than later ones. Woodwell concluded that complex ecosystems were
"more vulnerable to disturbances than simpler systems such as the [weed]
field, which has little ecological structure and little dependence on it."[38]

Though Brookhaven's Irradiated Forest Experiment seemed applicable
only to the activities of its sponsor, the AEC, it actually revealed more universal patterns of ecological disturbance. Woodwell realized that the spatial
configuration of the forest's radiation damage seemed to mimic the temporal
stages of succession. In other words, the area closest to the gamma source and
subject to the greatest exposures ended up completely devoid of trees and
higher plant life, while zones at increasing distances contained progressively
more diverse shrubs, oaks, and pines. This damage gradient resembled others
caused by very different forms of environmental stress, such as fire, salt spray,
temperature extremes, or exposure to sulfur dioxide pollution. As Woodwell
noted, the species that survived high radiation at Brookhaven were ones
"commonly found in disturbed places, such as roadsides, gravel banks, and
areas with nutrient deficient or unstable soil."[39]

Various types of disturbances, then, including manmade activities like
pollution, caused common and predictable changes in ecosystem diversity,

complexity, and structure. Woodwell's irradiated forest on Long Island and Likens's denuded forest in New England demonstrated a similar divergence from normal patterns of biogeochemical activity under stress. In both cases, reductions in plant diversity diminished the "total inventory of nutrient elements held within the system." Such nutrient imbalances not only impoverished terrestrial communities but, as Hubbard Brook demonstrated, also tended to overload aquatic environments, reducing biological complexity and stability in both systems.[40]

Woodwell concluded that the integrity of an ecosystem's biogeochemical cycles, as established on an evolutionary scale, could be compromised by manmade disturbances operating within a much briefer time frame. This conception of "ecosystem integrity" informed his understanding of how environmental pollutants should be measured and managed. Toxicologists and sanitary engineers focused on the immediate hazards that toxic substances posed to human health. Ecologists, too, concerned themselves with human welfare, but, according to Woodwell, they also recognized that "toxicity to humans is but one aspect of the pollution problem, the other being a threat to the maintenance of a biosphere suitable for life as we know it." The key for Woodwell, then, was to determine "what effects such pollutants have on the structure of natural ecosystems and on biological diversity, and what these changes mean to physiology, especially to mineral cycling and the long term potential for sustaining life."[41]

Woodwell's other major research effort in the sixties traced how one toxic substance in particular, DDT, behaved biogeochemically and what impact it had on ecosystem integrity over time. He conducted some of his earliest investigations in the forests of Maine and eastern Canada, which had been subjected to aerial DDT spraying during the 1950s to control the spruce budworm. While Woodwell concluded that the pesky budworm posed more of a threat to higher plant life than the DDT, he did find "abundant evidence . . . that food chains are contaminated in various ways." He further warned that "the persistence of residues of DDT in soils for as much as a decade is ample reason to examine the cycling of this and other noxious products through ecological systems with great care."[42]

Silent Spring had first alerted the public to the potential risks associated with the new generation of postwar insecticides, but Rachel Carson had not undertaken any original research on the subject. Carson wrote about "pollution of the total environment of mankind" and recounted how DDT accumulated in food chains, but her book focused primarily on direct threats to human health. And although *Silent Spring* inspired public debate, congressional hearings, and a PSAC study, it did not significantly alter the use or regulation of pesticides.

The real period of transition occurred between 1963 and 1968. In the wake of more vigilant environmental monitoring, advances in detection technology like the gas chromatograph, and increasing interdisciplinary attention by researchers, scientists were able to present a more compelling account of what one historian described as DDT's "mobility, persistence, bioconcentration, and effects on non-target species." In turn, this new information fueled grassroots challenges to individual spraying programs on the local level. George Woodwell participated actively in both roles.[43]

When residents of Long Island filed suit to stop the Suffolk County Mosquito Control Commission from applying DDT to local marshlands in 1966, Woodwell and several of his colleagues at Brookhaven agreed to serve as expert advisors and witnesses. The plaintiffs' petition to the court, filed by thirty-one-year-old trial lawyer and area resident Victor Yannacone, contended that repeated applications of chlorinated hydrocarbon pesticides would cause ecological damage and "adversely affect the people of Suffolk County . . . either personally or through destruction of . . . natural resources." Yannacone won a temporary injunction based on the authoritative testimony of his scientists, who claimed that further use of DDT would diminish the size and variety of local fish and wildlife populations. Among other evidence, Woodwell cited his own recent investigation of DDT residue concentrations in a salt marsh at the eastern end of Long Island's Great South Bay.[44]

Woodwell's marsh study provided evidence that DDT residues cycled between organisms and the environment in much the same way other organic nutrients or inorganic minerals did. DDT in soil was leached by water, moved by erosion, and taken up by algae, microorganisms, and other mud-dwellers, who were consumed in turn by creatures occupying higher trophic levels. In an example of "biological magnification," the marsh's chain of plant and animal life accumulated the fat-soluble toxin at an exponential rate. DDT concentrations found in carnivorous birds generally reached ten to one hundred times those in the fish they ate, and exceeded the original residue levels in the water by up to a million-fold. Woodwell concluded that the concentrations of DDT in the marsh's food web were approaching "the maximum levels observable in living organisms, and now occasionally reach acutely lethal levels in both birds and fish."[45]

The manifestations of ecosystem disturbance in the Long Island marsh followed a familiar pattern. DDT, like radiation or other stresses, reduced the number of higher species, diminished food web diversity, and upset biogeochemical cycles. Moreover, as Woodwell noted in a widely reproduced 1967 *Scientific American* article, chlorinated hydrocarbons circulated far and wide within the global biosphere, following the same pathways of wind, water, and soil that carried other toxic elements like strontium 90.[46]

Woodwell's concern over the "dysfunctional" policies that state and federal governments pursued with respect to pesticides like DDT drew him into the political arena. In 1967, he joined with six other biologists and ecologists as founding trustees of the Environmental Defense Fund, the litigation-oriented public interest group that Victor Yannacone established in connection with his Long Island crusade. He also served as the chairman of the Environmental Defense Fund's Environmental Advisory Committee. Since he believed that human societies lacked the information necessary to manage ecosystems in a "stable and sustained fashion," Woodwell viewed the Environmental Defense Fund as a "direct means of bringing science to bear on environmental issues." For Yannacone, the only place this could be done effectively was in a courtroom, where "a scientist [can] present his evidence, free of harassment by politicians," and "bureaucratic hogwash can be tested in the crucible of cross-examination." But while the Long Island attorney preferred to "sue the bastards," Congress demonstrated its own interest in what ecologists had to say.[47]

Ecologists for Muskie?

The professional careers of Woodwell and Likens help put their later advice to the Senate Public Works Committee in its proper technocratic context but do little to explain how or why they came to advise the committee in the first place. The senator most likely to express an interest in ecology, Edmund Muskie, never showed the enthusiasm that other legislators, like Emilio Daddario, Gaylord Nelson, John Dingell, or even Henry Jackson (D-Wash.) had begun to demonstrate. Although the media would dub him "Ecology

Ed," Muskie merely paid lip service to ecological ideas in the late sixties and proved hesitant to apply them to his pollution control legislation.

Even the opportunistic Thomas Jorling dealt with Muskie only in passing. In 1968, Jorling volunteered to work with a number of like-minded ecologists who had decided to query the presidential candidates about their environmental policy positions. The Humphrey-Muskie campaign was the only one that responded to their initiative. As a consequence, a group that included Woodwell, Likens, and Bormann ended up lending advice, information, and support to the Democratic ticket. "Ecologists for Humphrey" failed to tip the balance in the Minnesotan's favor, but Jorling took solace in the somewhat Panglossian idea that they had come close to having an "influential relationship on [sic] the presidency."[48]

In time, Jorling, Likens, and Woodwell came to exercise that influence within the legislative branch. Even before the latter two had signed on as ecological advisors for the Public Works Committee in 1970, Jorling accepted the job as its minority counsel in 1969. His training and professional associations took on a new significance in 1969–1970. As other legislative entrepreneurs began to dabble with alternative approaches for protecting the natural world, the committee members—and Muskie—realized they could no longer take their expert status or jurisdiction in environmental matters for granted.

5

From Pollution Control to Environmental Quality

The Challenge of NEPA

During the first half of the sixties, Edmund Muskie used his status as a Senate specialist to build public awareness of the nation's water pollution problem and congressional consensus in support of a regulatory solution. Before environmentalism had become a fixture of the nation's political culture, Muskie articulated a national policy that encouraged the incremental enhancement of water quality. The system of ambient stream standards he inaugurated with the 1965 Water Quality Act relied upon the cooperative efforts of administrators and sanitary engineers on the state and federal levels. To advance a new environmental agenda over the ambivalence of local government officials and outright corporate opposition, Muskie chose to work with recognized experts and within preexisting institutional arrangements. And he continued to stress how pollution control, by ensuring adequate water supplies, could satisfy a growing population's need for recreational activities and economic growth alike.

In the years after 1965, however, as popular concern for protecting the natural world gathered momentum, public opinion began to catch up with Muskie. By decade's end, ecological justifications for pollution control proved more persuasive than developmental rationales; indeed, growth itself seemed environmentally suspect. A new generation of public interest advocates in the early seventies turned the senator's sincere belief in federalism and local control into political liabilities. In the span of just a few years, the once-proactive visionary seemed to fall behind the curve.

Although Muskie's pollution control philosophy came under fire from external critics, the first serious challenge to his authority in the late sixties arose within Congress. During that time, other chairs responded to the institutional incentives of the congressional committee system just as Muskie had earlier in the decade. They mobilized available committee resources to accommodate emerging environmental constituencies, focus on new issues, and seek out new bases of knowledge and expertise. In the process, these legislative entrepreneurs explored alternative methods for protecting the environment that challenged Muskie's regulatory apparatus and his Subcommittee on Air and Water Pollution's exclusive jurisdiction over it.

Ecology emerged as a significant mode of thought in this contested realm of regulatory politics. The study of ecosystems had recently gained stature in Congress as a practical form of systems analysis—that is, as a science capable of promoting rational, sophisticated environmental management. Now public officials began to contemplate an administrative system capable in turn of managing all federal activities that had ecological impacts. This involved much more than just pollution control or a compartmentalized concern with individual media like water or air. It pointed toward a comprehensive, government-wide policy for the "total environment" of the sort that came to be embodied in the landmark National Environmental Policy Act (NEPA).

The two years leading up to NEPA's enactment on 1 January 1970 mark a period of transition for Ed Muskie and his colleagues on the Senate Public Works Committee. Prior to the direct challenges they faced from environmental interest groups in the wake of Earth Day, the senators sought to adapt both the existing pollution control system and their own committee to solve the new ecological and bureaucratic problems that NEPA purported to address.

Thermal pollution, which emerged as a prominent issue during this time, served as the catalyst for the committee. The policy question at hand was straightforward: how could the AEC be made to consider the effects of heated cooling water on aquatic ecosystems when deciding whether to license privately operated nuclear power plants? The answers it prompted, however, underscored the competing conceptions of environmental regulation at stake. Muskie himself had no intention of attempting to transform the commissioners into environmentalists—determining the impact of waste heat was a job for traditional pollution control experts. But as the senator came to realize, NEPA, if approved by Congress, would not necessarily recognize the pollution control administrators he oversaw as the final arbiters of environmental quality. Instead, it stood to establish a more universal responsibility among all government agencies to assess the environmental consequences of their actions, regardless of their mission.

Blurring the line between the regulators and the regulated was precisely what NEPA's sponsor, Henry "Scoop" Jackson (D-Wash.), had in mind. Jackson, the chairman of the Interior Committee, had nothing against pollution control and much in common with Muskie. Both were Democrats from predominantly rural states who shared a concern for balancing environmental protection, natural resource development, and economic growth. But Jackson and his committee staff believed that the responsibility for environmental administration belonged to all government agencies, whose officials would choose wiser alternatives if prompted by NEPA to solicit and apply the right information. Such a comprehensive approach better suited the interdependent natural world that ecologists described. Moreover, it transcended the jurisdiction of the Public Works Committee, promising new opportunities for the Interior Committee to guide the transformation of government policy.

The conflict between Muskie and Jackson over NEPA may have reflected institutional tensions internal to Congress, but the resulting law reverberated beyond the capitol in ways neither man could have predicted. Muskie's efforts to modify NEPA and preserve the primacy of pollution control expertise did not prevent federal judges from interpreting the statute expansively in response to public interest lawsuits. It remained to be seen whether a new generation of environmental activists, operating through the courts, would allow the pronouncements of such experts to go unexamined or unchallenged.

Thermal Pollution: Licensing an Ecological Dilemma

The public's desire for environmental protection in the latter half of the sixties coincided with an exploding national demand for energy. In 1968, the Office of Science and Technology predicted that 250 "mammoth" power plants would be needed by 1990 to meet a consumer demand for electricity that had nearly doubled in each decade since the forties. Since fossil fuel facilities belched millions of tons of sulfur dioxide, nitrogen oxides, and carbon dioxide into the air, utility companies looked to emission-free nuclear energy as a way to satisfy the concurrent call for power and environmental quality. In 1968, nuclear plants provided only about 1 percent of the nation's 260 million kilowatts of generating capacity, but experts believed that by 1980 fission could produce 30 percent of the anticipated 530-million-kilowatt requirement.[1]

Given the impending number, size, and character of future steam-generating plants, the possible effects of elevated stream temperatures on fish and marine invertebrates became a more prominent concern between 1965 and 1970. In 1965, electrical plants discharged 48 trillion gallons of heated water. Within fifteen years, the volume was expected to approach 108 trillion gallons. The likely proliferation of nuclear reactors, which discharged 50 percent more waste heat than conventional plants, confounded the difficulty. "Everyone thought thermal pollution wouldn't be a problem for five to ten years, so we've been grappling with the more obvious aspects of pollution," observed an Interior Department official in 1967, "but all of a sudden there's been an explosion of nuclear plant construction, and we found ourselves fighting a whole new series of brushfires."[2]

The broader debate over thermal pollution grew out of a series of internal disagreements between the Fish and Wildlife Service and the AEC in the mid-sixties. The latter assumed that its authority to regulate commercial nuclear power plants under the 1954 Atomic Energy Act did not extend beyond the realm of radiological health and safety. It relied instead on informal cooperative relationships with other federal agencies to assess environmental questions that arose during the licensing process. Under a 1964 agreement, the Fish and Wildlife Service reviewed applications to evaluate the impact of proposed reactors on aquatic animal and plant species. The AEC dutifully passed this information on to the states and potential licensees but was not obligated to alter the prevailing permit conditions. The AEC made no other effort to weigh the environmental consequences of waste heat and refused to consider it as a mitigating factor that might justify the delay or rejection of an applicant's license. By 1966, certain officials in the Fish and Wildlife Service had grown impatient with the AEC's habitual evasion and began insisting that it take account of possible thermal effects when hearing licensing cases.[3]

Before long, the matter began to play out before Congress as well. John Dingell (D-Mich.), chairman of the House Subcommittee on Fisheries and

Wildlife Conservation, took up on behalf of his subcommittee's mission. Appearing before the Joint Committee on Atomic Energy, Dingell asserted that the AEC's actions deliberately skirted the intentions of the Fish and Wildlife Coordination Act of 1958. That legislation required federal agencies to consult the Fish and Wildlife Service "with a view to the conservation of wildlife resources," if the activities they proposed to undertake or license "impounded, diverted . . . controlled or modified" a body of water. Dingell charged that the AEC was promoting nuclear power plant development "without due care for either the enhancement or the preservation of fish and wildlife values." In response, the AEC conducted an internal legal review of its thermal pollution policy that confirmed the original, narrow interpretation of its 1954 enabling legislation. The AEC's general counsel concluded that the Fish and Wildlife Coordination Act did not apply to atomic facilities or expand the regulatory authority of the AEC.[4]

This question of the AEC's regulatory reach occupied Congress into the next decade. Following the AEC's declaration of limited liability, legislators proposed various strategies to compel it to incorporate environmental values directly into its licensing procedures. The ensuing course of events drew Edmund Muskie and his subcommittee into the fray in 1967, shifting the locus of the issue from the discrete realm of fish and wildlife to the broader arena of pollution control.

Muskie in Hot Water

Muskie's subcommittee took up thermal pollution at a time when budgetary constraints forced him as chair to explore alternative means of maintaining the water pollution program's momentum. As the 1966 Clean Water Restoration Act's generous construction grant authorizations fell victim to the Vietnam War, Muskie and his colleagues labored unsuccessfully to devise alternative financing solutions that would allow states and local governments to pay for waste treatment facilities. By contrast, policing federal licensing procedures for compliance with state water quality standards promised "significant results . . . without undue delay or excessive federal financial outlays." As Muskie informed the undersecretary of Interior, "This philosophy applies not only to the Atomic Energy Commission . . . all federal agencies . . . through licenses, permits, and leases, and through their contractual activities should require maximum efforts to comply with water quality standards."[5]

Although Muskie framed the issue in universal terms, the AEC served as his target of opportunity in 1967–1968, a fact partly attributable to the vicissitudes of geography. In November 1966, the Vermont Yankee Nuclear Power Corporation applied for a construction permit for a 514,000-kilowatt power plant on the Connecticut River at Vernon, Vermont. The most vocal thermal pollution controversy to date soon unfolded right in Muskie's own backyard. Residents of New Hampshire, Massachusetts, and Connecticut eyed the prospect of the new facility with considerable trepidation. The Interior Department estimated that the proposed plant would require 60 percent of the maximum flow of the Connecticut River for cooling and would release enough heated effluent to elevate stream temperature by 15 or 20 degrees. One official feared that such massive thermal discharges might "kill the river biologically," rendering it little more than "the cooling system for Vermont Yankee." Moreover, Vermont Yankee's waste heat threatened to violate Massachusetts's recently approved water quality standards, which did not allow temperature increases in interstate streams. All the states involved, even Vermont, criticized the AEC's refusal to consider thermal effects as a mitigating factor in the licensing process.[6]

It was against this backdrop that the senator from Maine addressed a letter to AEC chairman Glenn Seaborg in September 1967, questioning the AEC's licensing practices and its commitment to pollution control. Muskie believed that the provisions of the Water Quality Act and of Executive Order 11288 obligated the commission to regulate thermal effluents from its licensed reactors. The latter compelled federal installations, as well as those supported by federal loans, grants, or contracts, to conform to water pollution standards, including the maintenance of "water temperatures within acceptable limits." AEC officials responded a month later by reiterating their general counsel's earlier legal analysis: although the AEC complied with state-federal standards with respect to its own installations, it could not compel the plants it licensed to do the same.[7]

Muskie pursued the matter with a growing sense of annoyance, but also with a greater sense of personal urgency. On 5 October, the Maine Yankee Atomic Power Company applied for its own permit for an 830,000-kilowatt reactor to be located on Baily Point, Wiscasset, north of Bothbay Harbor. The senator queried Seaborg about the AEC's efforts to consider waste treatment requirements for thermal pollution "at the earliest feasible stage of planning"

for the proposed plant. When the AEC chairman's response proved unsatis-
factory, Muskie announced the subcommittee's intention to hold hearings in
New England on the matter of thermal pollution from nuclear power generating plants. Those proceedings marked a significant departure from the
subcommittee's past fact-finding efforts.[8]

Factoring Ecology

Prior to 1968, the Subcommittee on Air and Water Pollution did not solicit,
and witnesses rarely presented, testimony that asserted ecological principles
as a technical or philosophical justification for water pollution control. The
subcommittee committed itself to improving stream conditions, upgrading
waterways to the highest possible beneficial uses, and protecting unspoiled
rivers; it also emphasized public health concerns whenever pertinent. But
maintaining an ample water supply capable of supporting economic growth
and a range of practical applications remained the leading justification for a
state-federal regulatory system.

The water quality standards and criteria required by statute remained
grounded in traditional expertise. Sanitary engineers from government
agencies and industry and economists from natural resource think tanks appeared regularly as witnesses when technical pronouncements were required.
The majority of testimony came from state, federal, and local officials, interest group representatives, conservationists, and plant operators, who debated
the need for more federal regulatory authority or the amount of money required to finance treatment plant construction.

No professionally trained ecologists testified before the Subcommittee
on Air and Water Pollution between 1963 and 1967, and no more than an
occasional reference to ecology was made, even as the subcommittee's interests grew more diverse. In 1967, for example, legislation pending before
the subcommittee consolidated a number of separate concerns, including
acid mine drainage, oil pollution, and the deterioration of the Great Lakes.
Representatives from the oil and coal industries and the Bureau of Mines
dominated the witness list. Discussions of lake-related problems like eutrophication, which were beginning to gain wider public and media attention,
did not benefit from the input of limnologists; sanitary engineers sufficed.
Their testimony dealt with the practical consequences of eutrophication for
water users rather than with the well-being of aquatic ecosystems. The chief

sanitary engineer for the North Dakota State Health Department set the tone when he informed the senators in August 1967 that "the aging of a lake [eutrophication] is basically a recreational and aesthetic problem and is usually not of concern to public health, unless the lake deteriorates too far."[9]

By contrast, the subcommittee's 1968 thermal pollution hearings featured broad discussions of ecology. Muskie's opening remarks on 6 February stressed that "the need for a balanced environment will shift our focus from dealing only with crises and obvious toxic effects from pollution to a policy which takes into account long-term effects of waste discharges on ecological communities." The subcommittee also engaged ecological experts to provide technical background and an alternative source of information on the issue of power plant siting.[10]

It would be misleading, however, to imply that a single set of hearings transformed the subcommittee's modus operandi. The Senate Public Works Committee certainly became more receptive to ecological science between 1968 and 1971. It did so in response to a variety of internal and external stimuli: the perception of changing public values and priorities; the activities of other entrepreneurial committee chairs who had already begun staking claims to emerging environmental issues; and the influence of new advisors and staff. Nevertheless, this new responsiveness to ecology did not have an immediate, tangible impact on the substance of the committee's legislation. Relative to colleagues like Emilio Daddario and Henry Jackson, Muskie reacted slowly to emerging trends that favored a more holistic brand of environmental policymaking. The call for rational federal administration of the "total environment" in the late sixties implied a less compartmentalized regulatory strategy than Muskie's. It also called into question the administrative rationale upon which he had built his career.

The Muskie subcommittee's ultimate response to thermal pollution in 1969 underscored its commitment to the state-federal pollution control infrastructure it had pioneered. Muskie continued to defer to traditional repositories of expertise, rejecting strategies that might have employed ecological information as a wedge to modify the values and priorities of developmental agencies. The subcommittee did seek to change the federal permit process by requiring licensing boards to incorporate state water quality standards into their decision making. But the criteria for water quality standards did not necessarily account for all the variables ecologists deemed important. Nor did standards alone promise to transform bureaucratic environmental consciousness. So while the Public Works Committee began to talk the talk in the late sixties, it hesitated to translate rhetoric into statutory policy.

Legislating Environmental Awareness

Congressional committees other than Muskie's took an interest in addressing the AEC's regulatory responsibility for reactor waste heat in 1968, each according to its own agenda. The Joint Committee on Atomic Energy proposed to amend the Atomic Energy Act of 1954 and give the AEC the ultimate authority to consider an applicant's capacity to control thermal effluents. Members hoped that granting thermal pollution due consideration would contain environmental disputes while expediting reactor development. John Dingell's Subcommittee on Fisheries and Wildlife Conservation sponsored legislation requiring any federal agency, prior to issuing a license or permit, to obtain a certification from the secretary of the Interior Department declaring thermal discharges consistent with applicable water quality standards. This proposal essentially granted the Interior Department preconstruction approval authority over federally licensed activities, on top of its preexisting power to approve state-federal water quality standards.[11]

Muskie dabbled with both the Joint Committee on Atomic Energy and Dingell options but ultimately rejected them in favor of a solution, introduced in early 1969, that deferred to the institutional framework of the 1965 Water Quality Act. Before a federal agency could issue an operating or construction permit, the applicant had to seek a certification from the appropriate state water quality office verifying that the proposed facility would not violate established standards. All discharges, not simply waste heat, were to be considered. All licensing agencies, not simply the AEC, had to defer to the expertise of the certifiers, which meant that nuclear power plants would not be held to a distinctive set of environmental considerations and placed at a competitive disadvantage. By requiring, as Muskie put it, "water quality compliance as a precondition of federal activities," the subcommittee attempted to adapt the regulatory system it created to monitor the environmental impacts of facilities licensed by a broad array of government agencies.[12]

Muskie's certification procedure went otherwise unnoticed in a piece of legislation, the Water Quality Improvement Act of 1970, that addressed oil pollution and the notorious 1969 Santa Barbara spill. Fierce opposition by the petroleum industry delayed the bill for almost a year. Certification, however, proved quite popular among other industrial interests, particularly electric utilities, because it relieved the AEC, or any other licensing agency, from having to make unilateral determinations of environmental impact. It came as no surprise that a broad cross section of industrialists rejected John Dingell's plan to bring in the secretary of the Interior as an autonomous player in the licensing process. But other legislative proposals that required federal permitting agencies to assess environmental risks themselves and apply corrective measures were equally unpopular. According to the president of the Edison Electric Institute, such measures threatened to empower the AEC, an agency with no environmental expertise, to implement pollution control measures that met, or possibly superseded, water quality standards set by the states. Endowing all federal agencies with such discretion, the Manufacturing Chemists of America spokesman agreed, would dissipate control of water pollution programs at the federal level, drain the supply of specialists in the field, and encourage administrative discrepancies.[13]

Muskie's passive certification process precluded federal agencies from issuing any license or permit until state experts accounted for water quality concerns. It offered a way to dissipate the political heat generated by conservation organizations and journalists without violating the AEC's understanding of its own regulatory authority or putting nuclear power at a competitive disadvantage. Industrialists, utilities, and the AEC alike embraced the subcommittee's bill, whereas all had vigorously opposed an earlier version in 1968 without the state certification process. The shift in mood gave Ed Muskie pause. "As I understand your testimony, you have no objections to S. 7," the senator stated after the spokesman from the Manufacturing Chemists of America had finished his presentation. "That is correct sir, yes," he replied. "Maybe there is something wrong with it," Muskie noted sardonically.[14]

In 1971, a federal appeals court did find something wrong with it, but for that turn of events Muskie would have the 1970 National Environmental Policy Act, not industrial lobbyists, to blame. Developed by Henry Jackson's Senate Committee on Interior and Insular Affairs in response to broader contemporary political trends, NEPA sought to revolutionize the federal government's entire approach to administrative decision making with respect to the environment. Less constrained by conceptions of federalism, agency expertise, or other elements that were a part of the institutional experience of the Public Works Committee, the Interior Committee pursued a far more expansive vision of environmental regulation. The system it advocated in 1969–1970 posited information as a universal solvent, dissolving the bureaucratic boundaries that circumscribed environmental responsibility. In lieu of designating a pollution control infrastructure characterized by specialization, with NEPA, Congress declared a comprehensive national policy to rationalize and integrate federal management of the "total environment." Promoting environmental quality became, in theory, a universal bureaucratic goal that transcended narrow definitions of pollution control, the agencies that carried it out, or the congressional committee that oversaw it.

NEPA: A New Paradigm for Environmental Quality

In the late sixties, public officials concluded that a renewed national commitment to the environment demanded more precise management of two complex systems: nature itself and the federal government's sprawling bureaucracy. Ecosystem ecology seemed to offer the quantitative tools and holistic perspective necessary to master the first, prompting legislators like Emilio Daddario and Gaylord Nelson to seek more active government support for the discipline. But the ecological ethos of managing parts in relation to the whole seemed applicable to human institutions as well, especially those having an impact on the environment. If ecologists sought to comprehend how systems of interdependent organisms functioned in nature, then students of public administration hoped to promote a similar concinnity among government agencies, transforming a rudderless federal environmental agenda into a comprehensive policy.[15]

Contemporary academics emphasized how civic awareness of environmental deterioration had exposed deficiencies in the government's aggregate institutional response to the natural world. According to the most prominent critic, Indiana University professor of government Lynton Caldwell, federal agencies that promoted economic development—such as the AEC, the Corps of Engineers, or the Bureau of Reclamation—pursued unilateral agendas, as did the congressional committees overseeing them. Government-sponsored activities of this kind had environmental consequences, but they were compromised by inadequate knowledge and an ingrained philosophy of resource exploitation. Nor did anyone seem to be running the show. President Johnson's Citizens Advisory Committee on Recreation and Natural Beauty bemoaned the fact that "no single entity within the federal structure can be counted on to weigh each decision or measure each new program objective against the impact that it will have on the natural environment."[16]

The call for better management of environmentally significant government activities and, by extension, the "total" environment itself (defined ecologically) found a sympathetic audience in Congress between 1966 and 1969. The Senate Public Works Committee, however, demonstrated limited interest in the subject. Although the committee had opportunities to stake its jurisdictional claim, Muskie never seriously considered ecologically oriented legislation to review or coordinate government policy, choosing to remain focused on regulating specific media like air, water, and solid waste.[17]

Henry Jackson's Committee on Interior and Insular Affairs stepped in to fill the breach, but not without some persistent prodding by newly hired legislative counsel William Van Ness. Although Jackson had played an active role in advancing prominent conservation-oriented legislation, he did not perceive the environment as being on a par with other priorities, like national security. But Van Ness realized that the Interior Committee could position itself as the congressional leader in a field of burgeoning importance and oversee the restructuring of environmental institutions and agendas, if it outmaneuvered other committees with competing claims and took decisive action.[18]

The legislative counsel made his case with particular vigor beginning in January 1967, recounting the arguments of Caldwell and others that a compartmentalized government bureaucracy could never hope to manage (or avoid damaging) interdependent natural systems. The time had come, he concluded, to devise a comprehensive national environmental policy that would allow government officials to consider alternative courses of action and reserve a place for environmental value choices in the policy process. By summertime, Jackson was delivering speeches authored by his persistent counsel, addressing the need for a national policy on the environment and the coordinated institutions required to implement it, which the senator dubbed "environmental administration." In 1968, Jackson's committee and Emilio Daddario's House Subcommittee on Science, Research, and Development held joint hearings and produced reports on the subject.[19]

This frequent reference to national "policy" denoted less a set of specific directives than a recognition of the power of information, properly solicited and applied, to transform government behavior. Early versions of what would become NEPA made no effort to declare any particular environmental policy, but they did focus on the collection, analysis, and dissemination of information thought to be underrepresented in agency decision making. Van Ness's initial draft bills in 1966 and 1967 closely resembled the legislation Gaylord Nelson had introduced in 1965 to promote research and surveys in ecology. As late as February 1969, many of the provisions included in S. 1075 (the bill that would become NEPA) resembled little more than a solicitation of information on trends and changes in the natural environment, setting up the Department of Interior as a sort of clearinghouse for ecological data.[20]

For Lynton Caldwell, however, who by 1968 had become the Interior Committee's most influential expert advisor, Jackson's evolving bill did more than promote data gathering and organization. "The need for more knowledge has been established beyond doubt," he insisted, "but of equal and perhaps greater importance at this time is the establishment of a system to insure that existing knowledge and new findings will be organized in a manner suitable for review and decision as matters of public policy." Thus, Caldwell suggested, new and relevant information would help reinforce ecological priorities within the government.[21]

The bill's proposed council of environmental advisors, long advocated by politicians, academics, government reports, and conservation-minded editors, offered similar advantages. As a high-level reviewing agency responsible directly to the president, the council would, according to Caldwell, "bridge the gap between the functions of environmental surveillance, research, and analysis, on the one hand, and policy-making functions of President and Congress on the other." The drafters envisioned a body capable of undertaking broad, independent reviews of policy means and ends, elevating the environment to a level commensurate with national defense or the economy. Again, proper use of information would rationalize policy and balance competing values.[22]

While the legislation alluded to the power of interdisciplinary scientific information to mitigate ingrained bureaucratic biases or suggest unexamined options, prior to the summer of 1969 it provided no mechanism to ensure that such information would be incorporated into the policymaking process. Information altered the function of systems—be they mechanical, natural, or bureaucratic—only with the aid of proper feedback loops. So, as Lynton

Caldwell came to realize, any national environmental policy Congress put in place would need to reorder existing administrative procedures.

Caldwell suggested that any national environmental policy include an "action-forcing, operational aspect." As he informed Senator Jackson, "When we speak of policy we ought to think of a statement which is so written that it is capable of implementation . . . not merely a statement of desirable goals or objectives." Specifically, Caldwell envisioned a national policy that required federal agencies to anticipate and submit an evaluation of the environmental impact of any proposed activities. Agencies involved in licensing, such as the AEC, would also be required to incorporate environmental factors into their deliberations.[23]

The updated version of S. 1075 that Jackson presented to the Senate at the end of May reflected Caldwell's revised thinking. "As a nation, we have failed to design and implement a national environmental policy which would enable us to weigh alternatives, and to anticipate the undesirable side effects which often result from our ongoing policies, programs, and actions," the senator proclaimed. The amendments he introduced included an extended policy declaration; to make good on it, the act required reports on every proposed federal activity to include "a finding" by a "responsible official," confirming that all potential environmental impacts had been properly assessed. Any adverse consequences that could not be avoided by following reasonable alternatives had to be "justified by stated considerations of national policy." As Jackson explained, the official statement of policy, coupled with the departmental duty to undertake environmental findings, made the quality of the environment *everyone's* responsibility. "No agency," he concluded, "will . . . be able to maintain that it has no mandate or no requirement to consider the environmental consequences of its actions." As Jackson and Caldwell saw it, these procedures, buttressed by the coordinating oversight of a Council on Environmental Quality, would help incorporate new, relevant sources of information and expertise into bureaucratic deliberations. With the proper feedback loops in place to determine the consequences of federal activities, government officials could recalibrate national priorities and protect the environment.[24]

Muskie versus Jackson: Divergent Roads to Environmental Quality

At the time, few in Congress recognized how S. 1075's strategy to inculcate environmental values might disrupt the networks of power that had dominated government policymaking throughout the twentieth century. One of the few who did, House Interior Committee chairman Wayne Aspinall (D-Colo.), jealously guarded the independence of federal agencies charged with managing natural resources and promoting economic growth, particularly in the West. To neutralize Jackson's initiative, he made certain that the House version of the bill pledged not to alter "any responsibility or authority of any federal official or agency created by other provision of law." For Aspinall, whose own authority stemmed from the oversight of developmental agencies, and for client interests, whose privileged access to Aspinall's committee helped secure profits from mining, petroleum, and dams, the Senate bill threatened to impede customary policy objectives by introducing new sets of experts, government officials, interest groups, and perhaps even judges into an exclusive decision-making process.[25]

Yet the most serious challenge to S. 1075 came not from a champion of development in the House but rather from an environmentalist in the Senate: Edmund Muskie. His opposition stemmed not simply from a sense of jurisdictional propriety but rather from a concern that Jackson's approach to environmental policy ran counter to the Public Works Committee's accumulated knowledge and practical experience. As early as 1968, Muskie's new staff director, Leon Billings, had begun to eye Jackson's widening environmental activities warily. The joint colloquium with Daddario in particular raised red flags, since participants spoke of "solving" the problem of fragmented executive branch administration by vesting mission agencies with more independent environmental responsibility. As Billings reminded his boss, the subcommittee's dealings with "the Joint Committee on Atomic Energy, its relationship with the AEC and the latter's attitude on thermal pollution can serve as a reminder of the potential situation which might occur if both Mr. Jackson and Mr. Daddario were to be successful." The Water Quality Improvement Act's certification process indicated the Senate Public Works Committee's belief that mission agencies possessed neither the inclination, the technical competence, nor the administrative capacity to police themselves on matters of environmental quality.[26]

For Muskie, a clear dichotomy existed between "environmental impact" agencies, whose actions tended to harm the natural environment, and "environmental enhancement" agencies, empowered to improve environmental quality through regulation and oversight. The Subcommittee on Air and

Water Pollution had built the ethos of "enhancement" into its legislation over the last seven years. Those laws relied on administrators and experts to develop quantitative air/water quality criteria; set enforceable standards based on those criteria for local streams or air sheds; determine site-specific implementation plans; and apply the technology needed to achieve standards. By design, the locus of activity rested with state and local pollution control agencies and their counterparts on the federal level. This administrative process, Muskie and his colleagues believed, offered the best chance of improving air quality and upgrading beneficial use designations for waterways. They expected other federal agencies to defer to the expertise of pollution control officials; the AEC, for one, seemed willing to do so.[27]

S. 1075 proved troublesome because it circumvented this system, vesting "impact" agencies with the final say in environmental matters. It offered barely a nod to the state-federal pollution control apparatus, or its carefully delineated methods for achieving and enforcing environmental quality. Instead, the legislation threatened to shift the responsibility for environmental enhancement to the mission agencies themselves. According to Muskie, the Jackson bill "made every Federal agency an environmental agency—not just an agency concerned with the environment, which all Federal agencies should [be], but an action agency to protect the environment," a strategy that ran contrary to the philosophy and intent of his subcommittee's legislation.[28]

Muskie feared that the bill's vague "finding" provision offered an escape hatch, immune to judicial review, for developmentally minded departments to pay lip service to environmental values while advancing their own priorities. Henry Jackson viewed federal administrators as reasonable men who could be conditioned to solicit new information and consider policy alternatives according to S. 1075's procedures and mandates. Muskie thought facile requirements like the finding would do little to modify the behavior of mission agencies or their clients. The Senate Interior Committee, Muskie and his colleagues believed, did not comprehend how doggedly discrete economic interests would resist efforts to redistribute the costs of environmental quality, or how complicit federal developmental agencies would be in this effort. Of course, while Muskie considered Jackson's confidence misplaced, the senator from Maine continued to rely on state officials to administer his pollution control programs, despite their well-documented tendency to accommodate local economic interests.[29]

The members and staff of the Public Works Committee soon concluded that legislation of their own was needed to counteract Jackson's flawed strategy and protect the committee's jurisdictional interests. Despite an apparent agreement to consult with them before reporting S. 1075, Jackson had allowed the bill to slip through under the consent calendar. Such machinations only reinforced the staff's view of Jackson as a political opportunist and self-promoter, who, they sensed, already owned the momentum in the press, public, and conservation organizations. Nor did Muskie appreciate getting "scooped"; his relationship with Jackson was already contentious, dating back to the early sixties when the two had clashed in the Government Operations Committee over the propriety of a Defense Department contract for the TFX fighter plane.[30]

On 12 June, the senator from Maine introduced his own Environmental Quality Improvement Act of 1969 (S. 2391), a hastily assembled measure designed to outflank the Interior Committee. It provided for an Office of Environmental Quality in the Executive Office of the President, larger and supposedly better-equipped than Jackson's three-person Council on Environmental Quality. When the *Environmental Health Letter* referred to this latest legislative gambit as "old S. 2391," a Public Works Committee staff member noted the misnomer with amusement, describing the bill as "really quite new," having been "just pulled out of ESM's [Muskie's] bag of tricks!" Indeed, nothing ever became of the Office of Environmental Quality. Nevertheless, the bill sent a clear message: a national environmental policy could not be divorced from, and was in fact already "specifically enunciated" in, the piecemeal legislative efforts of the Public Works Committee, from pollution control to Appalachian regional development and flood control. When the Senate passed Jackson's bill in July, Muskie incorporated S. 2391 into the pending Water Quality Improvement Act. The enactment of both measures promised inevitable jurisdictional conflict in future matters of environmental oversight.[31]

Efforts between the two committee staffs to work out a compromise in late September and early October only underscored their differences. Within the Muskie camp, attempts to "revise" S. 1075 amounted to a gutting of the bill, including the excision of the "findings" clause. Interior Committee staffers, on the other hand, denied any intention to supplant Public Works' air–water–solid wastes programs but considered Muskie's labors as "yeoman work." The senator from Maine's piecemeal efforts, they suggested, did not translate into a comprehensive vision for the environment. As Jackson himself pointed out, "Legislative jurisdiction over 'pollution control' does not . . . mean that the Public Works Committee—or any other committee—has jurisdiction over all matters which relate to maintaining and improving the quality of the human environment."[32]

NEPA, Environmental Impact Statements, and the Seeds of Discord

It took another contentious week of negotiations before Jackson and Muskie could finally announce a compromise on 8 October. The new version of Jackson's bill they reported on the Senate floor, however, represented a more consummate realization of Lynton Caldwell's original vision: a congressional act capable of transforming administrative priorities by restructuring the channels of information that informed them.[33]

The most far-reaching revisions to S. 1075 were designed to mitigate Muskie's misgivings. First, to force mission agencies to justify their decision making in a judicially reviewable document, Muskie dispensed with the troublesome vagueness of a "finding" in Section 102, substituting a requirement for a "detailed statement." He also sought to ensure that the federal pollution control agencies his committee oversaw retained a definitive say in the assessment of environmental impact. Before any detailed statement could be undertaken, "responsible officials" from developmentally minded departments were required to solicit the views of agencies having "jurisdiction or special expertise" with respect to the potential environmental impact involved. The statute encouraged those external reviewers to reexamine the fundamental assumptions underlying developmental policies. Again at Muskie's behest, the committee staffs inserted language calling for all impact statements to articulate specific alternatives to proposed actions. Copies of the impact statement and outside commentary would have to be made available to the president, the president's environmental quality advisors, and the public as well.[34]

The revisions of S. 1075 were designed to expose mission agencies to a broader, more-stringent review process, but Muskie also wanted to ensure that the process would not vitiate specific pollution control mandates. The Water Quality Improvement Act never intended the Corps of Engineers or the AEC to investigate the environmental consequences of effluent discharges

Senate Majority Leader Mike Mansfield (D-Mont., center) urged Senators Muskie (on his immediate left) and Henry Jackson (D-Wash., on his immediate right) to settle their differences over the National Environmental Policy Act. Courtesy of the Edmund S. Muskie Archives and Special Collections Library.

independently. The subcommittee had deliberately cast such licensing agencies as passive actors who deferred to the expertise of state water pollution control officials. Yet Section 102's environmental impact statement (EIS), as amended, stood to saddle these agencies with an obligation to reassess state certification, overruling the authority of water pollution agencies and slowing the permit process to a crawl. Muskie insisted that licensing bodies be exempted from the EIS requirement on the subject of water quality. Jackson agreed to new language qualifying the impact statement provisions, which, he confirmed, did not "in any way affect the specific statutory obligations of federal agencies to comply with environmental standards . . . or to condition their actions upon state or federal certifications."[35]

The certification issue was just a variation on a larger problem that would surface again with respect to NEPA. If developmentally oriented agencies could not be expected to police themselves in environmental matters, as Muskie believed, then it stood to reason that enhancement agencies ought to be left alone to carry out their mandates free from interference or second-guessing. But that conclusion was far from self-evident. The revisions Muskie demanded did not insulate enhancement agencies from Jackson's legislation. They merely absolved licensing agencies from the obligation of second-guessing state certification. They did not necessarily shield environmental agencies from having to reconsider the broader consequences of their own expert conclusions.

The real issue, then, was the extent to which environmental bureaucracies themselves were subject to, and their edicts contingent upon, the provisions of NEPA. Muskie did not begin to address this issue until the release of the House-Senate conference report on S. 1075 in December, when he convinced Jackson to insert a paragraph into an official document entitled "Major Changes in S. 1075 as Passed by the Senate." "Many existing agencies such as . . . the Federal Water Pollution Control Administration and the National Air Pollution Control Administration already have important responsibilities in the area of environmental control," it emphasized. "The provisions of section 102 . . . are not designed to result in any change in the manner in which they carry out their environmental protection authority." Muskie then reiterated the point on the Senate floor.[36]

The senator and his colleagues scrambled as best they could to pad the floor debate and legislative history on NEPA with their institutional perspective, since they had no say in the final form of the conference report. The Senate colloquy on 20 December attempted to underscore the fact that S. 1075 was directed at agencies other than those with a mandate for environmental improvement. As enacted, however, NEPA did not explicitly exempt environmental agencies from filing impact statements on their various activities. And nowhere in their otherwise thorough presentation did any Public Works Committee member suggest that environmental agencies were immune from the impact statement process. The idea may have been implied in Muskie's otherwise unambiguous presentation. But when President Nixon ushered in the "environmental decade" by signing NEPA into law on New Year's Day, 1970, the issue remained in doubt.[37]

Environmental Impacts

Ed Muskie grounded his state-federal pollution control system in the principle of administrative and technical specialization. He intended Section 102 of NEPA to reaffirm the unique mandate of environmental regulatory agencies and the autonomy of pollution control experts. But a new generation of public interest litigants and judges showed little inclination to distinguish between trustworthy and untrustworthy bureaucrats. They came to believe that the narrow outlook and insular authority of pollution control specialists ran counter to the open-ended, multifaceted process environmental impact assessment seemed to demand. Even as the Senate Public Works Committee broadened its own access to environmental expertise, environmentalists and the courts used NEPA to challenge the very concept of specialization Muskie believed he had preserved.

Help Wanted

Henry Jackson's legislation did not unilaterally inspire the Senate Public Works Committee to reassess its legislative priorities between 1968 and 1970. That process had commenced independently. But initiatives like NEPA underscored the political and policy implications of the environment, lending greater urgency to the committee's ambitions for incorporating environmental values into its legislative agenda. The most significant changes undertaken during this time were organizational in nature. Upgrades to the committee's technical capacity and staff base helped restructure the channels of information and expertise that had traditionally characterized water pollution policy networks in Congress. The 1972 Water Pollution Control Act Amendments would reflect these institutional changes most fully.

By 1969, the Subcommittee on Air and Water Pollution needed help. A burgeoning workload taxed human resources and threatened to overwhelm members and staff alike. Legislation commanded more time as the issues involved grew more complex, but Muskie's office was also inundated with correspondence, press calls, and requests for information or technical assistance. The staff struggled to keep up; increasingly, the chairman himself appeared overwhelmed and uninformed on specific policy matters. In the fall of 1969, Muskie alerted Public Works Committee chairman Jennings Randolph to the perils of understaffing. Recent labors on the Water Quality Improvement

Act had consumed eleven executive sessions, all of which required extensive preparation at the expense of routine duties. "Not only did this inability
to maintain daily activities inhibit, if not prohibit, effective relations with
an interested public," Muskie warned, "it provided an opportunity for other
committees to move ahead on matters in which you and I, as well as other
members of the committee share a concern." This thinly veiled reference to
Henry Jackson's recent activities underscored the dire need for additional
staff support at a time when Muskie's authority as an environmental expert
was being challenged.[38]

The relationship between the subcommittee's personnel and its legislative
output, however, always transcended calculations of raw manpower. Muskie
never treated staffers as ciphers; they exercised enough autonomy and discretion to influence the substance of legislation. The 1965 Water Quality Act reflected Don Nicoll's faith in federalism and gradualism as much as Muskie's;
Leon Billings did not share that faith. The twenty-nine-year-old Montana
native, a former journalist and lobbyist for the American Public Power Association, joined the Subcommittee on Air and Water Pollution in 1966. Billings
was a strong-willed liberal with an intrinsic distrust of big business. When he
took over as subcommittee staff director in 1966, his confrontational style facilitated the shift to a more punitive approach to corporate polluters.[39]

Likewise, the committee's hiring of Thomas Jorling in 1969 secured someone capable of incorporating the insights of professional ecology directly
into the law. Ranking Republican Sherman Cooper had wooed the lawyer-
ecologist since the spring of 1968. His eagerness to tap a lifelong Democrat as
the committee's minority counsel underscored the membership's determination to find personnel with relevant technical training in environmental issues. Jorling initially rebuffed Cooper, but the senator from Kentucky proved
persistent, stressing the committee's history of bipartisanship and regaling
him with tales of his connections with the Kennedys. Jorling soon relented.
Although he had earlier viewed Henry Jackson and Emilio Daddario as the
best congressional outlets for the profession, the new minority counsel immediately set out to forge connections between the ecological community
and the Public Works Committee.[40]

Jorling was not the only person eager to forge more intimate connections
between scientists and legislators in 1969. Richard Royce, the chief clerk and
staff director of the Public Works Committee, developed plans that summer

to create a committee advisory panel, composed of "scientists of capacity . . . technologists, and potentially some comprehensivists [sic]." He envisioned a process in which the staff, in conjunction with expert consultants, labored to produce a viable environmental agenda. The advisory panel concept stemmed from Royce's broader ambitions for the Public Works Committee. As Billings observed, "It is . . . obvious that Mr. Royce has been able to convince Senator Randolph that the wave of the future lies in the environment; that to tie Public Buildings and Grounds, Economic Development, River and Harbors and Roads into this area [is] of lucrative political value."[41]

The Senate Public Works Committee followed through on the Environmental Advisory Panel in January 1970. Chairman Jennings Randolph claimed that the panel of consultants would "provide a new, more effective and more direct channel of communication between the scientific community and the legislative processes," particularly in the fields of ecological and environmental policy. The twelve-man panel consisted of chemists, geologists, sanitary engineers, lawyers, and regional planners. It also included three ecologists, including Woodhaven's George Woodwell and Cornell's Gene Likens. Over the next two years, these men would have by far the most direct impact on the substance of the Public Works Committee's legislative output, a fact attributable in part to the mediating influence of Thomas Jorling and his consistent advocacy on behalf of their contributions.[42]

The committee also benefited from external initiatives. The specter of thermal pollution in New England may have triggered the Muskie subcommittee's initial search for ecological expertise, but a similar dilemma in Ithaca, New York, pointed some ecologists Muskie's way. A group of Cornell scientists (including Likens), who in 1968 helped galvanize citizen opposition to a proposed nuclear electric generating plant on nearby Cayuga Lake, decided to address what they perceived as a disconnect between science and public policy. Under the leadership of distinguished biologist Tom Eisner, they formed the Faculty Committee for Information Exchange/Citizens for Ecological Action, raised money, and created a "Visiting Scholar in Ecology" fellowship with the American Political Science Association Congressional Fellows Program and the Public Works Committee. The first fellow, Walter Westman, a graduate student in plant ecology, advised Muskie's subcommittee in 1971–1972 during its intensive labors on the water pollution control act amendments. His persistent influence, together with Jorling's, ensured that an ecological perspective received due consideration.[43]

Between 1968 and 1970, then, the Public Works Committee prepared to make better use of new sources of environmental knowledge. If these actions were not directly prodded by NEPA, they seemed at least consistent with the spirit of Henry Jackson's legislation. What had not changed was the committee's regulatory philosophy.

Despite Muskie's efforts to circumscribe NEPA, however, a series of federal court decisions soon expanded its scope and influence beyond anything Muskie—or Jackson—had ever envisioned. The chairman's careful efforts to preserve the sanctity of the certification process, and, by extension, the primacy of pollution control agencies and experts, did not long endure judicial scrutiny.

Balancing Calvert Cliffs

The subcommittee's thermal pollution hearings foretold of the case that would take direct aim at its regulatory framework. In February 1968, Senator Joseph Tydings (D-Md.) inquired about the Baltimore Gas and Electric Company's new Calvert Cliffs nuclear facility, currently under construction in Calvert County. He wondered if anyone had conducted studies to determine the possible effects of thermal discharges on the Chesapeake Bay. But according to one witness, a marine biologist, "the pressure on the power industry has been so great that they have moved into an area, acquired a site, and begun their development before any serious and extensive consideration of interests other than those of the power plant in power production were undertaken." Once the utility had sunk a considerable investment into the project, licensing agencies were placed "in an extremely difficult position to make a wise and effective public judgment." In time, the ensuing Calvert Cliffs controversy became the focal point of a landmark legal case, as local and national environmental organizations sought to test NEPA's capacity to inject environmental values into the federal licensing process.[44]

Initially, the specter of NEPA did little to change the AEC's familiar interpretation of its own preemptive regulatory responsibilities. In November 1969, its general counsel informed the Senate Interior Committee that S. 1075 did not stand to broaden the AEC's authority "to deny or condition its licenses on the basis of environmental considerations." The AEC had reason for optimism: the Justice Department had already validated its long-standing position in 1968, and the circuit court of appeals followed suit a year later in *State of New Hampshire v. Atomic Energy Commission.*[45]

In June 1970, the AEC amended its regulations to accommodate the recent Water Quality Improvement Act, as well as the federal guidelines for NEPA, published by the Council on Environmental Quality in May. The AEC required an EIS from both applicants and, following public comment, its own regulatory staff. But several key qualifications applied. Although the staff needed to consider environmental factors, hearing boards did not, unless prodded by staffers or external interests. But such parties were not permitted to raise nonradiological matters at any hearing announced in the Federal Register prior to 4 March 1971—a rather generous grace period. Furthermore, if the AEC issued a construction permit for a facility before January 1970, environmental factors did not have to be considered for the subsequent operating license. The AEC did require water quality certification from state agencies. But the certification process foreclosed any additional probative action, since published rules expressly prohibited hearing boards from conducting independent assessments of water quality. So, by design, the rules governing the consideration of environmental impacts served to limit the AEC's latitude.[46]

Environmentalists played a minor role in NEPA's legislative development, but the courts' expansive interpretation of judicial standing in the early seventies encouraged them to file suit against federal agencies that used desultory approaches to impact assessment. In late June, a coalition of three environmental groups—the Sierra Club, the National Wildlife Federation, and the Calvert Cliffs Coordinating Committee—submitted extensive amendments to the AEC's proposed regulations. The commission's rejection of these revisions triggered two lawsuits in November and December; one dealt specifically with the licensing of the Calvert Cliffs plant; the other targeted the AEC's environmental regulations for all nuclear facilities. The Federal Circuit Court of Appeals for the District of Columbia consolidated the two and rendered judgment on both the following July.[47]

In *Calvert Cliffs Coordinating Committee, Inc. v. Atomic Energy Commission,* Judge J. Skelly Wright rejected the AEC's circumscribed mode of regulation as a violation of both the spirit and the letter of NEPA. "NEPA imposes a substantive duty upon every Federal agency to consider the effects of each decision upon the environment," he concluded, "and to use all practicable means, consistent with other essential considerations of national policy, to avoid environmental degradation." The statute did not set environmental protection apart as an exclusive goal, Wright asserted, but it did endeavor to reorder fundamental priorities, "so that environmental costs and benefits will assume their proper place along with other considerations" in agency decision making.[48]

In Wright's estimation, NEPA required federal agencies to perform a "finely tuned and systematic balancing analysis" in order to reconcile environmental values with other pertinent variables (economic, social, technical). The AEC's revised licensing regulations militated against such a balancing; indeed, the court found that its "crabbed interpretation" of NEPA made "a mockery of the Act." Wright failed to see the point in preparing an impact statement if a hearing board was at liberty to ignore it. The AEC could "not simply sit back, like an umpire, and resolve adversary contentions at the hearing stage. Rather, it must itself take the initiative of considering environmental values at every distinctive and comprehensive stage of the process beyond the staff's evaluation and recommendation." Likewise, the court condemned the AEC's efforts to impose arbitrary cutoff points and extended lag times for implementing NEPA's requirements.[49]

Wright found that the AEC's literal compliance with the Water Quality Improvement Act's certification procedure precluded the sort of case-by-case balancing judgment NEPA required. The court did not mean to reject such recourse to specialized expertise, but it did make a distinction between consultation and outright abdication. In Wright's view, the only agency in a position to balance the total spectrum of costs and benefits for a proposed federal activity was the agency with overall responsibility for it. The perspective of a certifying agency tended to be more one-dimensional, since it assessed only the magnitude of certain discrete environmental costs. Standards divorced from a comprehensive cost-benefit calculation were not sufficient to determine the viability of proposed federal actions. The court contemplated instances in which the AEC's balancing judgment might demand a licensee to install pollution controls more stringent than those required by a certifying agency.[50]

In sum, the circuit court posited mission agencies as the primary arbiters of environmental quality, interpreting NEPA as a springboard for the sort of administrative discretion that business interests had feared and Muskie had rejected. Although the court took note of the senator's caveats concerning "self-policing by Federal agencies which pollute or license pollution," it determined that NEPA's "rather meager legislative history" could not "radically affect its interpretation if the language of the statute is clear."[51]

Calvert Cliffs's prescription for a case-by-case balancing judgment subjected pollution control experts to unprecedented scrutiny. The mandate for developmental agencies to "look behind" promulgated environmental standards was novel enough. But the issue of whether so-called enhancement agencies were themselves beholden to impact analysis became a matter of growing legislative concern in 1972, as a new Clean Water Act, more beholden than ever to technical expertise, took form.

But that confrontation lay in the future. For the time being, Muskie and his colleagues had to endure the second major test of their authority. It was this more direct challenge, emanating from a broader political, social, and institutional base, that first prompted them to rethink, and ultimately to reconfigure, the fundamental goals, strategies, and mechanisms of their regulatory system.

6

The Movement's Moment
The Challenge of Environmentalism

The National Environmental Policy Act caused Ed Muskie quite a bit of trouble, but in 1970 his troubles were just beginning. NEPA's strategy for protecting the "total environment" threatened to subject pollution control officials to the same process of "environmental impact" review intended for other government policymakers. Muskie insisted that NEPA and its sponsor, Henry Jackson, acknowledge the expert authority of environmental "enhancement agencies" and the jurisdiction of the Public Works Committee. For the time being, he succeeded. Despite its efforts to infuse new kinds of environmental information into administrative decision making, Jackson's legislation never directly disputed the credibility of Muskie's experts or the feasibility of his pollution control system. As the decade turned, however, and a burgeoning environmental movement soared to national prominence, the Senate's "Mr. Clean" faced just such a challenge.

The sudden surge of environmentalism as a political force overtook Muskie like a tidal wave. A legislative entrepreneur whose interest in pollution control had outpaced the public's during the sixties now found that the public demand for clean air and water exceeded what he had been able to deliver. An energized national constituency and a host of new interest groups clamored for a more prompt and effective government response to pollution problems they saw as getting worse, not better.

Muskie misjudged what this swelling environmental sentiment portended for pollution control policy. He proved sluggish in response to criticisms of the basic pillars of his air and water programs:

federalism, incremental ambient standard setting, and compromise at the local level. Against a backdrop of grassroots political activism that had begun to redefine the scope of citizen participation in civic affairs, ordinary Americans showed less patience for compromise and demanded that politically powerful polluters be punished. The consensus tilted in favor of a greater federal presence in—and a more punitive approach to—environmental regulation. Aggressive new lobbyists, congressional rivals, and even the Republican White House questioned the cautious senator's commitment, and they proposed legislative solutions designed to overhaul his regulatory system. When the new politics of the environment collided with presidential politics, the pressure on Muskie to respond only increased.

It is tempting to view 1970 as the watershed of American environmentalism, a line of transition separating the shadowy past from a more enlightened political landscape. The highlights of that year—NEPA, the first Earth Day, the seminal Clean Air Act, the creation of the Environmental Protection Agency (EPA)—suggest that the momentum of a movement culture had compelled a transformation in the substance of environmental policy. The Senate Subcommittee on Air and Water Pollution was not immune to these pressures. Starting with the Clean Air Act, Edmund Muskie answered his critics and salvaged his institutional authority by abandoning the regulatory restraint that characterized his earlier career. As a consequence, the environmental legislation he produced after 1970, including the 1972 Federal Water Pollution Control Act Amendments, diverged markedly from what had come before. It was more complex, more detailed, more stringent, and more solicitous of federal power. Although relying, as always, on experts to diagnose, abate, and even prevent pollution, the laws also circumscribed their discretion by leaving fewer administrative details to chance and by demanding more public accountability. Polluters, meanwhile, lost the benefit of the doubt as cooperation and compromise at the local level fell out of favor.

To follow the history of water pollution policy into the seventies, then, is to contend with real and often drastic change. An overview of the modern environmental movement, culminating in 1970 with the passage of the Clean Air Act, will provide the necessary context for comprehending the impetus for and extent of that change.

But reviewing how Congress responded to new stimuli also prepares us to reassess the continuing relevance of older ideas. At first glance, traditional priorities such as economic development appear as passé in the "age of ecology" as other discredited conventions like federalism. Nevertheless, persistent postwar agendas still influenced, in unexpected ways, the new regulatory priorities of post-1970 environmental legislation. Discerning how that happened requires an understanding of how such regulatory priorities came about in the first place. That story unfolds amid the gap between promise, performance, and public expectations.

Flaws in the System

The government's desultory efforts to control water pollution in the sixties serve as a prologue to the environmental movement of the seventies. The Water Quality Act did not provide much detail regarding how local, state, and federal officials should administer the program Congress created in 1965. These experts had a relatively easy time dealing with familiar technical issues, like determining the quantitative criteria (dissolved oxygen, pH, mineral concentration) for industrial, recreational, or sanitary water-use designations. The more daunting challenges were political rather than scientific. "Who is to arbitrate the first decision dealing with the actual uses to which the stream is to be put?" one federal pollution control official inquired not long after President Johnson signed the act. With respect to Muskie's doctrine of "enhancement," he also wondered "just how far . . . the state [must] go in its attempt to reclaim a stream for a higher use than presently in effect," not to mention when or how often the federal government should override local water-use decisions. These questions anticipated the basic administrative dilemmas the federal water quality program experienced during the sixties.[1]

Administrators were left to fill important gaps where the legislation was vague. Consistent with its enhancement policy, the Public Works Committee intended ambient water quality standards to recognize a stream's potential for high-end uses in the future, rather than simply "locking in" present conditions. But since the House had opposed federally mandated effluent limits, Muskie had to assume that local administrators would determine the proper treatment technology for individual polluters on their own. The Interior Department subsequently promulgated guidelines for state implementation plans in May 1966. They specified that all wastes were to receive "the best practicable treatment or control," which was commonly understood as "secondary treatment" (removal of floating solids plus a percentage of oxygen-reducing organic materials), unless it could be demonstrated that a lesser degree would provide for water quality enhancement "commensurate with proposed present and future water uses."[2]

Both the supporters and the opponents of tougher water quality standards soon called this administrative strategy into question. In October 1967, Thomas Kimball, executive director of the National Wildlife Federation, informed Secretary Stewart Udall that his department's regulations tolerated the degradation of "pure water," since certain state standards now allowed for higher levels of contaminants than were currently found in given streams. Kimball also complained that the Interior Department's secondary treatment standard did not apply to toxic heavy metals or nutrients like phosphorus and nitrogen, which caused excessive algal growth and eutrophication. "The accumulative effect of several plants with primary and secondary treatment of even 85% effectiveness can completely degrade a stream and ruin it for most beneficial uses," he observed. Responding to this and similar criticism from congressional watchdogs, in February 1968 Udall introduced an explicit "non-degradation" directive to protect streams whose quality already exceeded state standards and compel new sources of pollution to provide the "highest and best degree of waste treatment available under existing technology."[3]

Despite its exemptions for "necessary economic or social development," the new nondegradation policy elicited a torrent of protest. The Western Governors Conference unanimously condemned Udall's initiative for its unprecedented intrusiveness into local industrial siting decisions. Members rued the prospect of seeking Interior Department approval for every new waste discharge into interstate streams. Industrial resistance proved no less ardent. In April 1968, the U.S. Chamber of Commerce challenged the Interior Secretary's statutory authority to demand effluent limits (like mandatory secondary treatment) or nondegradation requirements in state water quality standards.[4]

Overzealous enforcement of the Water Quality Act, however, was never likely. By 1971, only twenty-eight states could claim fully approved standards. Even though the 1967 statutory deadline had long passed, the Federal Water Pollution Control Administration (renamed the Federal Water Quality Administration in 1968) preferred a strategy of persuasion and bargaining to outright federal promulgation of standards; the agency convened only one standard-setting conference, for Iowa, in 1969. In practice, the Federal Water Quality Administration proved more wedded to the secondary treatment minimum than nondegradation. No approved state standards imposed specific effluent limitations other than the generic secondary treatment minimum. In other words, state implementation plans did not articulate any causal relationship between effluent limits and ambient standards that officials could defend in a court challenge.[5]

Lacking fundamental regulatory tools and hobbled by a series of legislative loopholes and administrative oversights, the federal enforcement program faced significant obstacles. Despite the Senate Public Works Committee's intentions, the new system was subject to the same jurisdictional tests as the old abatement procedure it was supposed to replace. The Interior Secretary could not bring an enforcement action merely by demonstrating that a discharger had violated ambient standards for a given stream or was not complying with a state implementation plan. The discharge in question had to be shown to endanger the health or welfare of persons living in a state other than that where the discharge originated. The federal government continued to cede enforcement authority to the states in intrastate waters, including many coastal areas, where industrial pollution was often quite severe. Even setting aside the interstate health and welfare provision, the government faced a considerable burden of proof. Without recourse to effluent regulations, it was difficult to identify individual discharges as the discrete cause of ambient water quality violations—especially in a highly industrialized area like the Cuyahoga River in Cleveland, which featured thirty-two industrial effluent sources and about one hundred storm water outfalls along a single four-mile stretch. Only one federal enforcement action was ever prosecuted in court.[6]

Industries and large corporate polluters had little trouble evading federal enforcement actions, delaying abatement orders, or blocking the approval of stringent water quality standards on the local level. Moreover, the federal government's limited capacity to enforce standards led to slippage in virtually all state compliance schedules. In 1968, Massachusetts reported that 75 percent of its industries and 70 percent of its municipalities were behind schedule. By 1970, 78 out of 110 cities along Lake Erie had failed to keep pace with established construction and abatement plans. A shortage of funds posed one of the most serious problems. In the wake of the Vietnam War, Congress appropriated only a fraction of the money the 1966 Clean Water Restoration Act had authorized for waste treatment construction grants, burdening localities with an underfunded mandate to implement state-federal standards.[7]

As these and other regulatory frustrations mounted, the public's patience began to wear thin. The inadequacies of the federal pollution control system stood out in even bolder relief during the late sixties and early seventies, as a growing cultural concern about the natural world captured the nation's attention. The environmental movement of this era coalesced within a broader context of grassroots protest politics and a growing suspicion of government and business institutions, serving notice to policymakers and polluters alike that the status quo would no longer suffice. With respect to pollution, the era of public complacency was coming to an end.

The New Sacred Issue: Responding to Environmental Crisis, 1966–1971

Environmental values and consciousness did not spring forth, fully formed, in the decade of the sixties. The social and cultural seeds of environmentalism were more deeply ingrained and germinated on an unprecedented scale amid the shifting demographics of a dynamic post–World War II society. The most notable trend proved to be the growth of an affluent, educated middle-class population, concentrated in urban or suburban centers, which tended to define "quality of life" with increasing reference to health, leisure, domesticity, and community. The natural world made up an integral component of this new standard of living, as pristine open spaces provided an antidote to the pressures and complexities of modern society. As the public demanded access to environmental amenities, the call to protect and preserve them increased. Yet for the first two decades following World War II, this shift in values did not translate into a viable political movement of national import, particularly in matters of pollution control. Concern for the environment was growing but was not yet capable of altering the developmental priorities and regulatory practices of federal policymakers or challenging the political influence of industrial interests.[8]

Within five years, however, the environmental cause had, in the words of journalist Theodore White, "swollen into the favorite sacred issue of all politicians, all TV networks, all good-willed people of any party." By 1970, over half the respondents to a Gallup poll considered pollution an important national problem, whereas only 17 percent had in 1965. This sudden upsurge in interest was ultimately a product of perception, since the rate of despoliation had not radically accelerated during this period. As Americans gazed at NASA's photographs of the Earth from space, the lonely globe's fragility hit home. What had changed by the turn of the decade was the public's sense of urgency, galvanized by an intensified mass media focus on environmental problems, a popular ecological vocabulary that helped frame those problems, and Vietnam-era suspicion of corporate and government institutions.[9]

In 1969–1970, a series of disturbing, well-publicized incidents created an atmosphere of environmental crisis that cast business interests and state officials in a negative light. When Cleveland's Cuyahoga River caught fire in June 1969, the bizarre spectacle of the burning water seemed to make what one historian has called "a direct challenge to progress." Beamed to television audiences worldwide, the oil-choked channel became a vivid symbol of the nation's decaying waterways, victimized by decades of industrial neglect. "Chocolate brown, oily, bubbling with sub-surface gases, it oozes rather than flows," *Time* magazine cringed. Although this was not the first time the river had ignited, the intensity of the conflagration, which almost completely destroyed two railroad bridges, appeared to mock government pollution control efforts.[10]

As dramatic an image as the Cuyahoga presented, the Santa Barbara oil spill proved to be the year's most traumatic environmental catastrophe. Dubbed "the accident that experts said wouldn't happen," the blowout from a Union Oil Company rig poured 200,000 gallons of crude oil across a 400-square-mile area off the coast of Santa Barbara, California, in January, blanketing 30 miles of beaches and killing thousands of sea birds. Interior Secretary Stuart Udall, who had approved the drilling leases for the outer continental shelf, referred to the high-profile incident as "a sort of conservationist Bay of Pigs." Although the Santa Barbara incident was not as severe as it first appeared, media coverage played up the area's befouled natural beauty and the failure of government or industry to prevent the disaster. The spill also victimized an affluent university community and mobilized an elite segment of society that could command the attention of local and national leaders. By underscoring the fact that everyone, not simply lower-class urban dwellers, was susceptible to the hazards of pollution, the blowout crystallized the problem for that segment of American society that would populate the mainstream environmental movement: younger, educated, middle- and upper-middle class whites.[11]

Popular ecology gave grassroots activists an appealing holistic framework with which to appreciate the workings of nature and critique the institutional attitudes that reduced the environment to a commodity or a sink. Authors like Carson, Leopold, and Commoner emphasized the fragile, interdependent relationship between human society and the earth's complex, self-sustaining natural systems. But they also questioned modern notions of progress that celebrated the scientific control or technological conquest of nature. These ideas resonated with many Americans who viewed the postwar world with a certain ambivalence, particularly the young. New Left activists who decried the "military-industrial complex" easily extended their critique of the unholy government-corporate alliance to the environmental realm—those who questioned "the system" were more inclined to value the authenticity of natural systems.[12]

Attempts to channel a countercultural spirit into more mainstream venues culminated with the first Earth Day in April 1970, one of the largest public demonstrations in American history. The mastermind behind the unprecedented event, Senator Gaylord Nelson (D-Wisc.), had built his reputation as a congressional environmentalist during the sixties by sponsoring or supporting outdoor recreation, natural resource planning, wild and scenic rivers, federally sponsored ecological research, and a ban on DDT, among other initiatives. Nelson first suggested the idea of a national "teach-in," describing the environmental crisis as "the most critical issue facing mankind," making "Vietnam, nuclear war, hunger, decaying cities, and all other major problems one could name . . . relatively insignificant by comparison." His organizational point man, Harvard law student Dennis Hayes, retained a distinctly New Left outlook ("our goal is not to clean the air while leaving slums and ghettos, nor is it to provide a healthy world for oppression and war"), but he did not wish to alienate the middle and working classes with the confrontational style of campus radicals. The organization he headed on Nelson's behalf, Environmental Teach-In, Inc., planned for a decentralized event on 22 April that would support a wide variety of local actions and obtain as much official support as possible. The coordinators hoped for a healthy mix of celebration and cultural critique.[13]

The subsequent success of Earth Day testified to the broad appeal of ecology and the environmental cause beyond the New Left. An estimated twenty million people participated nationwide, including a heterogeneous mix of students (over ten thousand schools and two thousand colleges), housewives, children, workers, and businessmen. Events from New York to Washington to Los Angeles garnered media coverage, as politicians of both parties made every effort to identify themselves with the cause. Unlike any other issue, "ecology" attracted support across a broad social spectrum, becoming, as one observer expressed it, "the political substitute for the word 'mother.'"[14]

The emergence of a not-so-silent majority altered the political landscape, but the proliferation of environmental interest groups had a tangible impact on the policymaking process itself. Motivated by ineffective state activity, the recalcitrance of persistent polluters, or just general concern about local environmental problems, community organizations proliferated across the country, reflecting the growth of place-based activism in the wake of the civil rights movement. This vigilant new organizational presence also made its presence felt on the national level, providing, for the first time, an effective counterforce to corporate interests that Congress had to take seriously. In June 1969, for example, the Citizens' Crusade for Clean Water, a coalition of two dozen conservation groups, labor unions, professional societies, and municipal and county government associations, lobbied the appropriations committees to restore full funding for the federal treatment plant construction grant program. In response, a House-Senate Appropriations Conference Committee increased the 1970 authorization from $214 million to $800 million.[15]

For conservation organizations of long standing, this new, diversified brand of activism reflected the growth and change that accompanied the late sixties and early seventies. Groups such as the Sierra Club (1892), National Audubon Society (1905), Izaak Walton League (1922), and National Wildlife Federation (1936) traditionally focused on threats to particular (and often remote) geographic sites, endangered species, or recreational opportunities, rather than the problems associated with more urban environments. These first-generation organizations played little or no role in the planning for Earth Day, and many seemed taken aback by the surge in interest regarding pollution and ecology. Nevertheless, urged on by younger members and staff, the old guard did manage to adjust to changing times. They also experienced a membership explosion between 1960 and 1969 indicative of the intensified public awareness of environmental issues. A nearly seven-fold collective increase, from 124,000 to 819,000 in this period, was followed by a 38 percent spike (300,000 additional members) between 1969 and 1972. The Sierra Club and the National Wildlife Federation in particular benefited from name recognition, simplified membership requirements, and modernized direct mail campaigns.[16]

The newly invigorated conservation groups soon expanded their focus to include urban environments. "If you can't save the cities, you can't save the wilderness," observed a spokesperson for the Izaak Walton League. By the late sixties, many of these environmental organizations had begun to employ a more aggressive strategy, trying their hand at policy reform. The National Wildlife Federation's decisive role in the 1968 nondegradation controversy was a testament to this stepped-up vigilance, as was the vocal response of conservationists to thermal pollution. Between 1969 and 1971, the number of environmental organizations with offices in the nation's capitol increased from forty-five to sixty-seven.[17]

Many Washington-based interest groups were in fact new organizations that shunned tax-deductible status in order to lobby openly for environmental causes. These included Friends of the Earth, the League of Conservation Voters, Zero-Population Growth, and Environmental Action. One historian distinguished this new generation from its predecessors by underscoring the sense of crisis and commitment to fundamental environmental reform, sensitivity to the "equity implications" of environmental issues, and ambivalence about legislative compromise or cooperation with business interests. Perhaps the most significant distinction, however, was a deep and abiding suspicion of growth-oriented policies that ignored the fragility of ecological balance.[18]

Although these organizations frequently worked in tandem on pollution issues in the early seventies, Environmental Action would play a particularly active role lobbying the Senate Public Works Committee. Environmental Action evolved from Environmental Teach-In, the ad hoc information committee that had sponsored Earth Day. From the beginning, the organization focused on urban issues, or what one member called "the ecology of the cities." It did not have an open membership. Low-paid staffers and volunteers operated out of a cramped office in DuPont Circle, coordinating the activities of a network of two thousand unaffiliated local groups—the grassroots network that remained from the original Earth Day coalition. Led by Dennis Hayes and fellow founders Sam Love and Barbara J. Reid, the organization waged media campaigns against corporations and elected officials, while pressing its case directly on issues ranging from air and water pollution to strip mining and occupational health and safety.

Likewise, the public interest movement inaugurated by Ralph Nader exerted a tangible influence in environmental politics and policy in the early seventies. Made up predominantly of young, middle-class, college-educated activists with access to legal expertise, "Nader's Raiders" vetted state and federal pollution control laws and administrative practices, publicizing deficiencies and pressuring lawmakers to correct them. The Naderites were particularly attuned to procedural inequities that allowed corporate polluters to avoid enforcement and shift the costs of environmental degradation onto the public. They were inherently skeptical of government experts and bureaucrats who accommodated industry rather than holding it accountable, believing, as did many prominent contemporary academics, that these regulators had in fact been "captured" by the interests they were meant to oversee. Their suspicion of corporate motives also resonated with broader public attitudes. At a time when faith in the overall soundness of the economy remained strong, Americans seemed more willing than ever before to hold big business accountable for broader social ills.[19]

Other public interest groups specialized in environmental litigation as well as research and advocacy. These organizations, most notably the Environmental Defense Fund (1967) and the Natural Resources Defense Council (1970), used the sort of legal and scientific expertise that government bureaucracies or corporate polluters had traditionally monopolized. The financial support of charitable institutions like the Ford Foundation helped nurture this judicial strategy. So, too, did a fundamental transformation in administrative law. Starting in the mid-sixties, federal courts began to revise the legal definition of "standing," which allowed broader classes of interests to sue private concerns or the government without having to demonstrate actual economic or physical injury.[20]

Even without prodding from public interest groups, the judiciary managed to transform environmental politics by indirect means during the sixties. In response to court-mandated reapportionment earlier in the decade, electoral districts began to reflect changes in postwar residential patterns more accurately. As a consequence, the balance of power in Congress shifted from rural to metropolitan regions. Regardless of ideology, elected officials tended to reflect their urban and suburban constituents' concerns about pollution, congestion, or the availability of outdoor recreation. Representatives from the Boston-Washington corridor alone, for example, produced one third of the congressional votes for initiatives addressing these issues in the late sixties and early seventies.[21]

Politicians of all stripes took note of the electoral support associated with environmental causes. Ed Muskie, for one, did not pass up an opportunity to partake of the Earth Day festivities, even though he had played no part in organizing them. For much of the sixties, the senator had labored proactively to make pollution control a prominent national issue. As one of his aides recalled, he saw the events of 22 April 1970 as "an opportunity to provide political strength to his lonely crusade." But by 1970, Muskie was not alone. A nationwide environmental constituency had joined his crusade. So, too, had many members of Congress, who were more inclined than ever before to support environmental initiatives—if not for their constituents, then for the opportunity to carve out their own position of influence in a decentralized legislative institution.[22]

The issue's political potency did not escape the attention of the executive branch, either. In the sixties, the Johnson administration had served as a reliable ally of Muskie's, and a malleable one as well. It deferred to the senator when necessary and did not go out of its way to steal his thunder. Beginning in 1969, however, the White House's new, enigmatic, Republican occupant altered that dynamic, and with it the course of environmental policymaking.

Raising the Stakes: Nixon and the Environment

Richard Nixon treated environmental policy much like the rest of his domestic agenda—as a means to an end. He envisioned himself as the architect of the next great realignment of American politics, poised to outmaneuver eastern liberal elites of both parties by uniting a broad coalition of blue- and white-collar middle-class voters behind him. Unfettered by the ideological principles of a Goldwater or a Reagan, Nixon did not hesitate to woo target constituencies, many of whom traditionally voted Democratic, with expansive federal programs geared to their problems and concerns. His opportunistic use of "big government" often made the Great Society look modest by comparison. The environment proved to be a case in point.[23]

The upsurge in national environmental consciousness that coincided with Nixon's first term offered the administration an opportunity to curry favor with a growing cross section of Americans. The president's domestic affairs advisor, John Ehrlichman, used polling data to emphasize the political cogency of the issue across lines of age, income, political affiliation, and gender. Nixon got the message. Though personally indifferent to such matters, the president purportedly instructed his domestic advisor to "keep me out of trouble on environmental issues." Under Ehrlichman's watch, the White House generated programmatic initiatives to keep pace with congressional Democrats and prevent potential rivals for the presidency from stealing the spotlight. If this meant occasionally violating the tenets of the "New Federalism" by proposing an expansion of federal regulatory jurisdiction at the expense of the states, Ehrlichman assented. But he and Nixon also understood their limits. "Don't try to 'out-clean' Mr. Muskie, there's no way you can do it," the president supposedly told his advisors. The anchor of Nixon's hopes for political realignment was a thriving economy, and he had no plans to sacrifice economic stability on the altar of environmental quality.[24]

Nixon's approach to the environment may have been opportunistic, but the administration did boast a number of knowledgeable and dedicated staffers who took the issue seriously. Ehrlichman himself had gained a keen understanding of various environmental concerns and regulatory strategies while practicing as a land-use attorney in Seattle. The White House's top environmental advisor, forty-two-year-old John Whitaker, had served as Nixon's cabinet secretary and campaign aide, but the former vice president of Litton Industries also held a doctorate in geology from Johns Hopkins. Officials who filled other key positions, including William Ruckelshaus, the first director of the EPA, John Quarles, the EPA's top water quality administrator, and Russell Train, chairman of Nixon's Council on Environmental Quality, all worked diligently and effectively with Congress.[25]

Contemporary critics who portrayed the Nixon administration as an inveterate defender of big business failed to take into account its cadre of competent, well-placed environmental advocates. They also miscast Nixon himself. As one historian observed, "Liberals who characterized him as the servant of corporate interests did not understand the man." His larger political ambitions, antipathy toward eastern elites, and "aprincipled" attitude toward free-market economics all undermined his fidelity. More often than not, the Nixon administration was obliged to leap to the defense of the business sector to compensate for its inability to assess and respond to potentially unfavorable environmental legislation.[26]

Thus Nixon's own political reputation discouraged more sympathetic assessments of his administration's environmental record. Despite the Subcommittee on Air and Water Pollution's cordial relationship with EPA and Council on Environmental Quality officials, Muskie's staff always eyed the president warily. "One has to remember the attitudes toward Nixon himself, the feeling that you couldn't trust him," recalled Don Nicoll, the senator's administrative assistant. "If not inherently evil, he was at least very suspect. . . . it was hard to give credence to virtually anything they were proposing, [and] only in retrospect can you look back and say 'gee, they weren't half bad.'"[27]

It is impossible to separate the course of environmental policymaking in the early seventies from the contours of partisan politics or the rivalry between Edmund Muskie and Richard Nixon. After 1968, both Muskie and the environment arrived on the national stage to stay. Following his favorable debut as Hubert Humphrey's running mate, Muskie gradually emerged as a leading candidate for the 1972 Democratic presidential nomination. It did not take long for Nixon to start worrying about his challenger's potential appeal among an environmentally conscious electorate. The senator, meanwhile, jealously guarded his reputation as "Mr. Clean," a political identity that reflected years of policy expertise accumulated in the relative obscurity of the Senate. He chafed at Nixon's efforts to co-opt the issue for his own advantage.

The battle lines between Muskie and the White House had formed before Earth Day. The two had already jousted on issues ranging from the nomination of Interior Secretary Walter Hickel, to the Alaska oil pipeline, to the supersonic transport. On New Year's Day, 1970, Nixon used the signing ceremony for NEPA to announce his administration's commitment to protecting the natural world. Muskie no doubt stewed watching the president stand alongside Henry Jackson, the act's sponsor and the senator's longtime rival, as both men basked in the media spotlight. Striking a tone of urgency, Nixon declared that it was "literally now or never. . . . the nineteen seventies absolutely must be the years when America pays its debt to the past by reclaiming the purity of its air, its water, and our living environment." Muskie responded two weeks later in Chicago, using a speech before the Magazine Publishers Association to characterize the administration's antipollution ambitions as "slogan-rich and action-poor."[28]

The White House soon followed up with specifics. In his State of the Union Address, as well as in a special message to the Congress on the environment in February, Nixon outlined several ambitious legislative proposals for pollution control. The agenda reflected the recommendations of an independent, interdepartmental task force on the environment, convened in the summer of 1969 and directed by John Whitaker with his twenty-three-year-old assistant, Chris DeMuth.[29]

The administration's proposal for clean air legislation formed part of the first broad offensive against Muskie's established pollution control reputation. The federal air quality program suffered many of the same administrative problems that plagued the water quality program. As it happened, dissatisfaction on the part of Congress, interest groups, the public, and the executive came together like a perfect storm to transform the air program first. In 1970, Muskie's first sustained encounter with this multiple-front challenge offered some important lessons about the new art of the possible in environmental politics, and he struggled to absorb them. By year's end, however, the landmark Clean Air Act gave testament to the ability of the chairman and his subcommittee to adjust to the demands of a new decade.

Clearing the Air

Throughout the sixties, Edmund Muskie believed that an effective program to control air pollution, like water pollution, required the administrative flexibility that only federalism could provide. In both cases, he preferred a system in which state officials took the lead setting and enforcing regionally specific ambient standards, while the federal government provided technical assistance and the threat of intervention if loose deadlines and expectations were not met. This strategy best accommodated preexisting institutional arrangements, local prerogatives, and environmental conditions that varied with geography. In Muskie's view, the ambient standard–setting process and the enumerated policy of "enhancement" found in both his air and water quality legislation represented the most practical way to ratchet up expectations and bring about steady, incremental improvements over time. Muskie stuck by this strategy even when the Johnson administration supported more stringent measures for pollution control. During deliberations on what would become the 1967 Air Quality Act, the senator rejected the White House's proposal for federally promulgated, national minimum standards on industrial emissions, because he judged them less amenable and adaptable to local exigencies and more likely to arouse political opposition.[30]

By decade's end, however, Muskie's advocacy of federalism had come at too high a political price. The senator soon discovered that deference to intergovernmental cooperation and decentralized control had assumed a more pejorative association with narrow-minded localism, resistance to progress, and corporate "capture" of regulatory agencies. The Air Quality Act's subpar performance seemed to confirm this negative appraisal, and it became a popular target among critics in the winter of 1969–1970.[31]

For the first time in his career, Senator Muskie saw his authority as a pollution control expert challenged, when congressional upstarts, the Nixon administration, and environmental groups began to champion bold new initiatives for air quality. In December 1969, the House Interstate and Foreign Commerce Committee's Subcommittee on Public Health and Welfare, under the leadership of Paul Rogers (D-Fla.), conducted aggressive hearings on the administration of the Air Quality Act. Observers questioned Rogers's motivations, commitment, experience, and expertise, but the congressman employed his status as novice outsider to his advantage, educating himself just enough to raise fundamental questions about the air program's direction and pace. Throughout the proceedings, witnesses scored the 1967 act's complicated provisions for state standard-setting, its byzantine intrastate regional designations, and its failure to clean the air. To that date, the states had designated only thirty-four air quality districts; not a single one had adopted an operative implementation plan for ambient standards.[32]

President Nixon's new air pollution legislation, announced in his message on the environment to Congress, sought to redress many of the complaints raised during the Rogers hearings. It called for federally determined national ambient air quality standards for specific pollutants or combinations of pollutants, coupled with national emissions standards for stationary sources (factories, power plants, or refineries with smokestacks) that contributed "substantially to endangerment of the public health or welfare." The plan simplified the process for designating air quality regions and required states to develop implementation plans within a year, although it mandated no timetables for actually achieving quality goals. Administration officials hoped the combination of uniformly applied standards would prove more equitable, rational, and easier to enforce than fifty independent efforts. The Rogers subcommittee organized hearings on Nixon's bill in March and reported an essentially identical version of it within ninety days.[33]

At the same time, public interest groups presented a vocal, united front on air pollution that outflanked a more lethargic business sector. Among the most prominent was Environmental Action, which formed a congressional clean air committee to lobby for even tougher automobile exhaust standards. Environmental Action also organized an informal coalition of leading environmental advocates to keep vigilant watch on legislative developments.

Times had changed. In 1967, the coal and electric utility industries successfully opposed limits on sulfur dioxide emissions, proving more organized and effective than conservation organizations. But by 1970, fragmented and complacent business lobbyists were caught flat-footed by the latest air quality proposals. They failed to adjust to changes in the politics of regulation, including the decentralization of power in Congress, the increased number of interest groups, the declining influence of parties, the expanded role of the media, the shifting public mood, and the more active role of the courts.[34]

As Ed Muskie soon learned, the new politics of regulation made his own environmental record subject to both scrutiny and censure. On 12 May, Ralph Nader's Center for the Study of Responsive Law released *Vanishing Air*, a stinging broadside against the federal air quality program that took the senator to task for his traditional caution and deference to federalism. Describing him as disinclined "either politically or temperamentally toward taking a tough stand against private industry," the authors accused Muskie of confusing conciliation for consensus:

> Muskie is, of course, the chief architect of the disastrous Air Quality Act of 1967. That fact alone would warrant his being stripped of his title as 'Mr. Pollution Control.' But the Senator's passivity since 1967 in the face of an ever worsening air pollution crisis compounds his earlier failure. Muskie has rarely interceded

on behalf of accelerated pollution efforts. . . . Perhaps the Senator should consider resigning his Chairmanship of the Subcommittee and leave the post to someone who can devote more time and energy to the task.[35]

Such well-aimed barbs angered the nation's leading environmental legislator and putative presidential candidate and attracted considerable media attention, just as Nader intended.[36]

Nader's rebuke, the recent Nixon and Rogers initiatives, and the pressure of heightened public expectations forced Muskie to reconsider his pollution control strategy. Although his subcommittee's own oversight hearings had highlighted the need to refine and expedite the administrative process governing air quality, the senator had not contemplated a radical overhaul of the 1967 act. But given the political context, any bill he sponsored had to contain, at minimum, provisions for national standards and emission controls. Even Don Nicoll, the primary staff architect of the 1967 legislation, saw the writing on the wall, though he was slow to abandon his faith in the old system.[37]

Others within the subcommittee proved more amenable to change. Staff director Leon Billings's willingness to nudge Muskie in the direction of stricter national standards for autos and stationary sources, often over Nicoll's objections, signaled his growing policy influence. The young Democrat may have resented Nader's attacks on his boss, but he shared the activist's confrontational style, punitive attitude toward corporate regulation, and dissatisfaction with Nicoll's incremental, intergovernmental approach. He believed the subcommittee's pollution control legislation needed to shift the legal burden of proof from the government officials who set stringent pollution standards to the industrial polluters who claimed those standards were not economically feasible. From a practical perspective, minority counsel Thomas Jorling and Senator Howard Baker (R-Tenn.) touted the technical and legal precision of emissions controls. Likewise, Senator Thomas Eagleton (D-Mo.) questioned the Nixon administration's unwillingness to attach strict timetables to stated air quality objectives. The 1969 Federal Coal Mine Health and Safety Act, which Eagleton had helped develop on the Labor and Commerce Committee, mandated reductions in airborne coal dust within a set time frame regardless of available technology. He suggested that similar "technology-forcing" standards and deadlines for air pollution would spur innovation and compel polluters nationwide to meet statutory requirements in a timely manner.[38]

Muskie did not simply adapt. He reestablished his control of the policymaking process and became the leading force behind the landmark 1970
Clean Air Act. Despite Paul Rogers's preemptive initiatives, the knowledge
and prestige the senator brought to bear enabled him to dominate the ensuing conference committee and dictate the final substance of the legislation
passed in December. During the late summer, an exhaustive series of hearings, as well as conversations with subcommittee members, staff, air pollution
experts, and Council on Environmental Quality officials persuaded Muskie
that air quality was deteriorating faster than his "evolutionary" regulatory
approach could respond, particularly as a consequence of auto emissions.
Once satisfied that more drastic standards and deadlines were administra-
tively feasible—and that industry's claims about their economic feasibility
were unreliable—Muskie reported a Senate bill that sharply reduced the discretion government administrators and polluters once enjoyed.[39]

The Clean Air Act's standards of compliance outstripped the Nixon administration's original bill in both rigor and specificity. With respect to automobiles, the legislation required unprecedented emissions targets by explicit
dates: 90 percent reductions in current carbon monoxide and hydrocarbon
levels for 1975 model cars and a 90 percent decrease in nitrogen oxides by
1976. When a skeptical reporter inquired whether the subcommittee had evidence that auto manufacturers were actually capable of meeting statutory
standards by 1975, Muskie informed him that it was not Congress's duty to
find technological solutions to air pollution problems but rather to provide
the health standards polluters had to meet. The burden of proof had shifted.
Similarly, Muskie assented to national ambient air quality standards based on
the protection of public health and federal emission standards for stationary
sources based on the "latest available control technology"—which included
outright prohibitions of the most hazardous pollutant discharges. To prevent
the "uneven and inadequate interpretation" of these legislative mandates, the
Senate version insisted that state implementation plans include emission requirements and compliance schedules, guarantees for adequate funding and
public participation, and assurances that the plan would meet national standards within three years of approval. The Muskie bill also featured a provision allowing citizens' suits against private firms and government agencies
that violated air quality standards, as well as against the EPA administrator if
this person failed to carry out "mandatory functions."[40]

From Clean Air to Clean Water

Political scientists interpret the 1970 Clean Air Act as a product of political bargaining behavior called "bidding up." Technology-forcing statutes of unprecedented regulatory scope and ambition, they argue, resulted from escalating partisan competition between Congress and the executive branch. Given a political climate newly receptive to strict environmental laws, Senator Muskie no longer needed to muster a constituency for his policy, as he had throughout the sixties; rather, a policy had to be developed for a solicitous majority. Freed from past restraints, and pressured by rival government actors, the Senate Public Works Committee is said to have abandoned incremental policy refinement for what one scholar has labeled "speculative augmentation." In order to meet the expectations of a demanding public, Congress mandated ambitious policy goals and deadlines unfettered by current technological, economic, or administrative limitations.[41]

Although commentators differ as to the rationality of this approach, they agree that the resulting legislation transformed the post–New Deal regulatory state. Generally speaking, the "new social regulation" of this period established complex bureaucratic systems designed to prevent a broad array of future harms, from pollution and racial imbalances in hiring to unsafe workplaces and consumer products. It concentrated costs within discrete business-industrial sectors to the benefit of broad, diffuse citizen constituencies, be they minorities, consumers, or users of environmental amenities. By restricting the discretion state and federal administrators once enjoyed, Congress no longer assumed that agency expertise would autonomously serve the public interest.[42]

The 1970 Clean Air Act and 1972 Clean Water Act that followed it were prominent examples of the "new social regulation." The two statutes emerged in succession from the same Senate committee, shared many of the same regulatory innovations, and raised many of the same questions concerning their ultimate effectiveness. But the policy processes that produced them were far from identical. Political bargaining and partisan competition alone cannot explain the regulatory strategy Muskie and his colleagues adopted for water pollution. The distinctive politics, discourses, and institutions associated with postwar water resources policy also informed the decisions they made.

Ecological ideas and Cold War systems thinking played a more prominent role in the committee's conception of water quality regulation. And though the experience gained by the Public Works Committee in the process of developing the Clean Air Act broadened the regulatory options Muskie and his colleagues were willing to consider, practical and political exigencies discouraged the committee from approaching water pollution control legislation as a mere carbon copy of its predecessor.

The congressional committee system accounted for basic differences in the evolution of the laws. Because the House of Representatives divided jurisdiction for air and water pollution between the Commerce and the Public Works Committees, its power did not compare to that of Muskie's specialized subcommittee. The subcommittee's surfeit of experience, expertise, and staff support allowed its chairman to regain control of an air pollution policy process that had gotten away from him. In matters related to water pollution, however, Muskie and his colleagues enjoyed less of an advantage. The House Public Works Committee boasted considerable knowledge and experience in the water resources field and employed capable personnel with superior technical abilities honed during years of service in various executive agencies. When the Senate staff met with them in early 1971 to hash out the structure of a revised water pollution bill, the House staff resisted unfamiliar innovations such as legislative deadlines and effluent limits, fearing the broader economic consequences of such a program. Over the next eighteen months, the House Public Works Committee provided a sympathetic outlet for more conservative voices otherwise shut out of the water pollution debate.[43]

The air and water pollution policy processes did share a notable constant, however, and that was the presence of environmentalism as a permanent fixture in American life. Its rise to national prominence in the late sixties and early seventies altered long-standing political discourse. Muskie no longer needed to raise the specter of shortage to justify an expanded federal pollution control program. At the start of hearings in March, the senator suggested that the nation's developmental ambitions would need to be tempered in order to stem the tide of pollution. "In a consumer-oriented society," he observed, "everything we produce leads to waste. . . . maybe we ought to set some limits on the standard of living." Muskie was never willing to forsake economic growth in the name of environmental quality in the way a new generation of environmentalists would be, but rhetorically, at least, the developmental priorities of decades past now seemed incompatible with the stringent pollution control the public demanded.[44]

Or perhaps not. In fact, older developmental discourses and institutional priorities not only persisted in the policy process, they also contributed in unanticipated ways to the substance and objectives of the new social regulation. Even as environmental activism at the grass roots, in Congress, and in court pressed for innovative improvements to the underachieving federal water quality program, one of the most cutting-edge solutions emerged from a policy context far removed from public perception. To understand how clean water legislation emerged in 1972, the place to begin is with perhaps the most unlikely environmentalist, the U.S. Army Corps of Engineers.

PART III

Synthesis

The Strange Career of the Corps of Engineers

Transforming Water Pollution Control Policy

In 1963, the U.S. Army Corps of Engineers announced its plan to build a series of sixteen dams along the Potomac River to serve the metropolitan area surrounding Washington, D.C. One of the principal motives the agency cited for this ambitious public works project was pollution control. To sustain anticipated growth, its study concluded, the region would require an abundant supply of water. Planners expected the dams to provide enough storage to augment the Potomac's flow during the summer months, allowing for the supplemental waste dilution that would help ease municipal water shortages and facilitate economic development. But conservationists and other concerned citizens did not want to alter the free-flowing river or inundate land otherwise suitable for farming, housing, business, or recreation (including a section of the historic C&O Canal). These critics succeeded in fighting the dams for the better part of a decade, dismissing the Corps' pollution control plan as at best "outmoded" and at worst insincere, just a cynical accounting trick to justify another boondoggle.[1]

One might be tempted to characterize the Potomac contretemps as par for the Corps—business as usual for the army's civil works bureaucracy. For most of the twentieth century, the Corps of Engineers advocated the total development of water resources to promote economic growth. The agency constructed thousands of dams, reservoirs, and diversions to channel water where officials claimed it was needed for navigation, irrigation, power production—and even pollution control, on occasion. But this unexamined bureaucratic mandate, encouraged by Congress with billions in appropriations, often proved destructive to the landscape. As public values changed in the sixties and seventies, and public officials responded to new, vocal constituencies, the Corps found its initiatives increasingly scrutinized, curtailed, and condemned. The agency's mission became a popular target of reproach, and critics characterized the agency itself as a relic from a bygone era.[2]

Environmental politics, however, can make for strange bedfellows. Defenders of the Potomac may have branded the Corps' opportunistic pollution control scheme a sham in 1963, but by 1970 a broad array of interests were encouraging the agency to reinvent itself as an aggressive water quality watchdog. Frustrated by ineffective post–World War II pollution laws and timid federal regulators, a coalition of liberal judges, entrepreneurial legislators, proactive administrators, media outlets, and motivated citizens "rediscovered" an underutilized nineteenth-century law known as the Refuse Act. With it, they sought to expand the Corps' century-old responsibility to maintain navigable waterways into a mandate to regulate industrial waste at its source. The resulting Refuse Act permit program placed the Corps at the center of an enhanced regulatory system. It also provided a model of enforcement that Senator Edmund Muskie and his Subcommittee on Air and Water Pollution could not afford to ignore as they drafted the Clean Water Act in 1971–1972.

Although unexpected, this turn of events does not necessarily subvert conventional wisdom. After all, the Refuse Act's revival reflected a new environmental consciousness at the grass roots and in government, less tolerant of corporate pollution as the price of progress and less patient with the bureaucratic status quo. The Corps of Engineers proved reluctant to assume new regulatory responsibilities so far afield from its traditional knowledge base; it took action only in response to mounting public pressure. Activists co-opted the navigational component of the agency's mission for their own ends while continuing to reject its developmental proclivities, which clearly had no affinity whatsoever with the new ecological ethic.

Or did they? In fact, the story is not so straightforward. The Corps of Engineers' most far-reaching contribution to Ed Muskie's groundbreaking clean water legislation did not turn out to be the Refuse Act after all. The agency helped precipitate other, even more fundamental transformations in the law's regulatory approach and underlying philosophy. It did so, however, by following through on the institutional priorities and expertise rooted in its developmental agenda.

By looking backward, the Corps of Engineers actually positioned itself to propel environmental policy forward. No grassroots movement clamored for the parallel program of "regional urban waste management" that the agency established in 1970–1971. It evolved instead as a by-product of more traditional concerns about water shortages and economic growth, expressed both in Congress and on the local level in the sixties. When the political ground shifted beneath the Corps, it responded by rethinking the relationship between water quantity and quality and reframing the pollution control problem in the broader context of regional water resources planning. Such an approach gelled with the agency's institutional capacities in ways that enforcement did not. Yet this same planning regime encouraged Corps officials to adopt an ecologically advanced waste treatment process even more eagerly than did existing federal water quality agencies and to promote more ambitious water quality goals than most pollution control experts did at the time. In short, the Corps went from relic to revolutionary without abandoning its original mission.

Conventional histories of the environmental movement overlook the strange career of the Corps of Engineers because they emphasize the ascent of new values, interests, and institutions to explain policy change. This story is not wrong, just incomplete. Older programmatic traditions persisted and continued to configure policy options in a governmental process known for its complexity and diversity. The Corps of Engineers experienced pressure to respond to new political and cultural priorities it would otherwise have ignored. Yet the same developmental orientation and expertise that environmentalists condemned allowed the Corps to articulate solutions to pollution that the Muskie subcommittee ultimately found appealing—more appealing, in many ways, than the Refuse Act.

Taken together, then, the Refuse Act and regional urban waste management underscore the multiplicity of values, discourses, and institutional priorities that shaped water pollution control policy in the early seventies. While the reemergence of the Refuse Act took place in a relatively public forum, the story of the waste management program played out in more obscure venues—and went largely unnoticed.

At the center of each, however, stood a most unlikely environmentalist. By the winter of 1970, the rival Nixon and Muskie camps had already proposed changes to the current federal water pollution control program. Despite an escalating war of words, both sought to expand the federal government's regulatory jurisdiction, expedite enforcement procedures, and ensure that specific, legally binding effluent limits accompanied state ambient water quality standards. Neither side had given any thought to the Army Corps of Engineers. Soon that would change.

Reinventing the Refuse Act

The Rivers and Harbors Act of 1899 consolidated a tangle of post–Civil War statutes and granted the Army Corps of Engineers extensive authority to maintain navigable waters. The backbone of the statute, Section 10, outlawed all activities designed to dredge, fill, erect structures in, or otherwise modify a navigable watercourse without a valid permit from the secretary of the army. But Congress went even further. Section 13, known independently as the Refuse Act of 1899, declared it unlawful to "throw, discharge or deposit . . . any refuse matter of any kind or description, whatever, other than that flowing from streets and sewers and passing therefrom in a liquid state, into any navigable water of the United States." It imposed monetary penalties for each violation up to $2,500 (and/or jail time) and entitled citizen whistle-blowers to collect up to half of the fine. No modern environmental law matched Section 13's resolute Victorian clarity.[3]

In the late nineteenth century, however, neither the members of the Senate Commerce Committee nor the army engineers who advised them envisioned the Refuse Act as an "antipollution" law apart from the specific matter of navigation. Federal officials merely intended to halt egregious dumping activities that threatened the free flow of shipping traffic. Literally construed, however, Section 13 made it a misdemeanor to deposit almost anything into a navigable stream without a permit from the secretary of the army.

In practice, the agency administered the statute narrowly. Section 10 became the focal point of the Corps' formal regulatory program over the next half century, and beginning in 1905 it issued thousands of permits to applicants seeking to build wharves or deepen channels. By contrast, the few permits the Corps did issue under Section 13 were handled on an ad hoc basis. Although the Corps pursued a significant number of prosecutions under Section 13, the enforcement rationale pertained strictly to navigation rather than water quality per se.[4]

The Refuse Act's renaissance began when the Warren Court rediscovered its untapped potential in a series of decisions bearing the imprimatur of William O. Douglas. The first of these, *U.S. v. Republic Steel* (1960), declared that industrial effluents conformed to the definition of "refuse" under the 1899 statute and were therefore just as subject to restriction as larger floating solids. The Court also ruled that the government could seek civil injunctive relief under Section 13 to force a polluter to halt its discharges. Six years later, in *U.S. v. Standard Oil*, the Court loosed the definition of refuse from its traditional moorings as a "navigational impediment," creating a much broader category of liability that included "all foreign substances and pollutants," not simply those that prevented ships from plying their way. A dissenting John Marshall Harlan speculated with alarm that "dropping anything but pure water into a river would appear to be a Federal misdemeanor." But Douglas, a noted conservationist, refused to "construe Section 13 . . . in a vacuum," interpreting the old statute as a new instrument to redress a modern environmental problem.[5]

And an intriguing instrument it was. The reinvented Refuse Act offered federal officials an opportunity to bypass the cumbersome enforcement mechanisms of postwar water pollution legislation, enjoin pollution at its source, and punish offenders with criminal penalties. Some within the government relished the prospect. In a report to Congress in December 1966, the comptroller general chastised the Corps of Engineers for not enforcing the Refuse Act consistently and urged a more aggressive response to industrial polluters. Others balked. The Department of Interior, which oversaw the federal pollution control program, displayed little enthusiasm for an arcane statute that threatened to inject the army into water quality matters.[6]

But the Corps' own internal resistance stifled vigorous Refuse Act enforcement during the sixties. Although a handful of administrators contemplated a more expansive program, official agency pronouncements insisted that "the concern of the Department of the Army in industrial wastes under [Section 13] lies in the effect [such effluents] have on the navigable capacity of the waterway," not with "minor illegal discharges of industrial wastes having no perceptible effect" on navigability. Other published regulations and official testimony before Congress throughout the decade confirmed the agency's conviction that Section 13 was to be administered "in the interest of navigation rather than of conservation, public health, or sanitation." Thus the Corps exhibited little enthusiasm for broadening its bureaucratic purview, despite the Supreme Court's overt invitation to address water pollution concerns.[7]

The next push for revitalizing the Refuse Act came from the executive branch. In the late sixties, the Nixon justice department began to employ the act more frequently against industrial polluters. Between October 1969 and April 1970, U.S. attorneys across the country pursued sixty-six prosecutions under Section 13, although continued Interior Department misgivings sometimes circumscribed these efforts. When the U.S. attorney in Chicago attempted to file complaints against high-profile companies like Republic Steel, Ford Motor Company, and United States Steel in February 1970, Federal Water Pollution Control Administration (FWPCA) officials refused to share relevant technical information. Commissioner David Dominick preferred state-level prosecutions under Illinois's own water quality laws, fearing that the fines levied under the Refuse Act provided corporate violators with a "cheap permit to pollute."[8]

Despite the FWPCA's resistance, Interior Secretary Walter Hickel and other environmentally concerned White House advisors came to realize that more expedient enforcement options were necessary. They feared that recent journalistic accounts were portraying the administration as "soft on enforcement." Particularly worrisome was conservationist Robert Boyle's widely publicized piece in the February 1970 *Sports Illustrated*, which detailed the bureaucratic lethargy endured by the Hudson River Fishermen's Association in its six-year effort to stop the Penn Central Railroad from dumping petrochemical wastes into the Hudson and Croton Rivers. Such embarrassing revelations drove the Interior Secretary to employ the rarely used "180-day notice," a procedure included in the 1965 Water Quality Act that threatened polluters in violation of state water quality standards with prosecution in federal court if they failed to undertake reasonable abatement remedies within six months.[9]

Hickel came to consider the Refuse Act as part of his arsenal. The secretary sought civil injunctive relief under Section 13 for the first time in March 1970, bringing suit to enjoin the Florida Power and Light Company from discharging large quantities of heated water into Biscayne Bay. The case attracted national attention, not simply for the mode of prosecution, but because its target involved thermal emissions. That summer, Hickel again turned to Section 13 to redress an even more urgent threat to the nation's waters—mercury contamination. The toxic metal was first detected in Michigan's Lake St. Clair earlier in the year, and by July studies revealed potentially dangerous levels in the fresh waters of fourteen eastern states, from New York to Louisiana. In subsequent cases where the government needed to halt discharges of industrial mercury immediately, the Refuse Act offered a rapid-response mechanism that modern federal water pollution control laws simply lacked (the heralded 180-day notice was the *fastest* statutory remedy available).[10]

The interior secretary well understood the Refuse Act's potential to regulate water quality. Nevertheless, Hickel continued to conceive of the statute in limited terms, preferring that the Interior Department apply it to "one-shot pollution cases" in "selective instances." He still believed that traditional state-federal enforcement forums offered the best opportunity to secure lasting improvements in regional water quality, especially if updated legislation could expedite their procedures.[11]

But the Refuse Act also attracted the notice of entrepreneurial members of Congress searching for opportunities to reshape environmental policy. Specifically, the efforts of Representative Henry Reuss (D-Wis.) in 1969–1970 contributed to the eventual demise of Hickel's "one-shot" strategy. Reuss, a Harvard-trained attorney and influential player on the House Banking Committee, also served as chairman of the House Government Operations Committee's Subcommittee on Conservation and Natural Resources. His investigations of Great Lakes pollution in the mid-sixties, particularly the link between phosphate detergents and eutrophication, introduced him to the frustrations of federal enforcement and positioned him as one of the more vocal environmental advocates in Congress. Following a staff briefing on Section 13, Reuss decided to use his subcommittee to publicize the obscure provision as a viable alternative to the Water Quality Act's moribund conference-hearing procedure.[12]

In March 1970, the Reuss subcommittee released a well-publicized report calling on the Corps of Engineers to enforce the Refuse Act much more vigorously. Citing recent judicial interpretations and the limits of conventional pollution control legislation, the report recommended that the Corps, the

FWPCA, and the attorney general work together to "institute injunction suits against all persons whose discharges or deposits . . . violate the Refuse Act and are not promptly cleaned up or stopped by the polluter." This approach envisioned Section 13 as a remedy for persistent pollution, rather than as a stopgap for anomalous or extraordinary discharges.[13]

Reuss intentionally appealed to local activists who were fed up with intransigent industrial dischargers and longed to take matters into their own hands. His office released a "handy kit," instructing citizen informers how to bring suit against polluters under Section 13 and collect their share of the fines. U.S. attorneys across the country ultimately had to cope with the civic revival Reuss helped inspire in 1970. After Earth Day, the Justice Department's regional offices fielded a flood of calls from environmental groups and other motivated tipsters. Such unchecked citizen participation, coupled with the specter of virtually unlimited corporate liability, threatened to overwhelm the Justice Department's limited resources. Since only 266 stationary industrial plants in the entire country held valid permits, practically every industry with an outfall pipe was in technical violation of the law.[14]

To avoid biting off more than it could chew, the Justice Department formulated a policy of deference to federal and state water pollution officials. By July, an internal directive discouraged U.S. attorneys from attempting to punish or prevent discharges "of a continuing nature resulting from the ordinary operations of a manufacturing plant," especially if those plants possessed state permits or had agreed to comply with established water quality standards. This call for prosecutorial discretion exposed Justice Department officials to vehement criticism from Congressman Reuss and his allies, particularly Senator Philip Hart (D-Mich.). Nevertheless, in certain jurisdictions, particularly the Southern District of New York, discretion did not prevent aggressive enforcement. Nor did the Justice Department abandon the Refuse Act. Its Land and Natural Resources Division created a sizable pollution control section in October 1970 to deal specifically with Section 13 prosecutions.[15]

As U.S. attorneys discovered, the advantages of the Refuse Act were not limited to expediency. In the Southern District of New York, industry executives were subpoenaed to appear before special grand juries, where detailed information on illegal discharges could be compiled under oath. By contrast,

*Representative Henry
Reuss (D-Wis.).
Courtesy of the Office of
House Photography.*

plant owners were not compelled to testify before (or even attend) the enforcement conferences and hearings convened under federal water pollution control laws. Likewise, the Corps' authority under Section 13 applied
to navigable waters both interstate and intrastate; the federal government's
jurisdiction under the 1965 Water Quality Act extended only to interstate waters. Moreover, court-ordered injunctions typically required defendants to
implement quite specific levels of treatment and effluent quality. Refuse Act
settlements often mandated a more stringent code of compliance than the
standards New York State implemented under the Water Quality Act.[16]

Toward a Permit Program

By 1970, then, the Refuse Act's inherent regulatory benefits had energized its proponents, who pressured the Corps to become more actively involved in policing pollution. As the summer approached, Corps officials concluded that the agency could no longer sidestep this new, externally imposed responsibility; indeed, it could no longer afford to go without a formal Section 13 permit program. The current strategy of scattershot litigation promised more confusion than clean water in the long run, especially if the prosecutions were not coordinated in any way with state and federal water quality agencies. If instead the Corps began issuing permits to industries that specified acceptable effluent content, that would allow for more systematic enforcement. But it would also create an entirely new regulatory apparatus. As such, the initiative drew inevitable responses from the Nixon White House, environmentalists, and the Muskie subcommittee, which oversaw the existing pollution control program.

The Corps did not shed its Refuse Act reticence until late in the game, suggesting a lingering reluctance to engage the issue. On 5 April 1970, the new chief engineer, Lt. Gen. Frederick J. Clarke, called the first general press conference in the Corps' 168-year history. The planned topic of conversation was not Section 13 but rather the recently enacted NEPA. Clarke announced the formation of a new Environmental Advisory Board to guide regional offices "on how they should consider the environmental impact of proposed projects" as required by NEPA. To Clark's dismay, the press all but ignored the board announcement, bombarding him instead with questions about the Corps' lax enforcement of the Refuse Act. The chief engineer was forced to admit that his agency's narrow administrative focus on navigation was out of sync with the changing popular climate. A month later, the Corps began to respond to some of the recommendations in the Reuss subcommittee's March report. Between May and July, the Department of the Army set about to devise a separate permit program to bring all industrial effluent sources into compliance with the Refuse Act.[17]

The army's resolve prompted the Nixon administration to take a more active role in institutionalizing the Refuse Act. Members of the president's newly convened Council on Environmental Quality did not believe that the

Corps of Engineers could reconcile permit effluent requirements with state water quality standards on its own. In the fall of 1970, the Council on Environmental Quality took charge of drafting the executive order that would create a national permit program administered by the Corps but coordinated by the new Environmental Protection Agency. Officials reasoned that the timing for such an initiative was right, with the EPA poised to absorb all federal water pollution programs by year's end and with Muskie's subcommittee too preoccupied with air pollution legislation to act on the water pollution proposals Nixon had announced in February.[18]

By the time the chair of the Council on Environmental Quality, Russell Train, convened an interagency meeting in November, little resistance to a Refuse Act permit program remained. In contrast to their past reservations, water quality officials now viewed a permit system as an ideal mechanism to impose more rigorous effluent limitations on industrial plants. The fact that the EPA was certain to circumscribe the Corps' autonomy likely contributed to the turnaround. Even the Commerce Department preferred uniform regulations to the vicissitudes of litigation.[19]

President Nixon inaugurated the Refuse Act Permit Program with the release of Executive Order 11574 on 23 December 1970. It required all dischargers to hold a valid federal permit by 1 July 1971. The secretary of the army reviewed, issued, or denied the permits, and the EPA identified all discharges that diminished water quality and made the recommendations that formed the basis of the secretary's decisions. The details of this unprecedented system owed little to either interest groups or members of Congress, despite their earlier critical activism, since the Council on Environmental Quality denied them any substantive participation in the administrative drafting process.[20]

Environmental advocates soon voiced their misgivings about the permit program's bifurcated authority. A coalition of organizations led by the Natural Resources Defense Council feared that de facto EPA administration of the permit system would enervate the Corps' mandate under the original 1899 statute to halt pollution at its source. The EPA had given them reason for concern. The overwhelming number of permits to be processed (over 40,000) forced the agency's reliance on "state certification." Instead of establishing stringent limits or prohibitions for industrial discharges, the EPA allowed the states to review permit applications on its behalf and approve effluent controls sufficient to meet existing (and sometimes lax) ambient stream standards. The agency also seemed hesitant to review and override inadequate certifications, particularly on intrastate waters.[21]

Edmund Muskie and the staff of the Subcommittee on Air and Water Pollution had their own concerns about the new system. The emergence of the Refuse Act had already complicated staff director Leon Billings's ambitious plans to conduct hearings and complete amendments to the Water Pollution Control Act by the end of March 1971. But the dilemma involved more than just bad timing. The Refuse Act permit program stood as a parallel system of water pollution regulation that had sprung up independent of any legislative authority, including Muskie's. Moreover, the White House had claimed it as its own and promoted it aggressively.[22]

Whereas environmentalists feared the permit program was too conjoined with existing state water quality programs, the Muskie subcommittee dreaded its potential for overlap and confusion. Billings warned that the Corps was set to issue permits by 1 July, meaning that "all industrial waste dischargers in the country would be operating under a compliance schedule at least one full year ahead of the effective date of any implementation plans approved as a result of the legislation the subcommittee is now considering." Would industries bear the capital costs to comply with the permit program if they suspected that new legislation would alter its requirements in two years? Would the content of Corps permits become de facto nationwide standards, established unilaterally and arbitrarily by the EPA, rendering the states' role superfluous? And since thirty-two states employed their own permit systems, would dischargers end up holding conflicting federal and state permits? Minority staff director Tom Jorling concluded that the "present redundant Refuse Act Permit Program" promised only litigation, an erosion of public confidence, and a lingering water pollution problem.[23]

Nixon administration officials downplayed these concerns, focusing instead on how the permit program might make the state-federal regulatory system work the way Muskie had intended it. Although the 1965 Water Quality Act required states to set ambient stream standards, state officials tended to neglect the far more technically complicated task of determining the volume and content of waste flows necessary to meet those standards. In lieu of precise, site-specific effluent limits, the majority of state implementation plans followed the Interior Department's 1966 guidelines and required "best practical" treatment for waste discharges. For municipal sewage, this meant "secondary treatment," or filtration combined with microbial decomposition of oxygen-depleting organic materials. But for the complex admixture of chemical compounds found in industrial run-off, sanitary engineers could speak only in terms of a vague "secondary equivalent," never adequately defined for any industry. As a consequence, if effluent limits were promulgated at all, they rarely pushed the technological envelope, and in many cases proved insufficient to achieve ambient standards.[24]

The Refuse Act held out the prospect of a more workable system. EPA officials argued that federal permits would help tailor treatment technologies to the unique chemistry of both individual streams and the industrial effluent discharged into them. They might also facilitate installation of the "best available and feasible technology . . . within the shortest practical time," a standard that courts and enforcement conferences increasingly demanded. By March 1971, senators from the states bordering Lake Michigan had joined environmental groups in urging the administration to use the permit program in this way.[25]

But practical concerns clouded this vision of the future. Program administrator John Quarles confessed that technical complexity, manpower limitations, and a 1 July deadline limited the EPA to promulgating specific performance standards for only the most flagrant polluters, at best a select minority. Moreover, environmentalists complained and Quarles all but admitted in June 1971 that the Nixon administration would hesitate to set strict effluent limits unless Congress granted legislative reaffirmation of the permit program.[26]

When judges, politicians, activists, and administrators rediscovered the Refuse Act, the Corps of Engineers found itself confronting a new regulatory responsibility it had not asked for. Once the Corps conceded to this external pressure and the Refuse Act permit program took form, Edmund Muskie faced a complex new regulatory program he had not asked for either. Now his subcommittee's pending clean water legislation would have to clarify all these issues. For their part, environmentalists had prompted the Council on Environmental Quality to issue revised regulations in April 1971 that increased public hearings and access to permit information. Nevertheless, Muskie and his colleagues remained ambivalent about an initiative developed entirely apart from the pollution control system they had devised and now oversaw. But the subcommittee staff demonstrated considerably more enthusiasm for another Corps initiative—urban waste management—that environmentalists had not directly demanded and knew little about.[27]

Regional Urban Waste Management

Perceived flaws in the nation's water pollution control system inspired both the Refuse Act permit program and the regional urban waste management program. The Corps accepted the former out of a sense of obligation, but it pursued the latter as an avenue of opportunity. Although federal and state water quality officials had underperformed in their enforcement duties, the Corps never felt entirely comfortable stepping in as a surrogate police force. The agency stood on much firmer ground, however, redressing another defect that came to light in 1969–1970: the inability of state or federal entities to build waste treatment facilities systematically within river basins. Construction and planning—that was something that the Corps knew how to do. Even better, the institutional structure already existed and proved to be a more natural fit for the new endeavor than anyone would have anticipated.

The Corps of Engineers' inclination and capacity to launch a regional urban waste management initiative in 1971 grew out of its response to renewed legislative concerns about water supply and development in the mid-sixties. Haunted by the debilitating effects of the recent northeastern drought and the specter of a chronic water shortage in that region, Congress turned the Omnibus Rivers and Harbors Act of 1965 into a vehicle to promote the long-range planning necessary to avert future disaster. The $2 billion public works bill included authorizations for two comprehensive, Corps-led surveys of the problem area, the North Atlantic Regional Study (NARS) and the North Eastern Water Supply Study (NEWS).[28]

The evolution of NARS and NEWS as planning systems gradually laid the technical groundwork for incorporating environmental objectives into the Corps' developmental mission. Congress's renewed commitment to maximize northeastern water resources awakened the agency not only to the urban demand for clean water but also to the importance of offering flexible alternatives to help communities meet that demand.

NARS began as a routine "Type I" study of the region, designed to estimate supplies of and demands for water over a fifty-year period and prioritize future infrastructure investments. But the Corps' North Atlantic Division responded to outside consultants who called for authentic interdisciplinary planning. Between 1967 and 1969, its Special Studies Branch adopted the "multiobjective" approach first developed in the 1950s by the Harvard Water Program and its founders, political scientist Arthur Maass and professor of public administration Maynard Hufschmidt. Using the latest in systems analysis and computer modeling, the Special Studies Branch rejected the narrow assessments of economic efficiency that had determined how planners prioritized regional water uses in the past. Instead, they accounted for different public preferences by choosing three broad objectives—national income, regional development, and environmental quality—and then developing alternative land- and water-use policies on the basis of those objectives for twenty-one subregions and various target dates up to 2020. The study's director, Harry Schwarz, was a distinguished hydraulic engineer and planner with distinct memories of the inflexible Potomac River study and the controversy it generated. He championed the new approach and sought out a wide array of experts to implement it, including civil and sanitary engineers, biologists, landscape architects, hydrologists, economists, and other social scientists.[29]

The debates in Congress surrounding initiatives like federally funded ecological research and NEPA demonstrated how policymakers could enlist systems analysis to serve environmental ends. NARS reflected the same trend at the same time in a different forum. Schwarz and the study's coordinating committee sought an interdisciplinary methodology to manage a complex system—in this case, a river basin planning process with conflicting agencies, agendas, and social priorities. With multiple-objective planning, the committee believed it had found the flexibility to provide "maximum information on alternatives . . . not only to update programs but to change the planning assumptions and objectives to create new programs."[30]

Environmental quality factored into these alternatives, but not simply as a cost-benefit sleight of hand to justify traditional bricks-and-mortar solutions. Agency framework plans in other areas of the country continued to recommend conventional construction programs as the only option to address future water problems. The NARS report analyzed the needs of its subregions from multiple perspectives. The study advised that the largest investments be made for waste treatment facilities and land management practices, rather than for dams and Potomac-style low-flow augmentation. The Corps of Engineers had not turned its back on its developmental ethos or aspirations by any means, but nevertheless found a way to advance a putative environmental agenda in the context of its traditional mission.[31]

If NARS and its multiple-objective planning process broadened the Corps' own sense of its institutional priorities, then the North Eastern Water Supply Study provided the platform to advance its bureaucratic ambitions in the field of water quality management. Again, this was not exactly what Congress had in mind. The House Public Works Committee had inserted NEWS into the Rivers and Harbors Act as a means to address the long-term urban crisis foreshadowed by the drought. The Senate conceived NARS as a general framework study, but the House expected NEWS to provide specific plans for the Corps to construct, operate, and maintain the infrastructure required to meet urban water supply needs in the Northeast corridor. Prior to this explicit mandate, the agency had exercised marginal responsibility for managing urban water supplies outside the District of Columbia.[32]

The planning conducted under NEWS explored a broad range of alternatives, from standard storage structures to investigations of groundwater, local reservoir interconnections, and elaborate interregional transfer schemes. But its urban focus also led the Corps to reconsider the link between quality and quantity. Specifically, the study raised the prospect that waste management on a regional or river basin level could help mitigate the Northeast's water supply woes. When the North Atlantic Division initiated its investigation in 1966, its early work focused on selecting the areas most vulnerable to chronic future shortages. In each instance, whether in New York, Newark, Boston, or Washington, D.C., a grossly polluted river stood out as one of the most promising sources available to meet metropolitan water demands. As the Corps' technical surveys grew more sophisticated, their analysis of engineering options focused increasingly on wastewater reclamation and reuse. By the spring of 1970, studies of southeastern New England determined that the befouled Merrimack River offered the greatest potential for alleviating the Boston Metropolitan Area's long-range water supply problems. In so doing, NEWS implied that environmental quality as a social objective need not conflict with urban economic growth. Indeed, the Corps might just be able to deliver both.[33]

Such conclusions buttressed a growing sentiment within the Corps of Engineers that its active participation in the field of waste management could yield mutual benefits for both the agency and the broader federal pollution control effort. On the one hand, the Corps felt compelled to respond to the growing chorus of critics who lambasted its relentless developmental ethos and environmental insensitivity. The same impetus to convene an Environmental Advisory Board, inaugurate a Refuse Act permit program, and adopt multiple-objective planning led agency officials to look favorably upon a new mission to implement wastewater reclamation projects, especially if it could be done in the name of metropolitan regional development.

But the timing of the Corps' initiative also coincided with mounting scrutiny of the current water pollution control program's overall effectiveness. Analyses conducted by government auditors indicated that the postwar federal effort to rejuvenate the nation's waterways had failed to make significant progress. These critics attributed the poor performance in part to ineffective planning mechanisms. If this were true, then the Corps' own institutional capabilities—so evident in the execution of NARS and NEWS—seemed to offer just what the auditors ordered.

The GAO and the Promise of Planning

Before the Corps of Engineers could act to fill a bureaucratic vacuum, someone had to point out that one existed and needed to be filled. The General Accounting Office (GAO) obliged in 1969, when it released its influential and widely cited study of the FWPCA's construction grant program. Corps officials took notice and interpreted the GAO's critique as an invitation to broaden their mission.

The report told a story of misallocated resources and lost opportunities. Between 1957 and 1969, FWPCA awarded $1.2 billion to states, municipalities, and intergovernmental agencies to assist in the construction of over 9,400 treatment works, estimated at a total cost of $5.4 billion. Although these projects helped stem the tide of water pollution, the GAO concluded that the program had not derived optimal benefits from its considerable investment. Many of the sewage plants financed with federal funds operated along waterways where nearby industrial and municipal sources persisted in discharging raw or inadequately treated waste. These effluent loads curtailed the impact of capital-intensive treatment. Such results were inevitable, the GAO concluded, when the agency administering the grant program prioritized treatment projects purely as a function of local financial capacity or pollution abatement needs. Ideally, administrators needed to judge an individual project's contribution to water quality relative to the aggregate activity along a particular stream. Such planning would prove even more essential in the future, given shrinking domestic budgets.[34]

To account for these variables, the GAO called for a now-familiar solution—the "application of systems analysis techniques to water pollution problems." A more thorough systems approach would allow planners to coordinate individual treatment plants within a framework designed to achieve a particular standard of ambient quality in the most cost-efficient manner. The auditors based their conclusions on an external study of the Merrimack, the river that had helped inspire the Corps of Engineers' own reassessment of water quality planning.[35]

Environmental policymakers concurred with the GAO's assertion that ineffective planning had hampered the federal water pollution control effort. In its 1970 report to Congress, *The Economics of Clean Water*, the FWPCA admitted that the allocation of funds for treatment plant construction had been "unguided by effective priority considerations." It encouraged the formation of river basin organizations to manage waste despite the practical political resistance from industry and local officials who resented "such special purpose governmental units." The Council of Environmental Quality's first annual report in 1970 touted a similar system. When the EPA took over from the FWPCA in 1971, it, too, hoped to base future construction grants on river basin or metropolitan regional plans for water pollution abatement, drawn up by state and local agencies.[36]

The Institute for Water Resources and the Power of Planning

The government's environmental watchdogs may have concurred with the GAO's assessment, but by 1970–1971 the Corps of Engineers was addressing the problem head on. The Corps' own analysts reiterated the GAO's diagnosis but prescribed a novel remedy derived from the agency's experience in water resource planning in the Northeast.

In April 1969, the army's new Institute for Water Resources (IWR) opened for business. The IWR represented another effort on the part of the Corps' leadership to adapt their civil works program to shifting public preferences. It convened an interdisciplinary team of engineers, economists, sociologists, and environmental scientists in an attempt to integrate a broader set of social and environmental values into the agency's water resource planning process. The IWR released one of its more intriguing analyses in October 1970, entitled *The Role of the U.S. Army Corps of Engineers in Water Quality Management.*[37]

The report contended that the Corps of Engineers' unique institutional capabilities qualified it for a more expansive role in the federal government's water quality management program. "Since the Corps primarily has built up an expertise in the area of water resources," it asserted, "and water pollution is now the largest part of the challenge in water resources, the emphasis of the Corps should be obvious." Though known best for its navigation and water supply projects, the Corps' recent activities demonstrated that it was no neophyte on the pollution front. The authors cited the agency's authority to plan reservoir storage for low-flow augmentation, its stepped-up Refuse Act permit activity, and the NEWS study, where the Corps was "necessarily relating water quality to water supply" for Northeast metropolitan areas.[38]

These programs, however, only hinted at the Corps' potential to revitalize the nation's pollution control system. The agency had many assets at its disposal: a capacity to manage large, complex construction and public-planning programs, an extensive field organization, and a set of unique institutional arrangements with local governments, Congress, and the executive branch. With these advantages, the authors suggested, the Corps could "achieve integration and proper balance between water quality improvement and all other water resources uses."

The key to success rested first with what the authors viewed as the agency's foremost talent: its ability to plan. Planning represented the unexploited opportunity in pollution control. The findings of IWR's own investigation comported with those of the GAO and the FWPCA concerning the gap between planning and treatment plant construction. The report faulted water quality bureaucracies for a certain narrowness of vision. These agencies, it noted, had always viewed planning objectives as functions of regulation and enforcement, rather than overall public investment. The limited basin planning that water quality agencies carried out provided no coordination with other water resource uses and offered nothing like a regional water quality investment plan.[39]

The next generation in pollution control, the authors suggested, required a more sophisticated approach. It had to involve the "organization of waste management systems by metropolitan region, with investments rationalized over the long term by river basin and integrated to overall resource development." Water quality agencies remained essential for setting and enforcing stream standards, but they lacked the capacity to "balance this set of activities against other water resource development investment." Only an agency "skilled in the management of complex multiple-purpose projects and already involved in other water resource investments" could fill this role. The Corps of Engineers was the obvious choice. Not only could the Corps plan, the IWR report insisted, the Corps could also broker deals between Congress, the executive branch, and local governments to forge the necessary regional management units.[40]

The IWR report cited NEWS as an inspiration for the kind of Corps-implemented regional waste management system it envisioned. NEWS impressed the authors with its "mix of organizational as well as technological evaluation." It allowed the Corps to present a wealth of information and a broad array of alternative plans to local governments, encouraging them to consider their water supply needs in a regional context. Moreover, the study's findings on wastewater renovation led the authors to recommend giving reuse alternatives "careful and explicit consideration" in future Corps planning for municipal and industrial water supplies, hinting that such options could provide more environmentally acceptable alternatives to "traditional storage solutions." The report also called for a new study, using NEWS as a springboard, that focused specifically on waste management.[41]

The office of the chief of engineers soon followed through on this suggestion, directing Harry Schwarz to design a study in the winter of 1970–1971. Choosing the well-surveyed Merrimack River Basin, Schwarz drew on personnel and consultants affiliated with NARS to complete a proposal that, when implemented, would rely on interdisciplinary expertise and offer up to seven flexible planning alternatives. Meanwhile, Lt. Gen. F. J. Clarke appeared before the House and Senate Public Works Appropriation Subcommittees on 8 and 9 March 1971, to request a reallocation of NEWS funds to pay for the Merrimack study. He also asked that Congress reorient funds committed to four other survey areas in order to create similar pilot programs in Cleveland-Akron, Detroit, Chicago, and San Francisco. Clarke described the proposal as the "missing link" in the Corps' ability to carry out total water resources planning, and as an opportunity to develop "comprehensively alternative systems of waste water management control."[42]

When Clarke spoke of "comprehensively alternative systems," he referred not simply to the sophisticated planning techniques recommended by the GAO, refined in NARS and NEWS, or touted by the IWR, but also to cutting-edge waste treatment technologies that complemented the Corps' regional emphasis. One in particular, known as land disposal, captured the imagination of agency officials and assumed a central place in their water quality planning endeavors—Clarke singled it out for specific endorsement during his congressional testimony. The technology held out the promise of re-claiming urban wastewater and rehabilitating urban rivers in a fashion that would delight environmentalists and developers alike. It also seemed ideally suited for the regional scale of the Corps' wastewater management programs, so much so that the agency best known for dredging and damming proved far more aggressive in advocating land disposal initiatives than the federal government's own water pollution bureaucracies.

Getting Back to the Land

For the Corps of Engineers, the road to regional urban waste management ran through New England, but it also branched off into Pennsylvania and Michigan. In these states, university scientists and resource planners devised the nation's most advanced systems of land-based waste treatment. These designs sought to replace the conventional hardware and outlook of sanitary engineering with a process more attuned to natural ecological cycles.

This was just what the Corps was after. Ecology helped the Corps to define its pollution control niche more clearly, since established water quality agencies relied almost exclusively on sanitary engineers for their expertise. Ecology's focus on interdependent systems also fit well with regional planning techniques. Moreover, events in State College and Muskegon demonstrated how more traditional concerns about water supply and economic growth could stimulate ecological innovation.

The practice of dumping urban sewage in an open field may seem antithetical to ecology, technology, and regional planning. Yet prior to the ascendance of modern metropolitan sewerage systems and the sanitary engineering profession that advocated them, nineteenth-century farmers purchased the fetid contents of privy vaults for use as fertilizer. The flow of human excreta from cesspools to croplands linked town and country by cycling nutrients back into the earth. As populations grew denser, waste loads burgeoned, and the threat of enteric disease spread, however, city officials opted for a capital-intensive technological solution that redirected urban wastes away from the hinterland and into local watercourses. This method of conveyance efficiently flushed away filth and disease but, as some historians have suggested, it also "severed the connection between human wastes and the soil" and inadvertently taxed downstream communities with massive volumes of sewage discharged upstream.[43]

For its cadre of dedicated proponents, land-based wastewater management encouraged the proper scale of administrative organization and ecological engineering by extending the metabolism of cities back into the adjoining countryside. They envisioned the soil of unproductive farm acreage as a "living filter," ready to reconnect human communities with natural nutrient cycles, relieve urban rivers from their duties as waste sinks, and supply the pure water required for economic and environmental prosperity. Moreover, they imagined multiple metropolitan areas tied into collective regional systems, managing their wastes in an efficient, cost-effective manner. Prior to the sixties, hundreds of municipalities in the United States applied treated wastewater to land, but attempts to exploit the absorptive capacity of soil to treat effluent were limited to a few industries, usually food processing plants.[44]

When the northeastern drought began exposing the link between pollution and fresh water scarcity in State College, Pennsylvania, it compelled a team of Pennsylvania State University scientists to develop the first multiple-purpose land treatment system in the United States. Even as the college town's primary underground reservoirs dwindled, Spring Creek, the local watercourse, sacrificed its flow to dilute millions of gallons of treated sewage from the community's 33,000 residents. By sanitary engineering standards, the effluent was acceptable, but ever-increasing loads and the high concentrations of nitrogen and phosphorus that remained after treatment depleted dissolved oxygen levels. In 1963, geologists and soil experts designed a spray irrigation system to distribute 500,000 gallons of treated sewage per day to mixed hardwood forest and farmland acreage on a year-round basis, enlisting the soil's microbes, vegetation, and adsorptive properties to renovate the effluent.[45]

Extensive monitoring over the next three years led the scientists to conclude that land-based disposal systems offered a viable alternative to conventional treatment. Wastewater applied to agricultural and forested areas and filtered through twelve inches of soil experienced removal rates of 99 percent for phosphorous and 68 to 82 percent for nitrates. Approximately 80 percent of that weekly application was recharged to the groundwater reservoir, at a quality that met the PHS's drinking water standard. The effluent supplied fertilizing nutrients to the soil that resulted in increased corn and hay yields as well as taller trees. Extrapolations from the Penn State findings suggested that 116,000 acres—less than a half a percent of the state's agricultural and forest land—could treat the wastewater of all Pennsylvania communities with populations under 100,000.[46]

The fullest realization of the Penn State design occurred along the eastern shore of Lake Michigan, where an ambitious project called the Muskegon County Waste Management System caught the attention of influential observers in Washington, the Corps of Engineers foremost among them. A stagnant economy, rather than drought, inspired the Michigan area's turn to ecological planning in the late sixties. Throughout the twentieth century, industrial pollution and unregulated urban sprawl had contributed to the degradation of Muskegon's lakes and shorelines. In the 1950s, its ravaged natural resource base discouraged the migration of new industry. Population and property values fell, while unemployment climbed to twice the national rate by the end of the sixties.[47]

County officials attempted to break the cycle of economic and environmental decline in 1968 by creating the Muskegon County Metropolitan Planning Commission. That same year, the Lake Michigan Pollution Conference, an outgrowth of the state's burgeoning environmental movement, provided the commissioners with some specific water resource planning goals. Called in response to growing public pressure and intensified media focus on the deteriorating southern section of the lake, the four-state enforcement conference ordered industries and municipalities to provide a minimum of secondary treatment or its equivalent by the end of 1972 and set a goal for 80 percent phosphorus removal. It fell to the commission to translate these requirements into a blueprint for the county's renaissance.[48]

For assistance, officials turned to the University of Chicago's Center for Urban Studies, where they appealed to John R. Sheaffer, a research associate and resident expert in natural resources management. The 37-year old Sheaffer had earned his Ph.D. at Chicago and first attracted national attention as the architect of "Mount Trashmore," a 125-foot synthetic ski slope constructed entirely of garbage in DuPage County, Illinois. Sheaffer concluded that Muskegon County had pursued a one-dimensional industrial economy at the expense of agriculture or a recreational sector anchored around the nearby Muskegon, Mona, and White Lakes. He believed that advances in land treatment technology could redress both oversights, provide a long-term solution to the area's waste disposal problem, and place Muskegon County in the national spotlight. Through a network of professional contacts, Sheaffer remained well acquainted with recent advances in land-based systems, the Penn State project in particular. Based on his recommendations, in February 1969 the County Board of Commissioners contracted with Chicago's Bauer Engineering Company to design a comprehensive sewage disposal system based on but decidedly more advanced than Penn State's.[49]

By choosing land disposal technology, the County of Muskegon set out to achieve developmental ends through ecological means. County officials believed that "a reclaiming of the environmental quality could be the catalyst for regional redevelopment" and expected the innovative waste management system to diversify the area's economic base. In turn, John Sheaffer's public statements stressed the ecological foundations for what became known as "Muskegon-type" projects. He stressed that the environment was a closed, interdependent system in dynamic equilibrium, where matter and energy cycled between land, water, and air. Conventional waste disposal strategies erred in their linearity, treating natural media as limitless sinks for human society's by-products. The Muskegon system assumed that waste products were nothing more than potential "resources out of place." The same phosphates and nitrates that promoted eutrophication in streams would improve agricultural productivity if applied as fertilizer on land.[50]

The $36-million Bauer design converted this theory into practice on a grand scale. Its two main branches, serving Muskegon–Mona Lake and the surrounding regions, were intended to replace the county's four existing municipal facilities, which handled thirty million gallons of municipal and industrial effluent per day. According to the blueprint, an interceptor network would collect the sewage and pump it eleven miles east into three eight-acre lagoons. After aeration and bacterial decomposition reduced the effluent's biological oxygen demand (BOD) by between 70 and 90 percent, it was removed to two clay-lined basins. Their enormous capacity (5.1 billion gallons) prevented urban storm water run-off and combined sewer overflows from bypassing the system, while containing backlogs of partially treated sewage when toxic industrial waste accidentally killed BOD-reducing bacterial colonies. When withdrawn from storage, the wastewater would be chlorinated, pumped through open-air channels to an irrigation pumping station, and dispersed to the surrounding nutrient-poor soil at a rate of 2.5 million gallons per acre over a seven-month application period. Given the typical removal rates for BOD (99 percent), suspended solids (99 percent), phosphorus (90 percent), nitrogen (87 percent), coliform (100 percent), and viruses (100 percent), the purified product met the standards imposed at the 1968 Lake Michigan Conference. As an added bonus, the Muskegon system promised to transform 6,000 acres of "unproductive, droughty, infertile, sandy soils" into profit-generating farmland.[51]

The Muskegon Land Disposal System managed to overcome a number of obstacles. These included the skepticism of the Michigan Water Resources Commission's sanitary engineers (who balked on the grounds of feasibility and expense), skittish politicians, and even a lawsuit filed by environmentalists concerned about contaminated groundwater. The task of neutralizing the commission's opposition in particular fell to Guy Vander Jagt, the representative from Michigan's ninth district, who together with John Sheaffer proved most responsible for the Muskegon Project's approval and subsequent national recognition. As the ranking Republican on Henry Reuss's Subcommittee on Conservation and Natural Resources, Vander Jagt had learned first hand of the frustrating limitations of conventional pollution control technology. Linking his political identity with an innovative technology that held the promise of both environmental and economic renewal also struck Vander Jagt as a prudent strategy in an election year. The congressman became a tireless booster of Sheaffer's plan, exploiting his ties to the Nixon administration to muster critical federal support for it.[52]

The first airing of the Muskegon system in a national forum occurred in the House Government Operations Committee, during the Reuss subcommittee's December 1969 hearings on phosphate detergents. The Wisconsin congressman had pestered the soap and detergent industry since the mid-sixties in an effort to get them to find chemical alternatives to ABS, a phosphate ingredient in soap products that led to unsightly foaming and eutrophication in watercourses. Sheaffer appeared before the subcommittee touting land disposal as an ideal method for reclaiming the phosphorus, the putative resource out of place. He suggested that land-based waste management systems portended innovations in technology as well as in regional administration, since uncoordinated government activities on the federal, state, and local levels currently militated against the centralized planning required to manage the environment as a total system.[53]

After the hearings, Vander Jagt wasted little time bringing the land treatment system to the personal attention of every domestic and environmental official in the Nixon administration. The opposition of the Michigan Water Resources Commission soon crumbled. In September, Interior Secretary Hickel announced the Sheaffer-Bauer project as the recipient of the largest Federal Water Quality Administration research and demonstration grant ever awarded. When construction began in 1971, the project had garnered over $2 million in federal aid. Following Vander Jagt's successful reelection bid in 1970, he knew exactly who and what to thank. The congressman informed John Ehrlichman that "the most significant factor in the size of my margin in Muskegon, my most metropolitan and Democratic County, was the Muskegon County Wastewater Treatment System" that the administration had helped push "through the bureaucratic maze." The president's aides also understood Muskegon's political capital in the midst of the "environmental decade." One even visualized a presidential tour stop in the fall of 1972 "pointing to progress in this area" and suggested that the Federal Water Quality Administration funnel more demonstration grant money into similar endeavors.[54]

But the Corps of Engineers beat them to the punch. The Muskegon project's compatibility with regional water resource planning, not to mention its ability to garner both good press and federal funding, convinced the agency's top administrators that land disposal should continue as in-house technology. They wasted little time hiring the man most responsible for its success to date, offering John Sheaffer a position as scientific advisor to the secretary of the army. From his new post, the energetic Sheaffer preached the gospel of the living filter to Congress, the public, and the agency's own field staff.[55]

The Corps may have resisted its obligation to regulate water pollution under the 1899 Refuse Act, but it embraced the union of soil and sewage, another remnant of the nineteenth century, to establish itself in the field of urban waste management. As army officials saw it, Muskegon provided a way for the Corps to play to its institutional strengths while exploiting the Federal Water Quality Administration's limitations. With land treatment, the agency could reinvent itself as the plucky challenger of a status quo fixated on local, linear, and limited solutions to pollution. The combination of Sheaffer's land-oriented technology and the Corps' planning and construction capacity promised to restore the connection between urban and rural ecosystems—and the Corps' environmental standing—on a grand scale.

Agency planners saw no conflict between their new mission and current state and federal efforts, because their programmatic objectives outstripped conventional expectations. The Merrimack basin study was a case in point. Officials from the North Atlantic Division eschewed old pollution control remedies like "secondary treatment equivalent" and dilution in favor of "alternative advanced technologies which are capable of cleaning waste water fully and thus make the river available for a full range of uses regardless of present and future development on its shores." The Corps did not intend to abate pollution; it meant to eliminate pollution in order to achieve "maximum feasible purity of our waste discharges" and produce "super clean water" on a regional basis. By 1971, the goals the Corps espoused for water quality began to surpass those generally advocated by career pollution control officials. When dam builders denounced dilution, clearly times had changed.[56]

A skeptical observer would not confuse the Corps' latest policy path for the road to Damascus, however, nor overstate the significance of the agency's conversion experience. Despite enduring opposition, the Corps still pressed for a modified version of its original Potomac plan into the seventies. It persisted in citing low-flow augmentation as a justification for reservoir projects elsewhere, much to the chagrin of environmentalists and the delight of industrialists, who preferred taxpayer-supported dilution solutions in lieu of costly pollution control technology. And it generated multiple legal challenges by continuing to champion large-scale public works of questionable economic and environmental value.[57]

And yet, elements of the Corps' developmental agenda continued to hold currency in an environmental age. Concerns about water shortages and growth in the sixties transitioned smoothly into waste management schemes in the seventies. The IWR grasped the connection and the Corps' role, asserting that "the water supply problem is the water quality problem, and we will not become efficient in the solution of either until the supply agencies see themselves as having equal responsibility for the quality problem." Similarly, land-based waste treatment programs proved a natural fit for an agency fluent in the language of multipurpose and multiple-objective planning. The ecological discourse Sheaffer employed to promote Muskegon featured an emphasis on integrated, holistically coordinated systems on a regional scale that modern water resource planners could appreciate, because they shared similar aspirations for rational systems management.[58]

That same mode of systems thinking, in both an ecological and comprehensive planning context, proved irresistible to the Subcommittee on Air and Water Pollution. As the subcommittee struggled with the political and practical problems of drafting a water pollution law suitable for an environmental decade, they turned to the Corps for organizational and technological solutions. More so than the Refuse Act permit program, regional waste management encouraged members and staff to pursue new and ambitious policy goals for water quality, ranging from "swimmable-fishable" standards to "ecological integrity" and eventually to "zero-discharge." How they came to consider such objectives, and why they turned to the Corps for answers, is an intricate story taken up in the remaining chapters.

Drafting the Clean Water Act
Systems Thinking and the
"Ecologically Sound Society"

The 1972 Federal Water Pollution Control Act Amendments restructured the regulatory system that Congress had established to protect the nation's freshwater supplies during the fifties and sixties. In just seven years, the substance of national policy and the means of implementing it changed dramatically. The 1965 Water Quality Act encouraged decentralized administrative flexibility and gradualism. Its successor transferred authority from the states to the Environmental Protection Agency and rejected local ambient water quality as a measure of progress or a trigger for enforcement. The new law relied instead on federally promulgated, industry-specific, technologically defined limits on the volume and type of emissions discharged by polluters. These new effluent standards came with strict deadlines and were designed to achieve ambitious long-range objectives grounded in the principles of ecological science, including a total ban on discharges by 1985.

The Clean Water Act seemed to owe much of its content to the political and cultural context of the times. Hadn't the landmark Clean Air Act of 1970 introduced the regulatory innovations that were applied directly to water two years later? Hadn't Congress passed both pieces of legislation in response to the inexorable pressures of the environmental movement? And didn't Senator Edmund Muskie's quest for the presidency, and his need to outbid Nixon on the environment, explain the act's ambitious goals and methods?

All of these explanations contain kernels of truth, but taken together they still fail to account for one of the modern era's most influential and complex pieces of environmental legislation. The Clean Water Act was a textbook example of the seventies' "new social regulation," and it did materialize from the responsiveness of committees and subcommittees in Congress to the demands of newly empowered mass movements and interest groups. Moreover, environmental values and activism did help create a political context that encouraged politicians to push the limits on such legislation, especially in an election year. But to conclude the story there is to overlook how the internal legislative process itself shaped the new social regulation, and how that process often reflected other agendas that, while less obvious, proved no less important.

Understanding institutional processes and unveiling recondite agendas becomes a matter of taking the language policymakers used seriously. For Edmund Muskie, viable legislation conveyed broad objectives to the public and specific implementation instructions to administrators. What worked for one statute did not carry over seamlessly to another, regardless of the political climate. Choosing the right words to communicate unprecedented policy goals and the practical means to achieve them occupied the Subcommittee on Air and Water Pollution behind closed doors in the summer of 1971.

And where did those words come from? As the history of federal water pollution control suggests, legislators drew upon a multiplicity of familiar postwar discourses to conceptualize new policies. Even a groundbreaking statute like the Clean Water Act bore witness to these continuities. Edmund Muskie fostered a committee culture that encouraged open debate and active participation from members and staff alike. To revolutionize environmental regulation, they listened to environmentalists and pollution control experts. But they also turned to some unlikely environmentalists, including men who designed ballistic missiles and an agency that built dams. They looked as well to professional ecologists, who spoke a language of systems management that resonated with late-twentieth-century policymakers more accustomed to dealing with missile designers and dam builders. Reintroducing these variables does not marginalize environmentalism or the political context it helped create; it merely integrates them into a broader narrative of American political development.

The Clean Water Act serves as a point of convergence for all the diverse strands of our story thus far. But the final product represented more than just the sum of these parts. The contributions of environmentalists, aerospace engineers, ecologists, water resource developers, Republicans, Democrats, Nixon partisans, and loyal committee staffers combined to produce a bill whose final form no one anticipated.

Fittingly, the catalyst for some of the most significant policy transformations was himself a rather unlikely environmentalist—and a late arrival to Muskie's subcommittee. For this reason, although national electoral politics cannot account for everything the Clean Water Act said and did, it remains the place to begin.

Enter John Tunney

The turbulent midterm elections of 1970 did not turn out the way President Nixon desired. Nixon sought to muster the same blue-collar and Sunbelt voters who had backed him two years before, but this time in support of congressional Republicans. The appeal of cultural conservatism coupled with a cooperative economy, Nixon hoped, might just topple a shaky Democratic majority in the Senate.

But it was not to be. The Federal Reserve's anti-inflationary measures precipitated an ill-timed recession, the prodigal labor vote returned to the Democrats, and the president's law-and-order rhetoric failed to resonate as expected. Nixon's televised appearance on the eve of the election, excoriating the "hoodlums and thugs" whom he had goaded into a rock-throwing confrontation days earlier in San Jose, California, struck a sour note. By contrast, the Democratic Party trotted out Edmund Muskie to deliver a tempered rejoinder that rejected "the politics of fear." When the ballots were tallied, Democrats lost only two seats in the Senate, gained nine in the House, and captured a net eleven governorships. Few races in 1970 hinged directly on environmental issues, although the public interest group Environmental Action did target twelve congressmen dubbed "The Dirty Dozen"—seven lost their reelection bids. Muskie's own reelection in Maine was never in doubt; moreover, his statesman-like performance established him as the front-runner for the Democratic presidential nomination in 1972.[1]

Perhaps the most intriguing political figure to emerge from the 1970 national election soon took his place beside Muskie as the newest member of the Senate Public Works Committee. John Varick Tunney, thirty-six, became the youngest active U.S. senator when he wrested California's seat from incumbent Republican and Nixon loyalist George Murphy. Tunney, son of former heavyweight champion Gene Tunney, had taken up politics only six years earlier, sweeping into the House on the coattails of the Johnson landslide. Critics labeled the boxer's progeny a "lightweight" with a shallow intellectual grasp, disparaging his wooden demeanor and tendency to vacillate on key issues. But Tunney's clever campaign cast Murphy as a political insider beholden to special interests and derided the Republican's stark law-and-order rhetoric.[2]

Tunney also drew upon a resource with a proven track record against all things Nixonian: the Kennedy mystique. The young candidate cut a tall, handsome figure, replete with boyish face, blond hair, and a winning smile. "Teeth. That's what you remember about John Tunney," noted *Time* magazine's Los Angeles bureau chief. "He smiles—big, healthy, sparkling molars and incisors and canines. Surely they glow in the dark." His friendship with Senator Edward Kennedy, a University of Virginia law school classmate, only reinforced an affiliation that helped Tunney draw more votes in California than did Governor Ronald Reagan in his reelection bid.[3]

Barely six months into his first term, the young political upstart caused quite a stir in the policy realm as well, although fewer people noticed. In June 1971, John Tunney introduced a deceptively simple proposal that led the Public Works Committee to shift its focus, alter the content of its pending legislation, and ultimately transform the nation's regulatory approach to water pollution control. Nothing in his resumé hinted at this turn of events. Tunney had scuba dived to the bottom of the Santa Barbara Channel to demonstrate his concern for offshore pollution to the media, but otherwise his environmental record lacked substance. Youth and inexperience appeared to preclude him from a significant role on a committee manned with experienced legislators like Caleb Boggs (R-Del.), Lloyd Bentsen (D-Texas), Howard Baker (R-Tenn.), and Muskie.

By the time the Public Works Committee concluded public hearings and settled into its schedule of executive sessions that June, the basic contours of a future water pollution bill had already emerged. Muskie and President Nixon both signed off on regulatory upgrades they had endorsed the year before: extending ambient water quality standards to all navigable waters, requiring state implementation plans to contain enforceable effluent limits, and expediting federal enforcement. They planned to increase funding for waste treatment plant construction as well, although Muskie wanted to spend a lot more ($25 billion over five years).[4]

The rival camps realized that the landmark Clean Air Act of 1970 had elevated public expectations about Washington's capacity to address the water pollution problem. Since a number of the statute's features were designed to reduce administrative discretion, the Public Works Committee and the White House imported them into their current water quality packages. Muskie's bill authorized the EPA to prohibit discharges of toxic substances altogether, subjected new industrial facilities to federally determined performance standards, and allowed citizen suits against both violators of standards and the EPA administrator. Nixon's offered similar, though somewhat less strictly worded, provisions. On the question of statutory deadlines, though, the Nixon administration hesitated to follow the clean air template so faithfully. Muskie's bill demanded that states adopt all water quality standards within a stated time frame and actually reach them no more than three years subsequent to EPA approval. By contrast, neither the president's 8 February environmental message to Congress nor his water quality bill contained any mention of deadlines, which the Office of Management and Budget opposed.[5]

Still, the White House legislation acknowledged the implications of recent environmental activism in ways Muskie's did not. When the courts, interest groups, and Congress "rediscovered" the Corps of Engineer's statutory authority to police industrial discharges, the administration created a permit program in 1970 to accommodate the imperatives of the so-called Refuse Act. Now the president's bill attempted to integrate this powerful but awkward appendage more seamlessly into the existing water pollution control bureaucracy. Muskie, however, worried about administrative redundancy. His bill remained silent on the matter of federal effluent limits for nontoxic pollutants and made no serious effort to deal with the permit program.

The Public Works Committee may have chosen to ignore the Refuse Act permit program, but its staff was determined to outshine the president's bill in most other regulatory matters. Throughout Ed Muskie's career, skilled and energetic staffers had enabled him to master large amounts of information, translate knowledge into political authority, and secure a niche for himself in the field of pollution control. By 1971, Thomas Jorling and Leon Billings were more willing than ever to exercise the autonomy Muskie traditionally bestowed. The committee had hired Jorling as its minority counsel in 1969 because of his professional training in ecology and law and his stated desire to place the latter in service to the former. The brash and talented Billings had served Muskie faithfully since 1966, most recently as the Subcommittee on Air and Water Pollution's staff director. As Don Nicoll shifted his attention to Muskie's presidential campaign, he relinquished day-to-day policy matters to the younger aide, who eschewed Nicoll's cautious incrementalism for a more aggressive approach to regulating corporate polluters.[6]

Billings and Jorling demonstrated their initiative by reworking Muskie's initial February bill, producing one of their own that became the committee's summer working draft.[7] The June staff print applied the Clean Air Act's regulatory, enforcement, and monitoring features with greater rigor. It did not propose any radical alternative to ambient stream standards but did exert greater statutory control over their substance as well as the content of the state plans designed to implement them. The minority counsel even tried to insert some ecological parameters that would define stream quality in terms unfamiliar to most sanitary engineers, such as "species diversity," or "normal population and community dynamics."[8]

In the months that followed, the Public Works Committee's most significant decision would be to reorient the structure and substance of the Clean Water Act according to ecological principles. The committee did not do so, however, just because the clean air precedent dictated it or a staff member penciled them in. Ecologically minded staffers proved essential, but Senator John Tunney put events in motion. His unexpected proposal prompted an extended conversation about policy means and ends in the seclusion of the Senate conference room. Tunney himself did not talk much about ecosystems per se. But by the time the conversation ended, the language of systems, ecological and otherwise, had inspired an even more far-reaching revision of the committee's legislation than the Clean Air Act, or even Tunney's original idea, had portended.

Swimmable Waters, Identifiable Goals, and the Military-Industrial Complex

At its most basic level, the so-called Tunney amendment defined clean water in terms of a person's ability to swim in it. It consisted of a "national target water quality standard" with a stated objective: to achieve a level of purity sufficient to allow body contact with all the nation's waters, without health hazard, by 31 December 1980. Tunney explained that this ambitious goal and fixed deadline would "focus national effort, provide an easily understandable measure of commitment, and encourage rational cost-effective program decisions." Congress had never contemplated anything like it with respect to water quality legislation. It seemed likely that the freshman's audacious idea had emerged in direct response to any number of contemporary inspirations, from the Clean Air Act to Earth Day.[9]

But it did not. The intellectual foundation of Tunney's bold initiative bore the imprint of the military-industrial complex, as transmitted by the leading executives of California's aerospace engineering industry. Even after Earth Day, legislators continued to address environmental problems by employing the traditional assumptions, institutional priorities, and professional discourses of postwar liberalism. Those of the national security state proved no exception. It is not surprising that an ambitious freshman senator chose environmental policy as his path to political relevance in 1971. It should be no less surprising that in his efforts to persuade a committee of seasoned veterans, he turned to the logic of systems thinking.

Tunney's Amendment grew out of discussions conducted in January 1971 with a number of influential constituents in the aerospace field, most prominently Cal-Tech professor and renowned corporate mogul Simon Ramo. An engineer by training, Ramo put the 'R' in TRW, co-founding the billion-dollar company in 1958. Following World War II, he had headed up the electronics division at Hughes Aircraft, which designed and manufactured such complex electronic systems as air-to-air missiles, radar, and cockpit displays. His managerial talent led him to national prominence in 1954, when he assumed the role of systems engineer and technical director for Project Atlas, the first stage of the Defense Department's $17 billion intercontinental ballistic missile program.[10]

Ramo's experience in weapons development fostered an ingrained faith in systems engineering and systems analysis. He championed the latter in his 1969 book, *Cure for Chaos*, as "an intellectual discipline for mobilizing science and technology to attack complex, large-scale problems in an objective, logical, complete, and thoroughly professional way." Ramo had applied such interdisciplinary, mission-oriented approach to Project Atlas. It was the only way to coordinate an ambitious military research and development program involving 20 principal contractors, 200 subcontractors, and a workforce of 70,000. In the context of the Cold War, military agencies and their industrial clients rapidly adopted this mode of management.[11]

By the 1960s, Ramo sensed a shift in the nexus of science and technology, away from the military-industrial complex and toward a new "social-industrial complex." He envisioned it as a hybrid of industrial, academic, and government organizations teamed up to solve problems within an array of "civic systems," ranging from transportation, medicine, and the environment to housing, poverty, and other urban concerns. These pressing domestic issues made up over half of the nation's gross national product, as compared to the military's 10 percent. Inevitably, he predicted, increasing pressure from voters would compel government to restructure itself in order to respond to these new imperatives. The private sector and the nation's technological talent pool needed to adjust as well, becoming more adept at "managing the application of science to society." During the sixties, Ramo sought to orient TRW's systems-engineering resources toward civil projects in California such as water resource management, land-use planning, and transportation systems.[12]

Ramo was confident that his interdisciplinary management style could coordinate plowshares as well as swords. He considered NASA's Apollo program, the peacetime descendant of Atlas, as the organizational model to apply to other large-scale civic endeavors. Many of his best engineers had gone on to important management roles in the space agency, and TRW had been a major NASA contractor.

Regardless of whether the impetus derived from domestic priorities or Cold War imperatives, however, well-articulated goals assumed paramount importance. At its core, systems analysis was mission oriented. Systems engineers were trained to transcend disciplines in order to grasp interconnections and were accustomed to communicating a central vision to more specialized engineers. A central vision, Ramo maintained, facilitated negotiations and trade-offs at the level of the subsystem. The challenge of environmental degradation provided a compelling example. In lieu of landing a man on the moon in a decade, Ramo frequently cited the idea of "depolluting" the Great Lakes in that same time frame. The act of defining the mission, he maintained, would mobilize the proper expertise, encourage resource budgeting, stimulate technological innovation, and force policymakers and the public to confront hard choices. Presumably for Ramo, congressional initiative would stimulate the proper systems response.[13]

Tunney's national standard incorporated all these ideas. As he later told the subcommittee, the common theme that all the systems engineers sounded during their discussions of environmental problems "was that unless you have a goal which is attainable . . . and unless you have a timetable to achieve that goal, there is no way that you can bring to bear available resources in the most feasible and practical way to achieve the goal. That was the whole basis of getting to the moon and it is what they say is so terribly difficult in getting the aerospace industry involved in mass transit or other problems that deal with society and politics." When Tunney first floated his proposal publicly in May 1971, the handsome young politician, who was so often compared to John Kennedy, appropriated both Kennedy's rhetoric and Ramo's example, wondering aloud whether cleaning the nation's waters in a decade was any more challenging than landing a man on the moon within that same time frame.[14]

Although Muskie did not express much initial enthusiasm for the Tunney amendment, its political implications soon became apparent. On 8 June, four days after the California senator had officially submitted his proposal, Leon Billings received a call from a *Newsweek* reporter, who wondered if Muskie's rumored opposition to the new "swimming standard" indicated that he had "gotten cold feet" regarding national standards and deadlines, just as he had with the Clean Air Act.[15]

Despite media speculation, however, Muskie had not snubbed the Californian's proposal. Far from being dismissed, the Tunney amendment became the centerpiece of the subcommittee's discussions and evolving draft bill over the next two months. Politics must have factored into the chairman's decision to devote so much time to the upstart ideas of a freshman senator. If Muskie planned to vie for the Democratic presidential nomination the following year, drawing the photogenic young senator's endorsement away from his friend Ted Kennedy would boost the campaign. Observers were already touting Tunney as a possible vice presidential nominee.[16]

Apart from the electoral angle, Muskie surely recalled the lessons of the Clean Air Act. With the public more amenable than ever before to ambitious environmental legislation, opportunities existed for entrepreneurial legislators and the White House to take bold initiatives. The idea of a uniform national ambient standard for water quality may have seemed as impractical to implement now as it had during the sixties, but if the chairman wished to retain his stature as the nation's primary pollution control expert, he could not afford to be perceived as inflexible or impervious to new ideas. Impracticalities aside, Tunney's national water quality standard distinguished the revamped bill from its predecessors and imposed tough sanctions on polluters.[17]

As the subcommittee's colloquy over the next month suggested, the standard's simplicity represented both its greatest strength and weakness. "We are saying that by 1980 you are going to be able to swim in water anywhere in the country if this law is enforced," Muskie informed his colleagues during a closed-session vetting of the Tunney amendment in early June. "We want to have a pretty good idea that is going to be done." It soon became clear, however, that the chairman harbored serious doubts about whether it could. Muskie described Tunney's proposal as "impossible through any realistic appraisal of the economic impact . . . on manufacturers, on jobs and so on." The staff estimated that the price tag could run as high as $40 or $50 billion.[18]

Staff director Leon Billings viewed the Tunney standard skeptically, but he did appreciate the potential advantages of its clarity. The value of any such standard rested in its ability to shift the burden of proof away from those who wanted to improve water quality to those who wished to degrade it. Currently, he noted, communities and industries armed with data on economic feasibility easily foiled attempts to upgrade local waterways. A statutory standard, however, would require those who wished to depart from it to justify their position. Placing that onus on polluters, Billings asserted, would constitute a complete restructuring of the national water quality program. Implicit in the staff director's argument was the precedent of the Clean Air Act. In 1970, the subcommittee had mandated national ambient air quality standards to protect human health, a straightforward policy goal that overrode counterarguments about technological or economic feasibility. The Tunney standard might prove useful because it articulated a goal the public understood and stood to promote uniformity in local implementation.[19]

For the chairman, however, simple was not synonymous with meaningful. Muskie viewed air and water pollution control as distinct fields with different policy histories, technological specifications, and implementation challenges. Although he believed the auto industry had the capacity to meet the

Clean Air Act's tough emissions standards, the same could not be said of all the various industries facing the Tunney standard. Likewise, he had doubts about a human health rationale for water pollution because its utility for defining and justifying ambient standards was limited. Localities traditionally determined the value of water as a function of many different beneficial uses and drew their fresh water supplies from distant reservoirs rather than local polluted sources—not an option for air. What the Tunney standard portended as a national standard was not any clearer than public health. Muskie pointed to the difficulty members and staff had in attempting to articulate what the standard actually meant as a measure of achievement. The public could hardly comprehend a national standard if the subcommittee could not define it satisfactorily for themselves.[20]

The vagueness of the Tunney amendment, the chairman feared, would be magnified in its implementation. The challenge facing the subcommittee remained the same as it had been in the sixties: how to compel the states to upgrade their designated water-use classifications, and by extension, the ambient condition of their lakes and streams. But a national "swimmable" standard promised none of the suggested uniformity or certainty—as a practical matter it couldn't be enforced the same way everywhere. The EPA would have to account for variations in regional economies as well as the physical characteristics of waterways, rendering the original national target "laughable and meaningless."[21]

When dealing with water, then, standard setting by legislative fiat carried inherent risks. Muskie emphasized the difficulties entailed in "setting a standard that then by some political process must be lowered to meet the practical [exigencies] of a local situation, whether it is economic or something else." The senator still bore the scars associated with having promoted a beet processing plant on Maine's Prestile Stream several years earlier. The potato processing industry had already befouled the Prestile where the plant was to be built, so no bank would finance the new venture. With Muskie's blessing, the legislature temporarily lowered the stream classification to allow for additional effluent discharge. Even though the new plant eventually employed a closed-cycle system, the senator still suffered a black eye among conservationists. Muskie also recalled the consternation that had ensued in 1968 in the wake of the deceptively simple federal "nondegradation" guideline, especially among underdeveloped areas that resented any potential restrictions on growth. "If there is that much difficulty in preserving the purity of water which is now pure," he feared "the task of . . . making those waterways which are now dirty meet a similar standard." Likewise, assigning a strict deadline to an ambitious water quality target like the Tunney standard promised to overwhelm and antagonize state administrators.[22]

Refining the Tunney Standard: The Search for Meaning

Nearly a month after Tunney introduced his proposal, Muskie determined that the subcommittee had still not identified a national standard that satisfied him, or one to which a timetable could be attached. The senator from California continued to lobby, but the chairman insisted that he still needed "some definition of it before we can react to it." The subcommittee spent a considerable portion of its time during the following month attempting to develop a suitable definition. Systems thinking had gotten Tunney only so far. As words themselves became the focus of debate, he decided to cast a wider net to fill in the details.[23]

The senator and his aides spent the next several weeks consulting with industrialists, environmentalists, committee members, and staff to add substance and specificity to the national minimum standard. Tunney decided at some point in late June or early July to couple the recreational component of his standard with one related specifically to fish and wildlife. The new language defined the national minimum water quality standard as "that level of water quality . . . which shall provide for the protection of any indigenous shellfish, fish and wildlife and allow recreational activities in and on the water." By 19 July, Tunney and the subcommittee staff had modified this language as well. Reviewers from the public interest group Environmental Action feared that the vague term "indigenous" would detract from the standard's enforceability. A slug worm content to ply the deoxygenated waters of a grossly polluted stream might be deemed indigenous, just as easily as the bass or trout that used to reside there. Partly on the basis of this objection, and in consultation with EPA water criteria specialists, the subcommittee staff substituted the phrase "the protection of a balanced population of naturally recurring shellfish, fish, and wildlife."[24]

Although Tunney proposed the new wording to add clarity to his intentions, Muskie viewed the revised draft as a Pandora's box of ambiguity. The often terse exchange between the chairman and the junior senator in executive session became, in essence, a debate about language. Muskie deconstructed the phrasing of Tunney's standard, demanding to know what each word implied about what Congress would require of the states.

The words "naturally recurring" drew most of Muskie's ire. It was unclear to the chairman exactly what "natural" meant, or what it implied as a policy prescription. Tunney's standard seemed premised on a baseline level of water purity, measured at some time prior to the onset of industrial society. Presumably, a stream existing in such a virgin state would be capable of supporting various species of aquatic life that may not have inhabited its waters in recent human memory. Salmon, for example, would qualify as a "natural" species of Maine's Kennebeck River, even though they hadn't been pulled out of its waters since the nineteenth century. Returning to the state of purity that General Arnold found when he paused to feed salmon to his Quebec-bound army, Muskie noted, would require state officials to eliminate the dams as well as the pollution. Muskie likewise echoed the objections expressed by Environmental Action over the word "indigenous." No one wanted a standard fit for a slug worm, he noted, but where should state officials draw the line, and on what basis, referenced to what point in time? To the chairman, the wording of the national standard, taken at face value, pointed toward an unworkable end. "Why don't you just say what you seem to mean," Muskie challenged Tunney, "that the objective is to restore every waterway to its pristine purity."[25]

Tunney responded to this interrogation with a defense of ambiguity in the service of ecology. The senator's replies suggested that his ultimate aim was for the revised standard to promote ecosystems in a reasonable state of equilibrium, although his words were hardly that precise or technical. "We decided that it would be advisable to be just a bit vague in the standard," he informed Muskie, "because I think a balanced population of naturally occurring shellfish, fish and wildlife certainly make it very clear that what you want is a balanced ecology." Such a functioning environment assumed "that you have fish and you assume that you have a food chain which will provide food for the fish to develop." Pollution, the senator implied, disrupted this balance, leading to practical manifestations of ecological and economic degradation, like reduced catches and a shrinking fishing industry along the coast of California. Tunney simply chose to express ecological ideas with a sanitarian's

vocabulary—state regulators always considered the maintenance of fish populations as a legitimate "beneficial use" of a stream—and preferred not to get
too wrapped up in the details.[26]

Unfortunately, traditional language failed to satisfy Muskie when policy
ambitions were without precedent and the precision of words took on even
greater significance. He contended that the standard's vague wording promised only to muddle the legislation's objective and complicate pragmatic regulatory action. "When you talk about setting a standard against which you
can prosecute people, apply enforcement procedures against . . . as well as
give plant managers and engineers some standard by which to design their
pollution control equipment, you have to have something that is pretty precise," Muskie insisted.[27]

Tunney remained confident that the committee could promulgate some
general standard capable of ordering national priorities, just as Simon Ramo
had advocated. He believed Muskie's concerns about vagueness were overstated, because the national standard was more grounded in the customs
and practices of the nation's water pollution officials than the chairman realized. He surprised Muskie by informing him that Environmental Action had
adapted its fish and wildlife language from a standard already instituted by
the Delaware River Basin Commission. Tunney later presented evidence il-
lustrating that water quality standards "at least as broad as the one which I
have proposed are currently being applied and enforced all over the country."
The senator's staff cited regulations from California, Texas, the Midwest, and
even federal statutes—all of which included language describing recreation
and maintenance of aquatic life as beneficial uses. The proposed national
standard, they argued, expressed goals that pollution officials nationwide
comprehended and accepted.[28]

Tunney's search for meaning, initiated at Muskie's behest, allowed environmentalists to influence the subcommittee's deliberations in a direct way.
Simon Ramo and the aerospace engineers may have inspired the concept
of the national standard, but its substance over time derived from the input of more traditional water pollution experts, as well as from public interest groups. When the Delaware River Basin Commission precedent caught
Muskie unawares, he called for further information on similar regulations.
Once again, Tunney's analysis stemmed from his staff's contact with seventeen or eighteen different state water boards and about ten university sci-

entists. They also returned to Barbara Reid, the director of Environmental Action, and to David Zwick, a Ralph Nader protégé and author of *Water Wasteland*, the companion piece to *Vanishing Air*. These environmental advocates already enjoyed more direct access to the subcommittee through sympathetic staffers like Billings and Jorling. But Tunney's need for experts increased their leverage, creating opportunities to enlist the media and press their advantage. Specifically, Reid served as the main source for a 23 July report in the *Washington Star* that promoted the Tunney amendment while portraying Muskie as a stubborn detractor who "raised all sorts of questions about [its] feasibility" and thus thwarted stronger federal legislation. Tunney was mortified at the negative coverage and attributed the story to his reliance on external expertise. Muskie responded by suggesting that members and staff exercise more discretion with the press but emphasized that he had not yet taken a firm position on the Tunney amendment.[29]

Whether Muskie admitted it or not, however, Environmental Action's public relations offensive all but precluded any retreat on Tunney's proposal. If the subcommittee's legislation didn't include a version of the national standard, it would need to boast of something similarly ambitious. The chairman's proclamations of neutrality aside, as of late July, he and the staff continued to hold out for a standard more meaningful than that provided by Tunney's recreation and wildlife language. Muskie offered no hint of what that alternative might be, however, until the pivotal 28 July executive session, when he interrupted a mid-afternoon discussion to alert his colleagues to "the idea that has come to me in the mail."

The Ecologist's Alternative: "Integrity"

Once again, systems thinking returned to the forefront and helped structure how legislators framed an environmental problem. The missive Muskie held up bore the letterhead of Brookhaven National Laboratories. Its author was George Woodwell, one of the scientific advisors the Public Works Committee had retained in 1970 following the passage of NEPA. In that capacity, the ecologist had reviewed the most recent print of the water pollution bill and offered over three pages of suggestions.

It was the letter's second paragraph that captured the chairman's attention, for it touched on the very issue of policy objectives that continued to trouble him. "There is nowhere in the bill, as I have seen it, a clear, technically defined statement of objectives in controlling water pollution," Woodwell asserted. "I would suggest that the objective be, in addition to those listed, *"maintenance of the chemical, physical, and biological integrity of all waters, including lakes, streams, rivers, estuaries, and oceans."* The chairman sensed an opening in these words. "We would have to define it the same way as we are trying to define this other thing," he noted, referring to the Tunney standard, but "one thing that strikes me about it is that it is an attempted definition of what the river ought to be in its natural state."[30]

John Tunney's unprecedented water quality standard relied upon a traditional "beneficial use" vocabulary that, Muskie worried, could never define the "natural state" of a stream with the precision necessary for proper implementation. But Woodwell resorted to an ecological idiom to describe similarly ambitious water pollution policy objectives. The chairman interpreted the shift in discourse as an opportunity to establish an element of exactitude only a systems-oriented science could provide.

"Integrity" served as the keystone for the entire endeavor. The term did not merely connote a static, utilitarian determination of a water body's condition at a discrete moment in time, as did beneficial-use designations. Rather, it suggested a quantifiable state of dynamic equilibrium. Woodwell's research experience led him to view human pollution as a source of chronic, short-term stress that compromised biogeochemical cycles calibrated through eons of evolutionary stimulus. Adopting the systemic perspective of the ecologist, he suggested, would enable policymakers to use a variety of yardsticks, from mineral cycling to biological diversity, to measure and articulate a standard of quality befitting the nation's waters. Woodwell himself preferred to prohibit "the release of any substance [into public waters] not represented in the natural flux of mineral and organic matter," and to limit the "modification of minerals and organics . . . to "10% of the natural flux."[31]

Muskie recognized that the idea of a self-contained, self-regulating system inherent in Woodwell's concept of "integrity" offered a practical remedy for a series of legislative dilemmas. Not the least of these was communicating the purpose of a policy that portended significant social costs. John Tunney had followed the prescription of systems engineers in his effort to stimulate rational, interdisciplinary responses to a complex environmental management problem. The chairman did not necessarily quarrel with Tunney's or Ramo's faith in systems thinking. In fact, he shared it, as did most postwar policy-makers seeking to manage complex systems, be they missile defenses, welfare programs, natural environments, or environmental bureaucracies.

His problem centered on Tunney's choice of words. The language the chairman preferred reflected the inherent systems-faith professed by ecosystem ecologists, whose highly technical discipline had, like Ramo's, come of age in the wake of thermonuclear explosions. By 1971, Ed Muskie looked to the ecologists to provide a working vocabulary for Ramo's social-industrial mission: articulating environmental objectives that the public could appreciate, experts and administrators could implement, and all parties would acknowledge as scientifically grounded. A natural system's steady state, measured and expressed in terms of thermodynamic equilibrium, nutrient cycling, and species diversity, afforded Muskie a conception of a stream's pre-industrial status that he could work with comfortably—indeed, that allowed him to contemplate such quality goals seriously. "I like the language in this letter," he informed his colleagues; "the natural condition is what we want to get. I think these words would tend to evolve that picture." By contrast, "old words" like those found in traditional statutory language about fish and wildlife presented an obstacle, since they delineated categories of water use rather than specific statutory objectives.[32]

The committee staff agreed that Woodwell's systems ecology provided a quantitative, scientifically based alternative to Tunney's vague swimmable/fishable language. The focal point of the policy, Leon Billings contended, "should be the ecological system," and "integrity . . . must be the key word," even if this new language did not comport with the sanitary engineering profession's conventional understanding. Of course, given the tangible transformations that had occurred in the political culture, the new terminology would also resonate beyond the realm of experts. "I think the words ecosystem, or ecological system or ecology [have] enough currency in the public at large," Muskie informed his colleagues, "so that the public at large would understand the thrust of this language."[33]

Muskie's and the staff's embrace of ecological integrity, however, did not yet signal a dramatic shift in legislative emphasis. Muskie's own grasp of the concept was still sketchy. The staff, meanwhile, had no firm idea where to insert the "Woodwell Policy" into the text of the bill. Nor did the new wording immediately replace the swimmable/fishable standard. Even John Tunney initially assumed that Woodwell's language could be incorporated seamlessly into the existing framework.[34]

In time, however, the committee would grasp "ecological integrity" as a wedge to displace Tunney's amendment and establish the technical and intellectual basis for an entirely new water pollution control strategy. By October, when the committee reported their completed work to the full Senate, their revised understanding of integrity gave rise to an alternative regulatory objective—"zero-discharge"—as ambitious as the Tunney standard.

Nonpoint Pollution, Regional Planning, and the Emergence of Zero-Discharge

Ironically, the Clean Water Act's transformation came about as the subcommittee continued to grapple with the practical and political implications of swimmable/fishable waters. Taking the unprecedented goal seriously compelled the staff to design an innovative blueprint for regional water quality planning, intended to solve a number of persistent pollution control problems that Congress had evaded in the past. This "waste management" program also emerged as a logical corollary of systems thinking and its alluring progeny, ecological integrity. Implementing it, however, required an agency sufficiently attuned to that logic, with the capacity to plan and manage water resource systems on the requisite scale. Once the weapons designers, environmentalists, and ecologists had their say, the Army Corps of Engineers stepped in to provide just the institutional synthesis the subcommittee was looking for.

For Leon Billings and Tom Jorling, the specter of nonpoint source pollution helped inspire their eventual turn to regional planning, and by extension, the wholesale revision of the subcommittee's legislation. Mining activities, agricultural practices, construction activities, and sewer overflows accounted for a significant volume of the pollution that drained into streams and watersheds. But since this waterborne waste could not be traced to any discrete source, remedying it meant broaching local land-use regulation, a political third rail Congress habitually eschewed.

Senator Tunney's amendment converted nonpoint source pollution from a chronic, ignored quandary into an urgent predicament in the summer of 1971. Billings and Jorling soon realized that if fishable and swimmable waters were to be seriously adopted as a national goal, then it was critical that the new federal pollution program address the control of diffuse run-off from rural and urban communities. The national standard, after all, was an ambient quality standard. Even if the legislation managed to tighten the spigot on industrial and municipal effluent, watershed drainage still contained a substantial-enough load of nutrients, pesticides, and other chemicals to render almost any waterway in violation of federal law.[35]

The logic of the Tunney amendment seemed to dictate much tighter regulations on nonpoint pollution, a trend Billings and Jorling independently supported, at least initially. But the staff soon had second thoughts. Although early bill drafts required state implementation plans to include "controls" for nonpoint pollution sources, by the end of July the legislation no longer applied statutory timetables to nonpoint pollution as it did to stationary sources. Criminal penalties, Billings explained, "do not seem applicable to this kind of pollution."[36]

Billings's evolving concern about regulating nonpoint pollution fueled a critique of the Tunney standard that focused less on its meaningfulness, per se, than on its achievability and economic justification. "Because implementation of [Tunney's] standard would require a major investment in such problems as combined sewer overflow, urban surface run-off, . . . agriculture waste management, mine waste control, controls over forest cutting practices, and a host of land use measures," he advised the chairman, it portended a de facto expansion of the federal pollution program's purview, and hence its price tag. Billings feared that many localities—particularly small farm communities—would bear a crippling financial burden if mandatory nonpoint controls were instituted. Even if the federal government possessed the technical knowledge to implement such controls, which he and Jorling doubted, "effective implementation would require an increasingly strong federal involvement in land use," something which agricultural interests explicitly opposed. Urban water officials, meanwhile, emphasized that most cities could not even expect to implement current quality standards without federal assistance to separate storm and sanitary sewers, a daunting task estimated to cost more money than Muskie's generous bill offered—between $15 and $47 billion. The staff director thus questioned whether the national standard was achievable by Tunney's "date certain" or was politically feasible to implement.[37]

Billings's caveats did not kill the Tunney standard, but they did alter the tactics staff members adopted to render it feasible. Accounting for technological limits and practical political barriers, they reasoned that no pollution control program could achieve national waters of swimmable/fishable quality, within a limited time frame, by attacking nonpoint pollution directly. Ignoring the issue, of course, invited failure. Ultimately, Billings and Jorling chose a flanking maneuver. They decided to concentrate their efforts where the current pollution control system exerted the most leverage in terms of technology and experience—at pipe's end. In order to have any hope of reaching the Tunney standard, the legislation would need to encourage an even more drastic reduction of point source effluent, with a heavier emphasis on recycling and outright reclamation of wastewater. This strategy would allow some latitude for a program of minimally coercive state incentives to begin to redress more diffuse nonpoint sources.[38]

The specific innovations Billings and Jorling pursued were organizational rather than strictly regulatory. The path to upgraded treatment technology did not run through the regulatory program (Title III). Instead, the staff opened up a second front by expanding the function of the grant program for sewage treatment plant construction (Title II). By combining legislative mandates and financial incentives to create new institutional arrangements, they hoped to facilitate authentic planning on a regional basis. To that end, Title II, Section 209, outlined a procedure to designate "waste treatment management" regions. These administrative units, geared toward the construction and systematic coordination of point source control, were also expected to address nonpoint pollution.[39]

Billings and Jorling had originally conceived Section 209 to address the 1969 GAO critique of the federal sewage treatment grant program. The idea for regional planning organizations grew out of the search for "a method of achieving a systems approach over a definable geographic area" to coordinate the administration of Title II grant applications, as the GAO had suggested. The staff sought to create, in Billings's words, "a specific stimulator mechanism in the law to force . . . metropolitan regions to get together and plan." Under Section 209, local operating agencies would be able to identify facility needs, establish priorities, and bolster treatment efficiency through the promotion of economies of scale. Regional planning units also offered the best hope of promoting integrated, comprehensive land-use management and industrial siting policies.[40]

The staff's innovation took on greater significance once they realized how it dovetailed with Tunney's nonpoint pollution dilemma. The staff and the comptroller general both recommended a systems approach to planning, but their reasons for doing so differed. The GAO looked to systems analysis primarily to optimize limited financial resources. Billings and Jorling, however, sought to optimize the purity of effluent loads. In order to meet the Tunney standard, coordinated regional management had to facilitate upgrades in treatment technology and encourage its application on a much greater scale. But if the committee hoped to replace conventional treatment methods and displace sanitary engineering's prevailing technical dominance, an ecological alternative that delivered on the promise of planning and wastewater recycling had to stand ready to take its place.

Land, Ecology, and the Corps

John Sheaffer and the Corps of Engineers were poised to provide that alternative. The Public Works Committee staff first learned of the Corps' innovative sewage treatment program in Muskegon County, Michigan, from Hugh Mields, the longtime spokesman for the U.S. Conference of Mayors. Mields had attended a 1970 conference on "achieving environmental quality in a developmental economy," where Sheaffer, the Muskegon project director, impressed him with a presentation on "total water resource management." If the Muskegon project performed as advertised, Mields told Muskie's aides, "we ought to take steps to make sure the waste treatment grants program starts to encourage . . . the eventual conversion of our entire system to this obviously superior approach." Coming from one of the most effective lobbyists for federal sewage treatment grants to cities, this was high praise indeed.[41]

In the context of the Tunney amendment, it made even more sense to expedite a shift in treatment technology by exploiting incentives in the federal grant program. By late July, the staff determined to take steps in this direction. Tom Jorling argued that Section 209's regional waste management approach facilitated the transition to the "most advanced, ecologically sound treatment" options. But because "traditional sanitary engineering" was "so woven into the water program," the provisions of the Title II grant program required explicit wording. Accordingly, the staff established "the recycling of pollutants and the reclamation of water, including confined and contained disposal on land of pollutants" as the grant program's first priority.[42]

Land disposal technology posed a tenable solution for the challenge presented by the Tunney standard, but its grounding in fundamental ecological precepts also resonated with the committee staff. Tom Jorling's positive response reflected his professional background, as well as the expert analysis of people he trusted, particularly the committee's scientific advisors, George Woodwell and Gene Likens. Likens cited his research at Hubbard Brook Experimental Forest to underscore how knowledge of biogeochemical cycles and other quantitative tools could "provide both a theoretical and a practical basis for the management and regulation of our freshwater resources." He criticized "technologists" (i.e., sanitary engineers) who ignored the complex interconnections between aquatic and terrestrial ecosystems and concluded that such sanitarian staples as dilution and partial (secondary) treatment were inadequate responses to current pollution loads. Woodwell concurred, telling Muskie that "the objectives of this bill will require much more than a simple proliferation of conventional sewage plants."[43]

John Sheaffer's pitch to the committee dovetailed perfectly with the analysis of its ecological experts and the needs of the staff. His formal presentation of the Muskegon system took place in executive session on 26 July, but staffers had already conducted an on-site inspection of the facility prior to that. By the time Billings and Jorling introduced the revised Section 209 program to Muskie on 27 July, the land treatment option had assumed an integral role in the blueprint. Jorling came to view Muskegon as a viable solution for the practical problems associated with the Tunney standard that also happened to conform to the professional prescription of the ecologists.[44]

Muskegon applied the concept of integrity to the process of municipal waste management. It promised ecologically sound alternatives for point and nonpoint pollution in precisely those challenging urban-industrial concentrations covered under Section 209. Jorling cited the Corps' five pilot studies in Boston, Cleveland, Detroit, San Francisco, and Chicago to suggest the project's general applicability. The land-based "living filter" eliminated receiving waters from the operation entirely, he noted, while containing, "in an integrated fashion for the entire region," the storm sewer overflows and urban run-off that threatened to render the Tunney standard unfeasible. Re-gional planning would force communities to ratchet up their technological capabilities and embrace the state of the art, which promised to save money in the long run. Moreover, Jorling argued, the Section 209 program allowed local communities to bypass the monopoly of expertise commanded by tra-ditional treatment grant bureaucracies and enlist the Corps' own repository of technical knowledge. Indeed, Section 209 did what the 1970 Institute for Water Resources Report had recommended: It recruited the Corps' planning capacity to serve the federal water pollution control program.[45]

The staff members' faith in the Corps' land disposal program had far-reaching consequences for the entire scope of the legislation. Not only did it inspire them, in late July, to weight the distribution of grant money in favor of such systems, it also led them to institute a de facto prohibition of mu-nicipal and industrial effluent within the context of Section 209. As Billings informed members of the committee, the definition of waste treatment man-agement "for the purposes of point sources in a designated region would be, unless otherwise shown, a no-discharge standard." Regional operating agen-cies would now be required to install land-based treatment facilities as their primary waste management apparatus. To foster compliance, traditional sanitary waste treatment works would no longer be eligible for federal grant money after 1974. Similar prohibitions did not apply to nonpoint pollution, but that was the intention. To begin to address nonpoint problems in a mini-mally intrusive way, while attempting to retain a national ambient standard, the legislation had to compel the elimination of point source pollution. The Tunney amendment effectively forced the issue.[46]

Muskie suddenly found himself with a grant program—John Blatnik's leg-acy of distributive politics—that set more stringent performance standards than the putative regulatory program did. He also discovered a planning pro-gram that broke with precedent and established centers of municipal popu-lation and industrial concentration, rather than geographically defined river basins, as the basic regional unit. Most important, even though the Tunney standard remained a point of reference, the focus of future regional operat-ing agencies would be effluent controls (and ultimately zero-discharge), not ambient standards per se. In other words, as Billings explained to Muskie, "in a river basin approach you are talking about the quality of the water, and in this approach you are talking about quality of waste discharge."[47]

John Tunney soon realized that the Section 209 program, though conceived with his amendment in mind, actually stood to displace the entire concept of a national ambient standard. Sheaffer's presentation had impressed the senator, and he supported the regional approach. But Tunney felt that the 1974 funding cutoff date for conventional treatment facilities instituted a de facto policy initiative that defined the legislation's overriding objective. This was not a choice the senators could make by default. Muskie immediately grasped the senator's point. "Obviously," the chairman observed, "if your objective is to prohibit all discharges into receiving waters, then you don't need a national minimum water quality standard." The former saw effluent control technology as the end in itself, while the latter approached technology as a means to an end.[48]

The Section 209 program called not only the Tunney standard into question, but all ambient standards. In so doing, it rekindled a debate first initiated by Senator Howard Baker back in June. Baker, an incisive legal mind with a talent for plain speaking and a background in engineering, emphasized that setting and enforcing effluent limits provided the most direct, uniform, and equitable way to apportion responsibility among polluters and track their compliance. The quality of water ultimately depended on the technology applied to reduce emissions, the Tennessee Republican reasoned, and relying on American technological prowess was the best hope for protecting the environment. The Clean Air Act's emission standards provided a model, but Baker contemplated going even further than the 1970 statute had. The senator suggested forgoing ambient standards entirely, which he admitted meant "in effect, repeal[ing] all of our water statutes and start[ing] over from scratch."[49]

Now the evolution of the bill's regional waste treatment provisions allowed Billings to articulate a "Baker option" alongside the Tunney proposal when summarizing various broad policy outlines. As the staff director understood it, Baker's approach treated ambient water quality as a measure of an effluent control program's performance, that is, as a general indication of progress, not as a legal basis for enforcement. Water quality was to be indexed strictly to available technology, qualified by some sort of economic feasibility test. The Refuse Act permit program presaged such a system, although the Nixon administration retained ambient quality as the programmatic end.[50]

As ambivalent as Ed Muskie remained about Tunney's strategy, however, he seemed unprepared to jettison an established regulatory precedent purely on the basis of an untested treatment technology, despite the staff's obvious enthusiasm. The Muskegon project was not even up and running, the chairman complained, "and yet on the basis of this one prototype, you are willing to make hard and fast comparisons to another system that didn't develop its weaknesses until it had been operated and tried and 5 billion dollars had been spent." The suddenness with which the staff had anointed land disposal also gave him pause. "It surfaced on the one day I haven't been here," Muskie told Billings pointedly, "and in that one day you found out the whole answer to the problem we have been laboring over all year."[51]

The chairman and the staff of the Senate Public Works Committee approached land disposal technology from different perspectives. Muskie viewed Muskegon as one of a number of technological approaches to the water pollution problem—innovative, promising, but as yet untried. Billings and Jorling seemed to view Muskegon as a technology that departed from the technological. It was "not . . . a technology that must be proved," Jorling insisted, but rather "the utilization of nature to perform its normal biogeochemical functions." Jorling distinguished the "technological instruments" of sanitary engineering from ecology's own brand of systems management. The former imposed a linear waste treatment methodology on complex ecosystems; the latter aligned human activities with the biogeochemical processes of nature, which, he concluded, was the only way "[we will] restore our nation's water quality on a long term basis."[52]

Muskie managed to overcome the reservations of minority members— and set aside his own—in time to preserve the original 6 August release date for the committee print of the bill. Apart from their concerns about an erosion of state autonomy, regional waste management proved to be a critical sticking point among Republicans because, as Billings reported, "it is new and because it implies land disposal of wastes." He urged the chairman to retain the bill in its entirety, including the controversial Section 209 section. "If a national goal is to be set and a meaningful deadline to be met for most waters," Billings pleaded, "*all* of these tools are necessary."[53]

The 6 August working draft, with its many complex, unreconciled segments, remained a work in progress. Although Muskie's ambivalence about the Tunney amendment had not abated, his legislation retained ambient standards as its central regulatory feature. It established a two-tiered program: states had to meet the ambient standards they approved under the 1965

Senators Howard Baker (R-Tenn.) and Muskie examine a steam-powered automobile, while staff director Leon Billings looks on. Courtesy of the Edmund S. Muskie Archives and Special Collections Library.

Water Quality Act no later than 1976 and devise plans to achieve swimmable/ fishable waters by 1980, unless they could demonstrate that the economic and social costs of the latter bore "no reasonable relationship" to the expected benefits (the so-called Bentsen test). On the other hand, Title II's planning and technology priorities introduced a separate, "no-discharge" benchmark that made effluent controls, not ambient quality, the key variable. This formulation, inspired by the Tunney standard's complications and the Corps of Engineers' water quality management aspirations, did not fit with the rest of the bill's content.

Executive Caveats

The legislation's final metamorphosis during the fall, however, tilted the balance in favor of emissions-only standards and "zero-discharge," a step Ed

Muskie had not taken before even in the context of the Clean Air Act. Absent Woodwell's evocative concept of ecological integrity, it is unlikely that the staff would have suggested, or the chairman would have signed off on, such a significant change. But the immediate catalyst for this October surprise was the Nixon administration. Its efforts to roll back what Nixon's point man on environmental issues, John Whitaker, called the summer's "radical rewrite" unwittingly inspired an even more radical alternative.[54]

The legislation's revised regulatory program posed the biggest stumbling block for the White House. Budget officials bemoaned the "damn-the-dollars-full-speed-ahead" authorizations for treatment plant construction and combined-sewer separation ($8 billion more than Nixon proposed). But the 1976 target date for current standards and the 1980 swimmable/fishable standard struck Whitaker and his colleagues at the EPA and the Council on Environmental Quality as "unachievable and irrational." Although the White House supported an enforcement strategy centered around ambient standards, statutory deadlines added a troubling degree of urgency reminiscent of the Clean Air Act. The prospect of enforcing a national swimmable/fishable standard on a deadline bothered the administration even more.[55]

In a long series of conversations, the EPA tried to dissuade the committee from imposing a single level of ambient water quality nationwide, particularly one so ambitious as Tunney's, by underscoring the inherent technical difficulties involved. The familiar problem of nonpoint source pollution came in for repeated emphasis. But no argument had more of an impact on the staff's thinking than the EPA's discussion of cause and effect. To achieve any desired level of ambient water quality, dischargers along a waterway had to reduce emissions in proportion to the degree of enhancement desired. For a given industrial process, it proved challenging enough to gauge the technology required to meet proposed effluent limitations, as EPA officials discovered during the administration of the Refuse Act permit program. But drawing a precise causal connection between the ambient condition of a waterway and the content of the effluent flowing into it was extremely difficult. As a matter of law, the agency argued, a regulatory program seeking to enforce standards and timetables would have problems ascribing liability among dischargers in a manner that could withstand legal scrutiny.[56]

EPA director William Ruckelshaus sensed the committee staff's receptivity to his arguments, and the administration began criticizing the Tunney amendment more publicly. In hearings before the House Public Works Committee on 16 September, Council on Environmental Quality chairman Russell Train bluntly rejected swimmable waters as a feasible goal by 1980. These stepped-up attacks drew the quick reproach of Environmental Action, Friends of the Earth, and the Sierra Club, who accused the White House and industrial interests of attempting to weaken Muskie's legislation. But the committee's staff had already taken the administration's protestations to heart.[57]

Rejecting Assimilative Capacity: The Ecological Advantages of Zero-Discharge

To the surprise of both environmentalists and the Nixon administration, Billings and Jorling, with Muskie's blessing, had not only decided to jettison the Tunney standard, but the entire mechanism of ambient quality control it exemplified. Instead, they introduced a regulatory system based exclusively on emissions controls. The EPA never intended its critique to push them that far. It meant only to neutralize the "extreme and unworkable" Tunney proposal and quiet the clamor for strict deadlines. Its appeal, however, resonated with a staff both dissatisfied with the Tunney standard and increasingly disposed to depart from an ambient strategy. The logic of ecology, specifically Woodwell's definition of integrity, nurtured this inclination. In this context, the EPA had not merely rebutted the Tunney amendment, it had helped expose the conceptual limitations of the 1965 Water Quality Act, discredit ambient standards as a viable regulatory mechanism, and legitimize another radical objective: zero-discharge.[58]

For the staff, the concept of integrity exposed the "ecological fictions" underlying the fundamental tenets of sanitary engineering. Sanitary engineers assumed that aquatic systems had a natural capacity to absorb pollutants that could be calculated mathematically and factored into sewage treatment requirements. Jorling and the committee's ecologist-in-residence, Walter Westman, insisted that streams could not function as waste sinks, since matter and energy moved in cyclical, not linear, pathways. But the "ultimate pitfall" of the engineering method, they asserted, was that it required "pollution enforcement officials to have the unassailable ability to predict the effect that an effluent will have on the ecology of a water body." Sanitary engineers measured organic wastes according to aggregate references (biological oxygen demand, pH, fecal coliform) and were ill-equipped to describe the chemical complexities of industrial emissions or their impact on aquatic ecosystems. Because accurate calculations of assimilative capacity outstripped contemporary technical abilities, ambient standards based on those calculations amounted to "rough estimates" more attuned to local economic considerations than ecological ones. Legal contrivances like mixing zones—areas around outflow pipes that were set aside for waste dilution and exempted from federal regulations—further compromised enforcement efforts.[59]

Faced with the scientific, legal, and practical shortcomings of assimilative capacity, the staff moved to embrace the full policy implications of its conceptual alternative—integrity. From a sanitarian's perspective, an objective like "integrity" or "natural purity" represented an impractical, prohibitively expensive abstraction, because water quality could not be defined apart from the impact of human society. The committee staff turned such thinking on its ear. Jorling later described his working definition of integrity in the most unflinching terms, as "that character of the aquatic ecosystem as it is determined by evolutionary factors including man, *but not technological man.* . . . It is that ecosystem which is a function of evolution. It is a mature non-successional community having been established over geologic time. It is 'background'" (emphasis added). Proper pollution controls had to ensure that human activities would not alter this "background" (the ecosystem's evolutionary rate of change) beyond an acceptable range of "flux." Westman affirmed that only a stream "at or close to pristine natural condition" resembled an ecosystem in balance. Restoring and maintaining its integrity, he suggested, would be more cost-effective in the long run than relying on assimilative capacity.[60]

By the third week of September, the policy implications had become clear enough to the committee staff. If the definition of integrity did not admit of any interaction between modern industrial society and the environment, then emission controls and a zero-discharge target were the only means capable of achieving the level of water quality implied by integrity. Thus a strategy that had emerged in July as an indirect response to nonpoint pollution, in the limited context of Title II's grant and planning programs, now applied to the entire regulatory apparatus.[61]

Over the next month, the staff reworked the bill's two-phased implementation structure to eliminate ambient standards, including Tunney's national standard, and incorporate what Billings had described as the "Baker option." Phase I defined effluent limitations exclusively as a function of treatment technology, with no reference to local receiving water conditions. It set a deadline for a minimum level of pollution control that Billings, Jorling, and EPA officials thought consistent with most current state plans to implement the 1965 Water Quality Act. Industrial polluters had to apply "the best practicable control technology currently available" by 1976, while municipal treatment works were required to install a minimum of secondary treatment by 1977. The staff settled on the term "best practicable technology'" (BPT) as shorthand for the "equivalent of secondary treatment for industry," a vague guideline first articulated by federal administrators in May 1966 and later refined by the EPA for use in the Refuse Act permit program. It was meant to represent "the average of the best existing performance by plants of various sizes, ages, and unit processes within each industrial category."[62]

Phase II, by contrast, moved industries and municipalities toward a considerably more ambitious target: zero-discharge by 1985. It required the installation, at minimum, of the "best available technology" (BAT) by 1981. The committee came to define BAT as a level of technology "that would always be better than something defined as 'best practicable technology,'" and that was determined in reference to at least the very best performer in an industrial category. In certain cases, particularly for new, state-of-the-art-plants, the committee assumed BAT could eliminate discharges—the legislation's new source performance standards, like those in the Clean Air Act, stated as much. Owners of older, marginal plants had the option of routing their effluent into a regional waste treatment management system along the Muskegon model. Phase II also provided for certain reasonable-cost safeguards for retrofitting older facilities with "new source" technology but purposely limited opportunities for case-by-case appeals.[63]

Faced with the evisceration of his celebrated national standard, John Tunney turned the tables on Muskie and the staff. The senator questioned whether their radical rewrite had produced a meaningful, economically justified, or reasonably achievable alternative. Eliminating all municipal and industrial discharges seemed an immensely expensive and "practically impossible" undertaking to him. Moreover, by divorcing technology-based effluent standards from any reference to desired ambient water quality, the program removed the most practical yardstick available to judge progress. Hadn't

Muskie always defended ambient standards for just this reason? Tunney argued that his own standard remained more technically feasible in the short run and communicated policy objectives more clearly.[64]

To be sure, Muskie's position had shifted during the fall, though his intentions had not. The task at hand, as he always understood it, was to establish a pollution control program whose implementation produced tangible results, avoided crippling legal challenges, sustained public confidence, and allowed for continuous advances. It was all too apparent to him by 1971 that the Water Quality Act had failed to do so. The senator realized as well that heightened public expectations demanded serious consideration of unprecedented environmental policy goals. But the question remained: Which strategy and objective would best compel measurable progress?[65]

Once more, the chairman rejected Tunney's standard, but his reasons for doing so this time reflected his staff's critique of all ambient standards as well as the EPA's recent caveats. "I submit that no-discharge is a clearer expression of ultimate intent than a lesser standard [swimmable/fishable waters] that can be said to rely on assimilative capacity," Muskie informed his colleagues. Muskie had never condoned the practice of loading streams to their maximum point of waste absorption and originally viewed ambient standards as a means to discourage it. Now his pejorative reference to "assimilative capacity" seemed to preclude *any* long-term reliance on a stream's absorptive abilities, which Muskie confirmed was "a very uncertain thing" and a dubious foundation for a pollution control policy. The chairman noted that Tunney's "aerospace friends" could not establish a foolproof method for determining the causal relationship between a point source and receiving water quality nor provide a meaningful deadline for swimmable/fishable waters or an accurate accounting of its cost. Over time, federal regulators would be forced to grant multiple exemptions to compensate for inadequate knowledge, program momentum would grind to a halt, and public confidence would dissipate.[66]

Emission standards offered a better alternative. Muskie came to accept Howard Baker's compelling argument that technology remained the only variable Congress could reasonably manipulate, industry could feasibly upgrade, and the administration could reliably monitor. "If you gear your process to increasing controls over effluent discharges, you will have a direct benefit on water quality," Muskie insisted, but working backward from ambient conditions to determine discrete effluent limits "was like trying to unscramble an egg." Emission standards, in short, promised regulatory certitude and national uniformity in a way ambient standards could not.[67]

Muskie may have rejected the particular brand of environmental systems management that John Tunney and Simon Ramo suggested, but the systems thinking of ecologists allowed him to rationalize the legislation's exclusive reliance on technology-based effluent control. Woodwell's concept of integrity not only helped the staff discredit ambient standards, it articulated a public policy goal that the chairman continued to find meaningful and scientifically valid. Neither emissions standards nor zero-discharge stood as detached ends in themselves. Instead, Muskie came to define the legislation's official objective as "restoring and maintaining the chemical, physical, and biological integrity of the waters of the United States through the elimination of the discharges of pollutants by 1985." Such a "clear and definite" statement of commitment gave him confidence to assign specific deadlines to the statute's various phases. In practice, the notion of defining a stream's "integrity" as a yardstick to judge program effectiveness glossed over a host of serious technical and administrative difficulties. For the committee, however, the "Woodwell clause" remained an appealing concept.[68]

The Corps of Engineers' recent institutional adaptations also helped ease the transition to effluent standards. The promise of advanced waste management planning and technology in Title II now meshed more consistently with the objectives of Title III's regulatory blueprint. But so too did the Refuse Act permit program. Having all but ignored it throughout the summer, in September and October the committee tapped the program to implement and enforce its technology-forcing effluent controls and no-discharge standard. Reconciling all the intergovernmental administrative inconsistencies of what would become the National Pollutant Discharge Elimination System (NPDES) remained a challenge. Yet more so than at any other time in the last seventy years, the literal interpretation of the Refuse Act matched the intent of Congress. The committee's bill, like the original 1899 statute, outlawed industrial discharges except where sanctioned by valid federal permits. The conditions and deadlines set forth in Title III were to become the basis for individual permits, which in turn would translate general policy into the quantitative limits for discrete outfalls. Taken together, the NPDES and the regional waste management program replaced state implementation plans as the mechanisms for planning and carrying out pollution control activities.[69]

The Nixon administration reacted with dismay to the committee's revisions, a predictable response that the staff managed not to foresee. From Billings and Jorling's perspective, the latest version of the bill delivered what the Nixon administration had lobbied for, since it abandoned the Tunney standard and included the permit program. Such optimism, however, proved misplaced. As Muskie surmised in October, the administration was "very cool to the idea of deadlines and national standards whether they are effluent standards or water quality standards." The causal link between effluent content and a stream's condition may have been difficult to establish, but the EPA still believed it essential to retain state ambient standards and, to the extent possible, establish discharge limits in reference to local water quality. Likewise, William Ruckelshaus urged the committee to rethink Phase II and its ultimate end, which he and others in the White House viewed as inflexible, unrealistic, and expensive.[70]

The administration's efforts to work through committee Republicans did not secure major changes to the bill before the full Senate approved it on 2 November. Minority members had expressed reservations about the final product, as questions about cost and the wisdom of a no-discharge objective dominated later executive sessions. They even managed to convince Muskie to convert the 1985 no-discharge deadline into a nonenforceable statement of policy. For the time being, however, Muskie and Billings's cost-related safeguards, including a promised "mid-course correction" report to Congress on Phase II, seemed to satisfy them, as well as wavering Democrats like Lloyd Bentsen. In fact, the administration grew frustrated with their repeated defense of the bill's ambitious policy objectives.[71]

Tom Jorling, the minority counsel, offered his own vindication of the committee's handiwork, but spoke as an ecologist rather than as a Republican. Jorling expected the legislation to instill "a new mode of . . . integrated thinking which will enable a comprehensive view of waste water production and waste water management, looking toward the elimination of discharge consistent with ecological principles." It remained to be seen, however, whether Congress, the Nixon administration, and the nation at large would embrace the Public Works Committee's blueprint for "the orderly transition to an ecologically sound society."[72]

9

Defending the Clean Water Act
Confronting Friends and Foes

Controversy and contention surrounded the Water Pollution Control Act Amendments for nearly a year after the Senate Public Works Committee first reported them in October 1971. Considering the legislation's radical break with the past, the prolonged reaction was hardly surprising. Its unorthodox ecological orientation, uncompromising regulatory requirements, unflinching enhancement of federal enforcement power, and unprecedented price tag roused a varied set of detractors. These interests, mobilized by the Nixon White House, demanded a venue to review, respond, and redact, opportunities denied by the Senate committee's summer seclusion. The House Public Works Committee proved much more responsive to their concerns, providing a legislative alternative to and a last line of defense against Ed Muskie's audacious initiative. During the ensuing House-Senate Conference, the struggle for the soul of the Clean Water Act unfolded in an argument over technical minutia that revealed fundamental differences concerning how the nation's water should be protected, and at what cost.

Beyond the conference committee, however, a number of other policymakers and interest groups sought to redraw the blueprints for federal environmental regulation in ways Muskie and his colleagues found troubling. Ironically, most of these actors belonged to the mainstream environmental movement of the early 1970s, precisely the constituency that had agitated for the uncompromising water quality legislation Muskie was busy trying to pass. But they were also of the opinion that Muskie's narrowly construed pollution control system was not the only, or even the most preferable, means to protect the natural world. In this regard, Henry Jackson's NEPA offered activists an enticing supplement. They viewed NEPA as a safeguard to ensure that government bureaucrats—including environmental regulators themselves—would consider the broadest array of information scientists and citizens could provide before taking actions that stood to affect the "total environment."

When environmentalists attempted to adapt NEPA's expansive model of administrative review to Muskie's impending water pollution control system, the senator found himself struggling to distinguish friends from foes. As it turned out, both the House conferees and NEPA's proponents favored broadening the range of variables federal environmental administrators had to factor into their regulatory decisions. By contrast, the members and staff of the Senate Public Works Committee concluded that strict enforcement required a narrower administrative focus. Their legislation may have reduced the discretion of EPA officials, but it retained Muskie's traditional approach to pollution control, which had always relied on specialized expertise. The Clean Water Act's grounding in ecology did not change that orientation or promote the more holistic approach to pollution control regulation that NEPA implied.

The committee's continuing trust in experts and the institutions they served reflected one of the more prominent articles of faith among post–World War II policymakers. By 1972, few environmentalists shared that faith. Of course, Muskie's Clean Water Act bore the stamp of other well-worn liberal discourses that the new generation of activists dismissed. Unlikely environmentalists, from dam builders to weapons engineers, had informed the act's unprecedented regulatory approach and prodded the Senate Public Works Committee to set ambitious objectives for national water quality. The question in 1971–1972 was whether the legislation's opponents, or for that matter, its putative supporters, would let the committee's complex handiwork see the light of day. For its part, the Nixon administration hoped a healthy dose of public participation would slow the Senate bill's momentum before it was swept up beyond reach in the wake of Muskie's presidential campaign.

Marshaling the Opposition

As October waned and their efforts to sway the senators failed, Nixon officials directed their full attention toward the House Public Works Committee.

If that committee could be convinced to convene extensive new hearings on the Senate's water pollution legislation, they reasoned, it could build a public record of opposition and produce a tangible alternative for the ensuing conference. The White House knew it had more traction with Republican members and staff in the House committee, particularly William Harsha (Ohio) and minority counsel Cliff Enfield, who were disturbed by the Muskie bill and proved particularly receptive to the administration's entreaties. The task at hand was to recruit a group of wavering Democrats to the cause and persuade the new committee chairman, John Blatnik, to go along.[1]

The administration's end run around the Senate returned Congressman Blatnik to the spotlight for a final brief moment in the fall of 1971. Blatnik's star had faded during the sixties, a time when influential conservatives like George H. Fallon (D-Md.) and William C. Cramer (R-Fla.) were content to pursue highway projects and block the Minnesotan's pollution control initiatives. Electoral defeats for both men in 1970 enabled Blatnik to assume the chairmanship of the full committee, but its members remained wary of radical regulatory reform, given the sustained pressures they faced from industrial lobbyists within their districts. Even Democratic staff members preferred the 1965 Water Quality Act's gradualist approach and worried about the economic consequences of the Senate bill. Frustrated environmentalists like Barbara Reid considered the committee "hopeless," full of "highway boys" who cared little about water pollution and rarely engaged citizen groups. These people retained a similar skepticism about its chairman. A new generation of activists criticized Blatnik's failure to fight as hard for federal enforcement power as he had for federal waste treatment grants and noted his support for Minnesota's Reserve Mining Company, a taconite refiner with a dismal record of polluting Lake Superior. The dedication to distributive politics and natural resource development that had fueled Blatnik's success as a pollution control advocate in the fifties came across as a liability by the seventies.[2]

Neither environmentalists nor the Nixon administration could predict how Blatnik would respond to the Senate bill. The chairman felt slighted because neither Muskie nor the Senate staff had bothered to consult with him. His criticism of uniform national standards and an exclusive reliance on effluent limits suggested his displeasure. On the other hand, Blatnik was loath to come across as "antienvironment" and seemed intent on passing a bill without additional hearings. Once Muskie and Leon Billings made an effort to secure his support and input, his public pronouncements began to favor the Senate legislation. But Blatnik soon learned of his committee's widespread bipartisan dissatisfaction with the Muskie bill. During their first mark-up session on 16 November, Democrats and Republicans alike demanded extensive new hearings. It was unlikely that Blatnik could have overcome this united front, but he never got the chance to try—a mild heart attack suffered that same day removed him as an active player. Four days later, the committee voted to convene additional hearings to consider a wide range of possible amendments to its pending legislation.[3]

Having secured a public forum to contest the Senate bill, the White House moved to assemble a coalition of the unwilling that included business and industrial organizations, state regulatory officials, and conventional pollution control experts. Although these interests had yet to coalesce as a unified bloc, most resented how radically Muskie's legislation had evolved behind closed doors during the summer and fall of 1971. Senate staff members had deliberately limited access to external petitioners. The committee's relationship with industrial organizations in particular was often antagonistic, but Leon Billings and Tom Jorling also kept environmentalists at arms length to avoid "endless sub-negotiations" over the "smallest details." Environmental Action's David Zwick, author of the Ralph Nader report, *Water Wasteland*, and a contributor to the Tunney standard, enjoyed fairly regular contact during the summer but had trouble discerning his precise influence on the staff. "I know of things in some sections [of the bill] that went in pretty much as we suggested them, but I am doubtful about how much we shaped the larger philosophy of the standards section, for instance," Zwick recalled. Following the August recess, Billings and Jorling refused to answer his phone calls, and he learned nothing of the legislation's development apart from rumors. Consequently, news of the shift to zero-discharge took environmental lobbyists by surprise. But although Muskie later made more of an effort to brief them, business interests and state officials remained largely shut out.[4]

The Nixon administration developed a coherent line of dissent against the Senate bill's regulatory strategy that all of its opponents adopted in one form or another. Their case consisted of two interrelated arguments. First, abandoning ambient standards in favor of technology-based effluent limits risked imposing an inflexible control mechanism that bore little relation to an individual stream's condition or a community's practical water quality needs. Second, the Senate's waste treatment strategy and zero-discharge objective threatened an exorbitant misallocation of national resources disproportionate to the benefits these resources might deliver. In a report compiled in mid-October, the EPA, the Council on Environmental Quality, and the Office of Management and Budget calculated that industries and municipalities would bear a $316.5 billion burden over a twenty-five-year period as the marginal costs of waste removal technology increased exponentially with each successive phase of the Senate bill. Ratcheting up treatment efficiencies to levels surpassing 95 percent and approaching 100 percent was expected to consume the bulk of the money, or almost $200 billion. That kind of price tag, the report warned, would precipitate marginal plant closures, increase unemployment, promote an unfavorable balance of trade, drive consumer prices and taxes higher, and drain funds away from other vital public services. Since advanced treatment techniques required much more energy and produced significant volumes of residual sludge, the quality of the total environment stood to suffer as well.[5]

When business lobbyists geared up in earnest to oppose the Senate bill, they followed the administration's basic script. As late as November 1971, most corporate leaders and small business owners remained uninformed and passive about the legislation, until the White House prodded them to organize and take action. The National Industrial Pollution Control Council and the National Association of Manufacturers adopted much of its subsequent critique from the October cost-benefit study. As the National Association of Manufacturers' director of environmental affairs summed it up, "Blind pursuit of absolutely pure water quality is a form of economic brinkmanship." Although state officials worried predominantly about the aggrandizement of federal enforcement power, their testimony in the House frequently underscored the cost angle. Much to Muskie's annoyance, "$316.5 billion" received wide airing in the press, a number he claimed "had no basis in fact, on the record or in any report." This did not stop other witnesses, from industrial engineers to New York governor Nelson Rockefeller, from inflating dollar estimates for zero-discharge into the trillions.[6]

With the cost of technology-based standards emerging as a major point of contention, the viability of "Muskegon-type" land disposal systems became a more prominent concern for both defenders and detractors of zero-discharge. The promise of the Corps of Engineers' regional wastewater management program and its "ecologically sound" centerpiece, soil-based sewage treatment, stood to neutralize two of the White House's most prominent arguments: that eliminating discharges by 1985 was not achievable or was otherwise prohibitively expensive. Boosters like Michigan congressman Guy Vander Jagt, who had fought to bring John Sheaffer's "living filter" to his district, projected Muskegon County's capital investment on a national scale and pegged the cost of the no-discharge goal at $32 billion, a fraction of the administration's estimate. An independent study conducted by Friends of the Earth concluded that it could be accomplished for $50 billion to $55 billion. The Friends of the Earth report coincided with a public relations offensive launched in March 1972 by a coalition of twenty-five public interest groups who, in seeking to defend the Senate bill, condemned the White House for deliberately overstating its price tag. Meanwhile, when the Corps of Engineers' own preliminary data indicated much higher costs than expected for land disposal technology in its five urban pilot programs, it promptly revised the numbers downward in a second "survey scope study" of the Chicago area.[7]

The White House refused to view land disposal as a "national panacea" and remained wary of the Corps' aggressive thrust into water quality planning. "It's push, push, push," one EPA official complained, "the Corps wants to run us out of business." William Ruckelshaus even attempted to terminate the five urban wastewater pilot programs, which he believed interfered with local planning efforts, but Vander Jagt and Henry Reuss blocked the effort. Instead, the EPA vetted the Corps' feasibility studies, questioning land disposal's performance, raising issues of toxicity and mineral contamination, and reassessing cost. The agency determined that to achieve 95 to 99 percent removal efficiencies nationwide, even advanced methods of mechanical distillation would cost less than land treatment. It concluded that favorable geological conditions and the ready availability of marginal land in western Michigan rendered Sheaffer's project less expensive than it would be in most other urban locations.[8]

The EPA also echoed the concerns of numerous sanitary engineers and state officials when it addressed the broader social costs of land disposal that the army avoided. Treating billions of gallons of metropolitan waste per day, critics noted, would consume millions of acres and necessitate the displacement of thousands of homes. One municipal official from Seattle pointed to the "serious political problems associated with the withdrawal of substantial acreage from the tax rolls of rural counties for the benefit of urban centers." In fact, the Corps' vision generated opposition in both urban and rural communities. The executive director of the Lake Michigan Federation noted the "terrific resistance to the Corps plans here and in Cleveland," adding that "we here in Chicago who know [John] Sheaffer well have been aghast at the apparent influence he has with the Senate Public Works Committee and Muskie."[9]

The Senate Public Works Committee promoted both land disposal technology and the no-discharge objective on the basis of certain ecological precepts that neither the Nixon administration nor the majority of pollution control experts shared. The White House skillfully encapsulated the voice of professional dissent in the so-called David Report—the product of a seven-member panel, made up predominantly of sanitary engineers and economists, that the president's science advisor, Dr. Edward E. David Jr., convened in December. As David quickly came to realize, "Much of the professional community is extremely critical of the approach to water quality control embodied in the proposed legislation." The report echoed the administration's defense of ambient standards, while describing both zero-discharge and uniform effluent limits of any kind as needlessly rigid and a drain on national resources. Panel members doubted that "any respectable professional economist or engineer" could support the Senate bill and condemned it as an example of "holy water syndrome" and "ecological overkill." They implicitly accepted what Tom Jorling denounced as "an ecological fiction": that the assimilative capacity of streams, lakes, and oceans remained a legitimate, cost-effective variable in the treatment process.[10]

The political significance of the David Report owed less to what it said than to who was saying it. Not only did the authors' professional affiliations lend weight to the report's content, but a number of those experts were either Democrats themselves or had worked for past Democratic administrations. As the Nixon administration took every opportunity to emphasize, many other prominent liberal academics were coming forward and echoing the report's conclusions, despite partisan enmity toward Nixon. "It just kills me to have to be on the same side as those SOBs," one self-described left-wing, peacenik, conservationist professor confessed.[11]

In the end, the House Public Works Committee accommodated the Senate legislation's many dissenters. Although the bill that the committee reported in the winter of 1972 mimicked the wording and two-phased structure of S. 2770, it deemphasized technology-based effluent limits, downgraded no-discharge, relaxed deadlines, and allowed states to retain more discretion in matters of enforcement. Having marshaled the forces of opposition, the Nixon administration looked on as state officials (led by the National Governors' Conference) and a host of industrial and trade organizations pressured their representatives to pass the bill without alteration. This decentralized lobbying effort proved successful. During the debates of 28–29 March, the House rejected a series of amendments offered by Henry Reuss, John Dingell, and forty other members on behalf of environmentalist organizations. Although White House officials approved of the House legislation's toned-down regulatory features, they still bemoaned its billions of dollars in additional authorizations for waste treatment grants. The fiscal consequences of such outlays troubled them as much as the private sector impact of the Senate bill's regulatory program did. The prospect of opposing the bill on account of its cost in the middle of an election year troubled them even more.[12]

The presidential race loomed large in the White House's political calculus on the Clean Water Act. As late as January 1972, Nixon and Muskie were running in a statistical dead heat. But despite a sizable war chest, the mantle of media front-runner, and early victories in New Hampshire and Illinois, the senator finished fourth in Wisconsin and Florida, barely registered in Pennsylvania and Massachusetts, and by 27 April had dropped out of the race. Muskie's lachrymose response on national television to the infamous "Canuck letter" notwithstanding, the senator failed to establish any tangible identity with voters, despite his command of environmental issues. Muskie's intellectual integrity, perhaps his greatest asset as a policymaker in the Senate, proved to be his greatest liability as a national candidate. As one frustrated observer put it, there was "not enough demagoguery in Muskie to be a good campaigner." He seldom offered pithy answers to policy questions or took a firm stand on complex issues, leaving his campaign without a unifying theme or a vision for the future.[13]

Contrary to White House prognostications, however, Muskie's political fortunes did not dictate the internal dynamic of the House-Senate Conference Committee. The committee convened almost forty times between May and September in its efforts to resolve the conflicting versions of the 1972 Water Pollution Control Act Amendments. Although all concerned wanted a water pollution bill and felt the weight of public expectations in an election year, sharp differences over substantive issues drove the deliberations of members and staff. At stake during the often contentious sessions was nothing less than the fate of the Senate's ecologically oriented, technology-forcing mode of regulation.[14]

Enforceability, Uniformity, and Finality: The Conference Committee

As the committee geared up for the conference, the Nixon administration downplayed the distinctions between the House and Senate legislation and accused opponents of the House version of undermining the clean water effort. In a widely publicized Earth Day speech before the American Bar Association, the EPA's assistant administrator for enforcement, John Quarles, noted that each bill's regulatory mechanisms were "essentially identical" through 1976 and both streamlined enforcement and permit procedures, increased penalties for polluters, extended federal jurisdiction, regulated toxic pollutants, and expanded the construction grant program. Much to Leon Billings's chagrin, a spate of eerily similar editorials published in April all urged Muskie to rise above partisan rivalries. "If the public (the press) can be convinced that it is politics and not philosophy which separates the two bodies," he cautioned, "then Muskie can get blamed for no legislation."[15]

For the members and staff of the Senate Public Works Committee, however, significant differences in legislative content and philosophy rendered the prospects of consensus with their House colleagues uncertain. Compromise proved easiest in matters of planning and distributive politics. Although the details were painstaking, the Senate conferees expressed a willingness to adopt the House position on almost every item relating to the Title II grant program, which resulted in a larger authorization ($18 billion) and more generous allocation formulas for funding waste treatment plants. Likewise, the House contingent acceded to the Senate bill's area-wide waste management program, but they also created a separate program authorizing additional multiple objective planning on the river basin level. In this instance, the two sides opted for redundancy to smooth over conflicts.[16]

William Harsha, the ranking Republican on the House Public Works Committee, points proudly to a sewage project in his Ohio district. From the William Harsha Papers, courtesy of the Mahn Center for Archives & Special Collections, Ohio University Libraries.

By contrast, Title III's regulatory framework inspired nearly intractable discord. Throughout the conference's five-month span, two issues generated the most consistent dissension: the mechanism for pollution control and enforcement, and the parameters used to determine the equitable cost of those controls. The House bill preserved ambient standards as the program's centerpiece. As Billings saw it, the intent was to ensure "that no regulations will be imposed on particular effluent sources which are not proved to be necessary for maintenance of specific beneficial uses." It also required state officials to determine "maximum daily loads" for individual bodies of water, or the amount of waste they could absorb per diem while still complying with ambient standards. Apportioning the assimilative capacity of individual water bodies in this manner, House members and staff believed, would force the states to correlate effluent limits with ambient quality as precisely as possible, a task they understood as difficult but necessary.[17]

The Senate conferees resisted the House approach. Ambient standards and maximum daily loads assumed that the assimilative capacity of a stream remained a legitimate variable in the control process, a practice they had concluded was unreliable and ecologically unsound. The Senate bill's clear intent after 1976 was to *eliminate* pollution as a means to restore and preserve what Billings called the "natural integrity" of the nation's waterways.[18]

The senators preferred technology-based effluent standards not simply for ecological reasons but also because they also reduced administrative discretion and limited the grounds for polluter appeals, particularly on questions of "reasonable cost." The only cost variables the EPA could consider when developing administrative definitions for "best practicable technology" (Phase I) or "best available technology" (Phase II) under the Senate bill were those pertaining to *internal* production processes, and then only as applied to categories or classes of plants, not individual facilities. Thereafter, the Senate bill allowed only a brief thirty-day window for challenging these guidelines in court. Suits against federal standards or individual permits had to be filed in the U.S. Court of Appeals rather than in district courts, and judges had no authority to conduct de novo reviews of standards during enforcement proceedings.[19]

Leon Billings had pushed the senators to reject a broad "economic-and-social-benefits-versus-cost test" for the regulatory program, but he feared his efforts during the previous fall would come to naught. "Even where the House bill appears to require establishment of effluent controls," he told Muskie, "it also requires that subjective economic, social, and environmental factors be considered in determining whether technology is practicable in Phase I or available in Phase II." The legislation extended the administrator's purview beyond the economics of internal plant engineering to encompass the community-wide implications of controls, including their impact on regional growth and employment, foreign competition, and collateral environmental costs related to land and air pollution.[20]

The House strategy, Billings informed Muskie, threatened to "vitiate the three principal elements of the Senate bill: enforceability, uniformity, and finality." Determining BPT and BAT as a function of internal engineering promoted uniform controls among like industries, regardless of geographic location, but, according to the staff director, there was "no way to adequately quantify the social and economic and environmental benefits of pollution control in relation to the cost associated with [them]." Even if there were, socioeconomic conditions varied with each locality; so the House approach would make it impossible to enforce strict effluent standards consistently on a national basis. Neither would standards bear any vestige of permanence, since "each decision which reflects one individual polluter will necessarily open the issue for his competitors." He also criticized the House bill because it sought to preserve de novo judicial review of standards during the enforcement process—and assigned such cases to district courts, which were more inclined to be sympathetic to local industries.[21]

As Billings predicted, the question of how administrators should define technology-based effluent controls and determine their reasonable cost emerged as the conference committee's most serious point of contention during the summer of 1972. The Senate conferees wished to close the loopholes that permitted time-consuming source-by-source appeals. They wanted the EPA to take the cost of applying emission controls into account when promulgating administrative guidelines for BPT and BAT, guidelines based on internal engineering factors applicable to broad industrial categories. They rejected external, socioeconomic qualifications, particularly for best practicable technology (Phase I), since BPT represented the codification of older, minimum requirements (secondary treatment or its industrial equivalent) that state programs had supposedly adopted after 1965.

The House fought to retain a community-wide perspective when defining BPT or BAT, and to allow plant-by-plant determinations of a proposed standard's economic impact. The Senate conferees soon realized, however, that their counterparts were more intent on mitigating BPT with socioeconomic qualifications than BAT, despite its conventional technological requirements and the EPA's vocal concerns about Phase II. True, the latter remained troubling. But while its 1981 deadline stood off in the future, the 1976 cutoff for Phase I loomed most ominously for influential industrial interest groups like the National Association of Manufacturers and the Chamber of Commerce. Likewise, the House contingent reasoned, if case-by-case economic feasibility judgments became standard operating procedure for determining

BPT, the momentum of the Refuse Act permit program—an independent White House initiative both they and state officials resented—might also be checked.[22]

To avoid protracted plant-by-plant challenges to effluent standards in the short term, particularly during the permit process, the Senate conferees acceded to a more inclusive economic test for BPT. EPA guidelines had to consider "the total cost . . . in relation to the effluent reduction benefits to be achieved," accounting for both external socioeconomic factors and internal technical ones. But the senators restricted this review process to broad "classes or categories of point sources" and emphasized that it should never occur "at the time of the application of an effluent limitation to an individual source within such a category or class." Dischargers retained the right to appeal the specific conditions spelled out in individual permits but could not use that opportunity to challenge the basic rationale of industry-wide standards. So while the House members managed to insert a broader social-cost test for Phase I, their Senate counterparts rigged the administrative process as best they could to limit the scope of appeals.[23]

The conferees took the opposite tack in devising a settlement on Phase II and BAT. The House agreed to forgo the total cost balancing test they had demanded for Phase I, while the Senate assented to a procedure for source-by-source appeals. The burden of proof rested with owners or operators to demonstrate that requested modifications represented "the maximum use of technology within [their] economic capability and will result in reasonable further progress toward the elimination of the discharge of pollutants." With this provision, Billings and the staff believed they had set the bar sufficiently high to discourage frivolous challenges and maintain program momentum after 1977.[24]

The reasonable-cost compromises on BPT and BAT validated the Senate's strategy to make effluent controls the regulatory centerpiece of the legislation. But the final conference bill still managed to preserve vestiges of the old system. Much to the staff's chagrin, the House continued to demand provisions that authorized implementation planning for ambient water quality standards and maximum daily load allocations as an alternative, "back up" approach to water pollution control. The Senate relented, but insisted that those sections remain secondary to the rest of the legislation's regulatory provisions. Indeed, Billings and Jorling deemed them as "irrelevant as a matter of Federal law," and, much like the human appendix, an atavistic appendage to be ignored.[25]

The Senate conferees combined tough negotiations with strategic concessions to preserve a water quality program with a narrow regulatory focus. To restore and maintain the ecological integrity of aquatic systems, they reasoned, the final legislation had to limit the EPA administrator's point of reference to the internal engineering of industrial point sources and the effluent content that emanated from their outflow pipes. Members of the House Committee, representing the forces of opposition, preferred an administrative process with a much broader purview.

Ironically, the forces of opposition were not the only ones that desired to expand the range of variables that EPA officials considered. Well before Ed Muskie and his colleagues had gained the advantage over their adversaries in conference, a number of environmentalist allies chose to pursue a course of litigation and lobbying that seemed certain to confound the senators' efforts. The activities of these activists did not suggest a lack of support for the Senate's technology-forcing approach to pollution control so much as an enduring faith in the information-forcing alternative offered by NEPA. Muskie had always feared NEPA's potential to undermine his method of regulation, and that fear had fueled his contentious battles with Henry Jackson over the statute's content and scope in 1969. But not even the suspicious senator foresaw how NEPA's evolving case law would inspire environmentalists and industrialists alike to challenge the judgment of environmental experts, and by extension, the entire system of environmental protection that deferred to them.

Environmental Impact and Pollution Control

In the two years following NEPA's passage, district and appeals courts interpreted the scope of environmental impact review broadly to halt a number of prominent federal construction projects. Public interest litigants won injunctions against the Cross Florida Barge Canal, the Tennessee Tombigbee Waterway, and Interstate 485 through Atlanta on the grounds that the agencies responsible for such "major Federal actions" had failed to submit adequate EISs. The courts also endeavored to clarify what constituted an "adequate" statement. They described NEPA as an "environmental full disclosure law" and insisted that EISs include a range of opinions from experts, concerned public or private organizations, and even "ordinary lay citizens." Federal agencies were compelled to perform an independent appraisal of environmental costs and benefits, rather than deferring to the analysis of interested parties. The U.S. Court of Appeals even declared an Interior Department EIS inadequate because its analysis of proposed petroleum extraction leases did not include a discussion of all reasonable alternatives, including those that could be implemented only by other departments, the president, or Congress. In other words, the court extended the planning process beyond the bounds of an agency's conventional expertise to ensure a multidisciplinary review.[26]

Neither Congress nor the Nixon administration had anticipated such a jarring court-mandated reordering of administrative priorities. Among the flood of judicial pronouncements, however, two decisions handed down in December 1971 provoked the most serious concerns about NEPA's long-term impact on the health of the economy, and, ironically, on the viability of the federal government's environmental regulatory program. Both cases in question descended from the landmark *Calvert Cliffs* decision, which ordered the AEC to carry out technically detailed "balancing judgments" that factored water quality into its licensing decisions, regardless of prior "certification" from state or federal pollution control agencies.

Because *Calvert Cliffs* portended delays in future nuclear power plant construction, the AEC adopted contingency plans to avoid critical shortages of electricity. In the fall, it began to issue licenses to about a dozen plants at various stages of construction, allowing them to operate at partial capacity. But when the Izaak Walton League contested the so-called Quad Cities reactors being constructed by Commonwealth Edison Company of Chicago, the D.C. District Court ruled that partial licenses still constituted "major Federal actions" requiring EISs.[27]

The second major decision cast a pall over the Nixon administration's Refuse Act permit program. The program already operated behind schedule and under fire from industrialists and state officials in 1971. Nonetheless, a dedicated cadre of EPA staffers worked with the Corps of Engineers to sort applications, gather data on industrial discharges, and bring suit against companies that had failed to file. While the EPA and the Corps anticipated conflicts with business interests or the states, however, they had not counted on run-ins with environmentalists like Jerome Kalur. A Cleveland attorney and Sierra Club member, Kalur made frequent recreational use of the Grand River in northeast Ohio. When the Corps issued permits to local chemical companies that specified, and thereby sanctioned, the volume and content of effluent discharges into that waterway, the avid canoer objected. He contended that Refuse Act permits constituted "major federal actions" that required the preparation of EISs.[28]

The White House assumed from the beginning that federal discharge permits were immune from the kind of external review Kalur demanded. In both its interim and final guidelines on NEPA, the Council on Environmental Quality deferred to the statements of Senator Muskie and the Public Works Committee regarding environmental "enhancement" agencies. "Because of the Act's legislative history," it concluded, "environmentally protective regulatory activities concurred in or taken by" the EPA did not require EISs. Although the Corps nominally ran the permit program, it deferred to the expertise of EPA and state pollution control agencies in all considerations of water quality, as required under Muskie's 1970 Water Quality Improvement Act.[29]

On 21 December 1971, U.S. District Court judge Aubrey Robinson's opinion in *Kalur v. Resor* decisively rejected the administration's—and Muskie's—position. Drawing liberally from the *Calvert Cliffs* precedent, he concluded that the permit program was not exempt from NEPA. The Corps had failed to file detailed EISs in matters concerned with water quality, in deference to the expertise and jurisdiction of environmental agencies. "NEPA did not permit the sort of total abdication of responsibility practiced by the Atomic Energy Commission in *Calvert Cliffs*," Robinson noted, and "it does not permit it here with the Corps of Engineers." Robinson reaffirmed that "licensing agencies" were responsible for conducting case-by-case balancing judgments under NEPA that considered a broader range of variables than environmental "certifying agencies." "Obedience to water quality certifications under the Water Quality Improvement Act is not mutually exclusive with the NEPA procedures," he insisted. "The Corps of Engineers can . . . go on to perform the very different operation of balancing the overall benefits and cost of a particular proposed project, and consider alterations above and beyond the applicable water quality standards that would further reduce environmental damage."[30]

Kalur v. Resor had momentous implications for the future of federal environmental regulation. In the short run, the decision enjoined the Corps from issuing Refuse Act permits until it amended its regulations to require EISs. The court did not explicitly state that each and every permit had to be accompanied by an EIS. But with upwards of 20,000 applicants awaiting permits, the additional administrative burden effectively ground the program to a halt, putting it "into a cocoon for nearly an entire year," as John Quarles recalled.[31]

The *Kalur* decision raised an even more troubling question for the long term: Did NEPA mandate EISs on the actions of federal agencies expressly charged with protecting the environment? Judge Robinson's opinion did not address the issue directly. Nevertheless, the EPA's autonomy and expertise had been indirectly challenged. If the water pollution legislation currently pending in Congress became law, it stood to vest the EPA with sole, uncontested control of the new National Pollutant Discharge Elimination System (NPDES). Would the *Kalur* ruling still hold then? Would the agency also be required to file EISs for actions taken with respect to radiation safety, pesticides registration, air quality regulations, or other matters falling within its broad jurisdiction? The scenario Ed Muskie had sought to avoid two years before now loomed as a distinct possibility.

More so than any other court rulings, *Kalur* and the Quad Cities case precipitated a flurry of proposals among members of Congress, industrial lobbyists, and White House officials designed to scale back NEPA. Although the administration's primary concern was preserving the Refuse Act permit program, *Kalur* had energy-related consequences as well, since it threatened to delay permits on conventional fossil fuel power plants currently under construction. The National Electric Reliability Council predicted that more than half the nation would suffer shortages of reserve generating capacity in the summer of 1972 as a result of the protracted environmental reviews required by the two December cases. As critics of NEPA pressed for revisions, the statute's supporters circled the wagons in an effort to protect its provisions. With the conference committee on the 1972 Water Pollution Control Act Amendments convening in the midst of this broader conflict, the fate of the two measures became inexorably intertwined.[32]

Reining in NEPA

Prior to December 1971, the Senate Public Works Committee had already included language in its water pollution bill to curb the reach of NEPA. The initiative came from Howard Baker, whose seat on the Joint Committee on Atomic Energy left him overexposed to NEPA-related issues. Baker reasoned that the EPA was best capable of promulgating optimal technology-based performance standards for new and existing facilities, which could then be treated as constant, or "frozen" costs in subsequent balancing judgments. The so-called Baker amendment excused any licensing agency from "determining on its own the standard of performance or effluent limitation that must be applied" once an applicant had obtained both a state certification and a federal discharge permit. The Tennessean's proposal passed with little fanfare during the 2 November Senate floor debate.[33]

Environmental interest groups, however, were less inclined to trust federal pollution experts or state bureaucracies and more concerned about preserving a role for citizen participation in the standard-setting process. The theory of NEPA, explained Sierra Club attorney Anthony Roisman, "is that no action should be authorized until all of the relevant facts have been developed and balanced in order to produce the optimum in environmental protection consistent with other national goals." He believed federal licensing proceedings provided the ideal public forum for citizens to supplement generic standards for effluent control technology, primarily by incorporating local viewpoints, cross-examining the experts, and challenging their conclusions. The Baker amendment, however, eliminated this opportunity.[34]

Above all, activists wanted to avoid narrow administrative interpretations of environmental impact. Since licensing agencies like the AEC had the best read on a project's overall environmental costs, economic benefits, and potential alternatives, NEPA proponents argued, such agencies should exercise the discretionary authority to adjust technological standards for pollution control in reference to their balancing judgments. In certain cases, they imagined, the standards imposed might even exceed those promulgated under the EPA's rule-making powers. But Roisman's line of argument met with considerable resistance from the staff of the Senate Public Works Committee, who doubted the value of "looking behind EPA's water-quality judgments." Billings even suspected that public interest legal expertise actually had a greater negative impact on participatory democracy than the EPA's administrative expertise.[35]

Because Howard Baker's amendment predated both the *Kalur* and Quad Cities decisions, it did not address the specific matter of EISs. But after the new year, the Nixon administration, together with the AEC and its congressional allies, stepped up their efforts to shield the permit program and nuclear energy development from the seemingly debilitating EIS. They discovered that doing so required direct revisions of NEPA itself, a task that John Dingell's Merchant Marine and Fisheries Committee—which exercised jurisdiction over the statute in the House—proved willing to consider.[36]

Congress, Dingell worried, was "literally dripping with amendments and bills that would gut the act." Responding with flexibility to discrete problems as they arose allowed him to preempt a more sweeping overhaul at the hands of NEPA's enemies. He described his Quad Cities remedy, developed in conjunction with the Joint Committee on Atomic Energy, as a "carefully worded, exquisitely narrow piece of legislation," which retained NEPA's spirit and substance while granting only "more leeway in time" to overburdened utilities. After the White House solicited his help with the permit program, the congressman dutifully responded with a bill to exempt the EPA from preparing EISs on federal permits until 31 December 1975. Despite his apparent willingness to grant the EPA a reprieve to comply with NEPA, Dingell disagreed with the administration's position and reaffirmed the agency's obligation to prepare EISs for all its regulatory activities.[37]

Environmental interest groups uniformly backed Dingell's comprehensive construction of NEPA but objected to any mitigation of the statute's mandate, no matter how pragmatic or targeted. Dingell's Quad Cities and Refuse Act bills, together with the perceived machinations of the Nixon administration, the AEC, and Howard Baker, pointed to what Anthony Roisman called an "ominous linkage of private interest groups with Congressmen and Federal agencies to destroy NEPA one way or the other." In response, a coalition of prominent environmental organizations launched the "Save NEPA" campaign in April 1972, uniting in opposition to any and all alterations of the two-year old statute. They feared that a slippery slope of well-meaning exemptions, fueled by various socioeconomic imperatives, would rapidly spell the end of NEPA's revolutionary procedural safeguards. The campaign issued a newsletter to hundreds of local and state environmental groups nationwide in an attempt to erect a grassroots firewall.[38]

The "Save NEPA" strategists proved adept at deflecting initial congressional efforts to circumvent the act. John Dingell succumbed to the campaign's entreaties to hold off temporarily on the Refuse Act bill. Much to the EPA's irritation, he agreed to wait for the outcome of the House-Senate water pollution conference. "I know their motives are the purest," one agency administrator complained of environmentalists, "but I cannot understand how they fail to see that to force us to prepare thousands of impact statements will only delay the water-pollution abatement program and frustrate the very purpose of NEPA." Thomas Jorling likewise described NEPA as a "procedural trap for the environmental movement" and "simply a bad piece of legislation" that contained "no substantive requirements for either Federal agencies or in turn for private industrial polluters." Believing the activists' zealous faith in NEPA misplaced, the Public Works Committee veteran insisted that "over the long run, it's the regulatory programs—in air, water, solid wastes, pesticides, and so forth—that are going to count."[39]

A Two-Edged Sword

Recent events suggested that the balancing judgments demanded by NEPA stood to undermine the very system Jorling prized, and in ways no one had anticipated. So far, court-induced administrative delays in environmental regulatory activities had come about as by-products of public interest legal challenges. Activists targeted pollution control standards that they believed did not take into account broader environmental costs. Environmentalists, however, were not the only parties to discover the fruits of litigation. Industrial interests soon began using NEPA to attack pollution control standards that they believed were indifferent to broader socioeconomic costs. In both instances, litigants were using the courts to challenge a perceived monopoly of government expertise.

Observers soon began to refer to the statute as a "two-edged sword." Late in January, four operating companies of the American Electric Power System asked the U.S. Circuit Court of Appeals in the District of Columbia to review EPA emission standards for new sources of air pollution promulgated under the 1970 Clean Air Act. The attorneys hinted that the suit might become an important NEPA test case, since the EPA had determined stationary source regulations unilaterally without recourse to broader environmental impact analysis. Industries seeking similar judicial relief from federal environmental decrees included automobiles, copper, chemicals, and petroleum. In twenty-five cases brought by utilities contesting EPA air quality regulations, fifteen cited failure to prepare impact statements as their primary rationale. One advocate for the electric utilities industry characterized new source emission standards as "piecemeal environmentalism at its worst," since the EPA had failed to consider viable alternatives for the regulations or determine their potential impact vis-à-vis water pollution, solid waste disposal, or energy shortages. "Only when the government has developed a precise and explicit balancing of costs and benefits—as required by NEPA—will it have the basis for rational decision making."[40]

The fact that both industrialists and environmentalists could appropriate *Calvert Cliffs*'s cost-benefit vocabulary underscored one of the principal tensions between technology-forcing regulatory statutes and information-forcing balancing procedures. Leon Billings's mantra of "enforceability, uniformity, and finality" expressed what the Senate Public Works Committee had attempted to accomplish with the Clean Water Act. Muskie and his colleagues had reduced administrative discretion by coupling clear national goals and explicit statutory directives with strict timetables. They expedited enforcement by keeping measurements at a polluter's outflow pipe, dispensing with the causal uncertainties of relating effluent content to receiving water quality. They based effluent standards strictly on technological factors, in order to prevent external socioeconomic factors from reducing pollution controls to their lowest common denominator. They limited broad cost-benefit tests that threatened to vitiate uniformly tough standards and minimized opportunities for powerful interest groups to contest administrative determinations. Throughout the summer, Billings and the Senate conference delegation fought to defeat all House amendments aimed at altering or nullifying these legislative features.

If NEPA's procedural requirements for case-by-case balancing judgments applied equally to environmental regulations, however, then public interest advocates and the courts had arguably accomplished the House conferees' mission. The EIS promised to have virtually the same effect as many of the

House bill's provisions: expanding the list of criteria for determining standards beyond technological judgments, introducing new evidence to challenge government expertise, and focusing on water quality per se (and thus external community values), rather than internal engineering factors, as the point of reference for controls. As one EPA official noted, any EIS filed on behalf of proposed discharge standards would "require primarily a discussion of how the standards would affect the quality of the receiving waters." Thus, "the validity of the effluent standards would be made to hinge upon a full consideration of the effect on the receiving waters, which is precisely the requirement that [the Senate Public Works Committee has] sought to avoid."[41]

In this context, it is not surprising that the House Public Works Committee exhibited little enthusiasm for the administration's desire to shield the permit program from NEPA. Achieving BPT by 1976 would require the rapid issuance of permits to polluters within the next twenty-four months. But if NEPA required EISs for each of them, then establishing the complex relationship between discharges and receiving water quality as part of the requisite balancing judgment would consume considerable time—just what the House desired.[42]

As the marathon conference committee wound down in the fall of 1972, the Senate Public Works Committee endeavored to disentangle the two most prominent environmental strategies of the early seventies. In an eleventh-hour maneuver during the last of the thirty-nine scheduled sessions, Senators Baker and Muskie introduced another amendment that explicitly exempted the EPA from filing EISs for most activities prescribed under the pending Clean Water Act (with two exceptions—permits for new pollution sources and construction plans for treatment works). The amendment also affirmed that NEPA did not authorize licensing or permitting agencies to review effluent standards, nor did it authorize them to mandate alternative discharge limits as conditions for permits or licenses. The House conferees ultimately relented, since their colleagues had already conceded to a number of key revisions in the effluent control requirements for Phases I and II, including a total-cost test for the former. Environmentalists both inside and outside Congress predictably condemned what they considered an "unwarranted attack on NEPA."[43]

In its defense, the Public Works Committee framed its latest amendment as a logical reconciliation of two innovative environmental statutes with distinct missions. "The mandate of NEPA is very broad," Muskie noted during Senate debate on the conference report; "the mandate of EPA is quite narrow." The "sole purpose" of the Clean Water Act, the senator reminded his colleagues, was "to establish a detailed regulatory mechanism for restoring and maintaining the chemical, physical and biological integrity of the Nation's waters," while "the goal of the Act" was "to eliminate the discharge of pollutants into the Nation's waters by 1985."[44]

Though revolutionary in scope, complexity, and specificity, the Senate bill still located environmental enhancement within a traditional network of state and federal agencies and experts. "Virtually every action required of the Administrator will involve some degree of agency discretion," the senator observed, including "judgments involving a complex balancing analysis of factors that include economic, technical, and other considerations." Committee members and staff designed the legislation to preempt the "capture" of environmental bureaucracies by regulated interests. But ultimately, the Senate Public Works Committee had to place its faith in the institutions, experts, and processes it created and oversaw. "If the general procedural or substantive reforms achieved in NEPA . . . were permitted to override, supersede, broaden, or affect in any way the more specific environmental mandate of the [EPA]," Muskie noted, "the administration of the Act would be seriously impeded and the intent of the Congress in passing it frustrated."[45]

In contrast, neither the activists nor the congressional entrepreneurs who backed NEPA unconditionally remained wedded to the administrative channels and processes the Public Works Committee devised. Innovators like Scoop Jackson or John Dingell supported other means to protect the environment. Allowing NEPA's information-forcing strategy to bypass traditional institutional arrangements created new opportunities for these legislators to carve out independent niches for oversight and policy. It also established their committees and subcommittees as points of access for the increasing numbers of environmental interest groups. In turn, decentralized administrative solutions appealed to the new generation of environmentalists, who liked "egalitarian inclusiveness" and "participatory openness" characteristic of movement cultures in the sixties and early seventies. They appreciated the way NEPA's procedural reforms reoriented the flow of information and made insulated, top-down decision-making structures more accountable to the judgments of diverse federal agencies, Congress, and citizens.[46]

NEPA also revealed a paradox of recent movement cultures—that even as social and political activists challenged traditional institutional authority, their vision of a society transformed depended increasingly on the involvement of the federal government. This combination of what one scholar referred to as "policy expectations and institutional suspicion" clearly characterized environmental public interest advocates. Not even an agency yoked to an explicitly detailed, technology-forcing congressional statute could be completely trusted without additional safeguards. For the new breed of activists, NEPA provided those safeguards. Indeed, reformers specifically dedicated to expanding the scope and vigor of the water pollution regulatory program, like David Zwick and Barbara Reid, had no qualms about supporting the initiatives of their colleagues who wished to "save NEPA."[47]

Environmental activists had faith that information-forcing and technology-forcing statutes were compatible. They doubted that most balancing judgments would conflict with the mandates of air or water quality statutes. Furthermore, recent case law suggested judicial receptivity to flexible administrative solutions in instances where deadlines or emergencies were imminent. Nor did they believe that federal courts would be particularly amenable to business interests attempting to vitiate pollution control standards with a "two-edged sword."[48]

Edmund Muskie held no such optimism. He believed that environmental decisions had to be made by environmental agencies, and he had no reservations about preventing agencies like the AEC from imposing higher standards. In short, Muskie did not subscribe to environmental protection by other means. His water pollution legislation strove to preserve both ecological integrity and the integrity of a distinct mode of government regulation.[49]

The 1972 federal Water Pollution Control Act Amendments survived the machinations of both friend and foe. The bill became law on 18 October, when Congress approved it by overwhelming margins (74–0 in the Senate and 366–11 in the House) and easily overrode President Nixon's veto. The final product retained the essential features that Muskie, his colleagues, and his staff had advocated throughout the year. Its two-phased timetable—requiring polluters to install BPT by 1977 and BAT by 1983—established a rigorous new set of benchmarks for environmental quality. The much-publicized objective to halt all discharges into the nation's waters by 1985 remained an

unenforceable goal. But by shifting the trigger for enforcement from ambient standards to strict, technology-forcing effluent standards via NPDES
permits, the Clean Water Act adopted the rationale of ecosystems ecology as
a means to ratchet up program expectations, narrow the discretion of federal
administrators, and—so its sponsors hoped—transform the nation's landscape.

Conclusion

This book recasts the history of environmental policymaking by emphasizing continuity in a story previously defined by change and upheaval. It reveals how long-standing political, professional, and institutional agendas both inspired the federal government's response to water pollution before the emergence of a mass environmental movement and informed policymakers well after Earth Day. These agendas embodied assumptions and priorities shared broadly across party lines and branches of government in the postwar era, and they often had little to do with environmentalism. Indeed, purveyors of economic development, pork barrel politics, and technocratic systems analysis were "unlikely environmentalists" precisely because their role in promoting water pollution control grew out of a set of counterintuitive values and concerns.

The contributions of these unlikely environmentalists to the policy process came to the fore once Congress took its place at the center of the narrative during the post–World War II era. Certainly the grass roots and the executive branch remained critical actors in the story of water pollution politics, but Congress took the lead in placing the issue on the national agenda in the fifties and sixties. Its decentralized committee structure and career norms encouraged legislative entrepreneurs to address the problem proactively, before the wider public took notice of it. At the same time, the committee system's idiosyncratic jurisdictional boundaries conditioned legislators to interpret water pollution as a function of preexisting agendas associated with traditional interest group clients and affiliated experts. Historians have elsewhere demonstrated how "policy communities" and "issue networks" configured legislative policymaking in the post-1945 era, but they have tended to focus on highly insulated, esoteric, or "top-down" government activities such as atomic energy or fiscal policy. As this book demonstrates, Congress operated as a complex, active, and historically bounded institution even when confronting emerging policy areas such as environmental quality that were subject to considerable "bottom-up" public participation.

If this new look at Congress can provide a more nuanced account of how environmental policies were developed, it can also help explain why they have persisted. Clearly, the environmental movement permanently altered the political landscape of the United States, and its values and priorities changed the structure and function of the regulatory state. But policies like water pollution control had roots that reached deeper into the postwar past—and deeper into institutional channels of the legislative branch—than the movement itself.

In his last-ditch effort to derail the 1972 Clean Water Act, Richard Nixon discovered the issue's staying power. The president vetoed what his advisor, John Whitaker, called the "most important piece of environmental legislation before the Congress this year, symbolically and politically," because of the perceived fiscal impact of the waste treatment grant program. Though the legislation's regulatory features and their private sector costs remained a strong point of contention, the Office of Management and Budget feared that the grant program's absolute cost ($700 million to $800 million over the executive branch budget for 1973—and up to $1 billion over in 1974) would exacerbate inflation and trigger tax increases. The White House's point man on the Senate Public Works Committee, Howard Baker, tried to warn Nixon off. "Baker strongly believes on the basis of his recent grass-roots campaigning that a veto would ignite the quiescent environmental issue," John Ehrlichman noted, "and permit the Democrats to have a tailor-made example of their theme that important domestic priorities (clean water) are being held hostage to continued high defensive spending and untrammeled big business (the 'polluters')."[1]

But the president had more than just grassroots activists and Democrats to worry about. The lure of treatment grant money also tended to convince Republicans who might normally have objected to the 1972 act's unprecedented expansion of state regulatory capacity. John Whitaker received an earful from local officials in Republican-controlled Suffolk County, New York. They let him know that "the campaign in Suffolk, and throughout the Long Island suburbs of New York City, would be severely hurt if the President vetoed the water bill." Long Island relied primarily on septic tanks to handle domestic waste, and population increases within the last few decades had seriously exacerbated groundwater pollution problems. Local governments estimated the costs of constructing a sewage system in Suffolk County alone in the billions of dollars. Consequently, as Whitaker discovered, Republicans viewed "water pollution [as] a hot local political item because of the tax increases that would be required to fund the local share of sewage plant construction."[2]

Even in the "environmental decade," John Blatnik's legacy of distributive politics remained a winning strategy. Nixon, like Eisenhower before him, had no answer for it. Indeed, the Clean Water Act owed its continued popularity in the ensuing decades to local pork as much as to a transformation in public values. Congress has allocated $75 billion to assist cities and towns in constructing waste treatment facilities since 1972. Although amendments in 1987 transformed the grant program into a loan program called the State Water Pollution Control Revolving Fund, Congress still allocates an average of $1.35 billion a year in capitalization grants. This is hardly surprising, given a 2003 EPA survey that pegged the amount of money necessary over the next two decades to upgrade wastewater infrastructure systems at $390 billion.[3]

This same long-range institutional perspective provides a more informed basis to assess Edmund Muskie's ambitious handiwork. Critics in the past have accused him of giving in to public pressure or engaging in partisan one-upsmanship with Nixon in 1972, which resulted in an unrealistic piece of legislation that promised more than it could deliver. Certainly politics cannot be ignored, but it turns out that Muskie was hardly so reactive. A multiplicity of ideas, individuals, and institutions shaped his committee's decision making, a process marked by robust debate and careful consideration of the language used to communicate legislative objectives and administrative details. In the end, the Clean Water Act's goals and regulatory requirements grew out of a philosophical approach to pollution control informed by ecosystems ecology specifically and postwar systems thinking in general.

Over the past three decades, the act has brought about a notable improvement in the quality of the nation's waterways with less of an impact on industrial output or employment than some of its harshest critics had predicted. The EPA's 2000 National Water Quality Inventory, which summarized data submitted by the fifty states, reported that 61 percent of assessed river and stream miles, 54 percent of assessed lake acreage, 49 percent of assessed estuarine square miles, and 22 percent of assessed Great Lakes shoreline miles completely met applicable water quality standards. These numbers suggest important progress, but it is evident that problems still remain: 300,000 river and shore miles and 5 million lake acres still suffer from excessive pollution. The act had its greatest success in reducing the volume of conventional organic sewage and suspended solids, which presented fewer technical challenges than more complex, potentially toxic chemicals and metals. It is estimated that nearly 50 percent of the nation's water pollution stems from nonpoint sources. Although the threat that agricultural and urban run-off posed led the staff of the Senate Public Works Committee to push for a much stricter water pollution bill in 1971, nonpoint pollution has garnered sustained attention only in recent years and remains a difficult political and technical problem. Meanwhile, the legislation's "no-discharge" goal and even some of its stricter technological requirements have gone unmet.[4]

The subsequent history of how the federal government and the states administered the Clean Water Act is a complex story that is beyond the scope of this book, although some brief observations can be offered here. In retrospect, the administrative requirements that Muskie expected EPA officials to fulfill proved too intricate and complex, despite his efforts to use precise and meaningful terms. The problem traces back to the allure of systems-oriented language. The concept of ecological integrity that Muskie found so appealing, when applied as a tangible policy goal, was no less difficult to define, and no less fanciful, than John Tunney's "swimmable-fishable" waters. Determining the technical parameters that actually described an aquatic ecosystem in equilibrium was no simple task, and one that outstripped the EPA's—and most ecologists'—scientific capacity. Integrity remained a rather abstract concept that did not translate easily into practical regulatory requirements. When followed to its logical conclusions, ecological integrity led the Senate Public Works Committee staff to define human beings out of "nature" entirely, positing preindustrial waters as the ideal type—just the conceit Muskie had pinned on Tunney and the sort of exercise that historians like William Cronon have advised against. Muskie's faith that ecosystems ecology would provide the foundation for more rational environmental management also led him to suppress his well-founded doubts about the cost and practicability of many elements of his committee's legislation, from zero-discharge to land treatment technology and the Corps' regional waste management scheme.[5]

In the ensuing years, when the EPA interpreted the Clean Water Act, it essentially overlooked the ecological implications of integrity. This is evident in the agency's year 2000 inventory, which evaluates water quality in terms of specific uses—such as fish consumption, agriculture, drinking water supply, or primary contact recreation—rather than variables associated with aquatic ecology or biogeochemical cycles. The Senate Public Works Committee staff had explicitly repudiated such use-oriented designations and had criticized the Tunney standard for retaining them. Likewise, post-1972 administrative guidelines reintroduced ambient-based water quality standards, a regulatory tool the Senate had discarded on ecological grounds. In response to citizen lawsuits in the 1980s, for example, the EPA developed a set of regulations to implement a program organized around "Total Maximum Daily Loads." TMDLs articulate a set of "ceilings" for aggregate pollution discharges into receiving waters. They implicitly accept the idea that waterways will continue to absorb urban industrial wastes—another tenet the Senate Public Works Committee had rejected outright. These regulations, moreover, are couched in terms of designated uses, not integrity.[6]

Ironically, the provision for maximum daily loads was part and parcel of the 1972 Clean Water Act itself. It represented a time capsule buried in the legislation by the House Public Works Committee in an effort to vest ambient standards with some remaining measure of legitimacy. Senate staffers had dismissed the provision as a meaningless concession that had no operative function. Yet while technology-based effluent standards remain integral to the federal water quality program, TMDLs have become a centerpiece as well. Other recent innovations, like tradable watershed "pollution credits," also stray from the Senate Public Works Committee's ecologically driven aversion to discharges and embody a promising market-based approach to environmental quality that enjoyed neither political nor cultural viability in 1972.[7]

For the Army Corps of Engineers, however, ecology and the vicissitudes of bicameralism also created surprising new opportunities to shape policy and preserve the natural world. The final version of the 1972 Clean Water Act may have circumscribed the Corps' autonomy in regional waste management planning and vested the EPA with primary responsibility for regulating industrial waste discharges under its revised permit program, the National Pollutant Discharge Elimination System (NPDES, Section 402). But the statute still managed, inadvertently, to position the Corps as the lead agency in what would become another of the federal government's principal environmental endeavors: wetlands conservation.

The Corps' new mandate actually stemmed from its duty under Section 10 of the original 1899 Rivers and Harbors Act to oversee dredging and filling activities. Because the Clean Water Act defined the term "pollutant" broadly to include dredged spoil, rock, sand, and cellar dirt, the potential existed for overlap between the EPA's jurisdiction under the NPDES and that of the Corps under Section 10. In short, the "discharge" of dredge or fill material into navigable waters seemed to require both a Section 402 and a Section 10 permit. The House Public Works Committee's bill, unlike the Senate version, granted the Corps independent regulatory authority to deal with these materials under a separate Section 404. Although the two chambers managed to reconcile the respective duties of the Corps and the EPA, Section 404 sowed the seeds of future controversy.[8]

At issue was the precise definition of "navigable waters," and by extension, the scope of the Corps of Engineers' regulatory ambit. Case law characterized a body of water as navigable if it were subject to the ebb and flow of the tide, or if it once had, was currently, or could one day support shipping traffic. This definition happened to exclude many types of wetlands—broadly defined as transitional areas between open water and dry land—from the Corps' purview. Many coastal and inland freshwater wetlands (marshes, bogs, or swamps) for example, were not affected by tidal action. Nor were other areas that the Fish and Wildlife Service classified as wetlands, such as woodlands, meadowlands, prairie potholes, arctic tundra, and even desert furrows.[9]

Had the Clean Water Act retained the traditional legal definition of "navigable," the Corps' fate would not have become entwined with these waterlogged topographies. But Section 502(7) of the act defined "navigable waters" simply as the "waters of the United States." The ecological pathways of pollutants, rather than commercial shipping, informed the Senate Public Works Committee's vocabulary. Water, they reasoned, moved in hydrologic cycles, just as contaminants flowed through an aquatic ecosystem's biogeochemical cycles; older navigational boundaries applied to neither. In order to control water pollution at the source, the regulatory scope of the federal government had to extend to practically all bodies of water, including lakes and tributary streams that were not navigable in the traditional sense. Although the Clean Water Act did not mention wetlands by name, they, too, became subject to the legislation's enforcement provisions—primarily through Section 404, since dredge and fill activities represented one of the principal threats to these ecosystems.[10]

Thus, in the wake of the 1972 Clean Water Act, public interest advocates looked to the Corps of Engineers, once the foremost federal developer of wetlands, to serve as the principle protector of these endangered landscapes. They reasoned that the Corps' unmatched technical competence, together with its ability to plan and execute large-scale projects, could be successfully applied to such an important environmental mission. The agency itself was not so easily convinced. But with time, litigation, and multiple rounds of administrative rule making, the Corps came to accept its new charge. Once again, the legislative language of ecology helped prompt an unlikely environmentalist well-versed in systems planning to undertake a role in environmental protection.[11]

The legislative branch best embodied the diversity of ideas and interests that informed the politics of environmental regulation, one of the most pressing issues of the last forty years. No other institution proved as capable of balancing the knowledge of experts with the will of the people for the sake of nature. But there is a larger lesson here: reinjecting Congress into narratives of state-building, and paying heed to the internal logic and history of the legislative process, compels us to reconsider the pathways of policy development. In this sense, the story of unlikely environmentalists is unlikely to stand as an isolated case.

NOTES

ABBREVIATIONS USED IN THE NOTES

Cong. Rec.	*Congressional Record*
CQA	*Congressional Quarterly Almanac*
HCPW	House Committee on Public Works
HCSASSRD	House Committee on Science and Astronautics, Subcommittee on Science, Research, and Development
HEW	Department of Health, Education, and Welfare
HSCRH	HCPW, Subcommittee on Rivers and Harbors
JP	Thomas Jorling Papers, Williams College Archives and Special Collections
LBJ Library	Lyndon Baines Johnson Library
LHV1	SCPW, *A Legislative History of the Water Pollution Control Act Amendments of 1972*, 93d Cong., 1st sess., January 1973, vol. 1
LHV2	SCPW, *A Legislative History of the Water Pollution Control Act Amendments of 1972*, 93d Cong., 1st sess., January 1973, vol. 2
LWVP	League of Women Voters Papers, Library of Congress
MA	U.S. Senate: Senate Office, Edmund S. Muskie Archives and Special Collections Library, Bates College
NA	National Archives
NARA	National Archives and Records Administration
NEPA	National Environmental Protection Agency
NYT	*New York Times*
PPP	*Public Papers of the Presidents of the United States*
RG	Record Group
SAWP	Senate Committee on Public Works, Subcommittee on Air and Water Pollution
SCIIA	Senate Committee on Interior and Insular Affairs
SCNR	House Committee on Government Operations, Subcommittee on Conservation and Natural Resources
SCNWR	Senate Select Committee on National Water Resources
SCPW	Senate Committee on Public Works
SCPWES	Senate Committee on Public Works Executive Session
SENRE	Senate Committee on Commerce, Subcommittee on Energy, Natural Resources, and the Environment
SFWC	House Committee on Merchant Marine and Fisheries, Subcommittee on Fisheries and Wildlife Conservation
WHCF	White House Central Files
WP	John Whitaker Papers, White House Central Files, Nixon Presidential Materials, National Archives

INTRODUCTION

1. John T. Barnhill, "The Coming National Crisis in Water," *Information Service of the Municipal Reference Bureau and League of Minnesota Municipalities* (September 1960), pp. 3–5, Folder "Public Works H.R. 4036—Water Resource Needs, 87th Cong., 1st sess.," Box 59, John Blatnik Papers, Minnesota Historical Society Manuscript Collection. Other estimates put the "population equivalent" of municipal pollution at 55 million. See chapter one, note 31.

2. David Zwick and Marcy Benstock, *Water Wasteland: Ralph Nader's Study Group Report on Water Pollution* (New York: Grossman, 1971), pp. 4, 37–53, 67–68, 120–39; and Hugh S. Gorman, *Redefining Efficiency: Pollution Concerns, Regulatory Mechanisms, and Technological Change in the U.S. Petroleum Industry* (Akron, Ohio: University of Akron Press, 2001).

3. Donald Carr, *Death of the Sweet Waters* (New York: W. W. Norton, 1966), pp. 125–38.

4. Robert Gottlieb, *Forcing the Spring: The Transformation of the American Environmental Movement* (Washington, D.C.: Island Press, 1993); Hal K. Rothman, *The Greening of a Nation? Environmentalism in the United States since 1945* (Fort Worth, Tex.: Harcourt Brace, 1998); Samuel P. Hays, *Beauty, Health, and Permanence: Environmental Politics in the United States, 1955–1985* (New York: Cambridge University Press, 1987); Kirkpatrick Sale, *The Green Revolution: The American Environmental Movement, 1962–1992* (New York: Hill and Wang, 1993); Philip Shabecoff, *A Fierce Green Fire: The American Environmental Movement* (New York: Hill and Wang, 1993); and Benjamin Kline, *First along the River: A Brief History of the U.S. Environmental Movement* (San Francisco: Acada Books, 1997).

5. Julian E. Zelizer, *Taxing America: Wilbur D. Mills, Congress, and the State, 1945–1975* (Cambridge: Cambridge University Press, 1998); and Julian E. Zelizer, ed., *The American Congress: The Building of Democracy* (Boston: Houghton Mifflin, 2004).

6. On the link between Congress's internal structure and policy output, see Julian E. Zelizer, *On Capitol Hill: The Struggle to Reform Congress and Its Consequences, 1948–2000* (Cambridge: Cambridge University Press, 2004).

7. In *Beauty, Health, and Permanence,* Samuel Hays interprets shifting environmental ideals as a product of post-1945 socioeconomic trends and distinguishes them from narrower, more developmental attitudes about nature that prevailed prior to World War II, namely the "production-oriented" mind-set of Progressive-era conservationists. By contrast, postwar government efforts to preserve and protect open space or other environmental amenities are said to grow out of a set of "consumption-oriented" values shared by a much broader demographic cross section of the population. Hays's insightful analysis endures, although some scholars consider his dichotomy to be overstated. See Paul S. Sutter, *Driven Wild: How the Fight against Automobiles Launched the Modern Wilderness Movement*

(Seattle: University of Washington Press, 2002); and Adam Rome, *The Bulldozer in the Countryside: Suburban Sprawl and the Rise of American Environmentalism* (New York: Cambridge University Press, 2001), pp. 8–9, 12–13. Recent correctives notwithstanding, one dimension of Hays's dichotomy remains unexamined: the connection between "production-oriented" values and the evolution of environmental policies, like water pollution, after 1945.

8. Harrison W. Fox Jr. and Susan Webb Hammond, *Congressional Staffs: The Invisible Force in American Lawmaking* (New York: Free Press, 1977), pp. 169–70.

9. Adam Rome, "What Really Matters in History?" *Environmental History* 7 (April 2002): 304.

CHAPTER 1: SETTING THE AGENDA

1. Gordon McCallum and Mark D. Hollis, "The Pollution 'Balance Sheet'—Where Do We Stand?" *Wastes Engineering* (October 1960): 579–82.

2. Gordon McCallum, "Water Resources and the Municipalities," speech to the League of Virginia Municipalities, 23 September 1958, pp. 2–4, Folder "McCallum 1958"; "Water Pollution Abatement Needs," presented at the National Water Resources Institute, 18 March 1959, pp. 2–3, Folder "McCallum 1959"; "Pollution Control—Our Guarantee of Enough Water," ca. 1960, pp. 1–3, Folder "McCallum 1960"; and "Drinking Waters," Proceedings of the Fifth Southern Municipal and Industrial Waste Conference, April 1956, pp. 36–39, Folder "McCallum 1956"; all in Box 1, Publications and Speeches of Division of Water Supply and Pollution Control Chief Gordon E. McCallum, 1949–1965, RG 412.2.1, NARA.

3. Ch. 758, 62 Stat. 1155 (1948); and M. William Hines, "Nor Any Drop to Drink—Public Regulation of Water Quality, Part III: The Federal Effort," *Iowa Law Review* 52, no. 5 (April 1967): 805–10. I contend that water pollution became a national issue only in the post–World War II era. For an alternate view, see Martin Melosi, *The Sanitary City: Urban Infrastructure from Colonial Times to the Present* (Baltimore: Johns Hopkins University Press, 2000), pp. 213–34.

4. "Clearing Muddy Waters: The Evolving Federalization of Water Pollution Control," *Georgetown Law Journal* 60 (February 1972): 744–47.

5. "Evolution of the Enforcement Provisions of the Federal Water Pollution Control Act: A Study of the Difficulty in Developing Effective Legislation," *Michigan Law Review* 68 (May 1970): 1104–7. In 1953, the Department of Health, Education, and Welfare (HEW) replaced the Federal Security Agency.

6. House Committee on Appropriations, Subcommittee on Labor—HEW, *Hearings on Appropriations for 1956*, 84th Cong., 1st sess., 1955, p. 325; and ibid., *Hearings on Appropriations for 1957*, 84th Cong., 2d sess., 1956, pp. 405–7.

7. House Committee on Public Works (hereafter HCPW), *Comparative Print of Changes Proposed to Be Made in the Water Pollution Control Act*, 84th Cong., 1st sess., 15 February 1955, pp. 1–23; Senate Committee on Public Works (hereafter SCPW), Subcommittee on Flood Control—Rivers and Harbors, *Water Pollution*

Control, 84th Cong., 1st sess., April 1955, pp. 5–6, 43; and "Evolution of the Enforcement Provisions of the Federal Water Pollution Control Act," p. 1111.

8. SCPW, Subcommittee on Flood Control—Rivers and Harbors, *Water Pollution Control*, 84th Cong., 1st sess., April 1955, pp. 43–56, 92–93, 161.

9. HCPW, Subcommittee on Rivers and Harbors (hereafter HSCRH), *Water Pollution Control Act*, 84th Cong., 1st sess., 20 July 1955, pp. 23–33.

10. On the highway legislation of 1955 and 1956 (the National Interstate Highway Act), see *Congressional Quarterly Almanac* 11 (hereafter *CQA*), 84th Cong., 1st sess., 1955, pp. 431–42; and *CQA* 12, 84th Cong., 2d sess., 1956, pp. 391–407.

11. Sonosky Interview, 28 October 1998.

12. John W. Kingdon, *Agendas, Alternatives, and Public Policies* (New York: Harper-Collins College Publishers, 1995).

13. *Biographical Directory of the American Congress, 1774–1996* (Alexandria, Va.: CQ Staff Directories, 1997), p. 673; and Saul B. Cohen, ed., *Columbia Gazetteer of the World*, vol. 1 (New York: Columbia University Press, 1998), p. 643.

14. "Biography of John Anton Blatnik," in *John Blatnik: An Inventory of His Congressional Papers*, Minnesota Historical Society web site (www.mnhs.org/library/findaids/00366.html).

15. E. W. Davis, *Pioneering with Taconite* (St. Paul: Minnesota Historical Society, 1964), pp. v, 1–5, 6–40, 91–107; and Robert V. Bartlett, *The Reserve Mining Controversy: Science, Technology and Environmental Quality* (Bloomington: Indiana University Press, 1980), pp. 11–20.

16. "Biography of John Anton Blatnik"; and Sonosky Interview, 20 October 2000. On the Democratic-Farmer-Labor Party, see Steve M. Gillon, *The Democrats' Dilemma: Walter F. Mondale and the Liberal Legacy* (New York: Columbia University Press, 1992), pp. 6–8.

17. HSCRH, *Water Pollution Control Act*, 84th Cong., 2d sess., March 1956, p. 21.

18. Sonosky Interview, 28 October 1998; and Sonosky, "Profile of Professional Experience, 1954–94" (author's files).

19. Wallace R. Vawter, "Water Supply and Use," reprinted in HSCRH, *Water Pollution Control Act*, 84th Cong., 1st sess., 20 July 1955, pp. 113–29.

20. Ibid.

21. "Council Presentation: Conservation," April 1957, p. 1, Folder "Water Resources, Basic Documents, 1951–58," Box 562, Series IV, League of Women Voters Papers, Library of Congress (hereafter LWVP).

22. K. A. MacKichan and J. B. Graham, *Water Resources Review, Supplement 3: Public Water-Supply Shortages, 1953* (Washington, D.C.: Department of Interior Geological Survey, 1954). On postwar urban water supply infrastructures, see Melosi, *The Sanitary City*, pp. 296–310.

23. Francis Bello, "How Are We Fixed for Water?" *Fortune* 44 (March 1954): 120–48; "Plenty of Water—But Not to Waste," *Business Week* (9 September 1950): 82–86; "U.S. Running Short of Water," *U.S. News and World Report* 39 (8 July 1955):

38–42; "Will Water Become Scarce?" *U.S. News and World Report* 40 (27 April 1956): 84–91; and "Water Crisis Still a Reality," *American City* 71 (November 1956), p. 23.

24. HSCRH, *Water Pollution Control Act*, 84th Cong., 1st sess., 20 July 1955, pp. 111–12.

25. Sonosky Interview, 28 October 1998.

26. James Q. Wilson, "The Politics of Regulation," in *Social Responsibility and the Business Predicament*, ed. James W. McKie (Washington, D.C.: Brookings Institution, 1974), pp. 138–44.

27. *CQA* 12, 84th Cong., 2d sess., 1956, p. 573.

28. E. E. Schattschneider, *The Semisovereign People: A Realist's View of Democracy in America* (New York: Holt, Rinehart, and Winston, 1960); and Frank Baumgartner and Bryan Jones, *Agendas and Instability in American Politics* (Chicago: University of Chicago Press, 1993).

29. Arthur Maass, *Muddy Waters: The Army Corps of Engineers and the Nation's Rivers* (Cambridge, Mass.: Harvard University Press, 1951).

30. Sonosky Interview, 28 October 1998; HSCRH, *Water Pollution Control Act*, 84th Cong., 1st sess., 20 July 1955, p. 246; and Melosi, *The Sanitary City*, pp. 208–12, 218–20. On distributive politics, see Richard L. McCormick, *The Party Period and Public Policy* (New York: Oxford University Press, 1986), pp. 18–19, 113–221; and Stephen Skowronek, *Building a New American State: The Expansion of National Administrative Capacities, 1877–1920* (New York: Cambridge University Press, 1982), pp. 19–46.

31. John Ludwig to Gordon McCallum, "Significant Trends in Water Pollution Control Program," 11 July 1955, Folder "Water Pollution 2: Control Measures," Box 107, RG 90, NARA; Gordon McCallum, "Public Health Service Makes Striking Prediction: 6,685 Sewage Plants and Trunk Lines Will Cost $5.33 Billion," *Wastes Engineering* (October 1955): 504–7.

32. HSCRH, *Water Pollution Control Act*, 84th Cong., 1st sess., 20 July 1955, pp. 138–39, 244–48.

33. Sonosky Interview, 20 October 2000; and Thomas Sugrue, *The Origins of the Urban Crisis: Race and Inequality in Postwar Detroit* (Princeton, N.J.: Princeton University Press, 1996), pp. 125–52.

34. HCPW, Subcommittee on Roads, *National Highway Program—Federal Aid Highway Act of 1956*, 84th Cong., 2d sess., March 1956, pp. 266–352; and *CQA* 12, 84th Cong., 2d sess., 1956, pp. 392, 400.

35. Sonosky Interview, 28 October 1998; Bess Furman, *A Profile of the United States Public Health Service, 1798–1948* (USHEW Publication No. 73-39, 1973), pp. 446–47; and Rosemary Stevens, *In Sickness and in Wealth: American Hospitals in the Twentieth Century* (Baltimore: Johns Hopkins University Press, 1999), pp. 216–21. For the allotment formula, see Hines, "Nor Any Drop to Drink, Part III," p. 818, note 83.

36. Sonosky Interview, 20 October 2000.
37. HSCRH, *Water Pollution Control Act*, 84th Cong., 1st sess., 20 July 1955, pp. 184–226; and "Evolution of the Enforcement Provisions of the Federal Water Pollution Control Act," pp. 1108–12. Critics estimated that the act's various waiting periods granted immunity to a polluter for at least eighteen months after initial notification.
38. Sonosky Interview, 28 October 1998.
39. *CQA* 12, 84th Cong., 2d sess., 1956, p. 570; M. Kent Jennings, "Legislative Politics and Water Pollution Control, 1956–61," in *Congress and Urban Problems*, ed. Frederic N. Cleaveland (Washington, D.C.: Brookings Institution, 1969), pp. 101–9.
40. R. S. Green to McCallum, "Municipal Sewage Treatment Requirements and Trends," 12 February 1958, Folder "Disposal 3: Sewage," Box 125, RG 90, NARA. The Census Bureau expected the population to be 220 million in 1975 and 270 million by 1985; initial estimates were 210 and 236 million, respectively.
41. Hines, "Nor Any Drop to Drink, Part III," p. 816; HSCRH, *Water Pollution Control Act*, 84th Cong., 1st sess., 20 July 1955, pp. 135–36, 141, 148; and Gordon McCallum, "Federal Water Pollution Control Legislation, 1955," speech before the Federation of Sewage and Industrial Wastes Associations, Atlantic City, N.J., 11 October 1955, p. 2, Folder "McCallum 1957," Box 1, and McCallum, "Balancing Urban Needs and Financial Resources in Water Supply and Pollution Control," speech presented before the American Municipal Congress, 1960, pp. 1–10, Folder "McCallum 1960," Box 2, McCallum Papers, RG 412.2.1, NARA.
42. Hines, "Nor Any Drop to Drink, Part III," pp. 819–22.

CHAPTER 2: THE SOLUTION TO POLLUTION IS DILUTION

1. Richard Lowitt, *The New Deal and the West* (Bloomington: Indiana University Press, 1984); Gerald Nash, *World War II and the West: Reshaping the Economy* (Lincoln: University of Nebraska Press, 1990); Richard White, *"It's Your Misfortune and None of My Own": A New History of the American West* (Norman: University of Oklahoma Press, 1991), pp. 483–87, 522–26; Clayton R. Koppes, "Efficiency, Equity, Esthetics: Shifting Themes in American Conservation," in *The Ends of the Earth: Perspectives on Modern Environmental History*, ed. Donald Worster (Cambridge: Cambridge University Press, 1989), p. 242; Donald Worster, *Rivers of Empire: Water, Aridity, and the Growth of the American West* (New York: Pantheon, 1985); Marc Reisner, *Cadillac Desert* (New York: Viking, 1986); and Norris Hundley, *Water and the West: The Colorado River Compact and the Politics of Water in the American West* (Berkeley: University of California Press, 1975).
2. Mark Harvey, *A Symbol of Wilderness: Echo Park and the American Conservation Movement* (Albuquerque: University of New Mexico Press, 1994); John McPhee, *Encounters with the Archdruid* (New York: Farrar, Straus, and Giroux, 1971); and Elmo Richardson, *Dams, Parks, and Politics: Resource Development and Preser-*

vation in the Truman-Eisenhower Era (Lexington: University Press of Kentucky, 1973).

3. Stans to Robert Kerr, 27 July 1959, p. 1, Folder "Bureau of the Budget," Box 6, RG 46.22.2, NARA; Chester Pach and Elmo Richardson, *The Presidency of Dwight D. Eisenhower* (Lawrence: University Press of Kansas, 1991), pp. 167–69; Charles C. Alexander, *Holding the Line: The Eisenhower Era, 1952–1961* (Bloomington: Indiana University Press, 1975), pp. 37–38, 191–94; and Steven E. Ambrose, *Eisenhower: The President* (New York: Simon and Schuster, 1984), pp. 88–91, 223–24, 388–91, 495–97.

4. *Congressional Record* 103 (hereafter *Cong. Rec.*) (28 March 1957), p. 4602; *CQA* 12, 84th Cong., 2d sess., 1956, p. 574; and *CQA* 13, 85th Cong., 1st sess., 1957, p. 623. These sums do not even take into account authorizations for reclamation projects, which were determined separately.

5. Robert Griffith, "Dwight D. Eisenhower and the Corporate Commonwealth," *American Historical Review* 87 (February 1982): 87–122; Martin Reuss, "Coping with Uncertainty: Social Scientists, Engineers, and Federal Water Resources Planning," *Natural Resources Review* 32 (Winter 1992): 125; and "Report from the Hill" (No. 21), April 1957, p. 1, Folder "Water Resources Basic Documents, 1951–58," and "Board Briefing: The Economy, Foreign Aid and Water Resources," 4 April 1958, p. 1, Folder "Water Resources Basic Documents—1958," Box 562, Series IV, LWVP.

6. "Memorandum of Disapproval of Bill Authorizing Navigation, Shore Protection, and Flood Control Projects," 10 August 1956, *Public Papers of the Presidents of the United States* (hereafter *PPP*): *Dwight D. Eisenhower, 1956* (Washington, D.C.: GPO, 1957), pp. 680–81; "Veto of Bill Authorizing Appropriations for Rivers, Harbors and Flood Control Projects," 15 April 1958, *PPP: Dwight D. Eisenhower, 1958*, pp. 307–8; *CQA* 12, 84th Cong., 2d sess., p. 12, 84th Cong., 2d sess., 1956, p. 574; *CQA* 13, 85th Cong., 1st sess., 1957, pp. 622–24; "Annual Budget Message to Congress, FY 1960," *PPP: Dwight D. Eisenhower, 1959*, p. 45; *CQA* 15, 86th Cong., 1st sess., 1959, p. 315–17; and "Veto of the Public Works Appropriation Bill," 28 August 1959, *PPP: Dwight D. Eisenhower, 1959*, pp. 618–20.

7. Schad Interview, 7 January 1998.

8. Theodore M. Schad, "An Analysis of the Work of the Senate Select Committee on National Water Resources," *Natural Resources Journal* 2 (August 1962): 226. On the various executive branch reports on water resources, see Beatrice Hort Holmes, *A History of Federal Water Resources Programs, 1800–1960* (Washington, D.C.: U.S. Department of Agriculture Economic Research Service, Miscellaneous Publication No. 1233, 1972), pp. 38–42; and President's Materials Policy Commission, *Resources for Freedom, Volume V: Selected Reports to the Commission* (Washington, D.C.: GPO, 1952), pp. 83–89.

9. *Cong. Rec.* 105, pt. 1 (27 January 1959), pp. 1157–58.

10. Senate Committee on Interior and Insular Affairs (hereafter SCIIA), Subcommittee on Irrigation and Reclamation, *Development and Coordination of Water*

Resources, 86th Cong., 1st sess., 1959, pp. 7–12; and Robert and Leona Rienow, "The Day the Taps Run Dry," *Harper's Magazine* 217 (October 1958), reprinted in ibid., *Development and Coordination of Water Resources*, Appendix, pp. 35–40.

11. Roy Hamilton, "The Senate Select Committee on National Water Resources: An Ethical and Rational Criticism," *Natural Resources Journal* 2 (April 1962): 47–51.

12. Ibid., pp. 52–54.

13. Holmes, *History of Federal Water Resources Programs*, pp. 37–52.

14. On the evolution of congressional staffs in the postwar era, see Fox and Hammond, *Congressional Staffs*, pp. 12–28, 168–71; Kenneth Kofmehl, *Professional Staffs of Congress* (West Lafayette, Ind.: Purdue University Press, 1977); Susan Webb Hammond, "Congressional Staffs," in *Encyclopedia of the American Legislative System*, ed. Joel H. Silbey, vol. 2 (New York: Charles Scribner's, 1994), pp. 785–800; and Michael J. Malbin, *Unelected Representatives: Congressional Staff and the Future of Representative Government* (New York: Basic Books, 1980).

15. Robert S. Kerr, *Land, Wood, and Water* (New York: Fleet Publishing, 1960), pp. 168–69.

16. Anne Hodges Morgan, *Robert S. Kerr: The Senate Years* (Tulsa: University of Oklahoma Press, 1977), pp. 42–46; and Walter McDougall, *The Heavens and the Earth: A Political History of the Space Age* (New York: Basic Books, 1985), pp. 309, 373–75, 386–87.

17. *CQA* 13, 85th Cong., 1st sess., 1957, p. 624; "Board Briefing on Water Resources," October 1958, p. 1, Folder "Water Resources, Basic Documents, 1958," Box 562, Series IV, LWVP; Walter Hollander Jr., *Abel Wolman: His Life and Philosophy* (Chapel Hill, N.C.: Universal Printing and Publishing, 1981), pp. 244, 443–44, 957; and Kerr, *Land, Wood, and Water*, pp. 323–39.

18. Schad Interview, 23 March 1998; Theodore Schad Oral Interview, conducted by Dr. Martin Reuss of the Office of History, Headquarters, U.S. Army Corps of Engineers, 27 February 1989, pp. 220–25; SCIIA, *Establishing Committee to Study Matter of Development and Coordination of Water Resources*, 86th Cong., 1st sess., 1959, S. Rep. 145, pp. 5–9; and "Suggested Approach to Studies Authorized by S. Res. 48," 21 May 1959, Folder "Outlines and Memoranda," Box 1, RG 46.22.2, NARA.

19. Schad Interview, 7 January 1998.

20. "General Outline of Proposed Procedures," 11 June 1959, Folder "Staff Memoranda," Box 1, RG 46.22.2, NARA; Philip W. Warken, *A History of the National Resources Planning Board, 1933–1943* (New York: Garland, 1979), pp. 103–28.

21. Douglas R. Woodward, "Availability of Water in the United States with Special Reference to Industrial Needs by 1980," Thesis No. 143, Resident Course, Industrial College of the Armed Forces, 10 April 1957, Folder "84th Congress, 2nd session," Box 59, John Blatnik Papers, Minnesota Historical Society Manuscript collection; and President's Materials Policy Commission, *Resources for Freedom, Volume V: Selected Reports to the Commission*, pp. 93–94. For reaction to Wood-

ward, see George Burke to Arve Dahl, "Telephone Call from Douglas Woodward and Comments on Mr. Woodward's Draft Report," 1 July 1957, and R. S. Green to Chief, Division of Sanitary Engineering Services, "Water Use in the United States," 25 April 1958, Folder "Water 4: Studies/Surveys/Projects," Box 106, RG 90, NARA.

22. Schad Interview, 23 March 1998; Resources for the Future, "Our Future Water Needs: PMPC Forecast vs. RFF Estimate," undated draft of paper, p. 16, and Resources for the Future, Annual Report draft, 2 November 1960, pp. 2–3, Folder "Resources for the Future," Box 11, RG 46.22.2, NARA; and Senate Select Committee on National Water Resources (hereafter SCNWR), *Water Resource Activities in the United States—Water Supply and Demand*, 86th Cong., 2d sess., August 1960, p. 2, Committee Print No. 32.

23. Irving K. Fox, "Water—Supply, Demand, and the Law," 25 August 1959, pp. 17–18, Folder 62, Box 2, Henry Caulfield Papers, Records Collections, Office of History, Headquarters U.S. Army Corps of Engineers; White to Schad, 3 July 1959, Folder "Gilbert White," Box 11, RG 46.22.2, NARA; and Maynard M. Hufschmidt to Schad, 22 July 1959, Folder "Correspondence—Maynard Hufschmidt," Box 11, RG 46.22.2, NARA.

24. Theodore M. Schad, "An Analysis of the Work of the Senate Select Committee on National Water Resources," *Natural Resources Journal* 2 (August 1962): 234. Experts affiliated with the Geological Survey and the Army Corps of Engineers did make other significant contributions; the Bureau of Reclamation did not. See Nathaniel Wollman, "Errors in the 'Ethical and Rational Criticism' of the Select Committee by Roy Hamilton," *Natural Resources Journal* 2 (August 1962): 265.

25. Ralph C. Williams, *The United States Public Health Service, 1798–1950* (Washington, D.C.: Commissioned Officers Association of the USPHS, 1951); Fitzhugh Mullan, *Plagues and Politics: The Story of the United States Public Health Service* (New York: Basic Books, 1989); Mark Hollis Memo for the Record, "Water Resources in the National Health Structure," 22 August 1957, p. 2, Folder "Water 3—Standards," Box 105, RG 90, NARA; Leonard A. Scheele to Undersecretary of HEW, "Departmental Interest in Public Works for Water Supply and Sewerage," 8 February 1954, Folder "Community Facilities," Box 16, RG 90, NARA; and Hollis to Chief Sanitary Engineering Officer, "Representation for Sanitary Engineering Interests of the Department in Federal Inter-Agency Activities," 7 January 1954, Folder "Cooperation," Box 16, RG 90, NARA.

26. Gordon E. McCallum and Robert W. Haywood Jr., "1958 Federal Water Supply Act and Future Water Requirements," *Journal of the American Water Works Association* 52 (July 1960): 829–33; "General Notes: PHS Participation in Multi-Purpose Water Resource Projects—AWRBIAC Project," pp. 1–6, Folder "Water 4: Studies/Surveys/Projects," Box 106, RG 90, NARA; Report attached to Memorandum of S. C. Martin to All Basin Engineers, "Comments on Water Pollution Control Activities of the Public Health Service," 12 November 1953, pp. 13–14, Folder

"Water Pollution: Comments on Water Pollution Activities of PHS," Box 41, RG 90, NARA; Senate Committee on Appropriations, Subcommittee on the Departments of Labor and HEW, *Labor—Health, Education and Welfare Appropriations, 1959 (Public Health Service)*, 85th Cong., 1st sess., 1958, pp. 520–32; HEW, *Annual Report*, 1956 (Washington, D.C.: GPO, 1957), p. 143; and ibid., 1954 (Washington, D.C.: GPO, 1954), pp. 152–53.

27. Schad Interview, 23 March 1998; SCNWR, *Water Resources Activities in the United States—Water Quality Management*, 86th Cong., 2d sess., February 1960, pp. 1–3, Committee Print No. 24.

28. SCNWR, *Water Resources Activities in the United States—Water Quality Management*, 86th Cong., 2d sess., February 1960, pp. 3, 15, Committee Print No. 32. "Preliminary Draft Statement on National Water Problems and Trends," undated, p. 1, Folder "PHS Correspondence," Box 10, RG 46.22.2, NARA; and SCNWR, *Water Resources Activities in the United States—Water Requirements for Pollution Abatement*, 86th Cong., 2d sess., July 1960, p. 1, Committee Print No. 29.

29. Keith Krause to DWS&PC Personnel, "Request of the Senate Select Committee on National Water Resources for Information on Municipal Water Supply and Water Pollution Problems," 12 August 1959, p. 6, Folder "PHS Correspondence," Box 10, RG 46.22.2, NARA.

30. SCNWR, *Water Resources Activities in the United States—Water Quality Management*, 86th Cong., 2d sess., February 1960, pp. 3, 15, Committee Print No. 32, p. 3–4, 20; Schad Interview, 7 January 1998; and SCNWR, *Water Resources Activities in the United States—Pollution Abatement*, 86th Cong., 2d sess., 1960, Committee Print No. 9.

31. Schad Interview, 23 March 1998 and 7 January 1998; Theodore Schad Oral Interview, U.S. Army Corps of Engineers, pp. 230, 238; and Schad to C. H. J. Hull, 7 April 1960, Folder "Abel Wolman," Box 11, RG 46.22.2, NARA.

32. Schad Interview, 23 March 1998.

33. Reid to Schad, 4 August 1959, Folder "George Reid," Box 11, RG 46.22.2, NARA.

34. Schad to Reid, 26 August 1959, and Reid to Schad, 2 September 1959, Folder "George Reid," Box 11, RG 46.22.2, NARA; SCNWR, *Water Resources Activities in the United States—Water Requirements for Pollution Abatement*, 86th Cong., 2d sess., July 1960, p. 1, Committee Print No. 29, pp. 1–12. Waste treated to remove 80 percent of BOD required only half the volume of supplemental dilution water of that subjected to 60 percent removal.

35. Schad to C. H. J. Hull, 7 April 1960, and Schad to Abel Wolman, 6 April 1960, Folder "Abel Wolman," Box 11, RG 46.22.2, NARA; and Earnest Gloyna to Schad, 31 October 1960, Folder "Correspondence G," Box 2, RG 46.22.2, NARA.

36. Draft of Preliminary Staff Report, 30 March 1960, pp. 9–11, Folder "Staff Memoranda," Box 1, and Reid to Wollman, 30 May 1960, Folder "Reid," Box 11, RG 46.22.2, NARA.

37. Draft of Preliminary Staff Report, p. 9; Schad to John C. Geyer, 9 June 1960, Folder "Abel Wolman," Box 11, RG 46.22.2, NARA. Three alternative programs were postulated for each region: maximum treatment and minimum storage; minimum treatment and maximum storage; or minimum aggregate costs of treatment and storage. Treatment levels ranged from 50 percent to 97.5 percent of BOD removal. See SCNWR, *Water Resources Activities in the United States—Water Quality Management*, 86th Cong., 2d sess., February 1960, Committee Print No. 32, pp. 8–10, 27, 29–32; and Theodore Schad, "Address before the Missouri Basin Inter-Agency Committee," 20 April 1960, pp. 5–6, Folder "Correspondence H," Box 2, RG 46.22.2, NARA.

38. SCNWR, *Water Resources Activities in the United States—Water Quality Management*, 86th Cong., 2d sess., February 1960, Committee Print No. 32, pp. 4–5; Nathaniel Wollman, "Errors in the 'Ethical and Rational Criticism' of the Select Committee by Roy Hamilton," *Natural Resources Journal* 2 (August 1962): 261–62. Approximately 90 percent of estimated flows for 1980 and 2000 were believed to be required to dilute projected levels of waste discharge.

39. Bruce Bimber, *The Politics of Expertise in Congress* (Albany: State University of New York Press, 1996), pp. 95–96.

40. "Preliminary State of Findings and Recommendations," 12 May 1960, Folder "Staff Memoranda," Box 1, RG 46.22.2, NARA; and Schad Interview, 7 January 1998.

41. On Kerr and water agencies in the Arkansas-Red-White Basin, see Morgan, *Robert S. Kerr*, pp. 148–57.

42. McGee to Kerr, 28 November 1960, and Moss to Kerr, 15 November 1960, Folder "Correspondence—Members," Box 5, RG 46.22.2, NARA.

43. Schad Interview, 7 January 1998; and Theodore M. Schad, "An Analysis of the Work of the Senate Select Committee on National Water Resources," *Natural Resources Journal* 2 (August 1962): 237–38.

44. SCNWR, *Report of the Senate Select Committee on National Water Resources*, 87th Cong., 1st sess., 30 January 1961, S. Rep. 29, pp. 5–7, 17–19; and C. L. McGuinness, "Water for the United States—An Analysis of the Report of the Senate Select Committee on National Water Resources," *Natural Resources Journal* 2 (August 1962): 194–98.

45. "Percolations and Runoff," *Journal of the American Water Works Association* 53 (May 1961): 43–44.

46. "Message on Natural Resources Policy," 23 February 1961, *PPP: John F. Kennedy* (Washington, D.C.: GPO, 1962), pp. 115–17.

47. M. Granger Morgan and John M. Peha, "Analysis, Governance, and the Need for Better Institutional Arrangements," and Bruce L. R. Smith and Jeffrey K. Stine, "Technical Advice for Congress: Past Trends and Present Obstacles," in *Science and Technology Advice for Congress*, ed. M. Granger Morgan and John M. Peha

(Washington, D.C.: Resources for the Future, 2003), pp. 3–20 and 23–52; and Nathaniel Wollman, "Errors in the 'Ethical and Rational Criticism' of the Select Committee by Roy Hamilton," *Natural Resources Journal* 2 (August 1962): 262, 265–66.

48. SCNWR, *Water Resources Activities in the United States—Water Quality Management*, 86th Cong., 2d sess., February 1960, Committee Print No. 32, pp. 32–34; and National Water Commission, *Water Policies for the Future: Final Report to the President and to the Congress of the United States by the National Water Commission* (Washington, D.C.: GPO, 1973), pp. 11–17.

49. *CQA* 17, 87th Cong., 1st sess., 1961, pp. 267–69; Sonosky Interview, 28 October 1998; Jennings, "Legislative Politics and Water Pollution Control," pp. 93–101; SCPW, Subcommittee on Flood Control—Rivers and Harbors, *River and Harbor—Flood Control Act of 1957* (S. 497), 85th Cong., 1st sess., pp. 14–15, 140–43; and SCPW, Subcommittee on Flood Control—Rivers and Harbors, *Water Pollution Control*, 87th Cong., 1st sess., 1961, pp. 1, 14, 67.

50. Frank Graham Jr., *Disaster by Default: Politics and Water Pollution* (New York: M. Evans, 1966), p. 225. The 1961 amendments bypassed the surgeon general and placed the program directly under the supervision of the secretary of HEW, setting the stage for more sweeping future legislation.

51. HCPW, *Federal Water Pollution Control*, 87th Cong., 1st sess., 14 March 1961, pp. 244–52, 265, 290, 293, 295–96.

52. Ibid., p. 13; Hines, "Nor Any Drop to Drink, Part III, p. 823; and Public Health Service, HEW, *Proceedings, The National Conference on Water Pollution*, Washington D.C., 12–14 December 1960, pp. 556–67.

CHAPTER 3: THE EDUCATION OF AN ENTREPRENEUR

1. William E. Leuchtenburg, *Flood Control Politics: The Connecticut River Valley Problem, 1927–1950* (New York: Da Capo, 1972); and SCNWR, *Hearings on National Water Resources—Augusta, Maine*, 86th Cong., 1st sess., 7 December 1959.

2. SCNWR, *Hearings on National Water Resources—Augusta, Maine*, pp. 2780–88.

3. Ibid., pp. 2832–33; Mrs. John Freeman to Arthur E. Whittemore, 10 December 1959, Folder "Conservation: Water Resources," Box 870, Series III, LWVP; and "Rating of Rivers a Pollution Issue," *New York Times* (hereafter *NYT*), 16 March 1965.

4. "What about Water?" fact sheet prepared by the League of Women Voters of Maine (undated), Folder "Conservation: Water Resources," Box 870, Series III, LWVP; SCNWR, *Hearings on National Water Resources—Augusta, Maine*, pp. 2837–40.

5. SCNWR, *Hearings on National Water Resources—Augusta, Maine*, p. 2824; and Theodore Schad Oral Interview, U.S. Army Corps of Engineers, 27 February 1989, pp. 274–76.

6. Edmund S. Muskie, *Journeys* (Garden City, N.Y.: Doubleday, 1972), p. 83.

7. Martin Nolan, "Muskie of Maine," *Reporter* 37 (13 July 1967): 44; and *Biographical Directory of the United States Congress, 1774–1989* (Alexandria, Va.: CQ Staff Directories, 1989), p. 1555.

8. David Nevins, *Muskie of Maine* (New York: Random House, 1972), pp. 34–35, 147–49; and Duane Lockard, *New England State Politics* (Princeton, N.J.: Princeton University Press, 1959), pp. 79, 107–18.

9. Richard W. Judd and Christopher S. Beach, *Natural States: The Environmental Imagination in Maine, Oregon, and the Nation* (Resources for the Future: Washington, D.C., 2003), pp. 28–39.

10. Robert F. Blomquist, "What Is Past Is Prologue: Senator Edmund S. Muskie's Environmental Policymaking Roots as Governor of Maine, 1955–58," *Maine Law Review* 51 (1999): 92–97, 114, 126; Nevins, *Muskie of Maine*, pp. 152–53, 161; and Billings Interview, 21 November 1997.

11. Theo Lippman Jr. and Donald C. Hansen, *Muskie* (New York: W. W. Norton, 1971), pp. 85–86; Blomquist, "What Is Past Is Prologue," pp. 94, 99, 114–18; Muskie, *Journeys*, p. 81; Nevins, *Muskie of Maine*, p. 173; and Lockard, *New England State Politics*, p. 108.

12. Richard F. Fenno, *Congressmen in Committees* (Boston: Little, Brown, 1973); Nelson Polsby, "The Institutionalization of the U.S. House of Representatives," *American Political Science Review* 62 (March 1968): 144–68; Polsby et al., "The Growth of the Seniority System in the U.S. House of Representatives," *American Political Science Review* 63 (1969): 787–807; Steven Smith and Christopher J. Deering, *Committees in Congress* (Washington, D.C.: Congressional Quarterly Press, 1984), p. 40; Barbara Hinkley, *Stability and Change in Congress* (New York: Harper and Row, 1988); and Allan G. Bogue et al., "Members of the House of Representatives and the Process of Modernization, 1789–1960," *Journal of American History* 63, no. 2 (September 1986): 275–302.

13. Smith and Deering, *Committees in Congress*, p. 41; Charles O. Jones, "Joseph G. Cannon and Howard H. Smith: An Essay on the Limits of Leadership in the House," *Journal of Politics* 30 (August 1968): 617–46; and Raymond E. Wolfinger and Joan Heifetz, "Safe Seats, Seniority, and Power in Congress," *American Political Science Review* 59 (1965): 337–49.

14. Zelizer, *Taxing America*; Samuel P. Huntington, "Congressional Responses to the Twentieth Century," in *The Congress and America's Future*, ed. David B. Truman (Englewood Cliffs, N.J.: Prentice Hall, 1965), pp. 18–21; Donald R. Matthews, *U.S. Senators and Their World* (Chapel Hill: University of North Carolina Press, 1960); and David W. Rohde, Norman J. Ornstein, and Robert L. Peabody, "Political Change and Legislative Norms in the U.S. Senate, 1957–74," in *Studies in Congress*, ed. Glenn R. Parker (Washington, D.C.: Congressional Quarterly Press, 1985), pp. 148–52.

15. Rohde, Ornstein, and Peabody, "Political Change and Legislative Norms in the U.S. Senate," pp. 168–75; and Barbara Sinclair, *The Transformation of the U.S. Senate* (Baltimore: Johns Hopkins University Press, 1981), pp. 30–32, 38–43.

16. Sinclair, *The Transformation of the U.S. Senate*, pp. 33–34.

17. Robert Dallek, *Lone Star Rising: Lyndon Johnson and His Times, 1908–1960* (New York: Oxford University Press, 1991), pp. 467–540; Rohde, Ornstein, and Peabody, "Political Change and Legislative Norms in the U.S. Senate," pp. 158–67; Rowland Evans and Robert Novack, "The Johnson System," in *The Legislative Process in the U.S. Senate*, ed. Lawrence K. Pettit and Edward Keynes (Chicago: Rand McNally, 1969), pp. 177–99; and Robert Caro, *Master of the Senate* (New York: Vintage, 2003).

18. Some version of this tale is recounted in all of the biographical material on Muskie and in Rowland Evans and Robert Novack, *Lyndon B. Johnson: The Exercise of Power* (New York: New American Library, 1966), p. 217; and Dallek, *Lone Star Rising*, pp. 547–48.

19. Linton Interview, 28 July 1998. Kerr operated as de facto committee chair, supplanting the alcoholic Dennis Chavez (D-N.Mex.), who died three weeks before Kerr. 20. Randall B. Ripley, "Power in the Post–World War II Senate," in *Studies in Congress*, ed. Glenn R. Parker (Washington, D.C.: Congressional Quarterly Press, 1985), pp. 300–310; Sinclair, *The Transformation of the U.S. Senate*, pp. 44–45; Smith and Deering, *Committees in Congress*, pp. 42–43, 135–62; and Randall B. Ripley, *Power in the Senate* (New York: St. Martin's, 1969), pp. 109–30.

20. James Q. Wilson, *The Politics of Regulation* (New York: Basic Books, 1980), pp. 357–94; David Vogel, *Fluctuating Fortunes: The Political Power of Business in America* (New York: Basic Books, 1989), pp. 37–58; and Roger Davidson, "Subcommittee Government: New Channels for Policy Making," in *The New Congress*, ed. Dean E. Mann and Norman Ornstein (Washington, D.C.: American Enterprise Institute, 1981), pp. 99–133.

21. Sonosky Interview, 28 October 1998; and Linton Interview, 28 July 1998.

22. Linton Interview, 28 July 1998; Martin Nolan, "Muskie of Maine," *Reporter* 37 (13 July 1967): 45–46; and Nevins, *Muskie of Maine*, pp. 63–65.

23. Nicoll Interview, 13 October 1998; Linton Interview, 28 July 1998; and Sinclair, *The Transformation of the U.S. Senate*, p. 45.

24. Linton Interview, 28 July 1998; Lippman and Hansen, *Muskie*, p. 148; Senate Historical Office, Oral History Interviews, "William F. Hildenbrand, Secretary of the Senate," 20 March – 6 May 1985, pp. 39–61, Library of Congress; and Bernard Asbell, *The Senate Nobody Knows* (Garden City, N.Y.: Doubleday, 1978), p. 42.

25. Nicoll Interview, 20 October 1998; and Linton Interview, 28 July 1998.

26. Holmes, *History of Federal Water Resources Programs and Policies*, pp. 66–73; Kristin M. Szylvian, "Transforming Lake Michigan into the 'World's Greatest Fishing Hole': The Environmental Politics of Michigan's Great Lakes Sport Fishing, 1965–1985," *Environmental History* 9 (January 2004): 102–27; and Terence Kehoe,

Cleaning Up the Great Lakes: From Cooperation to Confrontation (DeKalb: Northern Illinois University Press, 1997), pp. 43–66, 73–78.

27. Linton Interview, 28 July 1998; and Walter A. Rosenbaum, *The Politics of Environmental Concern* (New York: Praeger, 1977), pp. 6–7.

28. SCPW, Subcommittee on Air and Water Pollution (hereafter SAWP), *Water Pollution*, 89th Cong., 1st sess., pt. 2, June 1965; Muskie Press Release, 8 April 1965, Folder 7, Box 572, U.S. Senate: Senate Office, Edmund S. Muskie Archives and Special Collections Library, Bates College (hereafter MA); and Nevins, *Muskie of Maine*, pp. 183–85.

29. Linton Interview, 28 July 1998.

30. *Troubled Waters*, RG 412.8, NARA.

31. "The Reason for the Drought in the Northeast," *NYT*, 22 August 1965; and Theodore Steinberg, *Down to Earth: Nature's Role in American History* (New York: Oxford University Press, 2002), pp. 247–48.

32. "Drought Forces City to Re-Evaluate Its Water Outlook for the Future," *NYT*, 5 July 1965; "More Water Curbs Threatened to Prevent a Famine in Winter," *NYT*, 5 July 1965; "City Acts to Tap Hudson to Ease Water Shortage," *NYT*, 9 July 1965; and Holmes, *History of Federal Water Resources Programs*, pp. 62–64.

33. "The Dry Season," *New Republic* 153 (21 August 1965): 5–6; "The People-Water Crisis," *Newsweek* 66 (23 August 1965): 48–52; and "Water Crisis—Why? Story of a Scarcity That's Getting Worse," *U.S. News and World Report* 59 (2 August 1965): 39–41.

34. Martin Melosi, "Lyndon Johnson and Environmental Policy," in *The Johnson Years, Volume Two: Vietnam, the Environment, and Science*, ed. Robert A. Divine (Lawrence: University Press of Kansas, 1987), pp. 113–49; "The Dry Society," *Time* 86 (20 August 1965): 22; and "U.S. to Send Water Teams to Study Crisis in 5 Cities," *NYT*, 12 August 1965.

35. "Water Problem Faces Entire U.S.," *NYT*, 20 December 1965; Donald Hornig to the President, "Reuse of Water by Cities," 10 September 1965, Folder "DI2 8/15/65–9/10/65," Box 2, White House Central Files (hereafter WHCF), Lyndon Baines Johnson Library (hereafter LBJ Library); and "Water Pollution: Federal Role Is Strengthened by Law Authorizing New Agency and Quality Standards," *Science* 150 (8 October 1965): 258.

36. SCPW, *A Study of Pollution—Water*, 88th Cong., 1st sess., June 1963, p. 3; Edmund Muskie, "We Can Have Lots of Water!" *Science and Mechanics* (November 1965): 56–67; Muskie Press Release, 27 April 1965, Folder 3, Box 388, MA; and SAWP, *Water Pollution Control*, 88th Cong., 1st sess., June 1963, p. 570.

37. SAWP, *Water Pollution Control*, 88th Cong., 1st sess., June 1963, pp. 29–40, 44–46, 128–29; Bureau of the Budget to Anthony Celebrezze, "Relationship of Storage and Treatment in Achieving Water Quality Objectives," 19 November 1964, Folder "Water 5: Standards and Quality," Box 27, RG 382, NARA; "Excerpt from Minutes of the Meeting of the Water Pollution Control Advisory Board," 26 May 1964,"

Folder 3, Box 581, MA; Malcolm Taylor to Don Nicoll, 28 December 1964, Nicoll to Taylor, 12 January 1965, Folder 3, Box 581, MA.

38. Linton Interview, 28 July 1998; and Nicoll Interview, 12 October 1998.

39. The best account of sanitary engineers as state administrators is Kehoe, *Cleaning Up the Great Lakes.*

40. Nicoll Interview, 12 October 1998; and Muskie, *Journeys,* p. 80.

41. Nicoll Interview, 12 October 1998; National Council for Stream Improvement, "A Panel Discussion: The Effects of River Developments on the Waste Assimilative Capacity of Streams," May 1963, pp. 1–9, 57–58, Folder 3, Box 581, MA; James Ridgeway, "Gunboats on the Raritan," *New Republic* 151 (1 June 1963): 17–19; Assistant to Sec. HEW to Dep. Assist. Sec., 3 October 1963, Folder "Congressional Correspondence II," Box 1, James Quigley Papers, RG 412.2.1, NARA; Kehoe, *Cleaning Up the Great Lakes,* pp. 32–33, 45; and J. Clarence Davies, *The Politics of Pollution* (New York: Pegasus, 1970), pp. 135–36.

42. *Cong. Rec.* 109, pt. 2 (31 January 1963), p. 1455; SCPW, *A Study of Pollution—Water,* 88th Cong., 1st sess., 1963, pp. 5–6, 8–10; SAWP, *Water Quality Act of 1965,* 89th Cong., 1st sess., January 1965, pp. 51–53, 84; *Cong. Rec.* 109, pt. 15 (16 October 1963), pp. 19643, 19646; SAWP, *Water Pollution Control,* 88th Cong., 1st sess., June 1963, pp. 547–57.

43. *Federal Water Pollution Control Act Amendments of 1963,* 88th Cong., 1st sess., 1963, S. Rep. 556, pp. 8–9; SCPW, *A Study of Pollution—Water,* 88th Cong., 1st sess., 1963, pp. 79–82; and *Cong. Rec.* 109, pt. 15 (16 October 1963), pp. 19646, 19650–51, 19666.

44. Nicoll Interview, 12 October 1998; and Zwick and Benstock, *Water Wasteland,* p. 273.

45. Nicoll Interview, 12 October 1998 and 20 October 1998; SAWP, *Water Pollution Control,* 88th Cong., 1st sess., June 1963, p. 80.

46. *Cong. Rec.* 109, pt. 15 (16 October 1963), p. 19673; SAWP, *Water Pollution Control,* 88th Cong., 1st sess., June 1963, p. 460; and HCPW, *Water Pollution Control Act Amendments,* 88th Cong., 1st sess., December 1963, p. 24.

47. Nicoll Interview, 12 October 1998; and SAWP, *Water Quality Act of 1965,* 89th Cong., 1st sess., 1965, pp. 79–80.

48. *Cong. Rec.* 109, pt. 15 (16 October 1963), pp. 19661–64, 19667; *Federal Water Pollution Control Act Amendments of 1963,* 88th Cong., 1st sess., 1963, S. Rep. 556, pp. 12–14; SAWP, *Water Quality Act of 1965,* 89th Cong., 1st sess., 1965, pp. 37–48; and CQA 19, 88th Cong., 1st sess., 1963, p. 241.

49. Henry Wilson to Lee White, 9 June 1964, and White to Wilson, 11 June 1964, Folder "Water Resources," Box 5, Aides' File—Henry Wilson, LBJ Library; and Philip Hughes to White, 22 May 1964, Folder "LE/HE8-4," Box 61, WHCF, LBJ Library.

50. "Special Message to Congress on Natural Beauty," 8 February 1965, *PPP: Lyndon Baines Johnson,* 1965, Book 1 (Washington, D.C.: GPO, 1966), pp. 155–65; "Presi-

dent Asks for Federal Power to End Pollution," *NYT*, 9 February 1965; Dean Coston
to Wilbur Cohen, 5 February 1965, Folder "Pollution," Box 16, Aides Files—Good-
win, LBJ Library; and Kermit Gordon to Henry Wilson, "Developments Affecting
Strategy to Secure Improved Water Pollution Enforcement Authority," 6 March
1965, Folder "HE 8-4: Water Pollution—Purification/Supply," Box 24, WHCF, LBJ
Library.

51. Mike Mantos to Larry O'Brien, 16 March 1965, Folder "Water Pollution," Box 10,
Aides Files—Wilson, and Cohen to O'Brien, "Water Pollution Control Legis-
lation—House Committee Action," 18 March 1965, Folder "LE/HE 8-4," Box 61,
WHCF, LBJ Library; *CQA* 21, 89th Cong., 1st sess., 1965, p. 746; House Committee
on Appropriations, Subcommittee on Department of Agriculture and Related
Agency Appropriations, *Department of Agriculture Appropriations for 1966, Part
I: Budget for the Department of Agriculture*, 89th Cong., 1st sess., 19 March 1965,
pp. 35–37; "Congress Considers Pesticides, Pollution," *St. Louis Post-Dispatch*, 25
April 1965, in Folder "LE/HE8-4 11/22/63–8/20/65," Box 62, WHCF, LBJ Library;
Wilbur Cohen to O'Brien, "Legislative Developments," 29 March 1965, Folder
"Water Pollution," Box 10, Aides Files—Wilson, LBJ Library; Hughes to Bill
Moyers, "Water Pollution Control Legislation," 8 April 1965, Folder "LE/HE 8-4,"
Box 61, WHCF, LBJ Library; and "Water Pollution: Federal Role Is Strengthened
by Law Authorizing New Agency and Quality Standards," *Science* 150 (8 October
1965): 129.

52. Don Nicoll to Mike Mantos, "S. 4—Proposals for a Compromise on the 'Water
Quality Standards' Section," 27 July 1965, Folder "Water Pollution," Box 10, Aides
Files—Wilson, LBJ Library; and Wilson to O'Brien, 23 August 1965, Folder "1965—
1 of 3," Box 1, Legislative Background—Water Pollution, LBJ Library.

53. P.L. 89-234, 2 October 1965; and Muskie to Lyndon Johnson, 2 September 1965,
Folder "LE/HE 8-4," Box 61, WHCF, LBJ Library.

54. SAWP, *Steps toward Clean Water*, 89th Cong., 2d sess., January 1966, pp. 2–15; Paul
C. Milazzo, "Legislating the Solution to Pollution: Congress and the Development
of Water Pollution Control Policy, 1945–1972," Ph.D. diss., University of Virginia,
2001, pp. 221–29.

CHAPTER 4: THINKING IN SYSTEMS

1. Edmund P. Russell III, "Lost among the Parts per Billion: Ecological Protection at
the United States Environmental Protection Agency, 1970–1993," *Environmental
History* 2, no. 1 (January 1997): 31–32.

2. Linda Lear, *Rachel Carson: Witness to Nature* (New York: Henry Holt, 1997); Donald Fleming, "Roots of the New Conservation Movement," *Perspectives in American History* 6 (1972): 34, 40–48; Robert Cameron Mitchell, "From Conservation
to Environmental Movement: The Development of the Modern Environmental Lobbies," in *Government and Environmental Politics: Essays on Historical Developments since World War II*, ed. Michael J. Lacy (Baltimore: Johns Hopkins

University Press, 1991), p. 86; Edmund P. Russell III, *War and Nature: Fighting Humans and Insects with Chemicals from World War I to Silent Spring* (Cambridge: Cambridge University Press, 2001); and "Fighting to Save the Earth from Man," *Time* 95 (2 February 1970): 56.

3. Shabecoff, *A Fierce Green Fire*, pp. 98–99; "Paul Revere of Ecology," *Time* (2 February 1970): 58; and Russell, *War and Nature*, pp. 221–28.

4. Donald Worster, *Nature's Economy* (San Francisco: Sierra Club Books, 1977), pp. 370–71.

5. Rome, *The Bulldozer in the Countryside*, pp. 154–65.

6. Jorling to Gordon Harrison, 24 January 1969, Folder 32, Box 8, and Jorling to John Cantlon, undated, Folder 28, Box 8, Thomas Jorling Papers, Williams College Archives and Special Collections (hereafter JP).

7. Jorling Interview, 3 December 1998; and Jorling to Harrison, and Jorling to Robert McIntosh, 20 February 1968, Box 6, Folder 1, JP.

8. Worster, *Nature's Economy*, p. 206; and Peter J. Bowler, *The Norton History of the Environmental Sciences* (New York: W. W. Norton, 1992), p. 519.

9. Sara Tjossem, "Preservation of Nature and Academic Respectability: Tensions in the Ecological Society of America, 1915–1929," Ph.D. diss., Cornell University, 1994, pp. 5, 75–76; Barton C. Hacker, *Elements of Controversy: The Atomic Energy Commission and Radiation Safety in Nuclear Weapons Testing* (Berkeley: University of California Press, 1994); and Robert Divine, *Blowing on the Wind: The Nuclear Test Ban Debate, 1954–1960* (New York: Oxford University Press, 1978).

10. Tjossem, "Preservation of Nature and Academic Respectability," pp. 91–93; Frank Golley, *A History of the Ecosystem Concept of Ecology* (New Haven: Yale University Press, 1993), p. 3; SCIIA, *Ecological Research and Surveys*, 89th Cong., 2d sess., 1966, p. 35; and John Cantlon to Jorling, 16 July 1969, Folder 28, Box 8, JP.

11. Jorling to Cantlon, undated, Folder 28, Box 8, JP; and Ecological Society of America, "Proposal to Establish an Office of Executive Director of the Ecological Society of America in Washington, D.C., undated, p. 8, Box 8, Folder 24, JP.

12. Jorling to Lamont Cole, 6 February 1968, Folder 25, Box 8, and Jorling to Cantlon, Cole, Auerbach, and Woodwell, 12 December 1968, Folder 24, Box 8, JP.

13. Stewart Udall, "A Message for Biologists," *Bioscience* 14, no. 11 (November 1964): 17–18; and SCIIA, *Ecological Research and Surveys*, 89th Cong., 2d sess., 1966, pp. 1–2, 19, 63–69, 73–76.

14. House Committee on Science and Astronautics, Subcommittee on Science, Research and Development (hereafter HCSASSRD), *Environmental Quality*, 90th Cong., 2d sess., 1968, pp. 2–3, 326–48; HCSASSRD, *International Biological Program, H. Con. Res. 273*, 90th Cong., 1st sess., 1967, pp. 51–80; SCIIA (and House Committee on Science and Astronautics), *Joint House-Senate Colloquium to Discuss a National Policy for the Environment*, 90th Cong., 2d sess., 1968, pp. 152–61; HCSASSRD, *Policy Issues in Science and Technology, Review and Forecast: Third Progress Report*, 90th Cong., 2d sess., 1968, pp. 26–28, 33–37, 53; and HCSASSRD,

Environmental Pollution, A Challenge to Science and Technology, 89th Cong., 2d sess., 1966, pp. 1–8, 12, 17–18. For an overview, see Ken Hechler, *Toward the Endless Frontier: History of the Committee on Science and Technology, 1959–79* (Washington, D.C.: U.S. House of Representatives Committee Print, 1980).

15. Joel B. Hagen, *An Entangled Bank: The Origins of Ecosystem Ecology* (New Brunswick, N.J.: Rutgers University Press, 1992), pp. 100–121; and Golley, *History of the Ecosystem Concept of Ecology,* pp. 72–74. For the symbiotic relationship between science and the state, see Brian Balogh, *Chain Reaction: Expert Debate and Public Participation in American Commercial Nuclear Power, 1945–1975* (Cambridge: Cambridge University Press, 1991); McDougall, *The Heavens and the Earth;* Don K. Price, *The Scientific Estate* (Cambridge, Mass.: Harvard University Press, 1965); David Dickinson, *The New Politics of Science* (Chicago: University of Chicago Press, 1988); Greg Herken, *Counsels of War* (Oxford: Oxford University Press, 1987); and Daniel J. Kevles, *The Physicists: The History of a Scientific Community in Modern America* (New York: Knopf, 1978).

16. Chunglin Kwa, "Representations of Nature Mediating between Ecology and Science Policy: The Case of the International Biological Programme," *Social Studies of Science* 17 (1987): 416–19; and Hagen, *An Entangled Bank,* pp. 118–21.

17. "National Academy of Sciences: Unrest among the Ecologists," *Science* 159 (19 January 1968): 287–89; and Thomas R. Dunlap, *DDT: Scientists, Citizens, and Public Policy* (Princeton, N.J.: Princeton University Press, 1981), p. 116. See also LaMont Cole, "The Impending Emergence of Ecological Thought," *Bioscience* 17, no. 7 (July 1964): 30–32.

18. Kwa, "Representations of Nature," pp. 415–16, 420–22; Hagen, *An Entangled Bank,* pp. 166–79; Robert P. McIntosh, *The Background of Ecology: Concept and Theory* (Cambridge: Cambridge University Press, 1985), pp. 213–20; and W. F. Blair, *Big Biology: The US/IBP* (Stroudsburg, Pa.: Dowden, Hutchinson, and Ross, 1977).

19. Kwa, "Representations of Nature," pp. 422–29. See also Public Affairs Committee of the Ecological Society of America, "The Importance of Ecology and the Study of Ecosystems," reprinted in SCIIA (and House Committee on Science and Astronautics), *Joint House-Senate Colloquium to Discuss a National Policy for the Environment,* 90th Cong., 2d sess., 1968, pp. 154–58; and Golley, *History of the Ecosystem Concept of Ecology,* pp. 2–3, 62.

20. Fred Kaplan, *The Wizards of Armageddon* (New York: Simon and Schuster, 1983), pp. 50–103, 220–33.

21. Thomas P. Hughes, *Rescuing Prometheus* (New York: Pantheon, 1998), pp. 3–139.

22. Ibid., pp. 141–95; Jennifer S. Light, *From Warfare to Welfare: Defense Intellectuals and Urban Problems in Cold War America* (Baltimore: Johns Hopkins University Press, 2003); Robert Lilienfeld, *The Rise of Systems Theory* (New York: John Wiley, 1978), pp. 2–4, 103–34, 227–46; Reuss, "Coping with Uncertainty," pp. 129–32; Arthur Maass, *Design of Water Resource Systems* (Cambridge, Mass.: Harvard University Press, 1962); David Major, "Impacts of Systems Techniques on the

Planning Process," *Water Resources Research* 8 (June 1972): 766–68; and HC-SASSRD, *Environmental Quality*, 90th Cong., 2d sess., 1968, p. 2.

23. A. G. Tansley, "The Use and Abuse of Vegetational Concepts and Terms," *Ecology* 16 (1935): 284–307; Worster, *Nature's Economy*, pp. 301–4; Joseph V. Siry, *Marshes of the Ocean Shore: Development of an Ecological Ethic* (College Station: Texas A&M University Press, 1984), pp. 117–27; and Bowler, *Norton History of the Environmental Sciences*, p. 525.

24. Eugene P. Odum and Howard T. Odum, *Principles of Ecology*, 2d ed. (Philadelphia: Saunders, 1959), p. 86; Raymond L. Lindeman, "The Trophic-Dynamic Aspect of Ecology," *Ecology* 23 (1942): 399–418; and Hagen, *An Entangled Bank*, pp. 62–68, 87–89.

25. Hagen, *An Entangled Bank*, pp. 90–99; and Golley, *History of the Ecosystem Concept of Ecology*, pp. 61–62.

26. W. Ross Ashby, *An Introduction to Cybernetics* (New York: John Wiley, 1958); Leroy L. Langley, *Homeostasis* (London: Chapman and Hall, 1965); Hughes, *Rescuing Prometheus*, pp. 21–22, 178; Worster, *Nature's Economy*, pp. 292–314; and Hagen, *An Entangled Bank*, pp. 69, 130.

27. Hagen, *An Entangled Bank*, pp. 68–74.

28. Ibid., pp. 103–6. Definition quoted in Golley, *History of the Ecosystem Concept of Ecology*, p. 66.

29. Golley, *History of the Ecosystem Concept of Ecology*, pp. 67–69; and Eugene P. Odum, "The New Ecology," *Bioscience* 14, no. 7 (July 1964): 14–16.

30. Worster, *Nature's Economy*, pp. 388–420; Donald Worster, "The Ecology of Order and Chaos," in *The Wealth of Nature* (New York: Oxford University Press, 1993), pp. 156–70; Michael G. Barbour, "Ecological Fragmentation in the Fifties," in *Uncommon Ground*, ed. William Cronon (New York: W. W. Norton, 1996), pp. 233–55; Dorothy Nelkin, "Scientists and Professional Responsibility: The Experience of American Ecologists," *Social Studies of Science* 7 (1977): 84–86; McIntosh, *The Background of Ecology*, pp. 216–17; and Hagen, *An Entangled Bank*, pp. 166–79.

31. Gene E. Likens, *The Ecosystem Approach: Its Use and Abuse* (Oldendorf/Luhe, Germany: Ecological Institute, 1992), pp. xxi–xxiv, 15–16; Golley, *History of the Ecosystem Concept of Ecology*, pp. 143–45; and Stephen Bocking, *Ecologists and Environmental Politics* (New Haven: Yale University Press, 1997), pp. 116–47.

32. Hagen, *An Entangled Bank*, pp. 181–88.

33. F. H. Bormann and G. E. Likens, "Nutrient Cycling," *Science* 155 (January 1967): 424–29; and Golley, *History of the Ecosystem Concept of Ecology*, pp. 145–51.

34. Golley, *History of the Ecosystem Concept of Ecology*, pp. 145–51; F. Herbert Bormann and Gene E. Likens, "The Nutrient Cycles of an Ecosystem," *Scientific American* 223 (April 1970): 92–101; G. E. Likens, F. H. Bormann, N. M. Johnson, and R. S. Pierce, "The Calcium, Magnesium, Potassium, and Sodium Budgets for a Small Forested Ecosystem," *Ecology* 48 (late Summer 1967): 772–85; and F. H. Bormann, G. E. Likens, and J. S. Eaton, "Biotic Regulation of Particulate and

Solution Losses from a Forest Ecosystem," *BioScience* 19 (July 1969): 600–610.
35. F. H. Bormann, G. E. Likens, D. W. Fisher, and R. S. Pierce, "Nutrient Loss Accelerated by Clear-Cutting of a Forest Ecosystem," *Science* 159 (23 February 1968): 882; and Likens, *The Ecosystem Approach*, p. 106.
36. Gene Likens, F. H. Bormann, and Noye M. Johnson, "Nitrification: Importance to Nutrient Losses from a Cutover Forested Ecosystem," *Science* 163 (14 March 1969): 1205–6; Likens, Bormann, et al., "Effects of Forest Cutting and Herbicide Treatment on Nutrient Budgets in the Hubbard Brook Watershed-Ecosystem," *Ecological Monographs* 40 (Winter 1970): 23–47; Hagen, *An Entangled Bank*, pp. 183–86; "National Forests in Danger? A Growing Dispute," *U.S. News and World Report* 70 (3 May 1971): 48–49; Bocking, *Ecologists and Environmental Politics*, pp. 130–31; Likens, *The Ecosystem Approach*, p. 107; and Golley, *History of the Ecosystem Concept of Ecology*, pp. 148–49.
37. "About the Authors," *Scientific American* 208 (June 1963): 28; *American Men and Women of Science*, 20th ed., vol. 7 (New Providence, R.I.: R. R. Bowker, 1998), 905; G. M. Woodwell, "Radiation and the Patterns of Nature," *Science* 156 (April 1967): 461–62; and Hagen, *An Entangled Bank*, pp. 74, 105–6, 130.
38. G. M. Woodwell, "Effects of Pollution on the Structure and Physiology of Ecosystems," *Science* 168 (April 1970): 429, 432; G. M. Woodwell and A. L. Rebuck, "Effects of Chronic Gamma Radiation on the Structure and Diversity of an Oak-Pine Forest," *Ecological Monographs* 37 (Winter 1967): 53–55; G. M. Woodwell, "The Ecological Effects of Radiation," *Scientific American* 208 (June 1963): 40–46; and G. M. Woodwell, "Effects of Ionizing Radiation on Terrestrial Ecosystems," *Science* 138 (2 November 1962): 572–77.
39. G. M. Woodwell, "The Ecological Effects of Radiation," 45–46; G. M. Woodwell, "Radiation and the Patterns of Nature," pp. 463–70; and G. M. Woodwell, "Effects of Pollution on the Structure and Physiology of Ecosystems," pp. 429–30.
40. G. M. Woodwell, "Effects of Pollution on the Structure and Physiology of Ecosystems," p. 431.
41. Ibid., pp. 429, 431; and Woodwell Interview, March 1999.
42. G. M. Woodwell, "Effect of DDT on Cone Production, Germination, and Seedling Survival in the Boreal Forest," *Ecology* 43 (Summer 1962): 396–402; G. M. Woodwell, "The Persistence of DDT in a Forest Soil," *Forest Science* 7 (September 1961): 194–96; G. M. Woodwell, "Toxic Substances and Ecological Cycles," *Scientific American* 216 (March 1967): 30–31; G. M. Woodwell and F. T. Martin, "Persistence of DDT in Soils of Heavily Sprayed Forest Stands," *Science* 145 (July 1964): 481–83; and Hagen, *An Entangled Bank*, p. 141.
43. Dunlap, *Scientists, Citizens, and Public Policy*, pp. 100–101, 130–44; Lear, *Rachel Carson*, pp. 110–30, 313–38; and Hays, *Beauty, Health, and Permanence*, pp. 174–75.
44. "Environmental Pollution: Scientists Go to Court," *Science* 158 (December 1967): 1552; Dunlap, *Scientists, Citizens, and Public Policy*, pp. 145–46; Frank Graham Jr., "Gathering Storm over DDT," *New Republic* 157 (24 June 1967): 17; and G. M.

Woodwell and Charles F. Wurster Jr., "DDT Residues in an East Coast Estuary: A Case of Biological Concentration of a Persistent Insecticide," *Science* 156 (12 May 1967): 821–22.

45. Woodwell and Wurster, "DDT Residues in an East Coast Estuary," p. 823; G. M. Woodwell, "Toxic Substances and Ecological Cycles," p. 31; and G. M. Woodwell, Paul Craig, and Horton Johnson, "DDT in the Biosphere: Where Does It Go?" *Science* 174 (10 December 1971): 1105.

46. G. M. Woodwell, "Toxic Substances and Ecological Cycles," pp. 26–30; G. M. Woodwell, Paul Craig, and Horton Johnson, "DDT in the Biosphere: Where Does It Go?" pp. 1105–6; and Frank Graham Jr., "Taking Polluters to Court," *New Republic* 158 (13 January 1968): 9.

47. Dunlap, *Scientists, Citizens, and Public Policy*, p. 147; Frank Graham Jr., "Taking Polluters to Court," p. 8. The Environmental Defense Fund's 1967 legal offensive against pesticide spraying on Long Island and in Michigan failed to convince federal judges to halt the programs or ban chlorinated hydrocarbons. See "New York Group Loses Its Fight to Block Pesticide in Michigan," *NYT*, 23 November 1967; and "Suit to Ban DDT in Suffolk County Is Dismissed," *NYT*, 2 December 1967.

48. "Ecology and Ecologists—Campaign 1968," pp. 1–4, undated, Folder 27, Box 8, JP; Jorling to John Oakes, 23 September 1968, Folder 31, Box 8, JP; and Jorling to Bormann, 12 December 1968, Folder 27, Box 8, JP.

CHAPTER 5: FROM POLLUTION CONTROL TO ENVIRONMENTAL QUALITY

1. J. Samuel Walker, "Nuclear Power and the Environment: The Atomic Energy Commission and Thermal Pollution, 1965–1971," *Technology and Culture* 30, no. 4 (October 1989): 964–65.

2. "Generating Plants Pose a 'Thermal Pollution' Threat to Rivers, Lakes," *Wall Street Journal*, 1 December 1967.

3. Walker, "Nuclear Power and the Environment," pp. 966–69; "Memorandum of Understanding with Regard to Procedures for Cooperation between the Atomic Energy Commission and the Department of the Interior Pertaining to Location and Operation of Proposed Nuclear Installations Subject to Licensing and Regulations by the Commission," March 1964, reprinted in SAWP, *Thermal Pollution—1968*, 90th Cong., 1st sess., 1968, pt. 3, pp. 999–1000.

4. Walker, "Nuclear Power and the Environment," pp. 975–77.

5. For discussions of treatment plant financing alternatives, see SAWP, *Water Pollution—1968*, 90th Cong., 2d sess., pt. 2, April 1968, pp. 485–550; and Muskie to David S. Black, 17 June 1968, Folder 4, Box 831, MA.

6. "Thermal Pollution: Senator Muskie Tells AEC to Cool It," *Science* 158 (10 November 1967): 755; SAWP, *Thermal Pollution—1968*, 90th Cong., 1st sess., pt. 1, 14 February 1968, pp. 337–38; and Walker, "Nuclear Power and the Environment," p. 980.

7. "Thermal Pollution: Senator Muskie Tells AEC to Cool It," *Science* 158 (10 November 1967): 756–56.

8. Ibid.; SAWP, *Thermal Pollution—1968*, 90th Cong., 1st sess., pt. 1, p. 280; Muskie to Seaborg, 25 October 1967, and Seaborg to Muskie, 8 November 1967, Folder 6, Box 818, MA.

9. SAWP, *Water Pollution—1967*, 90th Cong., 1st sess., pt. 1, June–August 1967, p. 473.

10. SAWP, *Thermal Pollution—1968*, 90th Cong., 1st sess., pt. 1, p. 2. For the committee's efforts to recruit ecologists, see Joan Jordan to Herbert Bormann, 12 January 1968, and similar correspondence in Folder 6, Box 831, MA; "Briefing Paper: Thermal Pollution," 6 February 1968, pp. 3–5, Folder 7, Box 818, MA; Jordan to Don [Nicoll], Staff, and Subcommittee, "Discussion on Thermal Pollution," 1 April 1968, pp. 1–7, MA; and Grundy to Nicoll, "Thermal Pollution Hearings," 21 March 1969, pp. 1–3, Folder 3, Box 1554, MA. For a complete list of scientists contacted, see Jordan to Don [Nicoll], Staff, and Subcommittee, "Discussion on Thermal Pollution," Appendix C, 1 April 1968, Folder 5, Box 831, MA. For examples of pertinent testimony, see SAWP, *Thermal Pollution—1968*, 90th Cong., 1st sess., 1968, pt. 3, pt. 1, pp. 44, 90–99, 100–108, 222–25, 278–83. Relevant scientific literature included John R. Clark, "Thermal Pollution and Aquatic Life," *Scientific American* 220 (March 1969): 20–23; and John Cairns Jr., "We're in Hot Water," *Scientist and Citizen* 10 (August 1968): 187–98.

11. Max N. Edwards, "Legal Control of Thermal Pollution," remarks delivered by the assistant secretary of the interior for water pollution control before the annual meeting of the American Bar Association, 6 August 1968, pp. 6–8, Folder 7, Box 831, MA; and Walker, "Nuclear Power and the Environment," p. 978.

12. For the evolution of the certification provision, see Muskie to David Black, 17 June 1968, Folder 6, Box 831, MA; *Cong. Rec.* 114, pt.16, 90th Cong., 1st sess. (10 July 1968): 20467, 20469; [Joint Committee on Atomic Energy chairman] John Pastore to Muskie, 5 September 1968, and John T. Comway to Pastore, "Summary Analysis of Section 5 of S. 3206," 27 August 1968, reprinted in SAWP, *Thermal Pollution—1968*, 90th Cong., 1st sess., 1968, pt. 3, pp. 978–81; and "Explanatory Statement by Senator Muskie," in *Thermal Pollution—1968*, pt. 3, Appendix 1, p. 976. For the final wording of the provision, see the Conference Report reprinted in *Cong. Rec.* 116, pt. 7, pp. 9071–72. Atomic facilities required both federal construction and operating permits; fossil fuel generating plants did not, but those located on navigable waters needed to obtain permits from the Corps of Engineers.

13. *Cong. Rec.* 115, pt. 1, 91st Cong., 1st sess., pp. 788–90; and ibid., pt. 21, p. 29053. On oil pollution, see "Comprehensive Water Pollution Control Act Cleared," *CQA* 26, 91st Cong., 2d sess., 1970, pp. 175–78; and SAWP, *Water Pollution—1969*, 91st Cong., 2d sess., pt. 1, pp. 84, 96, 98–99.

14. SAWP, *Water Pollution—1969*, 91st Cong., 2d sess., pt. 4, p. 1046. Joint Committee on Atomic Energy members also viewed Muskie's legislation as preferable to
their own. See SAWP, *Water Pollution—1969*, 91st Cong., 1st sess., March 1969, pt.
4, pp. 1042, 1047–48, 1056. For environmentalist pressure, see Robert Boyle, "The
Nukes Are in Hot Water," *Sports Illustrated* 30 (20 January 1969): 24–28; Walker,
"Nuclear Power and the Environment," p. 984; SAWP, *Water Pollution—1969*, 91st
Cong., 1st sess., February 1969, pt. 1, pp. 82–83, 100; "Congress Acts on Pollution
but Clears No Major Bills," *CQA* 24, 90th Cong., 2d sess., 1968, pp. 569–74; and
"Water Quality Improvement Act," *CQA* 25, 91st Cong., 1st sess., 1969, pp. 513–14.

15. HCSASSRD, *Environmental Pollution—A Challenge to Science and Technology*,
89th Cong., 2d sess., 1966, pp. 1–8; and ibid., *Managing the Environment: Report
of the Subcommittee on Science, Research, and Development*, 90th Cong., 2d sess.,
1968, pp. 5–6.

16. Lynton Caldwell, "Administrative Possibilities for Environmental Control," in
Future Environments of North America, ed. F. Fraser Darling and John P. Milton
(Garden City, N.Y.: Natural History Press, 1966), pp. 648–71; Lynton K. Caldwell,
"Biopolitics: Science, Ethics, and Public Policy," *Yale Review* 54 (1964): 1–16; Lynton K. Caldwell, "Environment: A New Focus for Public Policy?" *Public Administration Review* 23 (1963): 132–39; Jacob Beuscher, "Some New Machinery to Help
Us Do the Job," in *Environmental Quality in a Growing Economy*, ed. Henry Jarett
for Resources for the Future (Baltimore: Johns Hopkins University Press, 1966),
pp. 156–63; and *Cong. Rec.* 115, pt. 12, 91st Cong., 1st sess., p. 15547.

17. SAWP, *Need to Establish an Important Environmental Quality Policy*, 90th Cong.,
1st sess., 1968, pp. 164–65; and Terrence T. Finn, "Conflict and Compromise—
Congress Makes a Law: The Passage of the National Environmental Policy Act,"
Ph.D. diss., Georgetown University, 1973, pp. 218–22, 225–30.

18. Finn, "Conflict and Compromise," pp. 179–81, 184, 190–93, 199; and Robert G.
Kaufman, *Henry M. Jackson: A Life in Politics* (Seattle: University of Washington
Press, 2000), pp. 163–68.

19. Bill Van Ness to Senator Jackson, "A Proposed Legislative Program on the Prob-
lems of 'Environmental Quality and the Management of Natural Resources,'"
Cong. Rec. 113, pt. 27 (4 January 1967), 90th Cong., 1st sess., pp. 36856–57; Finn,
"Conflict and Compromise," pp. 194–99; and SCIIA (and House Committee on
Science and Astronautics), *Joint House-Senate Colloquium to Discuss a National
Policy for the Environment*, 90th Cong., 2d sess., 1968. Examples of Jackson's ad-
dresses are reprinted in *Cong. Rec.* 113, pt. 27, 90th Cong., 1st sess., pp. 36853–56.

20. *Cong. Rec.* 115, pt. 3 (18 February 1969), pp. 3698–701; and Finn, "Conflict and
Compromise," pp. 184, 193.

21. SCIIA, *A National Policy for the Environment*, 90th Cong., 2d sess., 11 July 1968,
reprinted in Appendix I of SCIIA (and House Committee on Science and Astronautics), *Joint House-Senate Colloquium to Discuss a National Policy for the Environment*, 90th Cong., 2d sess., 1968, pp. 96–115, especially 101–4 and 111–12.

22. Ibid., pp. 104–6; *Cong. Rec.* 113, pt. 27, 90th Cong., 1st sess., pp. 36849–53; SCIIA, *A National Policy for the Environment*, reprinted in Appendix I of SCIIA (and House Committee on Science and Astronautics), *Joint House-Senate Colloquium to Discuss a National Policy for the Environment*, 90th Cong., 2d sess., 1968, pp. 121–24; Robert Boyle, "How to Stop the Pillage of America," *Sports Illustrated* 27 (11 December 1967), reprinted in *Cong. Rec.* 113, pt. 27, 90th Cong., 1st sess., pp. 36851–53.

23. SCIIA, *Hearings on S. 1075, S. 237, and S. 1752*, 91st Cong., 1st sess., 1969, pp. 115–17; *Cong. Rec.* 113, pt. 27, 90th Cong., 1st sess., p. 36856; and Finn, "Conflict and Compromise," pp. 303–5.

24. SCIIA, *National Environmental Policy Act of 1969*, 91st Cong., 1st sess., 9 July 1969, S. Rep. 296, pp. 2–10; *Cong. Rec.* 115, pt. 11, 91st Cong., 1st sess., pp. 14346–47; and Lynton Caldwell, *Science and the National Environmental Policy Act* (University: University of Alabama Press, 1982), pp. 52–55.

25. Richard N. L. Andrews, *Environmental Policy and Administrative Change* (Lexington, Mass.: Lexington Books, 1976), pp. 10–11; and Steven C. Schulte, *Wayne Aspinall and the Shaping of the American West* (Boulder: University of Colorado Press, 2002).

26. Billings to Muskie, "The Colloquium," undated, Folder 5, Box 1961; and Billings to Nicoll, "Several Matters," 15 July 1968, Folder 7, Box 1961, MA.

27. *Cong. Rec.* 115, pt. 21, 91st Cong., 1st sess., pp. 29052–53; and ibid., pt. 12, p. 15547, and pt. 30, p. 40425.

28. "Draft Speech on NEPA, Re: 8 October Agreement," ca. 20 December 1969, p. 2, Folder 5, Box 1052, MA.

29. Jorling Interview, 2 December 1998; Richard A. Liroff, *A National Policy for the Environment: NEPA and Its Aftermath* (Bloomington: Indiana University Press, 1976), pp. 18–19; and Finn, "Conflict and Compromise," p. 465.

30. Finn, "Conflict and Compromise," pp. 447–53; Nicoll Interview, 20 October 1998; and Kaufman, *Henry M. Jackson*, pp. 140–60.

31. *Cong. Rec.* 115, pt. 12, 91st Cong., 1st sess., pp. 15544–46; Jorling Interview, 2 December 1998; Finn, "Conflict and Compromise," pp. 448, 454–58; "Environmental Amendment May Bring Fight on Water Bill," *Environmental Health Letter* 8 (1 August 1969): 5; attached memo to Don Nicoll dated 4 August 1969, Folder 6, Box 1090, MA; *Cong. Rec.*, 115, pt. 12, 91st Cong., 1st sess., pp. 15545–47, 28956; and "A Fight Over Who Cleans Up," *Business Week* (12 July 1969): 46.

32. Leon Billings to Don Nicoll, "Proposed Environmental Quality Compromise," 30 September 1969, Folder 2, Box 1090, MA; "Jackson, Muskie Nearing Environment Policy Compromise," *Washington Star*, 5 October 1969; and *Cong. Rec.* 115, pt. 21, 91st Cong., 1st sess., p. 29055.

33. "Agreed-Upon Changes in S. 7 and S. 1075," *Cong. Rec.* 115, pt. 21, p. 29058. The Nixon administration was skeptical of both bills, wanting to avoid accretions to the executive office. See "Legislation on Environmental Quality Organization in

the Executive Office," 10 October 1969, Folder "Water 4 of 5," Box 117, John Whitaker Papers, WHCF, Nixon Presidential Materials (hereafter WP), NARA.

34. Jorling Interview, 2 December 1998; Billings Interview, 21 November 1997; "Agreed-Upon Changes: Provisions Senate Conferees Will Support in Conference on S. 1075," *Cong. Rec.* 115, pt. 21, p. 29058; and Finn, "Conflict and Compromise," p. 503.

35. "Agreed-Upon Changes," *Cong. Rec.* 115, pt. 21, pp. 29056, 29059.

36. *Cong. Rec.* 115, pt. 30, 91st Cong., 1st sess., pp. 40418, 40423.

37. Ibid., 40423–25.

38. Muskie to Randolph, 17 November 1969, Folder 7, Box 1554; Billings to Richard Royce, "Water Pollution Consultant," 17 March 1969, Folder 5, Box 1961; and Billings to Nicoll et al., "Senator Muskie's Background for Hearings," 28 April 1970, Folder 5, Box 1961, MA.

39. Leon Billings Resume, ca. 1974, and "Background Statement," undated, Folder 11, Box 1961, MA; and Asbell, *The Senate Nobody Knows*, pp. 74–78.

40. Jorling Interview, 3 December 1998; and Jorling to John Oakes, 6 August 1969, Folder 31, Box 8, and Jorling to George Woodwell, 5 June 1969, Folder 27, Box 8, JP.

41. Billings to Nicoll, "The Environmental Quality Improvement Act and Appurtenant Committee Activities," 7 July 1969, p. 1, Folder 12, Box 1089, MA.

42. "Senator Randolph Establishes Environmental Advisory Group," Senate Committee on Public Works Press Release, 17 January 1970, Folder 4, Box 1053, and Billings to Royce, "The Scientific Advisory Panel," 10 May 1971, Folder 5, Box 1961, MA.

43. "Thermal Pollution: A Threat to Cayuga's Waters?" *Science* 162 (8 November 1968): 649–50; Dorothy Nelkin, *Nuclear Power and Its Critics* (Ithaca, N.Y.: Cornell University Press, 1971), pp. 40–106; Likens Interview, March 1999; Joy B. Zedler et al., "Wastelands to Wetlands: Links between Habitat Protection and Ecosystem Science," in *Successes, Limitations and Frontiers in Ecosystem Science*, ed. Michael L. Pace and Peter M. Groffman (New York: Springer, 1998), p. 73; and Jeffrey K. Stine, *Twenty Years of Science in the Public Interest: A History of the Congressional Science and Engineering Fellowship Program* (Washington, D.C.: American Association for the Advancement of Science, 1994), p. 21.

44. SAWP, *Thermal Pollution—1968*, 90th Cong., 1st sess., 1968, pt. 1, pp. 115–16.

45. Joseph Hennessey to Jerry Verkler, 12 November 1969, Folder "S. 1075," Box 34, RG 46.14, NARA.

46. "Calvert Cliffs Decision Requires Agencies to Get Tough with Environmental Laws," *National Journal* (18 September 1971): 1927; *Calvert Cliffs Coordinating Committee, Inc. v. Atomic Energy Commission* (D.C. Circuit, 23 July 1971), *Environmental Law Reporter* 1 (1971): 20350.

47. For a prescient prediction of NEPA's potential to attract litigation, given recent judicial interpretations of standing, see M. Barry Meyer to Jennings Randolph

and Muskie, "Subsection 101(b) of S. 1075, 'Standing to Sue,'" 24 September 1969, Folder 1, Box 1090, MA.

48. *Calvert Cliffs Coordinating Committee, Inc. v. Atomic Energy Commission, Environmental Law Reporter* 1 (1971): 20346–47.

49. Ibid., pp. 20348–52. See also "*Calvert Cliffs Coordinating Committee v. AEC* and the Requirement of 'Balancing' under NEPA," *Environmental Law Reporter* 2 (January 1972): 10003–6.

50. *Calvert Cliffs Coordinating Committee, Inc. v. Atomic Energy Commission, Environmental Law Reporter* 1 (1971): pp. 20353–54.

51. Ibid., p. 20355.

CHAPTER 6: THE MOVEMENT'S MOMENT

1. Richard Green to Keith S. Kraus, "Proposed Policy on Standards," 1 December 1965, Folder "Water 5—Standards & Quality," Box 27, RG 382, NARA.

2. Holmes, *History of Federal Water Resources Programs and Policies*, pp. 187–88; and "Statement by Secretary of the Interior Stewart L. Udall on Water Quality Standards," 19 July 1967, Folder 5, Box 656, MA.

3. Zwick and Benstock, *Water Wasteland*, p. 270; Luther J. Carter, "Water Pollution: Officials Goaded into Raising Quality Standards," *Science* 160 (5 April 1968): 49–50; and SAWP, *Water Pollution—1968*, 90th Cong., 2d sess., 1968, pp. 10–14.

4. "Administrative History of the Department of Interior," vol. 1, pt. 2, pp. 21–30, Box 1, DOI Administrative History, Lyndon Baines Johnson Presidential Materials, LBJ Library; Edward Dunkelberger to James Watt, 4 April 1968, Folder 8, Box 831, MA; Holmes, *History of Federal Water Resources Programs and Policies*, pp. 189–90; and Davies, *The Politics of Pollution*, p. 174.

5. Zwick and Benstock, *Water Wasteland*, pp. 271–80.

6. Ibid., p. 277; and Holmes, *History of Federal Water Resources Programs and Policies*, pp. 190–93.

7. Zwick and Benstock, *Water Wasteland*, p. 281; Holmes, *History of Federal Water Resources Programs and Policies*, pp. 99, 197–98, 219; and Peter Cleary Yeager, *The Limits of Law: The Public Regulation of Private Pollution* (Cambridge: Cambridge University Press, 1991). Congress approved only $203 million of the $450 million authorized for fiscal 1968 construction grants, and 214 million for fiscal 1969 and 1970. Authorizations for those years were $700 million and $1 billion, respectively.

8. Hays, *Beauty, Health, and Permanence.*

9. Rosenbaum, *The Politics of Environmental Concern*, pp. 6–7; and Mary Graham, *The Morning after Earth Day: Practical Environmental Politics* (Washington, D.C.: Brookings Institution Press, 1999), p. 37.

10. Rothman, *The Greening of a Nation*, p. 88; and "The Cities: The Price of Optimism," *Time* 94 (1 August 1969): 41.

11. Graham, *Morning after Earth Day*, p. 27; Hal K. Rothman, *Saving the Planet: The American Response to the Environment in the Twentieth Century* (Chicago: Ivan

R. Dee, 2000), pp. 127–28; and "Comprehensive Water Pollution Control Act Cleared," *CQA* 26, 91st Cong., 2d sess., 1970, pp. 175–78.

12. Hays, *Beauty, Health, and Permanence*, pp. 26–32; and Robert Gottlieb, "Beyond NEPA and Earth Day: Reconstructing the Past and Envisioning a Future for Environmentalism," *Environmental History Review* 19, no. 4 (Winter 1995): 8.

13. Gottlieb, "Beyond NEPA and Earth Day: Reconstructing the Past and Envisioning a Future for Environmentalism"; Gottlieb, *Forcing the Spring*, pp. 106–7; James Wagner, "Washington Pressures/Environmental Teach-In," *National Journal* (21 February 1970): 408–11; Thomas Huffman, *Protectors of the Land and Water: Environmentalism in Wisconsin, 1961–68* (Chapel Hill: University of North Carolina Press, 1994); and Bill Christofferson, *The Man from Clear Lake: Earth Day Founder Gaylord Nelson* (Madison: University of Wisconsin Press, 2004).

14. Gottlieb, *Forcing the Spring*, pp. 112–13; J. Brooks Flippen, *Nixon and the Environment* (Albuquerque: University of New Mexico Press, 2000), pp. 1, 8–16; and Russell, "Lost among the Parts per Billion," p. 32.

15. Holmes, *History of Federal Water Resources Programs and Policies*, p. 101.

16. Shabecoff, *A Fierce Green Fire*, pp. 118–19; Mitchell, "From Conservation to Environmental Movement," pp. 83–85, 96–97; Michael P. Cohen, *The History of the Sierra Club, 1892–1970* (San Francisco: Sierra Club Books, 1988); Harvey, *A Symbol of Wilderness*; Stephen Fox, *John Muir and His Legacy* (Madison: University of Wisconsin Press, 1981); and Christopher J. Bosso, *Environment Inc.: From Grassroots to Beltway* (Lawrence: University Press of Kansas, 2005).

17. Mitchell, *From Conservation to Environmental Movement*, p. 99; James R. Wagner, "Environmental Groups Shift Tactics from Demonstrations to Politics, Local Action," *National Journal* (24 July 1971): 1557–58; Robert Cameron Mitchell, Angela Mertig, and Riley E. Dunlap, "Twenty Years of Environmental Mobilization: Trends among National Environmental Organizations," in *American Environmentalism: The United States Environmental Movement, 1970–1990*, ed. Dunlap and Mertig (Philadelphia: Taylor and Francis, 1992), pp. 13–21; and Thomas Raymond Wellock, *Critical Masses: Opposition to Nuclear Power in California, 1958–1978* (Madison: University of Wisconsin Press, 1998).

18. Mitchell, *From Conservation to Environmental Movement*, p. 92.

19. Thomas R. Huffman, "U.S. Water Pollution," in *Water and the Environment since 1945: A Cross Cultural Perspective*, ed. Char Miller (New York: St. James / Gale, 2001), pp. 12–13; Gladwyn Hill, "The Politics of Air Pollution: Public Interest and Pressure Groups," *Arizona Law Review* 10 (Summer 1968): 40–43; David Vogel, *Kindred Strangers: The Uneasy Relationship between Politics and Business in America* (Princeton, N.J.: Princeton University Press, 1996), pp. 332–45; Marver Bernstein, *Regulating Business by Independent Commission* (Princeton, N.J.: Princeton University Press, 1955); and Theodore Lowi, *The End of Liberalism: Ideology, Policy, and the Crisis of Public Authority* (New York: Norton, 1969).

20. Graham, *Morning after Earth Day*, pp. 38–39; Mitchell, *From Conservation to Environmental Movement*, pp. 101–2; and Richard Stewart, "The Reformation of American Administrative Law," *Harvard Law Review* 88, no. 8 (1975): 1669–813. For the circumstances surrounding the landmark 1965 case on standing, *Scenic Hudson Preservation Conference v. Federal Power Commission*, see Allan R. Talbot, *Power along the Hudson: The Storm King Case and the Birth of Environmentalism* (New York: E. P. Dutton, 1972), pp. 100–140.

21. Richard N. L. Andrews, *Managing the Environment, Managing Ourselves: A History of American Environmental Policy* (New Haven: Yale University Press, 1999), p. 222. For the impact of redistricting on state-level environmental policies, see Huffman, *Protectors of the Land and Water*, p. 3.

22. Flippen, *Nixon and the Environment*, p. 9.

23. Joan Hoff, *Nixon Reconsidered* (New York: Basic Books, 1994), p. 8; and Hugh Davis Graham, *The Civil Rights Era: Origins and Development of National Policy* (New York: Oxford University Press, 1990).

24. Allan Matusow, *Nixon's Economy* (Lawrence: University Press of Kansas, 1998), pp. 1–4, 7–33, 117–48; Hoff, *Nixon Reconsidered*, pp. 8, 21–23; Flippen, *Nixon and the Environment*, pp. 8–79; and John C. Whitaker, *Striking a Balance: Environment and Natural Resources Policy in the Nixon-Ford Years* (Washington, D.C.: American Enterprise Institute, 1976), pp. 28–29.

25. Whitaker, *Striking a Balance*, pp. 29–39; "Nixon and Congress Consider Actions to Improve Environment," *National Journal* (20 December 1969): 370; and Russell Train, *Politics, Pollution, and Pandas: An Environmental Memoir* (New York: Island Press, 2003).

26. Matusow, *Nixon's Economy*, p. 2; and Hoff, *Nixon Reconsidered*, p. 3. For the business community's repeated failure to grasp the consequences of environmentalism, see Vogel, *Fluctuating Fortunes*.

27. Nicoll Interview, 20 October 1998.

28. James Reston, "Washington: 'It Is Literally Now or Never,'" *NYT*, 4 January 1970; and "Muskie Calls President's Anti-Pollution Drive 'Slogan-Rich and Action Poor,'" *NYT*, 16 January 1970.

29. Whitaker, *Striking a Balance*, pp. 27–39; Whitaker to Ehrlichman, "How the President Met the Environmental Issue," 25 January 1971, Folder "Environmental Legislation 1970–71, 3 of 3," Box 61, WP; "Muskie Hails Nixon's 'Concern' on Pollution but Asks Specifics," *NYT*, 24 January 1970; and "Nixon Urges End to 2-Party Fight over Pollution," *NYT*, 7 February 1970.

30. Charles O. Jones, *Clean Air: The Policies and Politics of Pollution Control* (Pittsburgh: University of Pittsburgh Press, 1975), pp. 77–83; Vogel, *Kindred Strangers*, pp. 330–32; David Vogel, "A Case Study of Clean Air Legislation, 1967–1981," in *The Impact of the Modern Corporation*, ed. Betty Bock (New York: Columbia University Press, 1984), pp. 309–86; Richard Tobin, *The Social Gamble: Determining*

Acceptable Levels of Air Quality (Lexington, Mass.: D. C. Heath, 1979), pp. 53–63; SAWP, *Air Pollution—1967 (Air Quality Act)*, 90th Cong., 1st sess., May 1967, pp. 2513–44; *CQA* 23, 90th Cong., 1st sess., 1967, p. 875–84; Davies, *The Politics of Pollution*, pp. 49–52; and Randall Ripley, "Congress and Clean Air," in *Pollution and Public Policy*, ed. David Paulsen (New York: Dodd, Mead, 1973), pp. 175–98.

31. Martha Derthick, "Crossing Thresholds: Federalism in the 1960s," in *Integrating the Sixties*, ed. Brian Balogh (University Park: Pennsylvania State University Press, 1996), pp. 64–80.

32. Davies, *The Politics of Pollution*, p. 53; "Tough Local Actions on Air Quality Boost Nixon's National Standards Plan," *National Journal* (9 May 1970): 968; and Jones, *Clean Air*, pp. 175–78.

33. "Special Message to the Congress on Environmental Quality," 10 February 1970, *PPP: Richard M. Nixon* (Washington, D.C.: GPO, 1971), pp. 100–104; and Jones, *Clean Air*, p. 181.

34. "Pressure for Stronger Bill," *National Journal* (15 August 1970): 1758; and Vogel, *Fluctuating Fortunes*, pp. 93–112.

35. John C. Esposito, *Vanishing Air: The Ralph Nader Study Group Report on Air Pollution* (New York: Grossman, 1970), pp. 259–98.

36. Billings Interview, 21 November 1997; "Muskie Criticized by Nader Group," *NYT*, 13 May 1970; and "Muskie Replies to Nader Criticism," *NYT*, 14 May 1970.

37. Leon Billings to Muskie, "Pending Air Pollution Legislation—Executive Sessions," 27 May 1970, Folder 4, Box 7, JP; and Nicoll Interview, 13 October 1998.

38. Billings Interview, 21 November 1997; Jorling Interview, 2 December 1998; Barry Meyer Interview, 2 June 1999; Billings to File, "The Clean Air Act," 5 May 1981, and "The Context of the Clean Air Act," 4 May 1981, Folder 13, Box 7, JP; Esposito, *Vanishing Air*, p. 291; SAWP, *Air Pollution—1970*, 91st Cong., 2d sess., 27 May 1970, pt. 4, pp. 1498–1506, 1511–12; Thomas Jorling, "A Political History of Federal Air and Water Pollution Control Legislation," June 1984, p. 21, Folder 61, Box 5, JP; *CQA* 25, 91st Cong., 1st sess., 1969, pp. 735–45; Jack L. Walker, "Setting the Agenda in the U.S. Senate: A Theory of Problem Selection," *British Journal of Political Science* 7 (October 1977): 437–40; Daniel J. Curran, *Dead Laws for Dead Men: The Politics of Federal Coal Mine Health and Safety Legislation* (Pittsburgh: University of Pittsburgh Press, 1993), pp. 109–39; and "Breaking New Ground to Make Mines Safe," *Business Week* (8 November 1969): 139–46.

39. SAWP, *Report of the Council on Environmental Quality*, 91st Cong., 2d sess., 11 August 1970, pp. 23–27; "Air Pollution Bill May Force Cities to Curb Use of Automobiles," *National Journal* (15 August 1970): 1756–57; Meyer Interview, 2 June 1999; and Tobin, *The Social Gamble*, p. 57.

40. Richard Corrigan, "Muskie Plays Dominant Role in Writing Tough New Air Pollution Law," *National Journal* (2 January 1971): 25–27; SAWP, National Air Quality Standards Act of 1970, 91st Cong., 2d sess., 1970, S. Rep. 1196; and "Air Pollution: Muskie Throws Down the Gauntlet," *Science* 169 (28 August 1970): 84.

41. John Gilmour, *Strategic Disagreement: Stalemate in American Politics* (Pittsburgh: University of Pittsburgh Press, 1995); and David Vogel, "Representing Diffuse Interests in Environmental Policymaking," in *Do Institutions Matter?*, ed. R. Kent Weaver and Bert A. Rockman (Washington, D.C.: Brookings Institution, 1993), pp. 237–71. Charles O. Jones advances the argument for "speculative augmentation" in *Clean Air*, pp. 175–210.

42. James Q. Wilson criticizes the Air and Water Pollution Acts of the early seventies in "The Politics of Regulation," pp. 135–68. For a more charitable view, see Helen Ingram, "The Political Rationality of Innovation: The Clean Air Act Amendments of 1970," in *Approaches to Controlling Air Pollution*, ed. Ann Friedlaender (Cambridge: MIT Press, 1978), pp. 12–56. For the "New Deal regulatory regime," see George Hoberg, *Pluralism by Design: Environmental Policy and the American Regulatory State* (Westport, N.Y.: Praeger, 1992). See also Robert L. Rabin, "Federal Regulation in Historical Perspective," *Stanford Law Review* 38 (May 1986): 1278–1315.

43. Edelman Interview, 9 March 1999; Billings Interview, 27 November 1997; and Meyer Interview, 2 June 1998.

44. Edmund Muskie, "Environmental Education: A Congressional Viewpoint," speech before the New England Conference on Environmental Management, 22 March 1968, and "Water Resources and the Legislative Branch," January 1967, Folder 8, Box 1026, MA; "Pollution Is Linked to Living Standard," *NYT*, 17 March 1970; "Muskie Tells Conservationists Economic Growth Must Go On," *NYT*, 19 April 1970; and Harvey Wheeler, "The Politics of Ecology," *Saturday Review* 53 (7 March 1970): 52.

CHAPTER 7: THE STRANGE CAREER OF THE CORPS OF ENGINEERS

1. U.S. Army Corps of Engineers, Baltimore District, *Potomac River Basin Report: Summary* (Baltimore: U.S. Army Engineer District, North Atlantic Division, 1963); "The Mess on the Potomac," *National Parks Magazine* 41 (April 1967): 2, 12; and "The Long Battle for the Potomac," *National Parks Magazine* 42 (January 1968): 2, 23.

2. Michael C. Robinson, "The Relationship between the Army Corps of Engineers and the Environmental Community," *Environmental Review* 13 (1989): 1–41; Andrews, *Managing the Environment, Managing Ourselves*, pp. 190, 287–88; and Holmes, *History of Federal Water Resources Programs and Policies*, pp. 111–17.

3. 30 Stat. 1152, 33 U.S.C. 401–15; Holmes, *History of Federal Water Resources Programs and Policies*, pp. 131–32; and 33 U.S.C. Section 407 (1971).

4. Albert E. Cowdrey, "Pioneering Environmental Law: The Army Corps of Engineers and the Refuse Act," *Pacific Historical Review* 46, no. 3 (August 1975): 331–42.

5. *United States v. Republic Steel* 362 U.S. 482 (1960); *United States v. Standard Oil Co.* 384 U.S. 224 (1966); and William H. Rodgers Jr., "Industrial Water Pollution

and the Refuse Act: A Second Chance for Water Quality," *University of Pennsylvania Law Review* 119 (1971): 770–73.

6. Department of the Army, Office of the Chief of Engineers, "Civic Regulatory Functions: Permits—Policy, Practice, and Procedure," 18 March 1968, reprinted in SAWP, *Refuse Act Permit Program*, 92d Cong., 1st sess., June 1971, pp. 4303–4; Edelman Interview, 9 March 1999; and Comptroller of the United States, *Need for Improving Procedures to Ensure Compliance with Law Regarding Deposition of Industrial Waste Solids into Navigable Waters* (Washington, D.C.: U.S. GAO, December 1966), pp. 10–11, 24–25.

7. Department of the Army, Office of the Chief Engineers, "Civil Regulatory Function: Illegal Deposits in Navigable Waters," Circular No. 1145-2-1, S-1, 17 February 1967, reprinted in House Committee on Merchant Marine and Fisheries, Subcommittee on Fisheries and Wildlife Conservation (hereafter SFWC), *Estuarine Areas*, 90th Cong., 1st sess., March 1967, pp. 173–76; and Rodgers, "Industrial Water Pollution and the Refuse Act," pp. 806–8. On the Corps' reticence to assume regulatory authority, see Jeffrey K. Stine, "Regulating Wetlands in the 1970s: U.S. Army Corps of Engineers and the Environmental Organizations," *Journal of Forest History* 27 (April 1983): 60–75.

8. Rodgers, "Industrial Water Pollution and the Refuse Act," pp. 792–93; and "Pollution Laid to 11 Companies," *NYT*, 10 February 1970.

9. Robert Boyle, "My Struggle to Help the President," *Sports Illustrated* 32 (16 February 1970): 32–34; Hickel to Whitaker, 4 May 1970, p. 1, and Haldeman to Whitaker, 17 February 1970, Folder "Water: 1 of 5," Box 116, WP; Kehoe, *Cleaning Up the Great Lakes*, pp. 118–19; SAWP, *Water Pollution Control Programs*, 92d Cong., 1st sess., February 1971, p. 77; and House Committee on Government Operations, Subcommittee on Conservation and Natural Resources (hereafter SCNR), *Mercury Pollution and Enforcement of the Refuse Act of 1899*, 92d Cong., 1st sess., 1971, pt. 2, pp. 1152–54.

10. "U.S. Making Initial Move against Thermal Pollution," *NYT*, 22 February 1970; "Dangerous Levels of Mercury Found in Lakes and Streams in 14 Eastern States by U.S. Investigators," *NYT*, 9 July 1970; and "U.S. Will Sue 8 Concerns over Dumping of Mercury," *NYT*, 25 July 1970.

11. Hickel to Whitaker, 4 May 1970, p. 2, Folder "Water: 1 of 5," Box 116, WP; "U.S. Shifts Fight on Dirty Water," *NYT*, 18 May 1970; and "U.S. to Continue Water Hearings," *NYT*, 29 May 1970.

12. Kehoe, *Cleaning Up the Great Lakes*, pp. 139–40, 147–49; and Edelman Interview, 9 March 1999.

13. SCNR, *Our Waters and Wetlands: How the Corps of Engineers Can Help Prevent Their Destruction and Pollution*, 91st Cong., 2d sess., 18 March 1970, H. Rep. 917, pp. 14–18.

14. James Reston, "Washington: The Politics of Pollution," *NYT*, 26 April 1970; "Rep. Reuss Pushes Pollution Action," *NYT*, 29 March 1970; "Reuss Urges Engineers to

Enforce Refuse Act," *Washington Star*, 31 July 1970, reprinted in SCNR, *Mercury Pollution and Enforcement of the Refuse Act of 1899*, 92d Cong., 1st sess., pt. 1, 1971, pp. 462–63; and Rodgers, "Industrial Water Pollution and the Refuse Act," p. 768.

15. "Justice Department Curbs Use of 1899 Pollution Act," *NYT*, 11 July 1970; SCNR, *Mercury Pollution and Enforcement of the Refuse Act of 1899*, 92d Cong., 1st sess., pt. 1, 1971, pp. 464–68, 1055–59; and Rodgers, "Industrial Water Pollution and the Refuse Act," pp. 793–94.

16. Ross Sandler, "The Refuse Act of 1899: Key to Clean Water," *American Bar Association Journal* 58 (May 1972): 468–71; "Administration Announces Refuse Act Permit Program," *Environmental Law Reporter* 1 (January 1971): 10010; and Senate Committee on Commerce, Subcommittee on Energy, Natural Resources, and the Environment (hereafter SENRE), *Refuse Act Permit Program*, 92d Cong., 1st sess., 1971, pp. 27–31.

17. "Army Engineers Join in Battle against Pollution," *NYT*, 5 April 1970; Martin Reuss, *Shaping Environmental Awareness: The United States Army Corps of Engineers Environmental Advisory Board, 1970–1980* (Washington, D.C.: Historical Division, Office of the Chief of Engineers, 1983), p. 5. Rodgers, "Industrial Water Pollution and the Refuse Act," p. 811; Cowdrey, "Pioneering Environmental Law," p. 347; SAWP, *Refuse Act Permit Program*, 92d Cong., 1st sess., 1971, pp. 4319–20; SENRE, *Effects of Mercury on Man and the Environment*, 91st Cong., 2d sess., pt. 2, pp. 428–29; and SCNR, *Mercury Pollution and Enforcement of the Refuse Act of 1899*, 92d Cong., 1st sess., pt. 1, 1971, pp. 460–61.

18. James R. Wagner, "Water Pollution Permit Plan Worries Conservationists, Industries Alike," *National Journal* (2 February 1971): 397; and Timothy Atkeson, "The Refuse Act Permit Program," Statement to the ALI-ABA Seminar on Environmental Law, 28 January 1971, reprinted in SENRE, *Refuse Act Permit Program*, 92d Cong., 1st sess., 1971, pp. 153–57. On the EPA, created by executive order in December 1970, see "Special Message to the Congress about Reorganization Plans to Establish the Environmental Protection Agency and the National Oceanic and Atmospheric Administration," 9 July 1970, *PPP: Richard M. Nixon*, 1970, pp. 578–87.

19. John Quarles, *Cleaning Up America: An Insider's View of the Environmental Protection Agency* (Boston: Houghton Mifflin, 1976), pp. 97–102. The Nixon administration could not just put the EPA in charge because no executive order could override the 1899 Rivers and Harbors Act.

20. Ibid., p. 104; Reuss to William Ruckelshaus, 4 December 1970, reprinted in SCNR, *Mercury Pollution and Enforcement of the Refuse Act of 1899*, 92d Cong., 1st sess., pt. 1, 1971, pp. 483–84; Wagner, "Water Pollution Permit Plan Worries Conservationists, Industries Alike," pp. 393–95, 397; "Statement on Signing Executive Order Establishing a Water Quality Enforcement Program," 23 December 1970, *PPP: Richard M. Nixon*, 1970, pp. 1153–54; and "Memorandum of Understanding," reprinted in SCNR, *Mercury Pollution and Enforcement of the Refuse Act of 1899*, 92d Cong., 1st sess., pt. 1, 1971, pp. 505–9.

21. National Resources Defense Council, "Ways to Improve the Administration's Refuse Act Permit Program," reprinted in SENRE, *Refuse Act Permit Program*, 92d Cong., 1st sess., 1971, pp. 71–72; Reuss to Train, 4 February 1971, reprinted in SENRE, *Refuse Act Permit Program*, p. 125, and also pp. 68–70, 72–74, 124, 138–40, 174–78; and Wagner, "Water Pollution Permit Plan Worries Conservationists, Industries Alike," p. 394. On "state certification" and the 1970 Water Quality Improvement Act, see chapter 5.

22. Billings to Muskie, "Schedule of Subcommittee Activities," undated, and Staff to Minority Members of the Senate Committee on Public Works, "A Very 'Tentative' Agenda for the Activities of the Subcommittee," 21 January 1971, Folder 7, Box 1961, MA.

23. Billings to Muskie, ca. March 1971, reprinted in SAWP, *Refuse Act Permit Program*, 92d Cong., 1st sess., 1971, pp. 4347–48; Jorling untitled memo, 23 June 1971, and Billings to Muskie, "Oversight Hearings," 4 February 1971, pp. 1–3, Folder "Refuse Act of 1899," Box 4, RG 46.18, NARA; Jorling[?] Memo, "The Refuse Act and the Federal-State Water Pollution Control Act," undated, pp. 3–4, Folder "Refuse Act of 1899," Box 4, RG 46.18, NARA; Billings to Muskie, "Oversight Hearings on the Water Pollution Program," 3 February 1971, Folder "Refuse Act 1971," Box 10, RG 46.18, NARA; SAWP, *Refuse Act Permit Program*, 92d Cong., 1st sess., 1971, p. 4351; and SAWP, *Water Pollution Control Programs*, 92d Cong., 1st sess., 1971, pp. 324–72. See also Billings to Baker, undated, Folder "Refuse Act 1971," Box 10, RG 46.18, NARA.

24. Billings to Muskie, "Refuse Act Permit Program," 23 June 1971, Folder "Refuse Act of 1899," Box 4, RG 46.18, NARA; SAWP, *Refuse Act Permit Program*, 92d Cong., 1st sess., 1971, p. 4340; Davies, *The Politics of Pollution*, p. 175; "Effluent Requirements for Industrial Wastes," EPA memo to independent research contractors, reprinted in SCNR, *Mercury Pollution and Enforcement of the Refuse Act of 1899*, 92d Cong., 1st sess., pt. 1, 1971, p. 901; and SAWP, *Refuse Act Permit Program*, 92d Cong., 1st sess., 1971, pp. 4340, 4343, 4358, 4371.

25. "Permit Program—Effluent Controls," Quarles to All Acting Regional Administrators, 15 July 1971, reprinted in SCNR, *Mercury Pollution and Enforcement of the Refuse Act of 1899*, 92d Cong., 1st sess., pt. 1, 1971, p. 934; "Effluent Requirements for Industrial Wastes," pp. 901–7; Wagner, "Water Pollution Permit Plan Worries Conservationists, Industries Alike," pp. 390–91; Rodgers, "Industrial Water Pollution and the Refuse Act," p. 815; and Kehoe, *Cleaning Up the Great Lakes*, pp. 123–24.

26. "Permit Program—Effluent Controls," p. 935; and SAWP, *Refuse Act Permit Program*, 92d Cong., 1st sess., 1971, pp. 4359, 4370.

27. James R. Wagner, "Industries Win Few Concessions as Pollution Permit Plan Moves on Schedule," *National Journal* (1 May 1971): 932–33, 938; SAWP, *Water Pollution Control Legislation*, 92d Cong., 1st sess., March 1971, pt. 2, p. 725; and SAWP, *Refuse Act Permit Program*, 92d Cong., 1st sess., June 1971, p. 4349.

28. "Water Problem in U.S.—What Can Be Done about It? Interview with the Chief of the Army Corps of Engineers," *U.S. News and World Report* 59 (25 October 1965): 66–75; *Cong. Rec.* 111, pt. 13 (27 July 1965), pp. 18337–41; "Congress Authorizes $2 Billion in New Water Projects," *CQA* 21, 89th Cong., 1st sess., 1965, p. 751; "Northeast Drought," and "Water Resources Planning Act Passed by Congress," *CQA* 21, 89th Cong., 1st sess., 1965, pp. 758–61; and Holmes, *History of Federal Water Resources Programs and Policies*, pp. 42–43, 45–46, 123, 249–61.

29. Harry E. Schwarz, "North Atlantic Regional Water Resources Study," American Society for Civil Engineers Conference paper, pp. 1–10, Folder 19–22, Box 56–60, Schwarz Papers; Harry Schwarz and David C. Major, "The Systems Approach: An Experience in Planning," *Water Spectrum* 3 (Fall 1971): 29–34; and Harry Schwarz, "The NAR Study: A Case Study in Systems Analysis," *Water Resources Research* 8 (June 1972): 751–54.

30. Harry Schwarz, "North Atlantic Regional Water Resources Study," p. 3.

31. Holmes, *History of Federal Water Resources Programs and Policies*, pp. 123–24, 259–60, 266.

32. *Cong. Rec.* 111, pt. 20, 20 October 1965, pp. 27698, 27702; "Congress Authorizes $2 Billion in New Water Projects" and "Northeast Drought," pp. 755, 758; and Holmes, *History of Federal Water Resources Programs and Policies*, p. 122.

33. Harry E. Schwarz, "Waste Water Management—A Regional Problem," undated paper, Folder 23–45, Box 61–62, Schwarz Papers; Harry Schwarz, "Scope of the NEWS Study," *Journal of the American Water Works Association* 63, no. 3 (May 1971): 313–14.

34. Comptroller General of the United States, *Examination into the Effectiveness of the Construction Grant Program for Abating, Controlling, and Preventing Water Pollution* (Washington, D.C.: U.S. GAO, 3 November 1969), pp. 1–68.

35. Ibid., pp. 80–98.

36. SCPW, *The Economics of Clean Water: Summary Report of the U.S. Department of Interior, Federal Water Pollution Control Administration, March 1970*, 91st Cong., 2d sess., December 1970, pp. 6, 16, 18; Council on Environmental Quality, *Environmental Quality: The First Annual Report of the Council on Environmental Quality* (Washington, D.C.: GPO, August 1970), pp. 55–59; and David J. Allee and Leonard B. Dworsky, "Where Now Clean Water?" *Water Spectrum* 2 (Winter 1970): 10–15.

37. Gregory Graves, *Pursuing Excellence in Water Planning and Policy Analysis: A History of the Institute for Water Resources, U.S. Army Corps of Engineers* (Washington, D.C.: GPO, 1996), pp. 1–56; and Reuss, *Shaping Environmental Awareness*, pp. 5–6.

38. David J. Allee et al., *The Role of the U.S. Army Corps of Engineers in Water Quality Management*, Corps of Engineers, Institute for Water Resources, Report 71-1, October 1970, pp. 7–12, U.S. Army Corps of Engineers Library, Washington, D.C.

39. Ibid., pp. 24–31, 48.

40. Ibid., pp. 13–18, 24–30, 41–42, 45, 49, 51–53, 66–70.

41. Ibid., pp. 19–20, 46, 65, 112–15.

42. Senate Committee on Appropriations, Subcommittee on Public Works, *Public Works for Water and Power Development and Atomic Energy Commission Appropriations Bill, 1972*, pt. 1, 92d Cong., 1st sess., 9 March 1971, pp. 8–9, 44, 46, 801–2; John Stennis to Lt. Gen. F. J. Clarke, 15 March 1971, reprinted in SCNR, *Phosphates and Phosphate Substitution in Detergents*, 92d Cong., 1st sess., October 1971, pp. 413–14; and Frank McGowan, Maria R. Eigerman, and Harry E. Schwarz, "The Merrimack Tapes," *Water Spectrum* 3 (Winter 1971): 1–10. On the history of the Merrimack and pollution, see Theodore Steinberg, *Nature Incorporated: Industrialization and the Waters of New England* (Cambridge: Cambridge University Press, 1991), pp. 205–39.

43. Steinberg, *Down to Earth*, p. 167; Joel Tarr, James McCurley, and Terry F. Yosie, "The Development and Impact of Urban Wastewater Technology: Changing Concepts of Water Quality Control, 1850–1930," in *Pollution and Reform in American Cities, 1870–1930*, ed. Martin Melosi (Austin: University of Texas Press, 1980), pp. 59–82.

44. R. Michael Stevens, *Green Land—Clean Streams* (Philadelphia: Temple University Center for the Study of Federalism, 1972), pp. 36–40.

45. Louis Kardos, William Sopper, and Earl Myers, "A Living Filter for Sewage," *Yearbook of Agriculture 1968: Science for Better Living* (Washington, D.C.: U.S. Department of Agriculture, 1968), pp. 197–99; Stevens, *Green Land—Clean Streams*, pp. 78–80; and Richard Parizek, Louis Kardos, et al., "The Pennsylvania State University Studies No. 23: Waste Water Renovation and Conservation," reprinted in SAWP, *Water Pollution—1970*, 91st Cong., 2d sess., May 1970, pt. 3, pp. 1017–18, 1025–33.

46. Parizek, Kardos et al., "The Pennsylvania State University Studies No. 23," pp. 1050, 1058–60, 1071–72; Kardos, Sopper, and Meyers, "A Living Filter for Sewage," pp. 199–201; Stevens, *Green Land—Clean Streams*, p. 89; William E. Sopper, "Effects of Sewage Effluent Irrigation on Tree Growth," reprinted in SAWP, *Water Pollution—1970*, 91st Cong., 2d sess., May 1970, pt. 3, pp. 989–92; and Richard R. Parizek and Earl A. Meyers, "Recharge of Ground Water from Renovated Sewage Effluent by Spray Irrigation," reprinted in SAWP, *Water Pollution—1970*, pt. 3, pp. 993–1010. See also Louis T. Kardos, "A New Prospect: Preventing Eutrophication of Our Lakes and Streams," *Environment* 12 (March 1970): 10–21.

47. "The Muskegon County Wastewater Management System," reprinted in HCPW, *Water Pollution Control Legislation—1971* (Amendments to Existing Water Pollution Control Laws), 92d Cong., 1st sess., 27 July 1971, p. 472.

48. Kehoe, *Cleaning Up the Great Lakes*, pp. 89–93; and "Great Lakes Pollution Poses 2 Problems for Nixon," *NYT*, 6 February 1970.

49. John R. Sheaffer, "Reviving the Great Lakes," *Saturday Review* 53 (7 November 1970): 63–64.

50. "Muskegon County, Mich., Mends Waste Lands with Waste Water," *American County* 35 (August 1970): 32–35; and "The Muskegon County Wastewater Management System," pp. 473, 483.

51. "The Muskegon County Wastewater Management System," pp. 474–482; and Stevens, *Green Land—Clean Streams*, pp. 92–105.

52. John R. Sheaffer, "Reviving the Great Lakes," *Saturday Review* 53 (7 November 1970): 65; and Leonard A. Stevens, "The County That Reclaims Its Sewage," *Readers' Digest* 107 (July 1975): 39–44.

53. Kehoe, *Cleaning Up the Great Lakes*, pp. 86–88, 130–31, 138–50; and SCNR, *Phosphates in Detergents and the Eutrophication of America's Waters*, 91st Cong., 1st sess., December 1969, pp. 209–15, 221–22.

54. SCNR, *Phosphates in Detergents and the Eutrophication of America's Waters*, pp. 215, 223; John R. Sheaffer, "Reviving the Great Lakes," *Saturday Review* 53 (7 November 1970): 65; "The Muskegon County Wastewater Management System," p. 485; Vander Jagt to Ehrlichman, 28 December 1970, Folder "Water Pollution/Water 1/1/71," Box 35, Subject Files HE, WHCF, Nixon Presidential Materials, NARA; and Whitaker to De Muth, 23 July 1970, Folder "Water: 1 of 5," Box 116, WP.

55. Daniel A. Mazmanian and Jeanne Nienaber, *Can Organizations Change? Environmental Protection, Citizen Participation, and the Corps of Engineers* (Washington, D.C.: Brookings Institution, 1979), pp. 114–15.

56. Frank McGowan, Maria R. Eigerman, and Harry E. Schwarz, "The Merrimack Tapes," *Water Spectrum* 3 (Winter 1971): 1–10; and "Corps to Assess Wastewater Systems," *Water Spectrum* 3 (Summer 1971): 43–44.

57. Anthony Wayne Smith, "Potomac River Dams," *Environmental Journal* 44 (September 1970): 23–26.

58. Allee et al., *The Role of the U.S. Army Corps of Engineers in Water Quality Management*, p. 64.

CHAPTER 8: DRAFTING THE CLEAN WATER ACT

1. "Election '70: The Democrats Shape Up" and "Ed Muskie—And the Pack," *Newsweek* 76 (16 November 1970): 30–32, 33–35; "And Now, Looking toward 1972" and "Issues That Lost, Men Who Won," *Time* 96 (16 November 1972): 15, 18; and Matusow, *Nixon's Economy*, pp. 55–83.

2. "California's John Tunney," *Time* 96 (16 November 1970): 20–21.

3. "The Great Tunney-Brown Fight," *Time* 95 (15 June 1970): 15; and Jacques Leslie, "John Tunney, Kennedy's Friend in Muskie's Corner," *NYT Magazine*, 26 December 1971, pp. 5–12.

4. *Cong. Rec.* 117, pt. 2, 92d Cong., 1st sess. (2 February 1971), pp. 1348–49. For Muskie's bill, S. 523, and Nixon's, S. 1014, see SAWP, *Water Pollution Control Legislation*, 92d Cong., 1st sess., 15 March 1971, pt. 1, pp. 193–240 and 306–35.

5. "Proposed Enforcement Legislation for Water Pollution Control," 5 February 1971, Folder "Environmental Legislation 1970–71, 1 of 3," Box 61, WP; "Special

Message to the Congress Proposing a 1971 Environmental Program," 8 February 1971, *PPP: Richard M. Nixon*, 1971, pp. 128–30. Certain initiatives, like deadlines, developed exclusively in the context of air pollution policy. Others, like new-source performance standards or citizen suits, were discussed concurrently during both the air and water debates in 1970.

6. The committee's general counsel, Barry Meyer, also played a central role in drafting the bill.

7. "Staff Proposal—Water Pollution Bill," 1 June 1971, Folder "Introduction of the National Water Quality Standards Act of 1971," Box 1, RG 46.18, NARA; Billings Interview, 21 November 1997; and "Outline of Water Pollution Issues," ca. April or May 1971, p. 1, Folder "Memos," Box 4, RG 46.18, NARA. The bill was reorganized into five discrete components: research and program grants (Title I); grants for construction of treatment works (Title II); standards and enforcement (Title III); permits and licenses (Title IV); and general provisions (citizen suits and emergency abatement) (Title V).

8. Jorling Memorandum on Policy Issues, 28 May 1971, pp. 2–6, Folder "Memos," Box 4, RG 46.18, NARA; Staff Print, 25 May 1971, pp. 15–22, Folder "Prints—S. 2770," Box 3, RG 46.18, NARA; Senate Committee on Public Works Executive Session (hereafter SCPWES), 29 June 1971, p. 10, Folder 1, Box 3044, MA; SCPWES, 10 June 1971, pp. 54, 61–79, Folder 6, Box 3043, MA; SAWP, Panel on Environmental Science and Technology, *Water Pollution Control Legislation: Waste Water Treatment Technology*, 92d Cong., 1st sess., 13 and 14 May 1971, pt. 8, pp. 3617–16; and SCPWES, 10 June 1971, pp. 66–67, 81–97, Folder 6, Box 3043, MA.

9. Tunney to Muskie, 3 June 1971, Folder "Tunney Standard," Box 4, RG 46.18, NARA.

10. SCPWES, 22 September 1971, p. 45, Folder 5, Box 3045, MA; "Caution! Si Ramo at Work," *Fortune* 82 (November 1970): 105–7; and Thomas P. Hughes, *Rescuing Prometheus* (New York: Pantheon Books, 1998), pp. 110–18.

11. Hughes, *Rescuing Prometheus*, pp. 69–70; Simon Ramo, *Cure for Chaos* (New York: David McKay, 1969), pp. v–x, 6–17, 27–37; and Simon Ramo, *Century of Mismatch* (New York: David McKay, 1970), pp. 141–62.

12. Simon Ramo, "The Systems Approach to Automated Common Sense," *Nation's Cities* 6 (March 1968): 14–19; Simon Ramo, "The Coming Social-Industrial Complex," *Vital Speeches* 38 (15 November 1971): 80–86; Hughes, *Rescuing Prometheus*, pp. 168–71; and Davis Dyer, *TRW: Pioneering Technology and Innovation since 1900* (Boston: Harvard Business School Press, 1998), pp. 259–93.

13. Dyer, *TRW*; and Hughes, *Rescuing Prometheus*, pp. 118–21.

14. SCPWES, 22 September 1971, p. 45, Folder 5, Box 3045, MA; Tunney to Muskie, 3 June 1971, Folder "Tunney Standard," Box 4, RG 46.18, NARA, p. 2; Claude E. Barfield, "Administration Fights Goals, Costs of Senate Water Quality Bill," *National Journal* (15 January 1972): 88; and SAWP, *National Environmental Laboratories*, 92d Cong., 1st sess., pt. 1, 6 May 1971, p. 481.

15. Billings to Dick Stewart, "Pending Water Pollution Legislation," 8 June 1971, Folder "Tunney Standard," Box 4, RG 46.18, NARA.

16. "Bandwagon Gambit," *Newsweek* 78 (20 December 1971): 27.

17. SCPWES, 10 June 1971, p. 11, Folder 6, Box 3043, MA.

18. Ibid., pp. 2–4, 9–10, 13–14; and Charles Gibbs to Billings, 16 June 1971, Folder "AMSA," Box 4, RG 46.18, NARA.

19. SCPWES, 10 June 1971, pp. 22–23, Folder 6, Box 3043, MA.

20. Ibid., p. 9; ibid., 29 June 1971, p. 15, Folder 6, Box 3043, MA.

21. Ibid., 10 June 1971, pp. 10, 19–23, 26–27, Folder 6, Box 3043, MA.

22. Ibid., pp. 22–24. "Senator Edmund Muskie: His Environmental Record, A Report from the League of Conservation Voters," 1971, pp. 8–9, Folder 5, Box 1603, MA; Don Nicoll to John McEvoy, "The Prestile and the Pulp and Paper Industry," 7 March 1972, Folder 7, Box 1603, MA; and SCPWES, 29 June 1971, pp. 12–14, Folder 6, Box 3043, MA.

23. SCPWES, 29 June 1971, pp. 13–14, Folder 6, Box 3043, MA; ibid., 21 July 1971, pp. 159–60, 192–93, Folder 3, Box 3044.

24. Ibid., pp. 164, 174, 178; Staff print, undated, p. 19, Folder "Committee Prints—S. 2770," Box 3, RG 46.18, NARA; and Billings to Muskie, "National Minimum Water Quality Standards," 19 July 1971, Folder "Memos," Box 4, RG 46.18, NARA.

25. SCPWES, 21 July 1971, pp. 167–70, Folder 3, Box 3044, MA.

26. Ibid., pp. 166, 169.

27. Ibid., pp. 172, 181.

28. Ibid., pp. 174–77, 183–85; "Meaningfulness of the National Minimum Water Quality Standard," undated, Folder "Tunney Standard," Box 4, RG 46.18, NARA. On the Delaware River Basin Commission, see Martha Derthick, *Between State and Nation: Regional Organizations of the United States* (Washington, D.C.: Brookings Institution, 1973), pp. 46–64; and Bruce Ackerman and James Sawyer, "The Uncertain Search for Environmental Policy: Scientific Fact-Finding and Rational Decision-Making along the Delaware River," *University of Pennsylvania Law Review* 120 (January 1972): 419–503.

29. SCPWES, 27 July 1971, pp. 87–91, 97–98, Folder 5, Box 3044, MA; and "Muskie Blocks Action, Conservation Unit Says," *Washington Star*, 23 July 1971.

30. SCPWES, 28 July 1971, pp. 242–43, 244, 246, Folder 1, Box 3045, MA; and Woodwell to Muskie, 9 July 1971, Folder "Science," Box 4, RG 46.18, NARA (emphasis added).

31. For an interpretation of the 1972 act that overlooks the significance of the integrity language, see Harvey Lieber, *Federalism and Clean Waters: The 1972 Water Pollution Control Act* (Lexington, Mass.: D. C. Heath, 1975), p. 41.

32. SCPWES, 28 July 1971, pp. 275–77, Folder 6, Box 3043, MA.

33. Ibid.; and Meyer Interview, 2 June 1999.

34. SCPWES, 28 July 1971, pp. 274, 277–78, Folder 6, Box 3043, MA; and Walter Westman to the Committee, "Points of Ecological Concern in New Draft of Water

Pollution Bill," 8 October 1971, Folder "Memos," Box 4, RG 46.18, NARA. For
the staff's various efforts to incorporate the Woodwell clause, see the 2 August,
3 August, and 6 August drafts in Folder "Committee Prints—S. 2770," Box 3, RG
46.18, NARA. Woodwell's language became the legislation's general statement of
purpose.

35. SCPWES, 28 July 1971, pp. 216–22, Folder 6, Box 3043, MA; and SAWP, *Water Pollution Control Legislation: Agricultural Runoff*, 92d Cong., 1st sess., 2 April 1971,
pt. 6, pp. 2515–677. See also N. William Hines, *Agriculture: The Unseen Foe in the
War on Pollution*, reprinted in ibid., Appendix, pp. 2679–99.

36. SCPWES, 10 June 1971, pp. 41–43, Folder 6, Box 3043, MA; Billings to Muskie,
"Other Comments on the Bill," 19 July 1971, Folder "Executive Sessions—Water,"
Box 4, RG 46.18, NARA; and SCPWES, 28 July 1971, pp. 236–37, Folder 6, Box
3043, MA. Compare Section 304 in August drafts with those in July for changes,
in Folder "Committee Prints—2770," Box 3, RG 46.18, NARA.

37. Billings to Muskie, "National Minimum Water Quality Standards," Folder "Executive Sessions—Water," pp. 1–3, Box 4, RG 46.18, NARA; John Tunney, "National
Minimum Water Quality Standard," 28 July 1971, Folder "Tunney Standard," and
Billings to Muskie, "Comment on the Attached Options for Executive Session on
Monday, July 26," undated, Folder "Memos," Box 4, RG 46.18, NARA; SCPWES,
27 July 1971, pp. 55–58, 191–92, Folder 5, Box 3044, MA; SCPWES, 28 July 1971, pp.
204–15, 220–25, 242–43, Folder 6, Box 3043, MA; and SCPWES, 21 July 1971, pp.
172–73, Folder 6, Box 3043, MA.

38. Billings to Muskie, "Today's Executive Session," 4 August 1971, p. 2, Folder "Executive Sessions—Water," Box 4, RG 46.18, NARA.

39. Staff print, undated, pp. 13–14, Folder "S. 2270—Committee Prints," Box 3, RG
46.18, NARA.

40. "Federal Water Pollution Control Act Amendments—Policies to Be Considered,"
undated, p. 2, Folder "Memos," Box 4, RG 46.1, NARA; and SCPWES, 27 July
1971, pp. 141–43, Folder 5, Box 3044, MA. The Clean Air Act's regional air-shed
approach also inspired the staff's thinking, but the idea of treating air sheds as
governable units was modeled after watersheds and river basins, where the concept of such planning had a longer policy history.

41. Mields to Don Nicoll, 19 November 1970, Folder "1971 Oversight," Box 10, RG
46.18, NARA.

42. Jorling to the Committee, "Waste Treatment Technology," 26 July 1971, Folder
"Regional Waste Management Information," Box 4, RG 46.18, NARA. See Section
201(b)(1) and 201(c) of the 6 August Committee Print in "Committee Prints—S.
2770." See also Zwick and Benstock, *Water Wasteland*, pp. 366–92.

43. SCPWES, 27 July 1971, pp. 76, 164, 165, Folder 5, Box 3044, MA; SAWP, *Water Pollution—1970*, 91st Cong., 2d sess., 26 May 1970, pt. 3, pp. 945–61; Likens to Muskie,
26 July 1971, Folder "Science," Box 4, RG 46.18, NARA; and Woodwell to Muskie,
9 July 1971, Folder "Science," Box 4, RG 46.18, NARA, p. 2.

44. SCPWES, 27 July 1971, p. 78, Folder 5, Box 3044, MA; and Jorling Interview, 2 December 1998. See also Jennings Randolph to Subcommittee, "Relationship of the Corps of Engineers to Waste Water Treatment," 2 June 1971, Folder "Memos," Box 4, RG 46.18, NARA.

45. SCPWES, 27 July 1971, pp. 59, 65–66, 77–78, 140, 152–53, 156–57, 180–83, Folder 5, Box 3044, MA.

46. Ibid., pp. 101–2, 103, 105, 111, 117–18, 160–62.

47. Ibid., pp. 128–30, 145, 175–76; and Nicoll to Billings, 10 September 1971, Folder "Memos," Box 4, RG 46.18, NARA.

48. SCPWES, 27 July 1971, pp. 153–55, 159, 188, Folder 5, Box 3044, MA.

49. Meyer Interview, 2 June 1999; J. Lee Annis Jr., *Howard Baker: Conciliator in an Age of Crisis* (New York: Madison Books, 1995), pp. 52–54; and SCPWES, 10 June 1971, pp. 5–6, 8, 15, 17, 31–32, Folder 6, Box 3043, MA.

50. Billings to Muskie, "Alternative Approaches to Water Quality Control," 23 July 1971, Folder "Memos," Box 4, RG 46.18, NARA. Given the problems EPA officials were having promulgating effluent standards for different industrial processes and individual plants, Billings preferred to discuss strict effluent controls in the context of integrated waste management systems. See SCPWES, 27 July 1971, pp. 184–87, Folder 5, Box 3044, MA.

51. SCPWES, 27 July 1971, pp. 79–80, 166–67, 169, 173, 180, Folder 5, Box 3044, MA.

52. Jorling to Committee, "Waste Water Treatment," 4 August 1971, pp. 1–4, Folder "Memos," Box 4, RG 46.18, NARA; and Richard D. Grundy, "Wastewater Treatment Processes," 5 August 1971, pp. 3–4, Folder "Memos," Box 4, RG 46.18, NARA.

53. Billings to Muskie, "Today's Executive Session," 4 August 1971, pp. 1–2, Folder "Executive Sessions—Water," Box 4, RG 46.18, NARA.

54. John Whitaker to John Ehrlichman, "Meeting to Discuss Water Quality Bill," 7 September 1971, p. 1, Folder "Legislation: 2 of 2," Box 117, WP.

55. Ibid.; and 6 August Committee Print with EPA Commentary, ca. 1 September 1971, pp. 47–50, Folder "Prints—S. 2770," Box 3, RG 46.18, NARA.

56. 6 August Committee Print with EPA Commentary, p. 47; Claude E. Barfield, "Administration Fights Goals, Costs of Senate Water Quality Bill," *National Journal* (15 January 1972): 90; Alm to Richard Fairbanks, "Alternative to 1976 Deadline Proposed in August 6 Senate Water Quality Print," 8 September 1971, Folder "Legislation: Water 2 of 2," Box 117, WP; SCPWES, 22 September 1971, p. 45, Folder 5, Box 3045, MA; and SCPWES, 21 July 1971, p. 173, Folder 3, Box 3044, MA.

57. Fairbanks to Whitaker, 9 September 1971, Folder "Legislation—Water 2 of 2," Box 117, WP; Billings to Muskie, "Pending Legislation," 12 September 1971, p. 2, Folder "Memos," Box 4, RG 46.18, NARA; HCPW, *Water Pollution Control Legislation— 1971* (Amendments to Existing Water Pollution Control Laws), 92d Cong., 1st sess., 16 September 1971, pp. 1582–83; and Environmental Action Press Release, 17 September 1971, Folder "Tunney Standard," Box 4, RG 46.18, NARA.

58. Bob Maynard to Billings, "Water Pollution Control Legislation—92d Congress," 21 April 1971, p. 8, Folder "General," Box 1, RG 46.18, NARA. The committee staff recognized—but did not emphasize—the "difficulty with relating effluent quality to water quality" during the summer. See "Effluent Limitation," undated, Folder 38, Box 8, JP.

59. Walter E. Westman, "Some Basic Issues in Water Pollution Control Legislation," *American Scientist* 60 (November–December 1972): 767–72; Jorling to Billings, "The Bangor Problem," 14 September 1973, Folder 16, Box 7, JP; Jorling Interview, 2 December 1998; Jorling, undated panel discussion remarks, ca. 1973, pp. 51–52, 55–58, Folder 15, Box 5, JP; Jorling to Committee, 18 October 1971, p. 1, Folder "Memos," Box 4, RG 46.18, NARA; Zwick and Benstock, *Water Wasteland*, pp. 276–77; Jorling Interview, 2 December 1998; and SCPWES, 22 September 1971, pp. 52–53, Folder 5, Box 3045, MA.

60. Walter E. Westman, "Some Basic Issues in Water Pollution Control Legislation," *American Scientist* 60 (November–December 1972): 767–772; and Jorling to James Range, 23 May 1974, p. 1, Folder 4, Box 6, JP. Billings reiterated the "natural" definition of integrity. See "Remarks Delivered to Environmental Law Conference, Columbia Law School," 23 March 1973, p. 3, Folder 11, Box 8, JP. The Senate Report on S. 2770 called for a "clearly set goal of natural water quality achieved through application of a no-discharge policy" (S. Rep. 414, 92d Cong., 1st sess., 28 October 1971, pp. 11–12).

61. Walter E. Westman, "Some Basic Issues in Water Pollution Control Legislation," *American Scientist* 60 (November–December 1972): 772; Jorling, "Comments on 'Integrity Statement,'" undated, pp. 2–3, Folder 7, Box 6, JP; and Jorling Interview, 2 December 1998. For the statutory guidelines on the administrative definition of integrity, see S. 2770, Section 304 (Information and Guidelines), in *LHV2*, p. 1613; SCPWES, 22 September 1971, p. 25, Folder 5, Box 3045, MA; and Committee Print, ca. 22 September 1971, p. 42, Folder "Committee Prints—S. 2770," Box 3, RG 46.18, NARA.

62. Committee Print, ca. 22 September 1971, pp. 43–46, Folder "Committee Prints— S. 2770," Box 3, RG 46.18, NARA; SCPWES, 22 September 1971, pp. 25–26, Folder 5, Box 3045, MA; Muskie to Albert C. Althenn, 26 January 1972, p. 1, Folder "Zero Discharge," Box 1, RG 46.18, NARA; undated panel discussion with Jorling and Billings, ca. 1973, pp. 18–19, Folder 23, Box 7, JP; S. Rep. 92-414, pp. 50–51; SCP-WES, 30 September 1971, pp. 19–20, Folder 6, Box 3045, MA; Leon G. Billings, "Remarks to the National Association of Manufacturers Environmental Quality Committee," 16 November 1972, pp. 1–3, Folder 11, Box 8, JP; and "Memorandum on Best Practicable Technology Currently Available," ca. March 1972, Folder "Phases I and II," Box 1, RG 46.18, NARA. Evidence from Muskegon and the Corps' Merrimack study indicated that secondary treatment facilities could be incorporated into more advanced systems. See SCPWES, 22 September 1971, pp. 7–10, Folder 5, Box 3045, MA.

63. Committee Print, ca. 22 September 1971, p. 42, Folder "Committee Prints—S. 2770," Box 3, p. 44, RG 46.18, NARA; SCPWES, 20 September 1971, pp. 2–6, Folder 5, Box 3045, MA; S. Rep. 92-414, pp. 50, 57–60; SCPWES, 22 September 1971, pp. 27–28, 34, Folder 5, Box 3045, MA; and Jorling/Billings undated panel discussion, p. 19, JP. See also "Remarks of Leon G. Billings, "Atomic Industrial Forum," 24 July 1974, p. 5, Folder 11, Box 8, JP. Unlike BPT, BAT did not imply that the technology had to be in routine use.

64. SCPWES, 22 September 1971, pp. 36–37, 49, Folder 5, Box 3045, MA. For a similar committee criticism of the Refuse Act permit program, see "Critique on Water Pollution Program," ca. June 1971, Folder "Memos," Box 4, RG 46.18, NARA.

65. SCPWES, 22 September 1971, pp. 43, 56, Folder 5, Box 3045, MA.

66. SCPWES, 30 September 1971, pp. 41–42, 44–50, Folder 6, Box 3045, MA. See also SCPWES, 22 September 1971, p. 40, Folder 5, Box 3045, MA.

67. SCPWES, 30 September 1971, pp. 48–49, Folder 6, Box 3045, MA; SCPWES, 4 October 1971, pp. 24–25, Folder 1, Box 3046, MA; Leon Billings, "Remarks Delivered to Environmental Law Conference—Columbia Law School," p. 4; and Leon Billings, "The 1972 Amendments," presented at the Water Quality Training Institute—Region X, Seattle, Washington, 1 March 1974, p. 3, Folder 21, Box 7, JP.

68. SCPWES, 30 September 1971, pp. 3–7, 10–12, 43–56, Folder 6, Box 3045, MA.

69. Ibid., pp. 14–15, 17; "Comments on the Refuse Act Permit Program," undated, pp. 1–2, Folder "Memos," Box 4, RG 46.18, NARA; and Claude E. Barfield, "Administration Fights Goals, Costs of Senate Water Quality Bill," *National Journal* (15 January 1972): 93.

70. SCPWES, 4 October 1971, pp. 18–20, Folder 1, Box 3046, MA. As a concession to Tunney and the administration, Billings retained the Tunney standard as an interim stage on the way to no-discharge, to be achieved by 1981 when a meaningful connection between ambient water quality and the effluent controls necessary to achieve it could be determined for specific streams. Reference to ambient standards in the Senate bill was limited to one other instance: cases where state standards implemented under the 1965 act imposed a greater degree of effluent control and/or an earlier date for compliance than Phase I. Billings repeatedly emphasized, however, that the new bill provided no legal authority to the administrator to enforce water quality standards. See Leon Billings, "Public Law 92-500: A Case for Strict Construction, Remarks to the American Law Institute—American Bar Association," 9 February 1973, pp. 3–4, Folder 11, Box 8, JP; Leon Billings, "The 1972 Amendments," 1 March 1974, p. 5, and "Remarks Delivered to Environmental Law School Conference," 23 March 1973, p. 6; SCPWES, 30 September 1971, pp. 24, 44–47, Folder 6, Box 3045, MA; Billings to Muskie, "Refuse Act Permit Program," 5 October 1971, p. 2; "National Water Quality Standards," undated but ca. 4 October 1971, pp. 1–4, Folder "Tunney Standard," Box 4, RG 46.18, NARA; and S. Rep. 92-414, p. 46.

71. Fairbanks to Don Rice and Don Crabill, "Water Bill—Meeting with Senators

Cooper, Boggs, and Baker," p. 1, Folder "Legislation—1 of 2," Box 117, WP; SCP-WES, 4 October 1971, p. 46; floor debate on S. 2770, in *LHV2*, pp. 1262, 1300–1301; and Claude E. Barfield, "Administration Fights Goals, Costs of Senate Water Quality Bill," *National Journal* (15 January 1972): 91.

72. Jorling to Committee, 18 October 1971, p. 1, Folder "Memos," Box 4, pp. 1–2, RG 46.18, NARA.

CHAPTER 9: DEFENDING THE CLEAN WATER ACT

1. Whitaker to Robert Fri, "Water Bill—House Side," 12 October 1971, Folder "Water Bill II," Box 114, WP; Whitaker to Ehrlichman, "Water Quality Bill Strategy," 18 October 1971, p. 2, Folder "Legislation—Water 1 of 2," Box 117, WP; and Claude E. Barfield, "Economic Arguments May Force Retreat from Senate Water Quality Goals," *National Journal* (22 January 1972): 137.

2. Barfield, "Economic Arguments May Force Retreat from Senate Water Quality Goals," p. 142; "Blatnik: 'Nice Guy' in a Tough Spot," *National Journal* (14 August 1971): 1718; Jamie Heard, "Water Pollution Proposals to Test Blatnik's Strength as Public Works Chairman," *National Journal* (14 August 1971): 1719, 1722; Edelman Interview, 9 March 1999; and Thomas Huffman, "Exploring the Legacy of Reserve Mining: What Does the Longest Environmental Trial in History Tell Us about the Meaning of American Environmentalism?" *Journal of Policy History* 12, no. 3 (2000): 339–68.

3. Billings to Muskie, "Meeting with Cong. Blatnik," November 1971, Folder 11, Box 1961, MA; Whitaker to Ehrlichman, "Water Bill—Meeting with House Republicans," 15 November 1971, pp. 1–3, Folder "Water Bill II," Box 114, WP; "House Unit Reopens Hearings on a Water Pollution Measure," *NYT*, 20 November 1971; and Edelman Interview, 9 March 1999.

4. Daniel W. Cannon, "How Clean Must Water Be?" *NAM Reports* (24 April 1972), Folder 3, Box 1704, MA; Harvey Lieber, *Federalism and Clean Waters* (New York: Lexington Books, 1975), pp. 52–53; and Claude E. Barfield, "Administration Fights Goals, Costs of Senate Water Quality Bill," *National Journal* (15 January 1972): 94–96. For the committee's frosty relationship with the Chamber of Commerce, see F. Ritter Shumway to Muskie, 14 April 1971 and 6 May 1971; and Billings to Berl Bernhard et al., 10 May 1971, Folder 9, Box 1861, MA. For examples of environmentalist input, see Zwick to Subcommittee Staff, 20 July 1971, Barbara Reid to Muskie, 20 September 1971, and Reid, Zwick et al. to Billings, 19 October 1971, Folder "1971 Bill: Comments—Citizens," Box 4, RG 46.18, NARA; and Zwick memo to Committee dated 30 January 197[2], Folder "Phases I & II," Box 1, RG 46.18, NARA.

5. HCPW, *Water Pollution Control Legislation—1971 (HR 11896, HR 11895)*, 92d Cong., 1st sess., 7 December 1971, pp. 201–8, 217, 221–23, 227–28, 254, 284–85, 288–93, 318–25; and Fairbanks to Whitaker, 14 October 1971, and "Environmental

and Economic Benefits and Costs Related to Various Water Pollution Abatement Strategies," pp. 1–14, Folder "Legislation—Water 1 of 2," Box 117, WP.

6. Vogel, *Fluctuating Fortunes*, pp. 67–112; Fairbanks to Whitaker, 1 November 1971, and "Suggested Talking Points" (attached), Folder "Legislation—Water 1 of 2," Box 117, WP; Karen DeW. Lewis, "Washington Pressures: NAM Turns Pragmatic in Opposing Federal Restraints on Industry," *National Journal* (3 June 1972): 940–47; "Connor Urges Delay on Clean-Water Bill," *NYT*, 7 January 1972; John T. Connor, "Zero Discharge: National Goal or National Calamity?" speech delivered to the Synthetic Organic Chemical Manufacturers Association, 6 January 1972, pp. 1–13, Folder "Zero Discharge," Box 1, RG 46.18, NARA; and HCPW, *Water Pollution Control Legislation—1971* (HR 11896, HR 11895), pp. 610, 617–20, 623–37, 653–54.

7. *Cong. Rec.* 117 (30 November 1971), pp. 43636–39; Whitaker to Vander Jagt, 21 December 1971, Folder "Water Bill I: 3 of 3," Box 113, WP; Vander Jagt to Whitaker, 7 January 1972, Folder "Water Treatment—Sewage 4 of 7," Box 116, WP; Vander Jagt to Whitaker, 6 March 1972, and Whitaker to Ruckelshaus, 9 March 1972, Folder "Water 2 of 5," Box 149, WP; "Cost of Clean Water Bill Overstated, Coalition Says," *Washington Post*, 7 March 1972; "Environmental Coalition Formed to Push Tougher Water-Quality Bill on House Floor," *National Journal* (18 March 1972): 493; "The Cost of Clean Water: An Analysis of the Administration's Figures," March 1972, Macro Folder "Conference Committee," Folder "General," Box 1, RG 46.18, NARA; "The Stormy Debate over 'Zero-Discharge,'" *Business Week* (5 February 1972): 71; "Pollution Plan Costs to Be Less," *Chicago Tribune*, 22 April 1972; and "Corps Makes First Wave in Waste Water Study," *Engineering News Record* 188 (11 May 1972): 23.

8. *Water Pollution Control Legislation—1971* (HR 11896, HR 11895), pp. 218, 328–29; "Draft: The Costs for Land Disposal Treatment Methods," ca. mid-March 1972, pp. 1–7, Folder "Water Bill—1 of 3," Box 113, WP; and Ruckelshaus to Harsha, 27 March 1972, pp. 1–3, Folder "Regional Waste Treatment," Box 1, RG 46.18, NARA.

9. Ruckelshaus to Harsha, 27 March 1972, p. 3; Charles V. Gibbs, "The Ecological Revolution: The Need for Local Solutions," undated speech, pp. 2–4, 6, Folder "Water: 2 of 5," Box 149, WP; *Water Pollution Control Legislation—1971* (HR 11896, HR 11895), pp. 424–28; and Lee Botts to Jim [Jordan?], 6 March 1972, Macro Folder "Conference Committee," Folder "General," Box 1, RG 46.18, NARA. For details about the Corps' dealing with rural antipathy toward urban sewage, see Mazmanian and Nienaber, *Can Organizations Change?*, pp. 119–31. For the committee's discussion of these potential problems, see SCPWES, 15 October 1971, pp. 27–29, and SCPWES, 27 July 1971, pp. 79–80, 169, Folder 2, Box 3046, MA, Folder 5, Box 3044, MA.

10. Richard Grundy to Leon Billings, "OST Report on Water Pollution Legislation," 11 December 1971, Folder "OST Report," Box 1, RG 46.18, NARA; David to John

Blatnik, 10 December 1971, Folder 199, Box 28, Arthur Maass Papers, Records Collections, Office of History, Headquarters, U.S. Army Corps of Engineers; Ad Hoc Panel to Advise on National Water Quality Problems, "Report to Dr. Edward E. David Jr., Science Advisor to the President," 6 December 1971, pp. 1–13, Folder 199, Box 28, Arthur Maass Papers; Walter Westman to Billings, "Response to OST Panel Report on Water Pollution Legislation," undated, Folder "OST Report," Box 1, RG 46.18, NARA; and Jorling, "Comments on the Report to Dr. Edward E. David, Jr., Science Advisor to the President," undated, Folder "OST Report," Box 1, RG 46.18, NARA.

11. "Nixon Gets Help from Liberals," *Washington Evening Star*, 14 December 1971; and Fairbanks to Howard Cohen, "OST Panel Report," 15 December 1971, Folder "Water Bill II," Box 114, WP.

12. Whitaker to Ehrlichman, "Water Bill—Developments in House," 13 March 1972, Paul Vander Myde to C. D. Ward, "Water Bill—House Vote," 17 March 1972, and Fairbanks to Ward, "Water Bill—House Vote," 17 March 1972, Folder "Water Bill: 1 of 3," Box 113, WP; "Environmentalists Fail to Amend House Water Bill," *National Journal* (1 April 1972): 580; "House Approves Water Pollution Bill," *NYT*, 30 March 1972; and Whitaker to Herb Stein, "Talking Points re: High Funding Levels in Water Pollution Legislation," 4 April 1972, Folder "Water Bill: 1 of 3," Box 113, WP.

13. Whitaker to Ehrlichman, "Water Bill—Political and Economic Impact," 9 March 1972, Folder "Waste Treatment—Sewage: 3 of 7," Box 115, WP; Theodore White, *The Making of the President—1972* (New York: Altheus, 1973), pp. 75–84; James M. Naughton, "The Taste of Defeat," *NYT Magazine* (16 May 1972): 13–14, 81–89; and Carl Bernstein and Bob Woodward, *All the President's Men* (New York: Simon and Schuster, 1974), pp. 127–29, 136–44.

14. "Memorandum to the File: The Water Bill," 3 May 1972, Folder "Water Bill—1 of 3," Box 113, WP.

15. Billings to Dan Lewis, "Water Pollution Conference," 13 April 1972, and Billings to Muskie, "Press Briefing on Water Pollution Legislation," 24 May 1972, Folder "General Conference Committee Memos," Box 2, RG 46.18, NARA. See also "A Time for Soft Talk," *Washington Evening Star*, 4 April 1972, and "Clean Water Politics," *Washington Daily News*, 11 April 1972 (photocopies in same folder); and Don Alexander to Billings, "John Quarles Speech," 25 April 1972, Macro Folder "Conference Committee," Folder "General," Box 1, RG 46.18, NARA.

16. Staff of the Subcommittee to Senate Conferees, untitled memoranda, 11 May 1972 and 17 May 1972, and Billings to Muskie, "Summary of Action and Discussion of Outstanding Issues in Title II," 31 May 1972, Folder "Title II," Box 2, RG 46.18, NARA; Staff to Senate Conferees, "Conference on S. 2770," 1 June 1972, pp. 1–5, Folder "GCCM," Box 2, RG 46.18, NARA; Edelman Interview, 9 March 1999; and Memorandum for the Record, "Summary to Date of House-Senate Staff and Conference Meeting on S. 2770," 24 May 1972, pp. 6–7, Folder "GCCM," Box 2, RG 46.18, NARA.

17. Billings to Muskie, "Status of Water Pollution Conference," 9 May 1972, p. 1, and Billings to Senate Conferees, "Differences in Pending Water Pollution Bills," 26 April 1972, pp. 1–2, Folder "GCCM," Box 2, RG 46.18, NARA; H.R. 11896, Section 303, in SCPW, *A Legislative History of the Water Pollution Control Act Amendments of 1972*, 93d Cong., 1st sess., January 1973, vol. 1 (hereafter *LHV1*), pp. 969–78; and H. Rep. 911, 92d Cong., 2d sess., 11 March 1972, pp. 104–7.

18. "Memorandum to the Conferees," 16 August 1972, Folder "GCCM," Box 2, RG 46.18, NARA; Staff to Senate Conferees, "Conference on S. 2770," 1 June 1972, pp. 1–2, Folder "GCCM," Box 2, RG 46.18, NARA; "Significant Weaknesses in House-Passed Water Pollution Legislation," undated, Folder "GCCM," Box 2, RG 46.18, NARA; H.R. 11896 in *LHV1*, pp. 897–900, 918–24, 994–98; and Staff of the Subcommittee on Air and Water Pollution to Senate Conferees, untitled memorandum, 11 May 1972, p. 3. Congress devoted curiously little discussion to the concept of "maximum daily loads." See the House debate on H.R. 11896, 27 March 1972, in *LHV1*, pp. 352–53, 489; and Billings[?] to John Barriere, "Summary of Principal Differences between House and Senate Water Pollution Legislation," 25 February 1972, p. 1, Folder "GCCM," Box 2, RG 46.18, NARA.

19. On judicial review, see P.L. 89-234 (2 October 1965), Section 5(5), p. 909; Billings to Senate Conferees, "Options to the House Proposal on Title III," 15 June 1972, p. 3, Folder "Conference Committee Session/15 June 1972," Box 2, RG 46.18, NARA; S. Rep. 414, 92d Cong., 1st sess., 1971, pp. 84–85; and Billings to Senate Conferees, "Differences in Pending Water Pollution Bills," 26 April 1972, p. 3.

20. Billings to Muskie, "Status of Water Pollution Conference," 9 May 1972, p. 1; and Barbara Reid (Environmental Policy Center) et al., general mailing to senators and representatives, 16 August 1972, Macro Folder "Conference Committee," Folder "General," Box 1, RG 46.18, NARA.

21. Staff to Senate Conferees, untitled memorandum, 11 May 1972, pp. 1–2, Staff of Subcommittee on Air and Water Pollution to Senate Conferees, untitled memorandum, 11 May 1972, pp. 1–3, Billings to Senate Conferees, "Options to the House Proposal on Title III," 15 June 1972, p. 2, Billings to Muskie, "Status of the Water Pollution Conference," 11 July 1972, p. 2, Folder "GCCM," Billings to Senate Conferees, "Options to the House Proposal on Title III," 15 June 1972, pp. 1–3, Memo for the Record, "Best Practicable Technology," 22 May 1972, Folder "Phases I and II," Box 2, RG 46.18, NARA. Sections 306 (new source performance standards) and 307 (toxic pollutants) of the House bill required similar economic, social, and environmental impact tests.

22. Staff to Senate Conferees, untitled memorandum, 11 May 1972, p. 2; Billings and Jorling to Muskie and Baker, "Outline of the Revised Section Applicable to 'Best Available Technology,'" 16 May 1972, pp. 1–2, Folder "Phases I & II," Box 2, RG 46.18, NARA; and Leon Billings to Author, 20 June 2000.

23. Handwritten Minutes of Conference Meeting Executive Session, 22 June 1972, pp. 1–5, Folder "Conference Committee Session—22 June 1972," Box 2, RG 46.18,

NARA; Senate Consideration of the Report of the Conference Committee, 4 October 1972, in *LHV1*, pp. 169–72; and S. Rep. 1236, 92d Cong., 2d sess., 28 September 1972, in *LHV1*, pp. 302–3, 307–8. Due to the length of the conference deliberations, the deadline date for BPT was pushed back from 1976 to 1977. A similar compromise applied to Section 307 on toxic substances. See Senate Consideration of the Report of the Conference Committee, 4 October 1972, and Conference Report, in *LHV1*, pp. 173, 312.

24. Billings to Author, 20 June 2000; Senate Consideration of the Report of the Conference Committee, 4 October 1972, and Conference Report, in *LHV1*, pp. 304, 308; House Consideration of the Report of the Conference Committee, 4 October 1972, in *LHV1*, p. 255; and John Whitaker to Ken Cole, "Water Bill Status," 8 September 1972, pp. 1–2, Folder "Water Bill III—1 of 3," Box 114, WP. The conferees employed a similar, though more restrictive, cost test for new source performance standards. See Senate Consideration of the Report of the Conference Committee, 4 October 1972, pp. 172–73, and Conference Report, pp. 311–12, in *LHV1*. The House agreed to drop its proposal to make Phase II contingent upon a National Academy of Sciences cost-benefit study, while the Senate agreed to "uncouple" the no-discharge objective from Phase II's new 1983 deadline. No-discharge remained an unenforceable national goal for 1985.

25. Undated panel discussion with Jorling and Billings, ca. 1973, pp. 20–21, Folder 23, Box 7, JP.

26. For a summary of nearly eighty relevant NEPA decisions, see SCPW, *National Environmental Policy Act*, 92d Cong., 2d sess., March 1972 (Joint Hearings with SCIIA), pp. 73–81, 47–48, 441–42.

27. Claude E. Barfield, "Exemptions from NEPA Requirements Sought for Nuclear Plants, Pollution Permits," *National Journal* (17 June 1972): 1025.

28. John Quarles, *Cleaning Up America: An Insider's View of the Environmental Protection Agency* (Boston: Houghton Mifflin, 1976), pp. 98–116.

29. *Kalur v. Resor* 1 ELR 20637 (D. D.C., 21 December 1971), p. 20641; and Claude E. Barfield, "Water Pollution Act Forces Showdown in 1973 over Best Way to Protect Environment," *National Journal* (9 December 1972): 1874.

30. *Kalur v. Resor*, pp. 20640–42.

31. SCPW, *National Environmental Policy Act* (Joint Hearings with SCIIA), pp. 429, 452, 463–64; and Quarles, *Cleaning Up America*, p. 111.

32. "Blackouts on the Horizon?" *National Journal* (26 February 1972): 347; and SFWC, *Interim Nuclear Licensing*, 92d Cong., 2d sess., March 1972, pp. 7–57.

33. Claude E. Barfield and Richard Corrigan, "White House Seeks to Restrict Scope of Environmental Law," *National Journal* (26 February 1972): 342; Baker to Muskie, 22 October 1971, Folder "NEPA," Box 2, RG 46.18, NARA; *LHV2*, pp. 1393–95; Billings to John McEvoy, "'Baker Amendment' to S. 2770," 17 April 1972, p. 1, Folder 4, Box 1603, MA; *LHV2*, p. 1394.

34. HCPW, *Water Pollution Control Legislation—1971 (HR 11896, HR 11895)*, 92d Cong., 1st sess., December 1971, pp. 366–67, 411–13.
35. Barfield and Corrigan, "White House Seeks to Restrict Scope of Environmental Law," p. 344.
36. Ibid.; Joint Committee on Atomic Energy, *H.R. 13731 and H.R. 1372, To Amend the Atomic Energy Act of 1954 Regarding the Licensing of Nuclear Facilities*, 92d Cong., 2d sess., 16 March, pp. 39–119; and "A Congressional Backlash on NEPA?" *National Journal* (17 June 1972): 1030.
37. Claude E. Barfield, "Exemptions from NEPA Requirements Sought for Nuclear Plants, Pollution Permits," *National Journal* (17 June 1972): 1026–28, 1033; SFWC, *Interim Nuclear Licensing*, 92d Cong., 2d sess., 1972; SFWC, *Temporary Exemption from Sec. 102 Statements*, 92d Cong., 2d sess., 30 June 1972; and Claude E. Barfield, "Water Pollution Act Forces Showdown in 1973 over Best Way to Protect Environment," *National Journal* (9 December 1972): 1873.
38. SCPW, *National Environmental Policy Act* (Joint Hearings with SCIIA), pp. 463–65; "Save NEPA," *NYT*, 2 May 1972; and Claude E. Barfield, "Exemptions from NEPA Requirements Sought for Nuclear Plants, Pollution Permits," *National Journal* (17 June 1972): 1028, 1029, 1031.
39. Barfield, "Exemptions from NEPA Requirements Sought for Nuclear Plants, Pollution Permits," pp. 1033–34; Barfield, "Water Pollution Act Forces Showdown in 1973 over Best Way to Protect Environment," *National Journal* (9 December 1972): 1880; and SCIIA, *Interim Nuclear Licensing*, 92d Cong., 2d sess., 28 April 1972, pp. 123–33.
40. Barfield and Corrigan, "White House Seeks to Restrict Scope of Environmental Law," pp. 348–49; Timothy Atkeson to Stewart Udall, 6 March 1972, p. 2, Macro Folder "Conference Committee," Folder "General," Box 1, RG 46.18, NARA; and Claude E. Barfield, "Water Pollution Act Forces Showdown in 1973 over Best Way to Protect Environment," p. 1881.
41. Assistant administrator for enforcement and general counsel to the administrator, "Applicability of NEPA to EPA's Regulatory Activities under Pending Water Bills," 23 May 1972, reprinted in SCPW, *National Environmental Policy Act*, 92d Cong., 2d sess., March 1972 (Joint Hearings with SCIIA), pp. 568–71. See also ibid., pp. 546–51, and Baker to Ruckelshaus, 21 March 1972, and Ruckelshaus to Baker, 23 May 1972, reprinted in ibid., pp. 564–68.
42. Ibid., p. 570.
43. See Section 511 of P.L. 92-500, "Other Affected Authority," 18 October 1972, in *LHV1*, p. 80; and Senate Consideration of the Report of the Conference Committee, 4 October 1972, in *LHV1*, p. 195.
44. Senate Consideration of the Report of the Conference Committee, 4 October 1972, in *LHV1*, pp. 179–83.
45. Ibid.

46. Hugh Heclo, "The Sixties' False Dawn: Awakenings, Movements, and Postmodern Policy-Making," in *Integrating the Sixties*, ed. Brian Balogh (University Park: Pennsylvania State University Press, 1996), pp. 39–44.
47. Ibid., pp. 50–57; Claude E. Barfield, "Exemptions from NEPA Requirements Sought for Nuclear Plants, Pollution Permits," *National Journal* (17 June 1972): 1034; Senate Consideration of the Report of the Conference Committee, 4 October 1972, in *LHV1*, pp. 200–205; and "Two Views of NEPA and EPA," *National Journal* (9 December 1972): 1873. See also Zwick's testimony in support of NEPA in House Committee on Merchant Marine and Fisheries, Subcommittee on Fisheries and Wildlife Conservation, *Temporary Exemption from Sec. 102 Statements*, pp. 207–12.
48. Claude E. Barfield, "Water Pollution Act Forces Showdown in 1973 over Best Way to Protect Environment," *National Journal* (9 December 1972): 1880–81; and Claude E. Barfield, "Exemptions from NEPA Requirements Sought for Nuclear Plants, Pollution Permits," *National Journal* (17 June 1972): 1034.
49. Senate Consideration of the Report of the Conference Committee, 4 October 1972, in *LHV1*, p. 198.

CONCLUSION

1. Whitaker to the President, "Decision on Possible Veto of Water Pollution Bill," 17 May 1972, pp. 3–5, Folder "Water Bill—2 of 3," Box 114, WP; and Ehrlichman to Chapin, "Schedule Proposal: Private Session with Senator Howard Baker of Tennessee," 2 August 1972, Folder "Water Bill—2 of 3," Box 114, WP.
2. Whitaker to Ed Harper, "Your Memorandum of October 17," 18 October 1972, p. 1, Folder "Water Bill [III]—1 of 3," Box 114, WP; and Dean E. Mann, "Political Incentives in U.S. Water Policy: Relationships between Distributive and Regulatory Politics," in *What Government Does*, ed. Matthew Holden Jr. and Dennis L. Dressang (Beverly Hills: Sage Publications, 1975), pp. 94–121.
3. Claudia Copeland, "Clean Water Act Issues in the 109th Cong.," 28 September 2005, Congressional Research Service Issue Brief, IB10142 (http://fpc.state.gov/documents/organization/54508.pdf), pp. 6–7.
4. U.S. Environmental Protection Agency, *National Water Quality Inventory: 2000 Report* (Washington, D.C., 2002), p. 3; Yeager, *The Limits of Law*, pp. 246–47; and Copeland, "Water Quality: Implementing the Clean Water Act," p. 5.
5. See William Cronon, "The Trouble with Wilderness; or, Getting Back to the Wrong Nature," in *Uncommon Ground*, ed. Cronon, pp. 69–90. In our 1998 interview, Thomas Jorling explained that the ecologists and staff were attempting to address the "gross impacts" of uncontrolled pollution rather than eliminate all discharges entirely. Such a strategy admitted that effluents might continue to cause alterations in ecosystem equilibrium, within an acceptable range. At some point in the future, with gross pollution controlled, policymakers could take the next step to decide whether eliminating the remainder of discharges was war-

ranted. Fluxes around background, rather than pristine conditions, seemed to be the goal. In fact, Jorling was somewhat critical of "presocial" standards. In the early seventies, however, Jorling tended, at minimum, to conjoin "fluxes around background" with "preindustrial" quality and advocated the latter more vocally, at least in the context of distinguishing the committee's position from the conventions of sanitary engineering.

6. U.S. Environmental Protection Agency, *National Water Quality Inventory: 2000 Report*, pp. 11–12; and National Research Council, *Assessing the TMDL Approach to Water Quality Management* (Washington, D.C.: National Academy Press, 2001), pp. 2, 11–15.

7. "EPA to Allow Polluters to Buy Clean Water Credits," *Washington Post*, 14 January 2003. For the EPA's administration of the Clean Water Act—and the courts' treatment of technology-based standards in particular—see Yeager, *The Limits of Law*, pp. 176–302.

8. Garrett Power, "The Fox in the Chicken Coop: The Regulatory Program of the U.S. Army Corps of Engineers," *Virginia Law Review* 63 (May 1977): 514–18, 522, 533; and *LHV1*, pp. 177–78, 1063–64.

9. Ronald Keith Gaddie and James L. Regens, *Regulating Wetlands Protection: Environmental Federalism and the States* (Albany: State University of New York Press, 2000), pp. 18–26.

10. Lee Evan Caplin, "Is Congress Protecting Our Water? The Controversy over Section 404, Federal Water Pollution Control Act Amendments of 1972," *University of Miami Law Review* 31 (Spring 1977): 447–50.

11. Stine, "Regulating Wetlands in the 1970s," 60–75.

ARCHIVAL SOURCES

John Blatnik Papers, Minnesota Historical Society Manuscript Collection, St. Paul

Lyndon Baines Johnson Presidential Materials, Lyndon Baines Johnson Library, Austin, Texas

Thomas Jorling Papers, Williams College Archives and Special Collections, Williamstown, Massachusetts

League of Women Voters Papers, Library of Congress Manuscript Division, Washington, D.C.

Edmund S. Muskie Archives and Special Collections Library, Bates College, Lewiston, Maine

Richard M. Nixon Presidential Materials, National Archives and Records Administration, Bethesda, Maryland

National Archives and Records Administration, Bethesda, Maryland

   Record Group 90, Records of the Public Health Service, Division of Sanitary Engineering Services

   Record Group 382, Records of the Federal Water Pollution Control Administration, 1965–1969

   Record Group 412.2.1, Records of the Environmental Protection Agency, Predecessor Agencies, Division of Water Supply and Pollution Control, and Its Successors

   Record Group 412.8, Environmental Protection Agency Motion Pictures (General), 1964–1976, Motion Pictures, Sound, and Video Branch

National Archives and Records Administration, Center for Legislative Archives, Washington, D.C.

   Record Group 46.14, Records of the Senate Committee on Interior and Insular Affairs

   Record Group 46.18, Federal Water Pollution Legislative Files, 1969–1974 (46-75-003), Records of the Senate Committee on Environment and Public Works and Its Predecessors

   Record Group 46.22.2, Records of the Senate Select Committee on National Water Resources

Records Collections, Office of History, Headquarters, U.S. Army Corps of Engineers

   Henry Caulfield Papers

   Howard Cook Papers

   Arthur Maass Papers

   Theodore Schad Oral Interview

   Harry Schwarz Papers

Senate Historical Office, Oral History Interviews, "William F. Hildenbrand, Secretary of the Senate," 20 March–6 May 1985, Library of Congress

U.S. Army Corps of Engineers Library, Washington, D.C.

INTERVIEWS CONDUCTED
Leon Billings
Lester Edelman
William Hildenbrand
Thomas Jorling
Gene Likens
Ronald Linton
Barry Meyer
Don Nicoll
Theodore Schad
Jerry Sonosky
George Woodwell

PUBLISHED CONGRESSIONAL HEARINGS AND REPORTS:
HOUSE OF REPRESENTATIVES

Committee on Appropriations
Subcommittee on Labor—Health, Education, and Welfare. *Hearings on Appropriations for 1956.* 84th Cong., 1st sess., 1955.
Subcommittee on Labor—Health, Education, and Welfare. *Hearings on Appropriations for 1957.* 84th Cong., 2d sess., 1956.
Subcommittee on Department of Agriculture and Related Agency Appropriations. *Department of Agriculture Appropriations for 1966, Part I: Budget for the Department of Agriculture.* 89th Cong., 1st sess., 1965.

Committee on Government Operations
Subcommittee on Natural Resources and Power. *Water Pollution Control and Abatement.* 88th Cong., 1st sess., 1963. Parts 1–6.
Subcommittee on Natural Resources and Power. *Water Pollution Control and Abatement.* 88th Cong., 2d sess., 1964. Parts 7–8.
Subcommittee on Natural Resources and Power. *Water Pollution—Great Lakes.* 89th Cong., 2d sess., 1966. Parts 1–4.
Subcommittee on Natural Resources and Power. *Pollution of Lake Michigan.* 90th Cong., 1st sess., 1967.
Subcommittee on Conservation and Natural Resources. *Phosphates in Detergents and the Eutrophication of America's Waters.* 91st Cong., 1st sess., 1969.
Subcommittee on Conservation and Natural Resources. *Our Waters and Wetlands: How the Corps of Engineers Can Help Prevent Their Destruction and Pollution.* 91st Cong., 2d sess., 1970. H. Rep. 917.
Subcommittee on Conservation and Natural Resources. *Mercury Pollution and Enforcement of the Refuse Act of 1899.* 92d Cong., 1st sess., 1971. Parts 1–2.

Subcommittee on Conservation and Natural Resources. *Phosphates and Phosphate Substitution in Detergents.* 92d Cong., 1st sess., 1971.
Subcommittee on Executive and Legislative Reorganization. *Reorganization Plan No. 2 of 1966 (Water Pollution Control).* 89th Cong., 2d sess., 1966.

Committee on Merchant Marine and Fisheries
Subcommittee on Fisheries and Wildlife Conservation. *Estuarine Areas.* 90th Cong., 1st sess., 1967.
Subcommittee on Fisheries and Wildlife Conservation. *Interim Nuclear Licensing.* 92d Cong., 2d sess., 1972.
Subcommittee on Fisheries and Wildlife Conservation. *Temporary Exemption from Sec. 102 Statements.* 92d Cong., 2d sess., 1972.

Committee on Public Works
Subcommittee on Rivers and Harbors. *Water Pollution Control Act.* 84th Cong., 1st sess., 1955.
Comparative Print of Changes Proposed to Be Made in the Water Pollution Control Act. 84th Cong., 1st sess., 1955.
Subcommittee on Rivers and Harbors. *Water Pollution Control Act.* 84th Cong., 2d sess., 1956.
Subcommittee on Roads. *National Highway Program—Federal Aid Highway Act of 1956.* 84th Cong., 2d sess., 1956.
Federal Water Pollution Control. 86th Cong., 1st sess., 1959.
Federal Water Pollution Control. 87th Cong., 1st sess., 1961.
Water Pollution Control Act Amendments. 88th Cong., 1st sess., 1963.
Water Pollution Control Act Amendments. 88th Cong., 2d sess., 1964.
Hearings on the Water Quality Act of 1965. 89th Cong., 1st sess., 1965.
Federal Water Pollution Control Act—1966. 89th Cong., 2d sess., 1966.
Federal Water Pollution Control Act Amendments—1968. 90th Cong., 2d sess., 1968.
Federal Water Pollution Control Act Amendments—1969. 91st Cong., 1st sess., 1969.
Water Pollution Control Legislation—1971 (Oversight of Existing Program). 92d Cong., 1st sess., 25 May–7 July 1971.
Water Pollution Control Legislation—1971 (Amendments to Existing Water Pollution Control Laws). 92d Cong., 1st sess., 13 July–9 November 1971.
Water Pollution Control Legislation—1971 (HR 11896, HR 11895). 92d Cong., 1st sess., 7–10 December 1971.
Federal Water Pollution Control Act Amendments of 1972. 92d Cong., 2d sess., 1972. H. Rep. 911.

Committee on Science and Astronautics, Subcommittee on Science, Research, and Development

Adequacy of Technology for Pollution Abatement. 89th Cong., 2d sess., 1966. Vol. 1.
Environmental Pollution—A Challenge to Science and Technology. 89th Cong., 2d sess., 1966. Committee Print.
International Biological Program, H. Con. Res. 273. 90th Cong., 1st sess., 1967.
Environmental Quality. 90th Cong., 2d sess., 1968.
Managing the Environment: Report of the Subcommittee on Science, Research, and Development. 90th Cong., 2d sess., 1968. Committee Print.
Policy Issues in Science and Technology, Review and Forecast: Third Progress Report. 90th Cong., 2d sess., 1968. Committee Print.

PUBLISHED CONGRESSIONAL HEARINGS AND REPORTS: SENATE

Committee on Appropriations
Subcommittee on the Departments of Labor and Health, Education, and Welfare. *Labor—Health, Education, and Welfare Appropriations, 1959 (Public Health Service).* 85th Cong., 1st sess., 1958.
Subcommittee on Public Works. *Public Works for Water and Power Development and Atomic Energy Commission Appropriations Bill, 1972, Part I.* 92d Cong., 1st sess., 1971.

Committee on Commerce
Subcommittee on Energy, Natural Resources, and the Environment. *Effects of Mercury on Man and the Environment.* 91st Cong., 2d sess., 1972. Parts 1–2.
Subcommittee on Energy, Natural Resources, and the Environment. *Refuse Act Permit Program.* 92d Cong., 1st sess., 1971.

Committee on Government Operations
Subcommittee on Intergovernmental Relations. *S. Res. 68 to Establish a Select Senate Committee on Technology and the Human Environment.* 90th Cong., 1st sess., 1967.
Subcommittee on Intergovernmental Relations. *S. Res. 78 to Establish a Select Senate Committee on Technology and the Human Environment.* 90th Cong., 2d sess., 1968.
Subcommittee on Investigations. *TFX Contract Investigation.* 88th Cong., 1st sess., 1963. Parts 1–10.
Subcommittee on Reorganization and International Organizations. *Interagency Coordination in Environmental Hazards (Pesticides).* 88th Cong., 1st sess., 1963.

Committee on Interior and Insular Affairs
Ecological Research and Surveys. 89th Cong., 2d sess., 1966.
Joint House-Senate Colloquium to Discuss a National Policy for the Environment. 90th Cong., 2d sess., 1968.
Hearings on S. 1075, S. 237, and S. 1752. 91st Cong., 1st sess., 1969.

National Environmental Policy Act of 1969. 91st Cong., 1st sess., 1969. S. Rep. 296.

Interior Nominations (Nomination of Russell Train, Chairman, Robert Cahn and Gordan James Fraser MacDonald to the Council on Environmental Quality). 91st Cong., 2d sess., 1970.

Interim Nuclear Licensing. 92d Cong., 2d sess., 1972.

Subcommittee on Irrigation and Reclamation. *Development and Coordination of Water Resources.* 86th Cong., 1st sess., 1959.

Establishing Committee to Study Matter of Development and Coordination of Water Resources. 86th Cong., 1st sess., 1959. S. Rep. 145.

Subcommittee on Public Lands. *Clear Cutting Practices on National Timberlands.* 92d Cong., 1st sess., 1971. Parts 1–3.

Committee on Public Works

Subcommittee on Flood Control—Rivers and Harbors. *Water Pollution Control.* 84th Cong., 1st sess., 1955.

Subcommittee on Flood Control—Rivers and Harbors. *River and Harbor—Flood Control Act of 1957* (S. 497). 85th Cong., 1st sess., 1957.

Subcommittee on Flood Control—Rivers and Harbors. *Water Pollution Control.* 87th Cong., 1st sess., 1961.

A Study of Pollution—Water. 88th Cong., 1st sess., 1963. Committee Print.

Special Subcommittee on Air and Water Pollution. *Water Pollution Control.* 88th Cong., 1st sess., 1963.

Federal Water Pollution Control Act Amendments of 1963. 88th Cong., 1st sess., 1963. S. Rep. 556.

Subcommittee on Air and Water Pollution. *Water Quality Act of 1965.* 89th Cong., 1st sess., 1965.

Water Pollution. 89th Cong., 1st sess., 1965. Parts 1–3.

Steps toward Clean Water. 89th Cong., 2d sess., 1966. Committee Print.

Water Pollution Control—1966. 89th Cong., 2d sess., 1966.

Air Pollution—1967 (Air Quality Act). 90th Cong., 1st sess., 1967.

Need to Establish an Important Environmental Quality Policy. 90th Cong., 1st sess., 1968.

Thermal Pollution—1968. 90th Cong., 1st sess., 1968. Parts 1–4.

Water Pollution—1967. 90th Cong., 1st sess., 1967. Parts 1–2.

Water Pollution—1968. 90th Cong., 2d sess., 1968. Parts 1–2.

Resource Recovery Act of 1969. 91st Cong., 1st sess., 1969. Part 1.

Water Pollution—1969. 91st Cong., 1st sess., 1969. Parts 1–4.

Air Pollution—1970. 91st Cong., 2d sess., 1970. Parts 1–4.

The Economics of Clean Water: Summary Report of the U.S. Department of Interior, Federal Water Pollution Control Administration, March 1970. 91st Cong., 2d sess., 1970. Committee Print.

National Air Quality Standards Act of 1970. 91st Cong., 2d sess., 1970. S. Rep. 1196.

Report of the Council on Environmental Quality. 91st Cong., 2d sess., 1970.

Water Pollution—1970. 91st Cong., 2d sess., 1970. Parts 1–4.

Federal Water Pollution Control Act Amendments of 1971. 92d Cong., 1st sess., 1971. S. Rep. 414.

National Environmental Laboratories. 92d Cong., 1st sess., 1971.

Refuse Act Permit Program. 92d Cong., 1st sess., 1971.

Water Pollution Control Legislation. 92d Cong., 1st sess., 1971. Parts 1–8.

Water Pollution Control Programs. 92d Cong., 1st sess., 1971.

Environmental Problems of the Lake Tahoe Basin. 92d Cong., 2d sess., 1972.

Federal Water Pollution Control Act Amendments of 1972. 92d Cong., 2d sess., 1972. S. Rep. 1236.

National Environmental Policy Act. 92d Cong., 2d sess., 1972. Joint Hearings with Committee on Interior and Insular Affairs.

A Legislative History of the Water Pollution Control Act Amendments of 1972. 93d Cong., 1st sess., 1973. 2 vols.

Select Committee on National Water Resources

Water Resources. 86th Cong., 1st sess., 1959. Parts 1–18.

Water Resource Activities in the United States. 86th Cong., 2d sess., 1960. 3 vols. Committee Prints 1–32.

Report of the Senate Select Committee on National Water Resources. 87th Cong., 1st sess., 1961. S. Rep. 29.

MISCELLANEOUS PUBLISHED CONGRESSIONAL DOCUMENTS

Congressional Record. 1956–1972. Washington, D.C.

Joint Committee on Atomic Energy. *H.R. 13731 and H.R. 1372, To Amend the Atomic Energy Act of 1954 Regarding the Licensing of Nuclear Facilities.* 92d Cong., 2d sess., 1972.

MISCELLANEOUS PUBLISHED GOVERNMENT DOCUMENTS

Chief of Engineers. U.S. Army Corps of Engineers. *Annual Report of the Chief of Engineers, U.S. Army, on Civil Works Activities 1967.* Washington, D.C.: GPO, 1967.

Comptroller of the United States. *Examination into the Effectiveness of the Construction Grant Program for Abating, Controlling, and Preventing Water Pollution.* Washington, D.C.: U.S. GAO, 1969.

Comptroller of the United States. *Need for Improving Procedures to Ensure Compliance with Law Regarding Deposition of Industrial Waste Solids into Navigable Waters.* Washington, D.C.: U.S. GAO, 1966.

Council on Environmental Quality. *Environmental Quality: The First Annual Report of the Council on Environmental Quality.* Washington, D.C., 1970.

Federal Security Agency. Public Health Service. *New England Drainage Basins: A Cooperative State-Federal Report on Water Pollution.* Washington, D.C., 1951.

National Water Commission. *Water Policies for the Future: Final Report to the President and to the Congress of the United States by the National Water Commission.* Washington, D.C.: GPO, 1973.

President's Materials Policy Commission. *Resources for Freedom.* 5 vols. Washington, D.C., 1952.

Public Health Service. Department of Health, Education, and Welfare. *Proceedings, The National Conference on Water Pollution.* Washington, D.C., 12–14 December 1960.

Public Papers of the Presidents of the United States: Dwight D. Eisenhower, 1956–1960. 5 vols. Washington, D.C.: GPO, 1957–1961.

Public Papers of the Presidents of the United States: John F. Kennedy, 1960–1961. 2 vols. Washington, D.C.: GPO, 1961–1962.

Public Papers of the Presidents of the United States: Lyndon B. Johnson, 1964–1968. 5 vols. Washington, D.C.: GPO, 1965–1969.

Public Papers of the Presidents of the United States: Richard M. Nixon, 1969–1972. 4 vols. Washington, D.C.: GPO, 1970–1973.

U.S. Army Corps of Engineers, Baltimore District. *Potomac River Basin Report: Summary.* Baltimore: U.S. Army Engineer District, North Atlantic Division, 1963.

U.S. Department of Health, Education, and Welfare. *Annual Report, 1956–59.* 4 vols. Washington, D.C.: GPO, 1955–1960.

U.S. Environmental Protection Agency. *National Water Quality Inventory: 2000 Report* (841-R-02-001). Washington, D.C., 2002.

JOURNALS AND PERIODICALS
American City
American County
Atlantic Monthly
Bioscience
Bulletin of the Atomic Scientists
Business Week
Chicago Tribune
Congressional Quarterly Almanac
Conservationist
Ecological Monographs
Ecology
Engineering News Record
Environmental Journal
Environmental Law Reporter
Field and Stream
Forest Science
Fortune
Harper's Magazine
Journal of Animal Ecology

Journal of Plant Ecology
Journal of the American Water Works Association
Journal of the Water Pollution Control Federation
National Journal
National Parks Magazine
National Review
Nation's Cities
Natural Resources Journal
New Republic
Newsweek
New York Times
New York Times Magazine
Playboy
Readers' Digest
Reporter
Saturday Evening Post
Saturday Review
Science
Science and Mechanics
Scientific American
Scientist and Citizen
Sports Illustrated
St. Paul Dispatch
Time
U.S. News and World Report
Vital Speeches
Wall Street Journal
Washington Star
Wastes Engineering
Water and Sewage Works
Water Resources Research
Water Spectrum

BOOKS, ARTICLES, DISSERTATIONS, AND MISCELLANEOUS

Ackerman, Bruce, and James Sawyer. "The Uncertain Search for Environmental Policy: Scientific Fact-Finding and Rational Decision-Making along the Delaware River." *University of Pennsylvania Law Review* 120 (January 1972): 419–503.

Alexander, Charles C. *Holding the Line: The Eisenhower Era, 1952–1961.* Bloomington: Indiana University Press, 1975.

Allee, David J., and Burnham H. Dodge. *The Role of the U.S. Army Corps of Engineers in Water Quality Management.* U.S. Department of the Army. Corps of Engineers. Institute for Water Resources, Report 71-1 (October 1970).

Ambrose, Steven E. *Eisenhower: The President.* New York: Simon and Schuster, 1984.
American Men and Women of Science. 20th ed. New Providence, R.I.: R. R. Bowker, 1998.
Anderson, Frederick R. *NEPA in the Courts.* Baltimore: Johns Hopkins University Press, 1973.
Andrews, Richard N. L. *Environmental Policy and Administrative Change.* Lexington, Mass.: Lexington Books, 1976.
———— *Managing the Environment, Managing Ourselves: A History of American Environmental Policy.* New Haven: Yale University Press, 1999.
Annis, J. Lee, Jr. *Howard Baker: Conciliator in an Age of Crisis.* New York: Madison Books, 1995.
Asbell, Bernard. *The Senate Nobody Knows.* Garden City, N.Y.: Doubleday, 1978.
Ashby, W. Ross. *An Introduction to Cybernetics.* New York: John Wiley, 1958.
Balogh, Brian. *Chain Reaction: Expert Debate and Public Participation in American Commercial Nuclear Power, 1945–1975.* Cambridge: Cambridge University Press, 1991.
———— "Reorganizing the Organizational Synthesis: Reconsidering Modern American Federal-Professional Relations." *Studies in American Political Development* 5, no. 1 (1991): 119–72.
Bartlett, Robert V. *The Reserve Mining Controversy: Science, Technology and Environmental Quality.* Bloomington: Indiana University Press, 1980.
Baumgartner, Frank, and Bryan Jones. *Agendas and Instability in American Politics.* Chicago: University of Chicago Press, 1993.
Bernstein, Carl, and Bob Woodward. *All the President's Men.* New York: Simon and Schuster, 1974.
Bernstein, Marver. *Regulating Business by Independent Commission.* Princeton, N.J.: Princeton University Press, 1955.
Beuscher, Jacob. "Some New Machinery to Help Us Do the Job." In *Environmental Quality in a Growing Economy,* edited by Henry Jarett, for Resources for the Future. Baltimore: Johns Hopkins University Press, 1966.
Bimber, Bruce. *The Politics of Expertise in Congress.* Albany: State University of New York Press, 1996.
Biographical Directory of the United States Congress, 1774–1989. Alexandria, Va.: CQ Staff Directories, 1989.
"Biography of John Anton Blatnik." In *John Blatnik: An Inventory of His Congressional Papers,* Minnesota Historical Society web site (www.mnhs.org/library/find-aids/00366.html).
Blair, W. F. *Big Biology: The US/IBP.* Stroudsburg, Pa.: Dowden, Hutchinson, and Ross, 1977.
Blomquist, Robert F. "'To Stir Up Public Interest': Edmund S. Muskie and the U.S. Senate Special Subcommittee's Water Pollution Investigations and Legislative Activities, 1963–66—A Case Study in Early Congressional Environmental Policy Development." *Columbia Journal of Environmental Law* 22, no. 1 (1997): 1–64.

——— "What Is Past Is Prologue: Senator Edmund S. Muskie's Environmental Policymaking Roots as Governor of Maine, 1955–58." *Maine Law Review* 51 (1999): 88–128.

Blythe, Barbara L. "The Conservation Philosophy of Stewart Udall, 1961–68." Ph.D. diss., Texas A&M University, 1977.

Bocking, Stephen. *Ecologists and Environmental Politics*. New Haven: Yale University Press, 1997.

Bogue, Allan G., Jerome M. Clubb, Carroll R. McKibbin, and Santa A. Traugott. "Members of the House of Representatives and the Process of Modernization, 1789–1960." *Journal of American History* 63, no. 2 (September 1986): 275–302.

Bosso, Christopher J. *Environment Inc.: From Grassroots to Beltway*. Lawrence: University Press of Kansas, 2005.

Bowler, Peter J. *The Norton History of the Environmental Sciences*. New York: W. W. Norton, 1992.

Boyle, Robert H. *The Hudson River: A Natural and Unnatural History*. New York: W. W. Norton, 1979.

Brownlee, W. Elliot, ed. *Funding the Modern American State, 1941–1995*. Washington, D.C.: Woodrow Wilson Center Press, 1996.

Caldwell, Lynton K. "Administrative Possibilities for Environmental Control." In *Future Environments of North America*, edited by F. Fraser Darling and John P. Milton, 648–71. Garden City, N.Y.: Natural History Press, 1966.

——— "Biopolitics: Science, Ethics, and Public Policy." *Yale Review* 54 (1964): 1–16.

——— "Environment: A New Focus for Public Policy?" *Public Administration Review* 23 (1963): 132–39.

——— *Science and the National Environmental Policy Act*. University: University of Alabama Press, 1982.

Caplin, Lee Evan. "Is Congress Protecting Our Water? The Controversy over Section 404, Federal Water Pollution Control Act Amendments of 1972." *University of Miami Law Review* 31 (Spring 1977): 445–95.

Caro, Robert. *Master of the Senate*. New York: Vintage, 2003.

Carr, Donald. *Death of the Sweet Waters*. New York: W. W. Norton, 1966.

Carson, Rachel. *Silent Spring*. Boston: Houghton Mifflin, 1994.

Christofferson, Bill. *The Man from Clear Lake: Earth Day Founder Gaylord Nelson*. Madison: University of Wisconsin Press, 2004.

"Clearing Muddy Waters: The Evolving Federalization of Water Pollution Control." *Georgetown Law Journal* 60 (February 1972): 742–70.

Cleaveland, Frederic N., ed. *Congress and Urban Problems*. Washington, D.C.: Brookings Institution, 1969.

Cohen, Michael P. *The History of the Sierra Club, 1892–1970*. San Francisco: Sierra Club Books, 1988.

Cohen, Saul B., ed. *Columbia Gazetteer of the World*, vol. 1. New York: Columbia University Press, 1998.

Copeland, Claudia. "Clean Water Act Issues in the 109th Congress." Congressional Research Service Issue Brief IB10142, 28 September 2005. http://fpc.state.gov/documents/organization/54508.pdf.

———— "Water Quality: Implementing the Clean Water Act." Congressional Research Service Issue Brief IB89102, 21 April 2005. http://www.ncseonline.org/nle/crsreports/05apr/IB89102.pdf.

Cowdrey, Albert E. "Pioneering Environmental Law: The Army Corps of Engineers and the Refuse Act." *Pacific Historical Review* 46, no. 3 (August 1975): 331–49.

Cronon, William, ed. *Uncommon Ground: Toward Reinventing Nature.* New York: W. W. Norton, 1995.

Cuff, Robert. *The War Industries Board: Business-Government Relations during World War I.* Baltimore: Johns Hopkins University Press, 1973.

Curran, Daniel J. *Dead Laws for Dead Men: The Politics of Federal Coal Mine Health and Safety Legislation.* Pittsburgh: University of Pittsburgh Press, 1993.

Dahl, Robert A. *A Preface to Democratic Theory.* Chicago: University of Chicago Press, 1956.

Dallek, Robert. *Lone Star Rising: Lyndon Johnson and His Times, 1908–1960.* New York: Oxford University Press, 1991.

Davidson, Roger. "Subcommittee Government: New Channels for Policy Making." In *The New Congress,* edited by Dean E. Mann and Norman Ornstein. Washington, D.C.: American Enterprise Institute, 1981.

Davies, J. Clarence. *The Politics of Pollution.* New York: Pegasus, 1970.

Davis, E. W. *Pioneering with Taconite.* St. Paul: Minnesota Historical Society, 1964.

Derickson, Alan. *Black Lung: Anatomy of a Public Health Disaster.* Ithaca, N.Y.: Cornell University Press, 1998.

Derthick, Martha. *Between State and Nation: Regional Organizations of the United States.* Washington, D.C.: Brookings Institution, 1973.

———— "Crossing Thresholds: Federalism in the 1960s." In *Integrating the Sixties,* edited by Brian Balogh. University Park: Pennsylvania State University Press, 1996.

———— *The Influence of Federal Grants.* Cambridge, Mass.: Harvard University Press, 1970.

Dickinson, David. *The New Politics of Science.* Chicago: University of Chicago Press, 1988.

Divine, Robert. *Blowing on the Wind: The Nuclear Test Ban Debate, 1954–1960.* New York: Oxford University Press, 1978.

Duffy, John. *The Sanitarians: A History of American Public Health.* Urbana: University of Illinois Press, 1990.

Dunlap, Thomas R. *DDT: Scientists, Citizens, and Public Policy.* Princeton, N.J.: Princeton University Press, 1981.

Dyer, Davis. *TRW: Pioneering Technology and Innovation since 1900.* Boston: Harvard Business School Press, 1998.

Esposito, John C. *Vanishing Air: The Ralph Nader Study Group Report on Air Pollution.* New York: Grossman, 1970.

Evans, Rowland, and Robert Novack. "The Johnson System." In *The Legislative Process in the U.S. Senate*, edited by Lawrence K. Pettit and Edward Keynes. Chicago: Rand McNally, 1969.

—— *Lyndon B. Johnson: The Exercise of Power*. New York: New American Library, 1966.

"Evolution of the Enforcement Provisions of the Federal Water Pollution Control Act: A Study of the Difficulty in Developing Effective Legislation." *Michigan Law Review* 68 (May 1970): 1103–30.

Fair, Gordon M., and J. C. Geyer. *Water Supply and Waste Disposal*. New York: Wiley, 1954.

Fenno, Richard F. *Congressmen in Committees*. Boston: Little, Brown, 1973.

Finn, Terrence T. "Conflict and Compromise—Congress Makes a Law: The Passage of the National Environmental Policy Act." Ph.D. diss., Georgetown University, 1973.

Fleming, Donald. "Roots of the New Conservation Movement." *Perspectives in American History* 6 (1972): 7–91.

Flippen, J. Brooks. *Nixon and the Environment*. Albuquerque: University of New Mexico Press, 2000.

Fox, Harrison W., Jr., and Susan Webb Hammond. *Congressional Staffs: The Invisible Force in American Lawmaking*. New York: Free Press, 1977.

Fox, Stephen. *John Muir and His Legacy*. Madison: University of Wisconsin Press, 1981.

Furman, Bess. *A Profile of the United States Public Health Service, 1798–1948*. USHEW Publication No. 73-39, 1973.

Gaddie, Ronald Keith, and James L. Regens. *Regulating Wetlands Protection: Environmental Federalism and the States*. Albany: State University of New York Press, 2000.

Gargan, John Joseph. "Beyond NEPA and Earth Day: Reconstructing the Past and Envisioning a Future for Environmentalism." *Environmental History Review* 19, no. 4 (Winter 1995): 1–13.

—— "The Politics of Water Pollution in New York State: The Development and Adoption of the 1965 Pure Waters Program." Ph.D. diss., Syracuse University, 1968.

Gilmour, John. *Strategic Disagreement: Stalemate in American Politics*. Pittsburgh: University of Pittsburgh Press, 1995.

Golley, Frank. *A History of the Ecosystem Concept of Ecology*. New Haven: Yale University Press, 1993.

Gorman, Hugh S. *Redefining Efficiency: Pollution Concerns, Regulatory Mechanisms, and Technological Change in the U.S. Petroleum Industry*. Akron, Ohio: University of Akron Press, 2001.

Gottlieb, Robert. "Beyond NEPA and Earth Day: Reconstructing the Past and Envisioning a Future for Environmentalism." *Environmental History Review* 19, no. 4 (Winter 1995): 8.

———— *Forcing the Spring: The Transformation of the American Environmental Movement.* Washington, D.C.: Island Press, 1993.

Graham, Frank, Jr. *Disaster by Default: Politics and Water Pollution.* New York: M. Evans, 1966.

Graham, Hugh Davis. *The Civil Rights Era: Origins and Development of National Policy.* New York: Oxford University Press, 1990.

Graham, Mary. *The Morning after Earth Day: Practical Environmental Politics.* Washington, D.C.: Brookings Institution Press, 1999.

Graham, Otis L., Jr. *Toward a Planned Society.* New York: Oxford University Press, 1976.

Graves, Gregory. *Pursuing Excellence in Water Planning and Policy Analysis: A History of the Institute for Water Resources, U.S. Army Corps of Engineers.* Washington, D.C.: GPO, 1996.

Greenstein, Fred I. *The Hidden-Hand Presidency: Eisenhower as Leader.* Baltimore: Johns Hopkins University Press, 1994.

Griffith, Robert. "Dwight D. Eisenhower and the Corporate Commonwealth." *American Historical Review* (February 1982): 87–122.

Hacker, Barton C. *Elements of Controversy: The Atomic Energy Commission and Radiation Safety in Nuclear Weapons Testing.* Berkeley: University of California Press, 1994.

Hagen, Joel B. *An Entangled Bank: The Origins of Ecosystem Ecology.* New Brunswick, N.J.: Rutgers University Press, 1992.

Harvey, Mark. *A Symbol of Wilderness: Echo Park and the American Conservation Movement.* Albuquerque: University of New Mexico Press, 1994.

Haskell, Elizabeth. *The Politics of Clean Air: EPA Standards for Coal Burning Power Plants.* New York: Praeger, 1982.

Hawley, Ellis. "Social Policy and the Liberal State in Twentieth Century America." In *Federal Social Policy: The Historical Dimension,* edited by Ellis Hawley and Donald T. Critchlow. University Park: Pennsylvania State University Press, 1988.

Hays, Samuel P. *Beauty, Health, and Permanence: Environmental Politics in the United States, 1955–1985.* New York: Cambridge University Press, 1987.

———— *Conservation and the Gospel of Efficiency.* Cambridge: Harvard University Press, 1968.

———— "Three Decades of Environmental Politics: The Historical Context." In *Government and Environmental Politics: Essays on Historical Developments since World War II,* edited by Michael J. Lacy. Baltimore: Johns Hopkins University Press, 1991.

Hechler, Ken. *Toward the Endless Frontier: History of the Committee on Science and Technology, 1959–79.* Washington, D.C.: U.S. House of Representatives Committee Print, 1980.

Heclo, Hugh. *Comparative Public Policy: The Politics of Social Choice in America, Europe, and Japan.* New York: St. Martin's, 1990.

———— "Issue Networks and the Executive Establishment." In *The New American Political System*, edited by Anthony King. Washington, D.C.: American Enterprise Institute, 1978.

———— "The Sixties False Dawn: Awakenings, Movements, and Postmodern Policy-Making." In *Integrating the Sixties*, edited by Brian Balogh. University Park: Pennsylvania State University Press, 1996.

Herken, Greg. *Counsels of War*. Oxford: Oxford University Press, 1987.

Hill, Gladwyn. "The Politics of Air Pollution: Public Interest and Pressure Groups." *Arizona Law Review* 10 (Summer 1968): 37–47.

Hines, M. William. "Nor Any Drop to Drink, Part II: Interstate Arrangements for Pollution Control." *Iowa Law Review* 52, no. 3 (December 1966): 432–57.

———— "Nor Any Drop to Drink—Public Regulation of Water Quality, Part III: The Federal Effort." *Iowa Law Review* 52, no. 5 (April 1967): 799–862.

Hinkley, Barbara. *Stability and Change in Congress*. New York: Harper and Row, 1988.

Hoberg, George. *Pluralism by Design: Environmental Policy and the American Regulatory State*. Westport, Conn.: Praeger, 1992.

Hoff, Joan. *Nixon Reconsidered*. New York: Basic Books, 1994.

Hogan, Michael. *A Cross of Iron: Harry S. Truman and the Origins of the National Security State, 1945–54*. New York: Cambridge University Press, 1998.

Hollander, Walter, Jr. *Abel Wolman: His Life and Philosophy*. Chapel Hill, N.C.: Universal Printing and Publishing, 1981.

Holmes, Beatrice Hort. *A History of Federal Water Resources Programs, 1800–1960*. Washington, D.C.: U.S. Department of Agriculture Economic Research Service. Miscellaneous Publication No. 1233, 1972.

———— *History of Federal Water Resources Programs and Policies, 1961–70*. Washington, D.C.: U.S. Department of Agriculture Economics, Statistics, and Cooperative Service. Miscellaneous Publication No. 1379, 1979.

Huffman, Thomas R. "Exploring the Legacy of Reserve Mining: What Does the Longest Environmental Trial in History Tell Us about the Meaning of American Environmentalism?" *Journal of Policy History* 12, no. 3 (2000): 339–68.

———— "Legislatures and the Environment." In *Encyclopedia of the American Legislative System: Studies of the Principal Structures, Processes, and Policies of Congress and the State Legislatures since the Colonial Era*, edited by Joel H. Silbey. New York: C. Scribner's, 1994.

———— *Protectors of the Land and Water: Environmentalism in Wisconsin, 1961–68*. Chapel Hill: University of North Carolina Press, 1994.

———— "U.S. Water Pollution." In *Water and the Environment since 1945: A Cross Cultural Perspective*, edited by Char Miller. New York: St. James/Gale, 2001.

Hughes, Thomas P. *Rescuing Prometheus*. New York: Pantheon, 1998.

Hundley, Norris. *The Great Thirst: Californians and Water, 1770s–1990s*. Berkeley: University of California Press, 1992.

———— *Water and the West: The Colorado River Compact and the Politics of Water in the American West.* Berkeley: University of California Press, 1975.

Huntington, Samuel P. "Congressional Responses to the Twentieth Century." In *The Congress and America's Future,* edited by David B. Truman. Englewood Cliffs, N.J.: Prentice Hall, 1965.

Ingram, Helen. "The Political Rationality of Innovation: The Clean Air Act Amendments of 1970." In *Approaches to Controlling Air Pollution,* edited by Ann Friedlaender. Cambridge, Mass.: MIT Press, 1978.

Jennings, M. Kent. "Legislative Politics and Water Pollution Control, 1956–61." In *Congress and Urban Problems,* edited by Frederic N. Cleaveland. Washington, D.C.: Brookings Institution, 1969.

Jones, Charles O. *Clean Air: The Policies and Politics of Pollution Control.* Pittsburgh: University of Pittsburgh Press, 1975.

———— "Joseph G. Cannon and Howard H. Smith: An Essay on the Limits of Leadership in the House." *Journal of Politics* 30 (August 1968): 617–46.

———— *The United States Congress: People, Place, and Policy.* Homewood, Ill.: Dorsey Press, 1982.

Judd, Richard W., and Christopher S. Beach. *Natural States: The Environmental Imagination in Maine, Oregon, and the Nation.* Washington, D.C.: Resources for the Future: 2003.

Kaplan, Fred. *The Wizards of Armageddon.* New York: Simon and Schuster, 1983.

Kardos, Louis, William Sopper, and Earl Myers. "A Living Filter for Sewage." *Yearbook of Agriculture 1968: Science for Better Living.* Washington, D.C.: U.S. Department of Agriculture, 1968.

Karl, Barry. *The Uneasy State.* Chicago: University of Chicago Press, 1983.

Karl, Barry, and Stanley Katz. "The American Private Philanthropic Foundation and the Public Sphere, 1890–1930." *Minerva* 19, no. 2 (Summer 1981): 236–70.

Kaufman, Robert G. *Henry M. Jackson: A Life in Politics.* Seattle: University of Washington Press, 2000.

Kehoe, Terence. *Cleaning Up the Great Lakes: From Cooperation to Confrontation.* Dekalb: Northern Illinois University Press, 1997.

Kerr, Robert S. *Land, Wood, and Water.* New York: Fleet Publishing, 1960.

Kevles, Daniel J. *The Physicists: The History of a Scientific Community in Modern America.* New York: Knopf, 1978.

Key, V. O., Jr. *Politics, Parties, and Pressure Groups.* New York: Cromwell, 1958.

Kingdon, John W. *Agendas, Alternatives, and Public Policies.* New York: HarperCollins College Publishers, 1995.

Kline, Benjamin. *First along the River: A Brief History of the U.S. Environmental Movement.* San Francisco: Acada Books, 1997.

Kneese, Allen V. *The Economics of Regional Water Quality Management.* Baltimore: Johns Hopkins University Press/Resources for the Future, 1964.

———— "Man and His Habitat: Problems of Water Pollution." *Bulletin of the Atomic Scientists* 21 (May 1965): 2–8.

Kofmehl, Kenneth. *Professional Staffs of Congress.* West Lafayette, Ind.: Purdue University Press, 1977.

Kopp, Carolyn. "The Origins of the American Scientific Debate over Fallout Hazards." *Social Studies of Science* 9 (November 1979): 403–22.

Koppes, Clayton R. "Efficiency, Equity, Esthetics: Shifting Themes in American Conservation." In *The Ends of the Earth: Perspectives on Modern Environmental History,* edited by Donald Worster. Cambridge: Cambridge University Press, 1989.

Krier, James E., and Edmund Ursin. *Pollution and Policy: A Case Essay on California and Federal Experience with Motor Vehicle Air Pollution, 1940–1975.* Berkeley: University of California Press, 1977.

Kwa, Chunglin. "Representations of Nature Mediating between Ecology and Science Policy: The Case of the International Biological Programme." *Social Studies of Science* 17 (1987): 413–41.

Langley, Leroy L. *Homeostasis.* London: Chapman and Hall, 1965.

Laycock, George. *The Diligent Destroyers.* New York: Doubleday, 1970.

Lear, Linda. *Rachel Carson: Witness to Nature.* New York: Henry Holt, 1997.

Leuchtenburg, William E. *Flood Control Politics: The Connecticut River Valley Problem, 1927–1950.* New York: Da Capo, 1972.

Lieber, Harvey. *Federalism and Clean Water: The 1972 Water Pollution Control Act.* Lexington, Mass.: D. C. Heath, 1975.

Light, Jennifer S. *From Warfare to Welfare: Defense Intellectuals and Urban Problems in Cold War America.* Baltimore: Johns Hopkins University Press, 2003.

Likens, Gene E. *The Ecosystem Approach: Its Use and Abuse.* Oldendorf/Luhe, Germany: Ecology Institute, 1992.

Lilienfeld, Robert. *The Rise of Systems Theory.* New York: John Wiley, 1978.

Lippman, Theo, Jr., and Donald C. Hansen. *Muskie.* New York: W. W. Norton, 1971.

Liroff, Richard A. *A National Policy for the Environment: NEPA and Its Aftermath.* Bloomington: Indiana University Press, 1976.

Lockard, Duane. *New England State Politics.* Princeton, N.J.: Princeton University Press, 1959.

Lowi, Theodore. *The End of Liberalism: Ideology, Policy, and the Crisis of Public Authority.* New York: Norton, 1969.

Lowitt, Richard. *The New Deal and the West.* Bloomington: Indiana University Press, 1984.

Maass, Arthur. *Design of Water Resource Systems.* Cambridge, Mass.: Harvard University Press, 1962.

———— *Muddy Waters: The Army Corps of Engineers and the Nation's Rivers.* Cambridge, Mass.: Harvard University Press, 1951.

MacKichan, K. A., and J. B. Graham. *Water Resources Review, Supplement 3: Pub-*

lic Water-Supply Shortages, 1953. Washington, D.C.: U.S. Department of Interior Geological Survey, 1954.

Malbin, Michael J. Unelected Representatives: Congressional Staff and the Future of Representative Government. New York: Basic Books, 1980.

Mann, Dean E. "Political Incentives in U.S. Water Policy: Relationships between Distributive and Regulatory Politics." In What Government Does, edited by Matthew Holden Jr. and Dennis L. Dresang. Beverly Hills: Sage Publications, 1975.

Marcus, Alfred A. Promise and Performance: Choosing and Implementing an Environmental Policy. Westport, Conn.: Greenwood, 1980.

Matthews, Donald R. U.S. Senators and Their World. Chapel Hill: University of North Carolina Press, 1960.

Matusow, Allan. Nixon's Economy. Lawrence: University Press of Kansas, 1998.

Mazmanian, Daniel A., and Jeanne Nienaber. Can Organizations Change? Environmental Protection, Citizen Participation, and the Corps of Engineers. Washington, D.C.: Brookings Institution, 1979.

McConnell, Grant. Private Power and American Democracy. New York: Knopf, 1966.

McCormick, Richard L. The Party Period and Public Policy. New York: Oxford University Press, 1986.

McDougall, Walter. The Heavens and the Earth: A Political History of the Space Age. New York: Basic Books, 1985.

McEvoy, Arthur F. The Fisherman's Problem: Ecology and Law in the California Fisheries, 1850–1980. Cambridge: Cambridge University Press, 1986.

McIntosh, Robert P. The Background of Ecology: Concept and Theory. Cambridge: Cambridge University Press, 1985.

McPhee, John. Encounters with the Archdruid. New York: Farrar, Straus, and Giroux, 1971.

Melnick, R. Shep. Regulation and the Courts: The Case of the Clean Air Act. Washington, D.C.: Brookings Institution, 1983.

Melosi, Martin. "Environmental Justice, Political Agenda Setting, and the Myths of History." Journal of Policy History 12 (2000): 43–71.

———— "Lyndon Johnson and Environmental Policy." In The Johnson Years, Volume Two: Vietnam, the Environment, and Science, edited by Robert A. Divine. Lawrence: University Press of Kansas, 1987.

———— The Sanitary City: Urban Infrastructure from Colonial Times to the Present. Baltimore: Johns Hopkins University Press, 2000.

Melosi, Martin, ed. Pollution and Reform in American Cities, 1870–1930. Austin: University of Texas Press, 1980.

Mintz, Joel A. Enforcement at the EPA. Austin: University of Texas Press, 1995.

Mitchell, Robert Cameron. "From Conservation to Environmental Movement: The Development of the Modern Environmental Lobbies." In Government and Environmental Politics: Essays on Historical Developments since World War II, edited by Michael J. Lacy. Baltimore: Johns Hopkins University Press, 1991.

Mitchell, Robert Cameron, Angela Mertig, and Riley E. Dunlap. "Twenty Years of Environmental Mobilization: Trends among National Environmental Organizations." In *American Environmentalism: The United States Environmental Movement, 1970–1990*, edited by Riley E. Dunlap and Angela Mertig. Philadelphia: Taylor and Francis, 1992.

Morgan, Anne Hodges. *Robert S. Kerr: The Senate Years*. Tulsa: University of Oklahoma Press, 1977.

Morgan, M. Granger, and Jon M. Peha, eds. *Science and Technology Advice for Congress*. Washington, D.C.: Resources for the Future, 2003.

Mullan, Fitzhugh. *Plagues and Politics: The Story of the United States Public Health Service*. New York: Basic Books, 1989.

Muskie, Edmund S. *Journeys*. Garden City, N.Y.: Doubleday, 1972.

Nash, Gerald. *The American West Transformed: Impact of the Second World War*. Bloomington: Indiana University Press, 1985.

———— *World War II and the West: Reshaping the Economy*. Lincoln: University of Nebraska Press, 1990.

National Research Council. *Assessing the TMDL Approach to Water Quality Management*. Washington, D.C.: National Academy Press, 2001.

Nelkin, Dorothy. *Nuclear Power and Its Critics*. Ithaca, N.Y.: Cornell University Press, 1971.

———— "Scientists and Professional Responsibility: The Experience of American Ecologists." *Social Studies of Science* 7 (1977): 75–95.

Nevins, David. *Muskie of Maine*. New York: Random House, 1972.

Odum, Eugene P., and Howard T. Odum. *Principles of Ecology*. 2d ed. Philadelphia: Saunders, 1959.

Orfield, Gary. *The Reconstruction of Southern Education*. New York: John Wiley, 1969.

Pach, Chester, and Elmo Richardson. *The Presidency of Dwight D. Eisenhower*. Lawrence: University Press of Kansas, 1991.

Picton, Walter L. *Water Use in the United States, 1900–1975*. Washington, D.C.: U.S. Department of Commerce, Business and Defense Administration, 1956.

Polsby, Nelson. "The Institutionalization of the U.S. House of Representatives." *American Political Science Review* 62 (March 1968): 144–68.

Polsby, Nelson, Miriam Gallaher, and Barry Spencer Rundquist. "The Growth of the Seniority System in the U.S. House of Representatives." *American Political Science Review* 63 (September 1969): 787–807.

Power, Garrett. "The Fox in the Chicken Coop: The Regulatory Program of the U.S. Army Corps of Engineers." *Virginia Law Review* 63 (May 1977): 503–59.

Price, Don K. *The Scientific Estate*. Cambridge, Mass.: Harvard University Press, 1965.

Quarles, John. *Cleaning Up America: An Insider's View of the Environmental Protection Agency*. Boston: Houghton Mifflin, 1976.

Rabin, Robert L. "Federal Regulation in Historical Perspective." *Stanford Law Review* 38 (May 1986): 1278–1315.

Ramo, Simon. *Century of Mismatch.* New York: David McKay, 1970.

——— *Cure for Chaos.* New York: David McKay, 1969.

Reisner, Marc. *Cadillac Desert.* New York: Viking, 1986.

Reuss, Martin. "Coping with Uncertainty: Social Scientists, Engineers, and Federal Water Resources Planning." *Natural Resources Journal* 32 (Winter 1992): 101–35.

——— *Shaping Environmental Awareness: The United States Army Corps of Engineers Environmental Advisory Board, 1970–1980.* Washington, D.C.: Historical Division, Office of the Chief of Engineers, 1983.

Richardson, Elmo. *Dams, Parks, and Politics: Resource Development and Preservation in the Truman-Eisenhower Era.* Lexington: University Press of Kentucky, 1973.

Ripley, Randall B. "Congress and Clean Air." In *Pollution and Public Policy,* edited by David Paulsen. New York: Dodd, Mead, 1973.

——— "Power in the Post–World War II Senate." In *Studies in Congress,* edited by Glenn R. Parker. Washington, D.C.: Congressional Quarterly Press, 1985.

——— *Power in the Senate.* New York: St. Martin's, 1969.

Robinson, Michael C. "The Relationship between the Army Corps of Engineers and the Environmental Community." *Environmental Review* 13 (1989): 1–41.

Rodgers, William H., Jr. "Industrial Water Pollution and the Refuse Act: A Second Chance for Water Quality." *University of Pennsylvania Law Review* 119 (1971): 761–822.

Rohde, David W., Norman J. Ornstein, and Robert L. Peabody. "Political Change and Legislative Norms in the U.S. Senate, 1957–74." In *Studies in Congress,* edited by Glenn R. Parker. Washington, D.C.: Congressional Quarterly Press, 1985.

Rome, Adam. *The Bulldozer in the Countryside: Suburban Sprawl and the Rise of American Environmentalism.* New York: Cambridge University Press, 2001.

——— "What Really Matters in History?" *Environmental History* 7 (April 2002): 303–18.

Rosenbaum, Walter A. *The Politics of Environmental Concern.* New York: Praeger, 1977.

Rothman, Hal. *The Greening of a Nation? Environmentalism in the United States since 1945.* Fort Worth, Tex.: Harcourt Brace, 1998.

——— *Saving the Planet: The American Response to the Environment in the Twentieth Century.* Chicago: Ivan R. Dee, 2000.

"Roundtable: The U.S. Congress in the Twentieth Century." *Social Science History* 24, no. 2 (Summer 2000): 307–93.

Rubin, Kenneth. "The New Federalism and National Flood Control Programs." In *The Flood Control Challenge: Past, Present, and Future,* edited by Howard Rosen and Martin Reuss. Chicago: Public Works Historical Society, 1988.

Russell, Edmund P. "Lost among the Parts per Billion: Ecological Protection at the United States Environmental Protection Agency, 1970–1993." *Environmental History* 2, no. 1 (January 1997): 29–51.

——— *War and Nature: Fighting Humans and Insects with Chemicals from World War I to Silent Spring.* Cambridge: Cambridge University Press, 2001.

Sale, Kirkpatrick. *The Green Revolution: The American Environmental Movement, 1962–1992.* New York: Hill and Wang, 1993.

Schad, Theodore M. "An Analysis of the Work of the Senate Select Committee on National Water Resources." *Natural Resources Journal* 2 (August 1962): 226–47.

Schattschneider, E. E. *The Semisovereign People: A Realist's View of Democracy in America.* New York: Holt, Rinehart, and Winston, 1960.

Schulte, Steven C. *Wayne Aspinall and the Shaping of the American West.* Boulder: University of Colorado Press, 2002.

Shabecoff, Philip. *A Fierce Green Fire: The American Environmental Movement.* New York: Hill and Wang, 1993.

Silbey, Joel H., ed. *Encyclopedia of the American Legislative System,* vol. 2. New York: Charles Scribner's, 1994.

Sinclair, Barbara. *The Transformation of the U.S. Senate.* Baltimore: Johns Hopkins University Press, 1981.

Siry, Joseph V. *Marshes of the Ocean Shore: Development of an Ecological Ethic.* College Station: Texas A&M University Press, 1984.

Skocpol, Theda, ed. *Bringing the State Back In.* New York: Cambridge University Press, 1985.

Skowronek, Stephen. *Building a New American State: The Expansion of National Administrative Capacities, 1877–1920.* New York: Cambridge University Press, 1982.

Smith, Steven, and Christopher J. Deering. *Committees in Congress.* Washington, D.C.: Congressional Quarterly Press, 1984.

Smith, W. B. "Statutory Treatment of Industrial Stream Pollution." *George Washington Law Review* 24, no. 3 (January 1956): 302–12.

Snyder, Lynne Page. "PHS in the Queen City: A Watershed Development." *Public Health Reports* 112 (July/August 1997): 347–50.

Steel, Ronald. *Walter Lippmann and the American Century.* New York: Vintage, 1980.

Steinberg, Theodore. *Down to Earth: Nature's Role in American History.* New York: Oxford University Press, 2002.

———— *Nature Incorporated: Industrialization and the Waters of New England.* Cambridge: Cambridge University Press, 1991.

Stevens, R. Michael. *Green Land—Clean Streams.* Philadelphia: Temple University Center for the Study of Federalism, 1972.

Stevens, Rosemary. *In Sickness and in Wealth: American Hospitals in the Twentieth Century.* Baltimore: Johns Hopkins University Press, 1999.

Stewart, Richard. "The Reformation of American Administrative Law." *Harvard Law Review* 88, no. 8 (1975): 1669–813.

Stine, Jeffrey K. *Mixing the Waters: Environment, Politics, and the Building of the Tennessee-Tombigbee Waterway.* Akron, Ohio: University of Akron Press, 1993.

———— "Regulating Wetlands in the 1970s: U.S. Army Corps of Engineers and the Environmental Organizations." *Journal of Forest History* 27, no. 2 (April 1983): 60–75.

———— *Twenty Years of Science in the Public Interest: A History of the Congressional Science and Engineering Fellowship Program.* Washington, D.C.: American Association for the Advancement of Science, 1994.

Sugrue, Thomas. *The Origins of the Urban Crisis: Race and Inequality in Postwar Detroit*. Princeton, N.J.: Princeton University Press, 1996.

Sutter, Paul S. *Driven Wild: How the Fight against Automobiles Launched the Modern Wilderness Movement*. Seattle: University of Washington Press, 2002.

Szylvian, Kristin M. "Transforming Lake Michigan into the 'World's Greatest Fishing Hole': The Environmental Politics of Michigan's Great Lakes Sport Fishing, 1965–1985." *Environmental History* 9 (January 2004): 102–27.

Talbot, Allan R. *Power along the Hudson: The Storm King Case and the Birth of Environmentalism*. New York: E. P. Dutton, 1972.

Tarr, Joel A. *The Search for the Ultimate Sink: Urban Pollution in Historical Perspective*. Akron, Ohio: University of Akron Press, 1996.

Tarr, Joel, James McCurley, and Terry F. Yosie. "The Development and Impact of Urban Wastewater Technology: Changing Concepts of Water Quality Control, 1850–1930." In *Pollution and Reform in American Cities, 1870–1930*, edited by Martin Melosi. Austin: University of Texas Press, 1980.

Tjossem, Sara. "Preservation of Nature and Academic Respectability: Tensions in the Ecological Society of America, 1915–1929." Ph.D. diss., Cornell University, 1994.

Tobin, Richard. *The Social Gamble: Determining Acceptable Levels of Air Quality*. Lexington, Mass.: D. C. Heath, 1979.

Train, Russell. *Politics, Pollution, and Pandas: An Environmental Memoir*. New York: Island Press, 2003.

Truman, David B. *The Governmental Process*. New York: Prentice-Hall, 1935.

Udall, Stewart. *The Quiet Crisis*. New York: Holt, Rinehart, and Winston, 1963.

Vogel, David. "A Case Study of Clean Air Legislation, 1967–1981." In *The Impact of the Modern Corporation*, edited by Betty Bock. New York: Columbia University Press, 1984.

——— *Fluctuating Fortunes: The Political Power of Business in America*. New York: Basic Books, 1989.

——— *Kindred Strangers: The Uneasy Relationship between Politics and Business in America*. Princeton, N.J.: Princeton University Press, 1996.

——— "Representing Diffuse Interests in Environmental Policymaking." In *Do Institutions Matter?*, edited by R. Kent Weaver and Bert A. Rockman. Washington, D.C.: Brookings Institution, 1993.

Walker, Jack L. "Interests, Political Parties, and Policy Formation in American Democracy." In *Federal Social Policy: The Historical Dimension*, edited by Donald T. Critchlow and Ellis W. Hawley. University Park: Pennsylvania State University Press, 1988.

——— "Setting the Agenda in the U.S. Senate: A Theory of Problem Selection." *British Journal of Political Science* 7 (October 1977): 423–45.

Walker, J. Samuel. "Nuclear Power and the Environment: The Atomic Energy Commission and Thermal Pollution, 1965–1971." *Technology and Culture* 30, no. 4 (October 1989): 964–92.

Warken, Philip W. *A History of the National Resources Planning Board, 1933–1943.* New York: Garland, 1979.

Wellock, Thomas Raymond. *Critical Masses: Opposition to Nuclear Power in California, 1958–1978.* Madison: University of Wisconsin Press, 1998.

Whitaker, John C. *Striking a Balance: Environment and Natural Resources Policy in the Nixon-Ford Years.* Washington, D.C.: American Enterprise Institute, 1976.

White, Richard. *"It's Your Misfortune and None of My Own": A New History of the American West.* Norman: University of Oklahoma Press, 1991.

White, Theodore. *The Making of the President—1972.* New York: Altheus, 1973.

Wiebe, Robert. *The Search for Order, 1877–1920.* New York: Hill and Wang, 1967.

Williams, Ralph C. *The United States Public Health Service, 1798–1950.* Washington, D.C.: Commissioned Officers Association of the USPHS, 1951.

Wilson, James Q. "The Politics of Regulation." In *Social Responsibility and the Business Predicament,* edited by James W. McKie. Washington, D.C.: Brookings Institution, 1974.

———— *The Politics of Regulation.* New York: Basic Books, 1980.

Wolfinger, Raymond E., and Joan Heifetz. "Safe Seats, Seniority, and Power in Congress." *American Political Science Review* 59 (1965): 337–49.

Woodward, Douglas R. "Availability of Water in the United States with Special Reference to Industrial Needs by 1980." Thesis no. 143, Resident Course, Industrial College of the Armed Forces, 10 April 1957.

Worster, Donald. *Nature's Economy.* San Francisco: Sierra Club Books, 1977.

———— *Rivers of Empire: Water, Aridity, and the Growth of the American West.* New York: Pantheon, 1985.

———— *The Wealth of Nature.* New York: Oxford University Press, 1993.

Worster, Donald, ed. *The Ends of the Earth: Perspectives on Modern Environmental History.* Cambridge: Cambridge University Press, 1989.

Wright, Gavin. *Old South, New South.* New York: Basic Books, 1986.

Yeager, Peter Cleary. *The Limits of Law: The Public Regulation of Private Pollution.* Cambridge: Cambridge University Press, 1991.

Zedler, Joy B., Meghan Q. Fellows, and Sally Trnka. "Wastelands to Wetlands: Links between Habitat Protection and Ecosystem Science." In *Successes, Limitations and Frontiers in Ecosystem Science,* edited by Michael L. Pace and Peter M. Groffman. New York: Springer, 1998.

Zelizer, Julian E. *On Capitol Hill: The Struggle to Reform Congress and Its Consequences, 1948–2000.* Cambridge: Cambridge University Press, 2004.

———— *Taxing America: Wilbur D. Mills, Congress, and the State, 1945–1975.* Cambridge: Cambridge University Press, 1998.

Zelizer, Julian E., ed. *The American Congress: The Building of Democracy.* Boston: Houghton Mifflin, 2004.

Zwick, David, and Marcy Benstock. *Water Wasteland: Ralph Nader's Study Group Report on Water Pollution.* New York: Grossman, 1971.